Origins of the Bronze Age Oasis Civilization in Central Asia

American School of Prehistoric Research
Bulletin 42

Peabody Museum of Archaeology and Ethnology
Harvard University

Origins of the Bronze Age Oasis Civilization in Central Asia

Fredrik T. Hiebert
Assistant Curator for Old World Archaeology
Peabody Museum, Harvard University

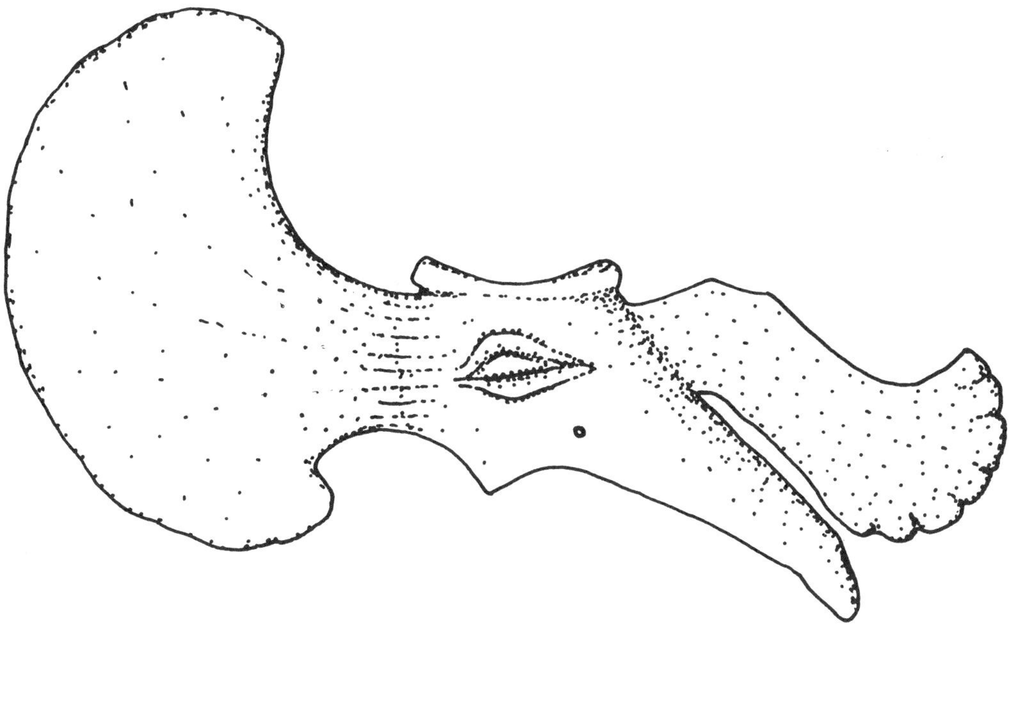

Peabody Museum of Archaeology and Ethnology
Harvard University
Cambridge, MA 1994

All photos and artwork by the author except as noted.

Portions of Chapters 8 and 9 were first published in *Antiquity*, vol. 68, no. 259: Hiebert, "Origins of the Oxus civilization," and Moore, Miller, Hiebert & Meadow, "Agriculture & herding in early Oxus oasis settlements." Republished with permission of *Antiquity*.

Designed by Janis Owens
Layout by Fredrik T. Hiebert and Amy Hirschfeld
Prepared by the Publication Department,
Peabody Museum

ISBN 0-87365-545-1
Library of Congress Catalog Card Number 94-066685
Manufactured in the United States of America

Contents

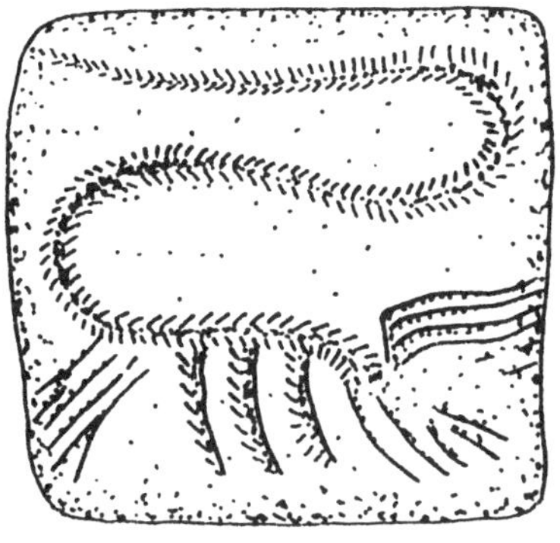

CHAPTER THREE

CHAPTER FOUR

CHAPTER FIVE

CHAPTER SIX

List of Figures

List of Tables

Foreword

Initiating an Archaeological Dialogue: The USA–USSR Archaeological Exchange

■

C. C. Lamberg-Karlovsky
Harvard University

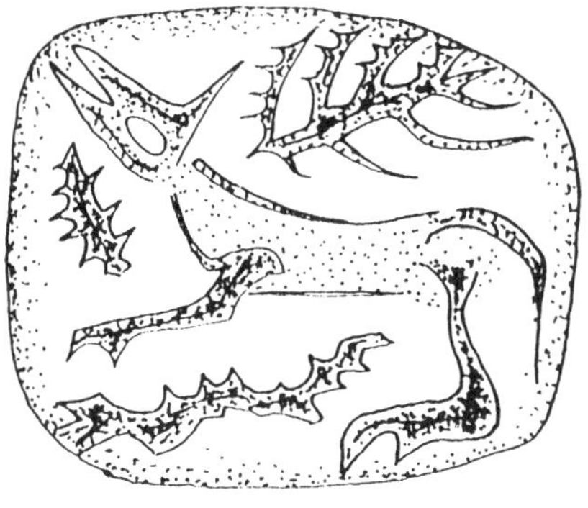

IN 1985 DRAMATIC CHANGES BEGAN TO SWEEP ACROSS THE former Soviet Union that were to profoundly affect the entire scientific community. Archaeology has not been immune from these changes (Dolukhanov 1993). The most profound involved the collapse of the Academy of Sciences of the USSR and a consequent decline in the funding of archaeological research and personnel. Within the former USSR the Academy of Sciences was the principal state organization supporting the sciences. Appropriations for the support of archaeology were derived from the academy's central office in Moscow. Today that academy no longer exists. It has been replaced by the Russian Academy of Sciences and by separate academies in each of the newly independent republics, or Confederation of Independent States (CIS): in the Baltics—Latvia, Estonia, and Lithuania; the Caucasus—Armenia, Georgia, and Azerbaijan; and Central Asia—Turkmenistan, Uzbekistan, Tajikistan, Kazakhstan, and Kirghizia. Financial problems remain acute in the Institutes of Archaeology throughout the former Soviet Union.

Today virtually all of the archaeological institutes face a reduction in their staffs. This is less than the disaster it might appear to be. In a recent article on "post-perestroika problems" in the USSR, Paul Dolukhanov (1993:150) begins with the statement "For about 70 years the USSR possessed the world's largest network of archaeological research." This statement is entirely true regarding the number of archaeologists affiliated with archaeological institutes. The Institute of Archaeology in Moscow employs more than two hundred archaeologists, and while it is only marginally larger than the institutes in Leningrad and Novosibirsk, it is considerably smaller than that in Tbilisi, Georgia SSR. In this regard the Institute of Archaeology in Moscow employs more archaeologists than twenty of the largest departments in American universities. On my first visit to Leningrad in 1970 I was quite impressed when the distinguished archaeologist Dr. Vladimir Lukonin informed me that there were more than three hundred scholars in the Oriental Institute concerned with aspects of the ancient Near East. Dr. Lukonin was not the last scholar affiliated with an institute to tell me, however, that less than 10 percent of the employed do all of the scientific work; the others sip tea. Over the years other Soviet scholars offered different percentages and/or a different beverage, but the message remained the same. I began to understand how the

USSR could structure a nation in which all were employed.

During the Soviet regime there were three All-Union institutions that were permitted to carry out archaeological excavations within any region of the USSR: (1) the Institute of Archaeology, Academy of Sciences of the USSR, Moscow; (2) the Branch of the Institute of Archaeology (of Moscow) in Leningrad; and (3) the Institute of History, Ethnography and Archaeology, Academy of Sciences of the USSR, Novosibirsk. All of the other republics maintained institutes or departments of archaeology within the framework of their respective republics' Academies of Sciences.

The disintegration of the Soviet state has led to the disruption of cooperation between the previous republics. Dolukhanov (1993:154), in writing about the past (USSR) and present (CIS) archaeological relations, observes that "even in the old days it was not always possible to obtain licenses for excavations from the republican archaeological authorities. *Now it has become much more difficult*" (emphasis mine). The reasons for the difficulties are numerous and involve lack of funds, ethnic conflicts that restrict access to archaeological sites, political conflicts (including open warfare) within the emergent new states, and an acting out of resentment toward the Russian "Big Brother" that previously dominated their affairs.

Under the Soviet regime, foreign collaboration within archaeology was severely restricted and tended to be monitored by the Moscow headquarters of the Academy of Sciences. The research reported on in this monograph began during the Soviet period, was sustained throughout the era of perestroika, and continues today with Russia and the independent nation of Turkmenistan. The historical background that laid the foundation for the USA–USSR archaeological collaboration, and ultimately for the publication of this volume, can be traced back to over fifteen years ago. The initial idea for an archaeological collaboration was proposed to two Soviet scholars attending a conference on the origins of agriculture at Åarhus, Denmark, in 1977. It was during this conference that I met Dr. Rauf Munchaev and Dr. Nikolai Merpert, both of the Institute of Archaeology, Moscow. After I confided in them that I would like to discuss the possibility of undertaking a collaborative excavation in the USSR, they graciously invited me to come to their room that evening for continued discussion. That evening was the first of many evenings I was to spend with Rauf and Nikolai sharing ample quantities of sausage, cheese, bread, pickles, and vodka that they brought with them from Moscow. That occasion was to be repeated in Boston, Washington, and New York. The conversation and the company varied, but the Russian sausage, bread, and vodka remained a constant. In Åarhus I made it clear that I wanted to collaborate on the excavation of a Bronze Age site in Soviet Central Asia. Dr. Munchaev made it equally clear that first a planning session involving a responsible committee of U.S. and Soviet scholars would have to be convened to formulate the protocol for such a collaboration. He urged that this planning session be held in the United States. We parted with Dr. Munchaev and Dr. Merpert being extremely encouraging about the opportunities for a joint project; they personally welcomed such an opportunity. It was 1977. Carter was in the White House and Brezhnev in the Kremlin; relations between our two countries were characterized by detente. In those days Dr. Munchaev was directing an important series of excavations in northern Iraq on a number of sites dated from the seventh to the fifth millennium B.C. Dr. Merpert, who annually participated in these excavations, was also directing his own archaeological project in Bulgaria. Both scholars had traveled widely and were well apprised of the advantages of international collaboration.

My interest in the archaeology of Soviet Central Asia was not occasioned by the opportunity of meeting Rauf Munchaev and Nikolai Merpert. The early 1970s excavations at Shahr-i Sokhta, under the direction of Dr. Maurizio Tosi, indicated that the site contained substantial amounts of Central Asian ceramics. Dr. Tosi's initial estimate that perhaps 40 percent of the early ceramics at Shahr-i Sokhta were of Central Asian type (Lamberg-Karlovsky and Tosi 1973) was later moderated by Dr. Rafaello Biscione (1973). My own excavations at Tepe Yahya, in southeastern Iran, were offering unequivocal and wide-ranging evidence for cultural contacts with Baluchistan, the Persian Gulf, and Mesopotamia (Lamberg-Karlovsky 1971). Tepe Yahya's parallels to Shahr-i Sokhta, and the Central Asian ceramics found there, offered the possibility of contacts with the distant north. Of even greater importance was the observation made by V. M. Masson and V. I. Sarianidi (1972) that clay figurines recovered from Altyn depe contained Proto-Elamite signs. The Proto-Elamite signary, circa 3200 B.C., represented the first writing known on the Iranian plateau. The discovery of Proto-Elamite tablets at Tepe Yahya in 1970 suggested the possibility of a link between these distant regions.

Maurizio Tosi and I shared an explicit concern for "interaction spheres" within the context of resource exploitation and economic networks of trade (Lamberg-Karlovsky and Tosi 1973; Lamberg-Karlovsky 1975). Tosi's study of the turquoise trade and the manufacture (1974a) and exchange of lapis lazuli (Tosi and Piperno 1973) was complemented by my own dealing with the distribution of carved chlorite bowls and market networks (Lamberg-Karlovsky 1975). At least three factors led me to an interest in the archaeology of Soviet Central Asia: (1) the remoteness of Tepe Yahya required one to look over long distances to establish both a relative chronology and to find parallels in its material inventory; (2) the relative absence of an understanding of the eastern Iranian plateau required the undertaking of a regional settlement analysis and an attempt to relate it to other settlement regimes (Prickett 1986); and (3) the clear evidence that Tepe Yahya was involved in a network of interaction that involved the manufacture and distribution of carved chlorite bowls (Kohl 1979). The fact that Dr. Tosi shared comparable experiences and concerns, as well as the fact that throughout the decade of the 1970s and early 1980s we were in continuous and productive contact, made it almost inevitable that we would both express an early interest in the archaeology of Soviet Central Asia (Tosi 1974b; Lamberg-Karlovsky 1973). Dr. Tosi was also in attendance at the Åarhus conference, and to those who know him it will come as no surprise that he was enormously supportive and generous in encouraging both me and our Soviet colleagues to proceed with a collaborative undertaking.

In 1978 I submitted the first of several proposals that were written over the course of a decade by either myself or my graduate students in order to gain support for participating in the USA–USSR archaeological collaboration. Most of the proposals were submitted to the International Research and Exchanges Board (IREX), a private organization that specializes in supporting research programs involving the United States, the USSR, and the Eastern European countries. For a decade IREX was the principal funding agency that supported our efforts in maintaining a USA–USSR archaeological exchange program. Without their financial support and the good offices of Dr. Wesley Fisher (secretary to the IREX Board), it is doubtful that the program would have gotten off the ground. An initial grant from IREX permitted the planning session to take place in the spring of 1979 at the Peabody Museum, Harvard University. Members of the Soviet delegation included Dr. Rauf Munchaev (chairman), Dr. Nikolai Merpert, and Dr. Vadim M. Masson, who within a year was to be appointed the director of the Leningrad branch of the Institute of Archaeology. Members of the U.S. delegation included Dr. Robert McC. Adams, then at the University of Chicago and currently the secretary of the Smithsonian Institution; Dr. Philip Kohl of Wellesley College; and myself as chairman. Philip Kohl and I shared a substantial interest in pursuing archaeological work in Central Asia.

In 1978 Phil Kohl directed an archaeological reconnaissance in Afghanistan. Following this wide-ranging survey he planned to undertake a full-scale excavation on one of the identified Bronze Age sites. This plan was one of many obliterated in 1979 by the Soviet invasion of Afghanistan. The first USA–USSR archaeological symposium, held at the Peabody Museum in 1981, could have been canceled because of the Soviet invasion of Afghanistan. The National Academy of Sciences in Washington, D.C., broke off bilateral relations with the Academy of Sciences of the USSR and was urging the cancellation of all scientific exchanges. Rather than cancel the meetings, which would result in a cessation of dialogue and an inevitable deterioration of relations, I chose, with the support of IREX, to maintain a dialogue and continue the plans for holding the first USA–USSR symposium. At this point it is perhaps appropriate to point out that my opposition to the political structure of the USSR was well known to my Soviet colleagues. They were well aware of the fact that I was born in Czechoslovakia and that, like most people of Central European background, I detested the various invasions of this region by the Soviet army no less than that of Afghanistan. I was both aware and openly critical of the social and political context in which the discipline of archaeology unfolded in the USSR. One can read of the positive achievements in Soviet archaeology in the recent work of Trigger (1989). This study offers deserved praise to their theoretical contributions but skims the surface of the painful context in which that discipline unfolded. The deaths, dismissals, and persecution that were visited on numerous archaeologists unwilling or unable to articulate the correct

Figure A

First USA–USSR Archaeological Exchange, Peabody Museum, November 1981. Standing from the left, top row—G. Dales, R. Stronach, A. Kempinski, M. Stopler, N. Yoffee, L. Levine, G. Possehl, F. Hole, J. Shaffer, G. Dollfus, J. Harlan, C. Redman, W. Sumner, G. Johnson; middle row—A. Zagarell, W. Fairservis, R. Meadow, E. Masimov, C. Cramer, V. Gulyaev, I. Winter, U. Islamov, M. Voigt; bottom row—P. Kohl, R. Dyson, V. Masson, N. Merpert, R. Munchaev, N. Negmatov, A. Muhammadzhanov, R. McAdams, C. C. Lamberg-Karlovsky. Photo: Hillel S. Burger.

Marxist perspective are captured in the early work of Miller (1956).

The initial planning session and the first archaeological symposium made it clear that collaborative excavations within Soviet Central Asia were out of the question. However, individual research trips to study museum collections and/or to archaeological institutes were encouraged. In fact, Phil Kohl had already taken advantage of this opportunity and in 1979 and 1980 had traveled to Soviet Central Asia to visit sites, study collections, and meet with colleagues. These research tours, funded by IREX, resulted in the publication of two notable works (Kohl 1981, 1984). The Soviet delegation favored the importance of symposia that were to be held every two years and that were to alternate between our two countries. The first conference was held at Harvard in the fall of 1981 and concentrated on the theme of urbanization in Central Asia. The Soviet delegation placed a special emphasis on bringing scholars from Soviet Central Asia to the symposia. The conference was attended by ten Soviet archaeologists and approximately twenty-five archaeologists invited from different departments in the United States. Threats of demonstrations by Harvard students over the Soviet invasion of Afghanistan never materialized, and after four days the symposium concluded its formal sessions. After a week in Cambridge, the Soviet delegation traveled to New York, Philadelphia, Washington, D.C., Chicago, and Santa Fe. The presence of four Central Asian archaeologists and two Russian archaeologists specializing in the archaeology of Central Asia did a great deal to reveal the exceptional importance and the richness of the Bronze Age in this region. It was also apparent that there were significant differences between scholars in the United States and those in the USSR concerning the chronology of the Central Asian Bronze Age. These differences, as is evident in this monograph, continue to this day.

The fact that the cold war was still being waged in some quarters—or was it simple paranoia?—is evident in the following incident. After the symposium Phil Kohl and I drove the Soviet delegation to New York City in a large van by way of the Brookhaven National Laboratories. Ed Sayre and Gar Harbottle had arranged to show the Soviet delegation the types of analytical work that were being done there in the field of archaeology. We took the ferry from New London, Connecticut, which passed by the Groton installation where nuclear submarines are both manufactured and visibly displayed at the docks. Someone on the sparsely inhabited ferry called the police and the FBI to inform them that a group of Russians were on board taking photographs of the submarines. The next day the *Hartford Courant* carried the story that the FBI was looking into the presence of unauthorized Soviets possibly "spying" on this nuclear facility. Two days later, on my return to Cambridge, I had a short and untroubled discussion with IREX and a lengthy, somewhat troubled conversation with our State Department. I attempted to explain to them that I simply did not know that any travel by the Soviet delegation, beyond that stipulated on their visas, had to be authorized by the State Department. Their visas did indicate that they would be in Boston and in New York. The assumption was that they would travel to these destinations by air; any other variant required permission. Ignorance was forgiven, and the delegation was permitted to continue with their itinerary.

Following this initial symposium, three other conferences were held in Samarkand, Uzbekistan SSR (1983), Washington, D.C. (1986), and Tbilisi, Georgia SSR (1988). A summary of each of the symposia was published in Russian in *Sovetskaya Arkheologiya*. During the second symposium, in Samarkand, mutual relations reached a point that permitted us to renew the question as to whether collaborative excavations would be allowed. This time the answer was more positive, and we were encouraged to consider working with Dr. Abdullah Isakov, who was excavating a very important chalcolithic settlement in Tajikistan. The site of Sarazm was said to be a surprisingly large agricultural site of the fourth millennium with ceramics that are better known from the Geoksyur oasis in Turkmenistan. Excavations in the Geoksyur oasis, directed by Vadim Masson and Viktor Sarianidi, revealed a number of agricultural villages engaged in canal irrigation by the first half of the fourth millennium. I first heard about this important work at a conference in Teheran in 1969 where Viktor Sarianidi reported on the results of these excavations. Little did either of us realize that a decade later our paths would once again cross in a productive collaboration. Sarianidi's report in Teheran caused a considerable stir, for it was the first evidence for an early-fourth-millennium settlement pattern in Central Asia. Furthermore, it was the first extensive evidence of an early irrigation agriculture beyond the confines of the Tigris and Euphrates rivers.

The site of Sarazm, located in Tajikistan on the second terrace of the Zeravshan River, was both the most easterly extension of Geoksyur ceramics and the earliest known agricultural village east of Turkmenistan. The conclusion seemed inevitable: the development of agriculture in this region was the result of its diffusion from the west, that is, from Turkmenistan. Only the process of its eastward expansion required examination. Thus, was agriculture adopted by local populations through a process of acculturation and stimulus diffusion or by an actual movement of western populations into this area? This seemingly succinct archaeological problem was layered with modern political concerns and conflicting ethnic identities. Today Central Asia is a mosaic of different ethnic groups that any daily newspaper indicates are not enamored of one another. Sarazm is located in Tajikistan, a Persian-speaking republic with strong historic and cultural ties to Iran. The modern-day republic of Turkish-speaking Turkmenistan, where the Geoksyur oasis is situated, is that region which allegedly introduced agriculture to Sarazm. Modern enthusiasms and antagonisms can have a profound effect on archaeological interpretation. We don't have the slightest notion of the ethnic identity, or of the linguistic affiliation, of the peoples that inhabited the Geoksyur oasis or the village of Sarazm in the fourth millennium. Nevertheless, pride in the past is inextricably related to the pride of place in the present. If the Geoksyur oasis offered agriculture to Sarazm, then it might be said that the lands of Turkish-speaking Turkmenistan offered agriculture to those of Persian-speaking Tajikistan. This might please a Turkmen but could easily offend a Tadzhik. Never mind that all of this happened more than six thousand years ago and that we have no idea about ethnicity within *any* archaeological context of that date. The past can be easily used to enhance or delimit ethnic tensions. It is not surprising that the Tadzhik excavator of Sarazm argues vehemently for the indigenous development of agriculture and thoroughly subordinates the role of the west (Turkmenistan) as playing any role in the origins of agriculture at Sarazm.

In 1985 Phil Kohl and I spent five weeks participating in the excavations at Sarazm. It was a thoroughly enjoyable and profitable experience. We were given the opportunity to open our own areas of excavation and to proceed in precisely the manner that we wished. It is impossible to imagine how Dr. Isakov could have been more hospitable or academically cooperative. He provided us with a number of metal samples from previous seasons of excavation that we were permitted to take back to the United States. With the assistance of Robert Maddin, we were able to publish a report on the metallurgical technology of the later-third-millennium settlement at Sarazm (Isakov, Kohl, Lamberg-Karlovsky, and Maddin 1987). Dr. Isakov enthusiastically encouraged us to continue our collaboration at Sarazm in forthcoming seasons. He planned to excavate the site for approximately a decade, a plan that he is in the process of carrying out. Perhaps we would have sustained the collaboration had it not been for an unexpected occurrence.

On the first day of our arrival at Sarazm, Dr. Isakov pointed out the trenches that were excavated by French archaeologists the summer before. We were fully aware of the fact that the French were quick to follow in our footsteps in establishing a protocol for an archaeological exchange with the USSR, but we were not informed by anyone that Roland Besenval and Bertille Lyonnet were already undertaking an excavation at Sarazm. No provision was made for a tripartite collaboration of Soviet, French, and U.S. excavations at Sarazm. Having three distinctive and uncoordinated expeditions on the same site struck Phil and I as extremely clumsy and potentially volatile. We decided to leave Sarazm in the hands of Isakov and his very capable French team, who were to spend the next five years excavating there. This was the first but by no means the last experience I had in the differences attached to the meaning of collaboration by Soviet and U.S. scholars. In Central Asia the Soviets saw no difficulty in inviting different teams to excavate on the same site without any provision as to how, or even whether, the different teams wanted to collaborate. Aside from the fact that this situation may give rise to logistical problems, let alone interpretive ones, there was (from the Soviet perspective) a very practical reason as to why this was done. Any archaeological project hosting a contingent of foreign collaborators was given a substantially greater amount of money by the Academy of Sciences of the USSR. Thus it was financially, and with regard to facilities also physically, advantageous to have as many foreigners participating as possible. Today the situation has changed. The Academy of Sciences is hard pressed for funds, and foreign expeditions operate on a completely different financial relationship.

The USA–USSR archaeological exchange offered an early model for the manner in which collaboration took place. The absolutely essential ingredient of the protocol was that there be equity between the two countries in all that was undertaken. Thus, with respect to the symposia, there had to be an equal number of participants visiting each other's country and the duration of the visit had to be the same. It was evident in the early years of the collaboration that Soviet archaeologists did not wish access to excavate or collaborate with American archaeologists in the field. However, this is what U.S. archaeologists wanted to do in the USSR. Soviet archaeologists wanted access to our centers of research. They wanted to have access to libraries and to travel to different universities. Thus, in return for the number of months that an American archaeologist worked on an excavation in the USSR, a comparable number of months was offered a Soviet archaeologist to visit the United States. Invariably, the Peabody Museum at Harvard University became the headquarters for our Soviet visitors. From there they visited New York, Philadelphia, Washington, Chicago, Ann Arbor, Santa Fe, Berkeley, and so on. Well over a dozen Soviet archaeologists visited the Peabody within the context of this agreement. The Soviet archaeologists came from virtually every corner of the USSR—from Georgia to Siberia and from Leningrad to Samarkand. Some, like

Dr. Valeri Gulyaev, fine scholar that he is, came to spend two months in the Tozzer Library filling box upon box of photocopied archaeological literature for shipment home. Others never entered the library and took maximum advantage of the shopping malls. Needless to say there was a very substantial expense to this undertaking. I was responsible for raising the money to support both the archaeological symposia and the visiting Soviet scholars in this country. The Academy of Sciences of the USSR expended a superficially inflated ruble to support U.S. scholars in the USSR. In the early 1980s the value of the dollar and the ruble was almost at parity: 1:1. Today the dollar is exchanged for several thousand rubles. The generous support of IREX, which funded the two conferences in the United States, was supplemented by substantial funds raised by the Peabody Museum, a circumstance facilitated by the fact that throughout the decade of the 1980s I served as the director of the Peabody Museum.

The last USA–USSR archaeological symposium was held in Tbilisi, Georgia SSR, in 1987. Our Soviet colleagues hoped that these conferences would continue and that within two or three years a fifth symposium would once again be held in the States. Unfortunately, this was not to occur. Dr. Wesley Fisher attended the symposium at Tbilisi and indicated that IREX had fulfilled its mission by bringing archaeologists from the two countries into a series of collaborative endeavors. With the loss of funding, the USA–USSR archaeological symposia had come to an end. Yet our own collaboration and that of many others from this country with archaeologists and philologists from Moscow, Saint Petersburg, Novosibirsk, Central Asia, and the Caucasus has expanded.

In the late 1980s a number of students in the Department of Anthropology were pursuing their interests in the anthropology of the Near East. None of these students, on entering the graduate program, had reason to believe that an opportunity existed for the undertaking of collaborative excavations in Soviet Central Asia. One of these students was Fred Hiebert. Fred came to Harvard from Ann Arbor, where he had completed his undergraduate studies at the University of Michigan. He was already an experienced field archaeologist having spent a number of seasons with a French expedition excavating a Bronze Age trade center on the island of Bahrain in the Persian Gulf. I suggested to Fred that opportunities existed for making an important contribution to the archaeology of Soviet Central Asia. His enthusiasm, although immediate, was tempered by a lingering doubt that permission for undertaking actual fieldwork might not become a reality. Fred, like Phil Kohl before him, began the long haul of taking maximum advantage of this potential opportunity; he obtained an IREX grant that permitted him to spend the summer in intensive Russian language study. I emphasize here that a commitment to working in the USSR was only a *potential* opportunity, for there were no guarantees that permission for a field collaboration would be granted. Before one could participate in such a collaboration, a facility in spoken Russian was essential. Although there are far more Soviet archaeologists who speak English than there are American archaeologists who speak Russian, a facility in spoken Russian remains essential for fieldwork in the former USSR. The asymmetry of linguistic skills that characterize CIS and American scholars is replicated in the unbalanced awareness of each other's archaeological contributions. It is a paradoxical fact that even though Western books and journals were very hard to come by in the Soviet Union, archaeologists there knew far more about the results of our research than American archaeologists, whose libraries could be filled with Soviet literature, knew of their research results. Within most of the Near East the English language is the archaeological *lingua franca*, but within the former USSR, particularly within Central Asia, spoken Russian remains an essential ingredient for a successful collaboration. Today a linguistic competence in Uzbek, Tadzhik, or Turkmen, depending on where one is working, might be more appreciated than Russian. Nevertheless, the one language shared by the Uzbeks, Tadzhiks, Mongols, and others is Russian, and, much as it might be resented by the Central Asians as the language of the imperialist period, it will remain for decades the *lingua franca* of this vast region.

Following the completion of his first year of graduate school, Fred spent his first summer studying intensive Russian at Middlebury College. This opportunity, as well as a subsequent grant that permitted him to travel to the USSR for a study tour of the major archaeological sites of Central Asia, was made possible by IREX. It was on that trip that Fred met Viktor Sarianidi, and we were able to arrange for a collaborative project of excavation at Gonur depe in Margiana. The successful results of that collaboration are reported on in this monograph as well as in volume 19 (1993) of the *Information Bulletin* (the Russian version

Figure B
First International Field Seminar in Margiana, fall 1990. At Togolok 21, left to right: A. Bader, V. Sarianidi, A. Paropla, E. Kuz'mina, L. P'yankova, C. C. Lamberg-Karlovsky.

edited by S. Potabenko and the English version edited by F. Hiebert).

Several other students expressed an interest in working in Central Asia, but the language requirement always seemed to mitigate against their final commitment to select this region as their research theater. One student not so troubled was John Schoeberlein-Engel. John was a social anthropologist with a keen linguistic facility. Adding Russian to his study of Persian and Turkish seemed to bother him not at all. He was much interested in undertaking research in Central Asia but not as an archaeologist. He wanted to study the changes brought about during the Soviet period in the relations of traditional pastoral society and their sedentary neighbors. Initially, to obtain permission to work in Central Asia, he had to frame his research request within an ethnoarchaeological format. In the mid-1980s it was simply not possible for a foreigner to work freely within Central Asia as a social anthropologist. Thus, to explore the possibilities of research in Central Asia, John obtained permission to collaborate with Dr. Numan Negmatov, an archaeologist who was excavating a site of the late medieval period in the mountainous region of Tajikistan. In 1985 I spent a month with Dr. Negmatov on one of his excavations in Tajikistan and it was relatively easy for me to establish a liaison for John. His participation in this excavation afforded him an initial access to the Tadzhiks within the Pamirs. As the process of perestroika unfolded and as John established his own contacts among Soviet ethnographers, he was able to expand on his interests and shed his adopted enthusiasm for archaeology. He was to spend a total of almost three years in various parts of Central Asia as a basis for his Ph.D. dissertation (Schoeberlein-Engel 1994).

Today the changes within the former Soviet Union occur with such rapidity and with such apparent unpredictability that it is impossible to fully comprehend what the future of that vast landscape holds for its inhabitants. When the research reported on in this monograph was undertaken, Turkmenistan was an autonomous republic within the USSR. Today it is an independent nation. In the past, permission to collaborate on an archaeological project in Central Asia had to be reviewed and approved by the Institute of Archaeology in Moscow. Today Moscow no longer holds the power of centralized authority. To work in any of the independent states of Central Asia, the Baltic, or the Caucasus, one must obtain the permission of the authority within the state that administers archaeological resources. No longer is there an outside authority monitoring their decisions. As indicated in the quote of Dolukhanov, "it has become much more difficult" to obtain permission to work in the newly independent states. But more difficult for whom? Certainly not for Western Europeans and Americans! Ironically enough Dolukhanov is referring to Russians. Russians, seen today as the old oppressors, are understandably having more difficulty in obtaining access and permission to work in their former colonies. All other foreigners are being not only welcomed but encouraged to undertake research in these newly founded nations. Within the past two to three years, the French, British, Italians, Japanese, Indians, Australians, and Americans have all actively initiated collaborative archaeological projects in Central Asia. Given the open enthusiasm expressed by the newly formed nation-states for collaboration, there is every reason to believe that more international projects will be initiated in the near future. Given a state of political stability, a condition that is far from evident but much to be hoped for, the Central Asian nations and those of the Caucasus, where there is greater political turbulence, have become the "in" regions for archaeological research in the 1990s.

On the one hand, the increase in archaeological collaboration is something to be applauded; on the other, it poses new threats and problems. In the past the foreigner collaborating in the USSR did not cover the costs for his/her stay in the USSR. The foreign researcher was inevitably an invited guest of the Academy of Sciences of the USSR, and that institution covered all costs. In fact, under the previous regime the foreign researcher was paid a salary while working in the USSR. When in 1981 I asked why I was receiving an allocation of funds, I was told, "The USSR does not exploit its workers!" In establishing reciprocal exchange visits, a formal necessity in days past, each country was responsible for paying all of the costs of the visiting scientists. Thus all the expenses of the visiting scientist, while in the USSR, were covered; a senior scientist, one of the endless array of hierarchical categories that existed in that would-be classless society, obtained in rubles the equivalent of about $15 per day (late 1980s). In reciprocating we covered the expenses of the visiting USSR scholars and offered them approximately $35 a day; paradoxically, no hierarchical categories existed in our own class society and all scientists, irrespective of rank or title, were given the same amount.

Today the entirety of this structure has changed. The collapse of the Soviet Union and the demise of the Academy of Sciences of the USSR have had profound consequences for international collaboration. The former USSR is simply unable to afford collaborative undertakings within the structure of financial reciprocity. The Academy of Sciences of Russia, and the Academies of the newly established nation-states, simply lack the funds to initiate reciprocal scientific exchanges. Today, in conformity with the normal procedures around the world, scientists desiring to collaborate in the former USSR must bear the burden of their own expenses. Under normal circumstances there is little reason to express concern for this turn of events. However, the circumstances within the former USSR are far from normal.

Every republic of the former USSR is in a state of financial crisis. Even those that are rich in valuable resources, oil, gold, diamonds, caviar, and so on are in financial straits. Archaeology, a science deemed less fundamental than biology, chemistry, or physics, is given a far smaller allocation of state funds than in previous days. To compensate for this new reality, archaeological institutes must raise their own funds not only to sustain their research programs but to maintain their personnel (Dolukhanov 1993). Archaeological institutes in Russia that lack substantial foreign collaboration—including The Institute of Archaeology in Moscow—have had to cut 25 to 30 percent of their staff, whereas those that have initiated strong international programs—Saint Petersburg and Novosibirsk—are faring somewhat better. Under the present condition there is reason to fear that archaeological institutes will become increasingly dependent on foreign capital. Today institutes must raise a significant portion of their own funds in order to survive and one of the likely sources is foreign collaborators. The extremely favorable exchange rate of virtually all foreign currencies, save those of Eastern Europe, against the ruble favors the foreign researcher. Today the salary of an academician within the Russian Academy of Sciences is less than $100 a month. This sum represents the highest salary offered a scientist working within an institute in Russia. There are still only a minuscule number of scientists who work for private concerns where the remuneration is substantially higher. A university professor would obtain significantly less than the above sum. Given the need of the archaeological institutes to increasingly support themselves and given the very low salaries of their personnel, it is not hard to imagine how much one can accomplish with a few thousand dollars. The average salary of a member of an archaeological institute is now less than $300 a year. In their need for foreign currency the institutes of archaeology may become entirely indiscriminate in offering permission to excavate archaeological sites. Even worse, but not surprising, is the emergence of an antiquities market involved in the sale of archaeological objects. It will not be long before archaeological objects looted from sites in the former USSR will be on sale in the international antiquities market. The greater the amount of international collaboration, the greater the flow of revenue, and the greater the revenue, the more viable the financial stability of the institute. When two parties undertake a scientific collaboration and one side engages mainly to gain revenue from the other, an asymmetrical relationship, one of dependence, is bound to emerge. In time this relationship will become resented by both parties. It is not the science that matters in such a collaboration but the money: one side will attempt to extort as much as possible, while the other may attempt to exploit his or her superior financial position.

In the past it was the administrative hierarchy of the institutes that benefited the most from foreign collaboration. The leaders of the institutes served themselves well. They traveled and they had access to foreign currency. Today precisely the same hierarchy remains in control of the most influential institutes of archaeology in Russia: Moscow, Saint Petersburg, and Novosibirsk. It is this same hierarchy that one negotiates with today. It is they who obtain the funds from the foreign collaborator and they who redistribute it within their institutes. It is not only President Clinton and President Yeltsin who express their concern for preventing foreign aid from falling into the hands of the Soviet "Mafia." Today there is no single model or structure by which archaeological collaboration unfolds in the former USSR. The rules for the preservation, conservation, and excavation of antiquities have not been formally written in any of the republics. Within Russia it remains uncertain as to whether the new laws of private property include or exclude the right to personally own an archaeological monument. Under the worst of possibilities, the law may permit an individual to buy an archaeological site. Should this situation emerge the former Soviet Union may revert to conditions that characterized the colonial era in which nation-states held a "concession" on a particular site for nearly a century, for example, the French at Susa and the Germans at Uruk.

With the same authorities in charge of most of the institutes, the process of meaningful change will take considerable time. Today the Russian Academy of Sciences contains virtually the identical membership of the former Soviet Academy. Names of institutes change, but the structures of authority and those wielding it remain virtually unchanged. The Academy of Sciences of the USSR was one of the very few institutions that favored the August coup of 1991. In recognition of the fact that institutions of power are unlikely to resign their authority, two distinguished scientists, the biologist A. Vorundstov and the physicist I. Kapitsa, founded an Academy of Natural Sciences in the hopes that this organization will be able to deal more readily and more honestly with the new changes that confront Russia. In Central Asia only Turkmenistan offers an illusion of being a beacon of stability. Ironically, this is due entirely to the fact that democracy has yet to make an impact on the leadership of that republic and alternative political expressions are severely repressed. Those in control are those who ruled the country years ago. On the other hand, Tajikistan is in a state of civil war, and Uzbekistan sustains a constant turmoil of political conflict among an increasing number of political parties. Internal tumult, even a war within a republic, need not necessarily affect an ongoing foreign collaboration. This is well attested to by Phil Kohl's successful archaeological project in Armenia and Georgia.

The political changes of 1989–90 have permanently altered the conditions for archaeological research in the former USSR. Institutes of archaeology, whether in Moscow or Tbilisi, are being forced to examine their overstaffed and underfunded programs. Funding for archaeological research has been drastically cut back, forcing major staff reductions. Institutes of archaeology, previously funded by the state through the Academy of Sciences of the USSR, are today required to raise significant portions of their own needed funds. This has led a number of archaeologists in the former USSR, with some success, to submit grant applications to Western funding agencies. Publication programs, irrespective of discipline, are confronting exceptional challenges. Journals and monographs confront paper shortages and rampant inflation, and have become both too expensive to produce and beyond the means of most to acquire. Even journals of outstanding significance, such as *Vestnik Drevnii Istorii*, are not immune from possible extinction. Several journals, mostly those produced in the ethnic republics, have already ceased to exist or suspended publication. With attempts and encouragement to transfer to a market economy, new methods have arisen in the search for funds. Some of these have been innovative; the Institute of Archaeology in Novosibirsk, for example, raises funds by sponsoring tours of Siberia for Western travelers and offers loan exhibitions of archaeological artifacts recovered from Siberian sites. Others are of more dubious merit—hunting expeditions in which fees are paid for the killing of a specific animal, for example, $5,000 for a Siberian bear. I have even heard it said that animals on the international list of endangered species—the snow leopard and the polar bear—could be hunted for a price.

Throughout the former USSR there is an increasing eagerness to engage the foreign archaeologist in a collaborative program. In part this new enthusiasm for collaboration is motivated by an access to much-needed foreign funds. Less than a decade ago there was not a single collaborative archaeological excavation in what was Soviet Central Asia; within the past five years there have been French, Italian, Japanese, British, Indian, and U.S. joint expeditions to this region. Sites of very major significance that only a few years ago could not be visited by foreigners, for either real or alleged security reasons, are today the scenes of collaborative excavations. Thus the site of Merv, one of the most important Iron Age cities in Central Asia, is the scene of a major collaboration that brings together archaeologists of the Turkmen Republic, the Institute of Archaeology in Saint Petersburg, and a British team. The possibilities for collaborative undertakings are exciting and at times disconcerting, for they have introduced perturbations into the archaeological environment. Because collaborative undertakings within the former USSR are a relatively new phenomenon, it is not always clear what rights and privileges pertain to the collaborating parties, as we ourselves experienced at Sarazm. The favorable exchange rate of foreign currency, particularly the dollar, against the ruble allows the foreign archaeologist to undertake a program of excavation for an extremely modest amount of money. This circumstance, as already indicated above, can lead to considerable tension when feelings of exploitation arise in the CIS archaeologist, who attempts, in turn, to compensate by charging the foreign archaeologist an amount thought by him or her to be excessive. There is little doubt that the new archaeological climate both welcomes and anticipates an increasing number of collaborative undertakings. Even though uncertainties and stress will prevail for the short term, the eventual outcome will be an internationalization of a more vigorous research climate. The new conditions within the former USSR allow for the emergence of a number of short-term problems and a singular long-term concern. In the short term, archaeological research, personnel, publications, archaeological sites, and museums are threatened by an absence of sufficient funds. Increasing political stability and long-range economic development offer promise for the resolution of the dominantly financial problems. A long-term concern, one without ready solution and familiar to all in capitalist countries, pertains to a new problem that did not exist in the former USSR: an antiquities market and the looting of archaeological sites. Under the Communist regime there simply was no market for the archaeological artifact. All archaeological sites were protected by law and were the inalienable property of the government. Infringement of these laws was severely punished, as was any attempt to market antiquities. Today archaeological artifacts, some allegedly taken from museum collections, can be seen for sale along the Arbat in Moscow. The fact that an antiquities market has begun to appear throughout what used to be called the Communist bloc is further evidenced by an article that appeared in the *New York Times* on March 15, 1992, titled, "East European Antiquities Shed Light on a Hidden World." Unfortunately, this world may seem "hidden" to government officials but not to the art dealers who profit from the sale of pillaged objects nor to the general public and scholars who lose the historical significance of an artifact when it is ripped out of its context. What Peter Bogucki (1993:148) has written regarding Eastern Europe has a precise resonance for the former USSR: "Previously, tight enforcement of national antiquities laws kept such behavior in check, but with borders now open and funds tight, one suspects that there will be more looting and trafficking in ill-gotten antiquities in years to come."

Not surprisingly, a spirit of independence and democracy has reached the most isolated regions of the USSR. In 1991 I participated in the excavations of a Scythian tomb located on the Beltek plateau in the Altai mountains of Siberia (Molodin 1992). Despite the spirit of international cooperation, including a film crew from NHK, Japanese national television, the tomb originally excavated was not the choice of the Russian excavator, Dr. Natasha Polosmak. Native villagers, some of whom are voicing a desire for independence from Russia, strongly protested the excavation of the tomb originally selected. They believed that those buried in the tombs were their ancestors, and they did not want them robbed or disturbed by archaeologists. The choice of a second, smaller tomb was made, one far distant from any settlement. In the summer of 1993 we were able to arrange for both a film crew from National Geographic Television and a team from *National Geographic* magazine to prepare a film and an article on the excavation of Scythian burials in the Altai mountains. The native peoples of the

Altai share the same attitude concerning the excavation of cemeteries as do the native peoples of the United States. In this instance, however, the belief of the Altai population is in error. The modern population is a distinctive people that colonized the Altai in the past millennium. Thus they cannot claim with any historical accuracy to be descended from the Iron Age Scythians. Perhaps the only peoples of the USSR with a degree of legitimacy in claiming descent from the Scythians are the Ossetes, who inhabit the northern regions of Georgia.

The research reported on in this monograph would not have been possible without the extraordinarily generous spirit of collaboration that characterizes Viktor Sarianidi and our colleagues in the Ministry of Culture and the Institute of Archaeology in Turkmenistan. It is hard to imagine a colleague more generous in spirit than Viktor Sarianidi. Excavations at Gonur depe in the fall of 1990 recovered a substantial and unique bar ingot. On the very day of its discovery, I expressed to Viktor an interest in having this important object analyzed. Without hesitation he handed me the object to take to the States for analysis. This is absolutely typical of his generosity; the analysis has been accomplished and the object is en route to Turkmenistan. In Moscow, Dr. Rauf Munchaev and Dr. Valeri Guliaev, deputy directors of the Institute of Archaeology, always supported our efforts to extend the reach of our collaborative endeavors. Dr. Valeri Alexeev, the late director of the Institute of Archaeology, was both dedicated to and responsible for an increase in international collaboration. He was one of the few scholars that endorsed, without equivocation or ambivalence, the political changes that were occurring within the USSR. It might be pointed out that the previous director of the institute, Dr. Boris Rybakov, who presided over the affairs of the institute from 1954 to 1988, informed me on the occasion of the second USA–USSR symposium in Samarkand, that there was neither need nor benefit in our two countries collaborating. In Uzbekistan, Dr. Ahmedali Askarov offered cooperation and assistance to all who came either to visit or to work on the archaeology of that country. In Tajikistan, the assistance of Dr. Alexander Ranov, Dr. Abdullah Isakov, and Dr. Numan Negmatov is gratefully acknowledged. Finally, the generous support of IREX made possible four USA–USSR archaeological symposia and funded, in part, the research that is reported on in this volume. Within the Peabody Museum, the generous support of Mr. Landon Clay and the American School of Prehistoric Research allowed for much to take place within the context of the USA–USSR collaboration, including the publication of this volume. To all of the above we are most grateful.

I close with a final word from Raphael Pumpelly. Quoted below is his grant proposal requesting the sum of $5,000 from the Carnegie Institution in Washington, D.C. The funding of this proposal permitted him to undertake the excavations at Anau in Turkmenistan in 1903 and 1904. The material remains recovered from the excavations at Anau were deposited at the Hermitage Museum in Saint Petersburg and at the Peabody Museum at Harvard University. In a search for additional documentation pertaining to the Pumpelly expedition, this document was recently recovered by Fred Hiebert from the files of the Carnegie Institution. In the summer of 1993, ninety years after Pumpelly "discovered" Anau, Fred Hiebert and I initiated a program of renewed excavations at Anau.

Pumpelly's impact on the archaeology of Asia was profound. This is particularly so with regard to his advancing the notion that environmental change was a causative factor in bringing about both settlement shifts and migratory movements (Wright 1971). Pumpelly's reconstruction of an oasis culture formed the foundation for what came to be known as the "oasis theory" for the origins of agriculture. This theory, which suggested that environmental desiccation was causative in bringing about the Neolithic revolution, was initially promulgated by Ellsworth Huntington, who had been a member of Pumpelly's staff at Anau. Later he was to be regarded by many as the *enfant terrible* of environmental determinism (Huntington 1945). Without doubt the most influential proponent of the "oasis theory" was V. Gordon Childe, whose writings on the subject go back to the 1920s.

Based on the materials recovered from Anau, Pumpelly believed that increasing aridity resulted in a collapse of settlement within the Bronze Age of Central Asia. This idea has withstood the test of time (see Dolukhanov 1988) even if some of the facts he relied on were in error—for example, there is little evidence to support the existence of a Central Asian sea larger than the Mediterranean. In 1908 Pumpelly published his two-volume report *Explorations in Turkestan: Expedition of 1904*. Beyond the expected report that details the nature of the excavated artifacts and the architecture and stratigraphy, his volumes contain chapters on the wheat and barley recovered from the excavations by H. C. Schellenberg; the animal remains, with a special emphasis on the horse, by J. Ulrich Duerst; the chemical analysis of metals by F. A. Gooch; the geologic and physiologic features by Ellsworth Huntington; and the physiography of deserts and oases with accompanying soil analyses by Raphael Pumpelly. Pumpelly's interdisciplinary approach to the study of a region and the excavation of a site was not to be duplicated in Asia until the passing of almost half a century, when Robert Braidwood began his Jarmo Project in Iraq. Pumpelly began his research in Central Asia by advancing the following specific hypotheses:

> If we try to retrace, through time and space, the steps of human progress, we find the various paths all converging towards the East in Southern Central Asia. Already at our start—whether in Egypt, Asia Minor, Mesopotamia, Persia, India, or China—we find highly developed civilizations existent at periods of some thousands of years before our era. In each instance, a veil hides the beginnings. On this side of the veil is already empire, organized civilization, luxury; beyond is the region of myth and tradition, a region of time and space in which our only guides are philology, ethnology, and archaeological research.
>
> All of these civilizations at the hither extremes of the diverging paths, retain features more or less common to each other, whether in language, tradition, customs, or religion.
>
> The meeting point of the converging paths was necessarily in the region beyond the Caspian Sea. The paths were irrevocably determined by the practicable passes through the great mountain ranges; and these routes were from prehistoric to recent times the great lines of trade. Moreover along these ways and in this region there were cities of the very ancient world—Bactria, Bamian, Samarkand, and others.
>
> Now there is reason to believe that this Trans-Caspian region, which is today largely desolate, enjoyed in prehistoric times a very different climate, capable of supporting large populations. This hypothesis is based on the following facts. The area which we will call the Trans-Caspian basin—an area of nearly one million square miles—and much larger than the Mediterranean—is a great plain, on which all the drainage is into the land-locked Caspian and Aral seas or into countless salt lakes and ponds. These smaller lakes are disappearing through evaporation, as shown on Russian maps of the past two centuries. If this shrinkage of water surfaces is due to a secular increase of evaporation over rainfall, there was evidently a time when these now separated lakes and seas were merged in one great body of inland water. This great inland sea was doubtless caused by the melting of that part of the glacial ice-cap that covered most of Eastern Russia west of the Ural Mountains, draining through the Rivers Volga and Ural, and by the then greatly enlarged glaciers of the Hindukush and Tienshan Mountains, draining through the Oxus, Jaxartes, and Tchou Rivers.
>
> With the disappearance of the Russian ice-cap and the shrinkage of the central Asiatic glaciers there began evaporation in excess of supply, and with this the climatic change toward aridity. This view is confirmed by the finding by the Russian geologists, of glacial clay beds carrying shells, of the glacial period, on the flanks of the Ural Mountains, in such a position as would show them to have been deposited on the border of this inland sea. It is evident that such a large body of water must have given to the countries surrounding it, a climate of agricultural possibilities very different from those now existing and capable of supporting large populations.
>
> With the diminishing area of water came a change of climate, a change probably in an increasing ratio at first lessening the productive capacity of the land, accompanied during the centuries by emigration of whole peoples to more favored regions East, South, and West. And in this I think lies the ultimate cause that sent the successive prehistoric, and later, waves of humanity into India, Persia, and Europe and to China. The tendency of geological reasoning is now toward a shortening of the time since the last stages of the glacial epoch, bringing it to within a period of prehistoric human life.
>
> The central abodes of the populations would be on the rivers, and on the great lines of intercourse, around the borders of the sea; and it seems probable that some of those of more ancient importance, were on the sites of those still existing towns, that were already old when mentioned, in what is to us, ancient history—as Bactria, Samarkand, Bamian.
>
> When we consider the physical geographical conditions, and the indications of remote contact between the eastern and western civilizations, it seems probable that this inland sea may have had an inter-reactionary influence in the development of civilizations similar to that exerted by the Mediterranean at a later date.
>
> And there can be little doubt, it would seem, that in these then fertile regions, empires arose and accumulated wealth; and that their cities were repeatedly destroyed and rebuilt on the old sites, leaving, in successive layers the traces of their organized life. Here may be hidden connecting links in the prehistoric life of the Aryan, Semitic, and Chinese races.

Assuming on apparently good reasons:

1st, That an inland sea larger than the Mediterranean once occupied the Caspian-Aral Basin and was derived from the melting of the glacial ice-cap in European Russia; 2nd, That the contemporaneous climate permitted the existence of large bordering populations; 3rd, That the drying up of the Sea, excepting the Caspian, Aral, and Balkash, was due to the disappearance of the Russian ice-cap; 4th, That the change of climate towards the present aridity caused the dispersion of these peoples to China, India, Western Asia, and Europe; 5th, That the cities, already old at the dawn of history—Samarkand, Bactria, and others on the great ancient trade routes between the far East and India, Persia, Western Asia and Egypt, were in more remote antiquity, the sites of centres of these dispersed populations.

It is desired to study the past and present physico-geographic conditions of this basin and its archaeological remains, the physical and archaeological studies to be correlative factors of an apparently well defined historical problem.

Raphael Pumpelly
Newport, Rhode Island
December 12, 1902

Preface

V. I. Sarianidi
Institute of Archaeology, Moscow

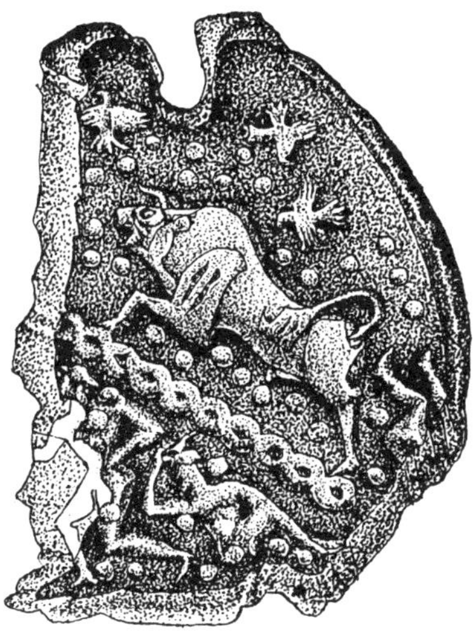

THE DISCOVERY OF LARGE BRONZE AGE OASIS SETTLEMENTS in Bactria and Margiana is one of the major events in the postwar archaeology of the greater Near East. Large-scale archaeological reconnaissance and excavation by Soviet and other researchers have revealed a separate center of ancient Near Eastern culture, with its own distinctive and local development of cultural complexity.

The monumental architecture of Bactria and Margiana was clearly built on distinctive plans, which employed sophisticated mathematic, geometric, and astronomic calculations. Our wide-scale excavations have revealed a uniform school of architecture, which takes its place in the system of the whole ancient Near East.

The oasis culture of Bactria and Margiana is characterized by a very high level of craft production such as pottery, metalsmithing, stonecutting, and sculpture. The style and artistic motifs found originating from these regions open a completely new page in the ancient history of Asia and, despite the lack of a writing system, have led our Western colleagues to suggest that this is a fifth center of Old World civilization (together with Mesopotamia, Egypt, India, and China).

It is almost twenty years since Bronze Age Bactria and Margiana were first investigated, and the subsequent long-term investigations have produced a large corpus of material concerning the origins and development of complex culture in Bactria and Margiana. It is this material that is the focus of the present book. The young American archaeologist Fredrik Hiebert has undertaken a multiyear project studying collections in many museums and, in particular, has participated in field expeditions in Turkmenistan, allowing him to draw a well-proportioned picture and document the life and culture of Bronze Age populations on the great Bactrian plain and in the ancient delta of the Murgab River. Hiebert presents the most current synthesis of these two Bronze Age regions, utilizing a framework that allows comparison with other Bronze Age civilizations.

Through systematic excavations and application of scientific methods of analysis of ecological data, the author not only generalizes the known archaeological data but presents a detailed description of Gonur depe in Margiana, revealing its distinctiveness in the system of the whole ancient Near East. It is this technique of presenting the whole archaeological culture as a systematic complex in relationship to adjacent

Figure C
Gonur south, fall 1993. Photo: Courtesy of V. Sarianidi.

cultures that has allowed him to create a general work that will be required text for all specialists engaged in the archaeology and ancient history of the Near East of the Bronze Age.

It is quite natural that the present book in its general synthesis has some points of discussion that require further investigation.

The first point concerns the origin of the Bactrian-Margiana Archaeological Complex. At present there are two principal viewpoints on the origin of the BMAC. Hiebert joins many archaeologists in suggesting that Bactria and Margiana were colonized from southern Turkmenistan during the Namazga V times and that the innovations of the BMAC are due to culture contact. It is my viewpoint that Margiana was founded by newcomers from southern Turkmenistan and practically simultaneously by migration of peoples from the west. Within this preface it is not possible to restate all the previously presented evidence to prove this or the other viewpoint (Sarianidi 1989a, 1990, 1992). For this purpose, new direct archaeological evidence is needed, and recent excavations in Margiana have brought to light such information, albeit in a preliminary form.

Thus the ongoing excavations at the south mound at Gonur (fig. C) in the area of the temple have uncovered steatite amulets and impressions of cylinder seals with images of winged birdmen holding in their hand the back feet of defeated animals. Similar compositions are unknown in Iran and Afghanistan, but they are very popular in the Syro-Anatolian region. In this respect a particular significance is given to the bull edicts with similar compositions from the archive in Acemhöyük which are well dated to 1800–1750 B.C. (Özgüç 1980). It is likely that the Margiana images are related to the Syro-Anatolian motifs, of which those images from the Acemhöyük archive are so far the earliest (fig. D). Although the actual mechanism of how this motif was propagated from the advanced centers of the Near East to distant Margiana is not yet clear, to my mind it penetrated this region together with the new tribes who arrived at the basin of the Murgab River delta, and despite the distance between these regions and the gaps in our understanding of the historical events of the supposed movements of populations, it is quite evident that the similarities in composition reflect mythological notions that existed among a related group or tribe. Even if one assumes that the Margiana populations were looking for resources in regions as far as Syria-Anatolia, it is unlikely that they would learn the mythological compositions while the mythological notions were foreign and strange to them. I would like to note that these are recently found objects in Margiana that were not available to the author of the present book.

Figure D
The image of a winged birdman from Acemhöyük (center) in relationship to similar images from Gonur south.

The problem of chronology also remains unresolved. Former Soviet and our Western colleagues traditionally diverge in opinion on the date of the late Bronze Age of Central Asia, including Bactria and Margiana, by at least five hundred years. Added to the previous radiocarbon dates, here are presented nine new dates obtained at the Beta laboratory in Florida. However, it should be mentioned that when the Bactrian-Margiana Archaeological Complex was first described almost twenty years ago, our Western colleagues were inclined to place the time of the existence of the complex entirely in the third millennium B.C. P. Amiet soon revised his opinion and remarked that the antiquities were not so archaic as they were *archaized* in such a way that, with time, he began to date the Bactrian-Margiana Archaeological Complex over a range from the late third millennium to the early second millennium B.C. (Amiet 1979). The new radiocarbon data substantially support the latter opinion, relating the time of the main existence of the Bactrian-Margiana Archaeological Complex to around 2000 B.C. At the same time, a paradoxical panorama is obtained when the sites of Margiana that existed in the second half of the second millennium fall out of the scale. As is known, the sites of Margiana form a chronologically *successive* line of development from the late Bronze Age to the early Iron Age and the Achaemenid and Parthian periods. It must be pointed out that both at Gonur south and at Togolok 21 there were some unique artifacts made of iron, a fact that does not allow the dates of the BMAC to be pushed back so far as suggested by the radiocarbon dates. To my mind, such a divergence in dates is explained either by the imperfect nature of the laboratory analyses or by some regional radiocarbon variation currently unrecognized by radiocarbon experts.

The author of the present book himself was in Margiana and could see how the occupation of sites generally shifted southward in a continuous occupation, like the baton of a relay race, passing from one time to another. For example, on the southern outskirts of Takhirbai 3 there are material remains of Achaemenid occupation, demonstrating occupational continuity and excluding chronological gaps in the occupation of Margiana. In other words, I wonder whether the chronological discrepancies in dates are due more to the imperfect nature of the technique than to the various approaches in the evaluation of the chronological framework.

The new excavations in Margiana offer additional data to the perspectives presented here. We found a few Andronovo ceramics among the masses of local pottery in the excavations of the temple buildings at Togolok 1 and Togolok 21. In 1992, during the excavation of the so-called tower complex (room 500, central building), at Gonur south, it was discovered that the northern set of towers is actually connected with the adjacent premises. We then discovered data that prove that the entire tower complex was associated with ritual steps of preparing and using the hallucinogenic beverage of a *haoma* or *soma* type. On the floor of one of the rooms, near a miniature column, was a sooted vessel with incised decoration—a ceramic typical of the Tazabag'yab steppe nomadic culture of Khorezm.

The consistency with which these ceramics of the nomadic tribes are found in the temples of Margiana, associated with the preparation of the hallucinogenic beverage or juices of *haoma/soma* type supports an old theory expressed almost one hundred years ago by the Russian orientalist V. Grigoriev and revised later by academician V. V. Struve. Both of these scholars paid attention to a statement by Ptolemy on the heterogeneity of the populations of Margiana, which included the Massagatai or "Big Saka." Thus, in an earlier period, the Eastern Saka and the "Amyrgioi" Saka penetrated this area, and both scholars applied the name "Amyrgioi" to the Murgab River. On the other hand, referring to Saka Amyrgioi, in ancient Persian writing the words "saka haumavarga" were used, that is, the "*haoma* manufacturing" people. As V. V. Struve states, the word *Haomavarga* represents an attempt to etymologize the Iranian ethnic name reflected in the Greek word *Amyrgiois*, but according to V. Grigoriev there is a similarity of sounds between the words *Haomavarga* and *Amyurgiami* (Struve 1949). The archaeological data allow us to suppose that the Amyrgioian Saka who lived in the basin of the Murgab River delta were already acquainted with the local settled population from whom they learned to use the ritual hallucinogenic beverage of *haoma/soma*. That is why they are mentioned as "*haoma* manufacturing" Saka in the ancient Persian texts. It should be added that another early Russian orientalist, V. Abaev, went so far as to suggest that Zarathustra himself was from Scythian descent (Abaev 1990).

If one collates the archaeological data with ancient Persian texts of Achaemenid date on the contacts between the settled and the nomad tribes who lived in the neighborhood of the Murgab River delta, it is possible to suggest that the pottery found in the BMAC temples in Margiana is not accidental but reflects their interaction. The hypothesis that the steppe Tazabag'yab tribes were acquainted with the settled tribes of their southern neighbors is supported both in the excavations in Margiana and in the excavations of Tazabag'yab tribes of Khorezm.

The process of collating the data produced by archaeology with the ancient texts certainly does not permit the resolution of the problem, but it raises it to a new level of research. All the texts are unanimous in the idea that Zarathustra was by origin from the ancient Iranian population. Professor V. Livshits, the preeminent scholar on the Avesta and the origins of Zoroaster, suggests that "in that epoch, nomadic cattle breeders gradually took up agriculture." In other words, the data and their implications now at our disposal take the study of the Zoroastrian problem to a new level of research.

In conclusion, the monograph written by F. Hiebert represents an in-depth review of the late Bronze Age of Margiana in the perspective of the greater Near East. Hiebert is currently the most qualified specialist on this subject due to his personal experience, and without any doubt he will continue to publish new works on the Bronze Age of this region.

Viktor I. Sarianidi

Acknowledgments

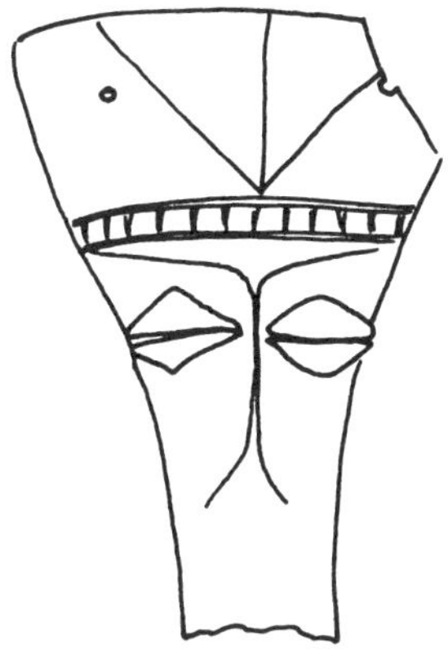

THIS RESEARCH WAS UNDERTAKEN AS A PRELIMINARY attempt to combine many disparate traditions in archaeology—Soviet, American, and western European—in the study of a region that until recently had remained terra incognita to much of the archaeological community. Such an undertaking could have been successful only as a part of a wide network of colleagues and institutions.

C. C. Lamberg-Karlovsky first suggested the area of Central Asia as an important arena for research. My research would not have been possible without his enthusiasm, encouragement, advice, and support. Our visit to Gonur depe in 1990 was a wonderful opportunity for me to see the site with new perspective. Kwang-chih Chang, Richard H. Meadow, Richard Frye, and Oleg Grabar have been enthusiastic supporters of this research in Turkmenistan.

This research program was made possible by the encouragement and generosity of Viktor Ivanovich Sarianidi (Institute of Archaeology, Moscow), who allowed me to join his expedition and study the materials from his previous excavations. He proposed that I join his expedition when everyone else considered collaboration in Turkmenistan impossible. His courage in bringing about this project and his support of young scholars will never be forgotten.

My language training and research in the Soviet Union (1987, 1988-1989) was sponsored by the International Research and Exchange Board (IREX). I was based at the Institute of Archaeology in Moscow and at the Turkmen State University in Ashkhabad, Turkmenistan. My official advisors in the Soviet Union were Professor Anagilide Gubaev, of the Turkmen State University, and the late academic Valeri Alexeev, former director of the Institute of Archaeology, Moscow.

My fieldwork consisted of two seasons. Katherine Moore and I joined V. I. Sarianidi's team in the spring 1989 field campaign at Gonur depe. Our participation in the project was supported by IREX. Additional support in Turkmenistan was provided by the Ministry of Culture, Turkmenistan, and the Institute of History and Archaeology of the Turkmen Academy of Sciences. I especially thank L. P'yankova and O. Rosenthal. I gratefully acknowledge two superb archaeologists based at the Academy of Sciences in Turkmenistan, I. Masimov and B. Udemuradov, who generously shared unpublished information with me. T. Khodzhanyazov, and M. Kurbansakhatov, of The Southern Turkmenistan Archeological Expedition

(IUTAKE) provided assistance in Turkmenistan. I especially acknowledge Galina Paul and her family for the hospitality and generosity they extended to me during my long stays in Ashgabat.

R. Munchaev, V. Gulyaev, and S. Potebenko in Moscow offered their assistance and advice. In the Saint Petersburg (formerly Leningrad) branch of the Institute of Archaeology, V. Masson, A. Niconorov, and A. Nikitin received me warmly and allowed me to study collections. I thank I. Khlopin for allowing me to study the collections from Namazga depe. I also studied collections in Tashkent, Samarkand, Pendzhikent, and Dushanbe. I especially thank A. Askarov, L. Al'baum, T. Shirinov, E. Rtveladze, and G. Pugachenkova for their assistance.

In France, J.-F. Jarrige, director of the Musée Guimée, and H.-P. Francfort allowed me to work in the laboratory of the URA 10 and to study the field reports from Mehrgarh and Sibri. S. Cleuziou showed me the study collections from Tureng tepe. Bertrand Bouchet of Paris shared his research on the traditional oasis while we were in Ashgabat.

In the United States, I studied collections in the University Museum, University of Pennsylvania with permission and assistance from R. Dyson and G. Possehl. C. C. Lamberg-Karlovsky gave permission for me to study the Peabody Museum's collections from Khurab and Tepe Yahya. I thank N. van der Merwe, D. Killick, S. Young, and R. Maddin for assistance in the analysis of the Central Asian metals. The analysis of the metals was funded through the Thaw Fellowship, Peabody Museum. I thank Naomi Miller, who greatly enriched this study with her analysis of the botanical remains and reconstruction of the plant ecology of Gonur. Kate Moore analyzed the faunal remains from Gonur. I would also like to thank Richard Meadow, Erika Evasdottir, Sharri Clark, and other members of the Central Asia Archaeology Seminar at Harvard University for their comments on this manuscript. Special thanks are due to Margaret R. Courtney (Publication Director, Peabody Museum) and Amy Hirschfeld (Department of Anthropology), for their assistance in the production of this volume. The Peabody Museum, the Department of Anthropology at Harvard University, and the American School of Prehistoric Research provided financial support for many aspects of this research.

Note on Translations and Transliterations

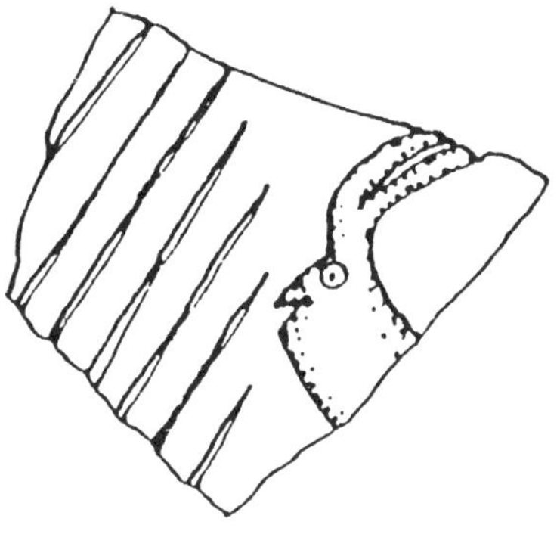

Russian and Turkmen Turkish vocabulary (both of which use the Cyrillic alphabet) is employed for specific archaeological forms and features, rather than the approximate translations of these in English. This allows the reader to compare most accurately this work with that of other published sources. The transliteration system used in the text and in the bibliography is based on the system recommended by the U.S. Board on Geographic Names. For example, the name of the archaeologist Хлопин is Khlopin, and not Hlopin, Klopin, Chlopin, or Xlopin. The journal Советская Археология is *Sovetskaya Arkheologiya*, and not *Sovetskaja Archeologija* or *Sovetskaia Arkheologiia*. I am consistent with Russian usage in the formation of plurals; for example, *khomcha* (singular) becomes *khomchi* (plural). This transliteration system is consistent with Kohl (1984).

Introduction

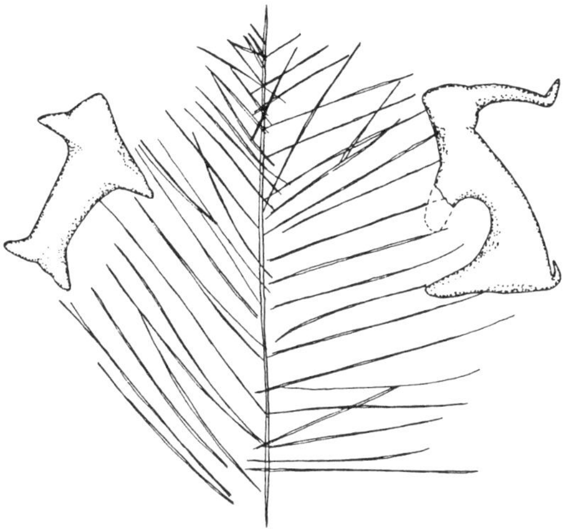

In the heart of the Kara Kum desert of Central Asia, surrounded by vast tracts of sand dunes, lie the remains of a sophisticated Bronze Age civilization, with a settlement and economic structure different from its Near Eastern and South Asian neighbors. This area is the source of finely made and distinctive artifacts that have been found throughout the greater Near East. The origins and development of the oasis culture in the Murgab River delta are the focus of this study.

The Bronze Age culture of Margiana was first described as the Margiana variant of the Namazga VI culture (Masson 1959). Soviet investigators discovered a related culture in southern Uzbekistan and northern Afghanistan during the late 1960s and early 1970s and labeled it the Bronze Age Bactrian civilization (Sarianidi 1977; Askarov 1977).

In attempts to distinguish the Bronze Age cultures in the oases areas from that of the foothill region, there has been a tendency to rename the oasis assemblage. Often Margiana is included under the name "Bactrian civilization" (Ligabue and Salvatori 1990). Recently the Bronze Age culture of Bactria and Margiana has been referred to as "the Oxus civilization" (Francfort 1989, Hiebert 1994, Lamberg-Karlovsky 1994a).

The Oxus civilization is characterized by a complex of specific ceramics, burial types, architecture and a specific small find assemblage called the Bactrian-Margiana Archaeological Complex (Sarianidi 1987b; Hiebert 1994). The Bactrian-Margiana Archaeological Complex includes stylistically distinctive carved stone objects, metal objects, and seals with zoomorphic, anthropomorphic, and geometric designs that co-occur with ceramics of the Central Asian type. In Bactria and Margiana, the assemblage is found in the context of a new form of architecture and settlement pattern. Prior to the investigations in this area, the Margiana-Bactria style objects were known primarily from isolated contexts in eastern Iran and northwestern South Asia.

GOALS OF THIS STUDY

For more than fifty years, Soviet researchers have investigated the archaeology of pre-Islamic Central Asia. The local development of prehistoric cultures in modern Turkmenistan, Uzbekistan, and Tajikistan included a Neolithic development of agriculture and, later, development of complex irrigation systems, urbanism, and highly complex production and trade networks by which this area was integrated into the greater Near Eastern and South Asian worlds. Excavations at the site of Namazga Depe carried out during the late 1950s defined the periods of the urban state-level Bronze Age culture in Central Asia (Namazga V and Namazga VI), with evidence of a region of settlements stretching for hundreds of kilometers along the Kopet Dag foothill plain.

The archaeology of Margiana is fundamentally tied into the Kopet Dag foothill chronological framework of the Namazga culture. Of prime importance has been the association of the monumental architecture in Margiana with numerous miniature stone columns, steatite bowls, bronze seals, and stone amulets. None of the materials of these objects is locally available, yet they have a style distinctive to the desert oases of Margiana and Bactria. The oasis sites have provided the first known cultural context for the Bactrian-Margiana Archaeological Complex. Viktor Sarianidi, who excavated Togolok 21, has interpreted this building complex as an Indo-Iranian temple with fire altars and remains of the ancient ritual drink *haoma,* suggested by finds of ephedra and opium poppy there (Sarianidi 1990). He has suggested that this distinctive culture is the result of migrations from Iran and Mesopotamia dating to the later second millennium. Due to the emphasis on wide-scale horizontal exposure of rooms at the expense of analysis of room function and chronology, the origins and development of the Bronze Age sites in the Murgab delta have remained elusive. Most of the research was carried out by Soviet archaeologists who worked separately from their Western counterparts, using different theoretical frameworks, having different goals, and often using different methods of research. This study is based on collaborative excavations conducted by V. Sarianidi and myself at the Bronze Age site of Gonur depe in Margiana. It is proposed here that the rapid occupation of sites in the Murgab delta oasis was contemporary with the late Namazga V settlement in the foothill region, which was the period of largest urban settlement at the site of Altyn depe. The present study proposes that the Bactrian-Margiana Archaeological Complex developed from local traditions at the beginning of the second millennium. In contrast to previously suggested reconstructions of the origins of the Bactrian-Margiana Archaeological Complex, I show that this development does not result from migrations from Iran, South Asia, or Mesopotamia, nor from the sedentarization of nomads.

The diverse geography and natural resources of Central Asia form a framework for the pattern of human settlement. The differential development of cultures in the areas of oasis and foothill plain is largely due to this diversity of environments.

The archaeological context of the Bronze Age sites of Margiana is special, in that very little post-Bronze Age occupation is found in the area. The Bronze Age architectural remains are preserved just below the surface. The area is highly deflated, leaving little more than the ground plan and a small amount of deposit just above the floors. These have been cleared over wide areas, exposing entire building complexes. The results of collaborative excavations at the best preserved of the Margiana Bronze Age sites—Gonur depe—are presented here.

The origins of the Margiana Bronze Age culture, and variation between the various Margiana sites, are addressed in the study of the ceramics. The ceramics are the key to the relative chronology and are one important database for the study of local and regional exchange. The absolute chronology is based primarily on a new series of radiocarbon dates, which came from the Margiana excavations, both from my own excavations at Gonur and from the previous excavations. The previous radiocarbon dates from Margiana and from other areas of Central Asia have provided unsatisfactory results for the archaeologists. Within the limitations of the technique, Margiana radiocarbon dates provide an absolute time period of the formation and development of this Bronze Age region.

Most of the excavations in Margiana have focused on the monumental architecture or large building complexes interpreted as palaces and temples. Excavations of nonmonumental, domestic architecture provides a contrast to the monumental architecture.

The development of the Margiana Bronze Age economy is based on analysis of materials from the excavations at Gonur and materials from other sites in Margiana provided by both V. Sarianidi and E. Masimov. The description of the oasis domestic economy is based on the archaeobotanical and archaeozoological analyses from the 1989 field season at Gonur. The oasis regions of ancient Bactria and Margiana developed their own artistic tradition on stone and metal artifacts despite the lack of the natural resources on which they were made. The distinctive material culture, described here as the Bactrian-Margiana Archaeological Complex (BMAC), is found in Margiana at Period 2 sites (Togolok 21, Togolok 24 burials), in Bactria (Sapalli and Dashli 3), and at sites well outside of Central Asia in Iran and Baluchistan. Notably, the distribution of this archaeological assemblage in Margiana includes burials, domestic areas, public areas, and production areas, indicating Margiana's core nature for this complex.

The development of oasis settlements in Margiana must be seen in the context of the Bronze Age traditions of Central Asia as a whole. The oasis settlements of Margiana are part of the long local development of culture in southern Turkmenistan as documented in the Namazga ceramic sequence and are a direct outgrowth of it. Adaptation to the oasis is the explanation for the development of the distinctive nature of the architecture, settlement, and production.

CHAPTER ONE

Region of Study

ANCIENT CENTRAL ASIA IS LOCATED IN THE COUNTRIES OF Turkmenistan, Uzbekistan, Tajikistan and Kazakstan (fig. 1.1). The modern borders of these former Soviet republics do not reflect the traditional cultural units of Central Asia. The artificial nature of the present borders is important, because most Soviet research was carried out through the auspices of the former republics' Academies of Sciences. Typically, researchers who had access to one republic did not have access to sites or information from the other republics, and thus they have been constrained by the modern political borders for their research. "Turkestan" and "Trans-Caspia" are synonyms for Central Asia that were primarily used prior to the Soviet period. The term "Central Asia" is used in this study to utilize the natural boundaries and is broadly similar to the terms "Soviet Central Asia" (Masson and Sarianidi 1972) and "Western Turkestan" (Kohl 1984:25).

Figure 1.1
Central Asia. Higlands above 1,000 m are shaded.

PHYSICAL ENVIRONMENT

Central Asia is bounded on the west by the Caspian Sea, on the south by the Kopet Dag and the Paropamisus mountains, on the north by the vast steppes of Kazakhstan, and on the east by the plain and valleys rising up to the Pamirs. The mountains

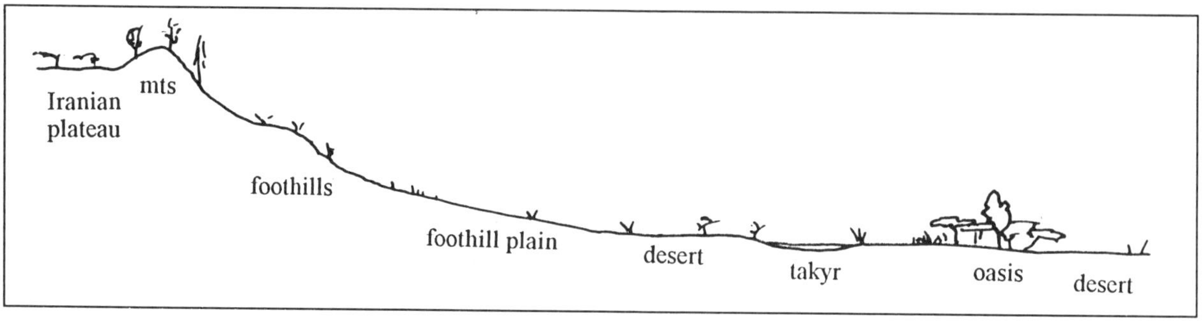

Figure 1.2
Schematic cross-section of the environments of Central Asia.

form a "U" around the large desert basin into which rivers from the southwest, southeast, and east flow. Many distinct environments are contained within this region (fig. 1.2) and the region is culturally diverse as well.

The Oasis

The primary emphasis of this study is on the settlements of the agricultural oasis of the Murgab River delta. In the deserts of Central Asia, agricultural oasis environments are created by clearing the thickets from natural river deltas and diverting the watercourses (Suslov 1961:510). Outside of oases, the desert climate is arid and sharply continental with quickly changing seasonal and daily temperatures.

The oases have more rainfall, higher humidity, and a more moderate climate than the natural delta; however, the annual precipitation (1.8 to 5.8 inches a year) in the Murgab delta is inadequate for dry farming (ibid., 439–440).

The productivity of the oasis fields is due to the rich loess from upstream suspended in the river water (fig. 1.3). The alluvial layer is up to 4 m deep in the contemporary Murgab oasis, and may have been deeper in the ancient oases before partial deflation (ibid., 510). High temperatures and intense sunlight in the oasis aid in ripening the late harvested (December) fruits and grains.

Today, wells in the Murgab delta are 1 to 3 m deep; on the periphery and in the sandy part of the desert the wells are 3 to 8 m deep (*Encyclopedia of Turkmenistan* 1984:59). Along the exterior edges of the agricultural lands in the oases are reedy marshes originating from the cast-off water of irrigation overflow. The marsh vegetation is salt adapted and has economically important stands of reeds (*Phragmites communis*) and saxaul (*Halaxyon persicum*).

Natural Delta Environment

The natural delta environment consists of uninhabitable reedy marshes and dense *tugai* thickets (fig. 1.4). At the turn of the century, the traveler/journalist E. O'Donovan described the marshy delta of the Atrek River:

> We crossed hundreds of acres of marshy ground, covered with bulrushes which overtopped a horseman's head, the horses sinking fetlock deep in the mixture of mud and tangled grass beneath our feet. Here and there broad belts of bamboo-like cane, growing from fifteen to eighteen feet high, and entirely impassable, forced us to turn aside. In the midst of

Figure 1.3
The modern oasis of Merv in the delta of the Murgab River.

Figure 1.4
Reedy marshes and *tugai* thicket.

> these cane brakes were shallow pools crammed with fish . . . vast flocks of water-fowl rose screaming from these pools as we approached. There were blue herons, swans, cormorants, flamingoes, frigate-birds, and even eagles and hawks together. Occasionally, too, a sudden plunge and crashing amid the cane announced the presence of a wild boar, and the animal would break out into the open and dash across the swamp.
>
> *O'Donovan, 1882, vol. 1:120*

Along the edges of the reedy marshes is a dense vegetation called *tugai* forest. These forests form a narrow broken belt along the edges of the riverbed as it flows along the plain and spreads out in the delta. The *tugai* vegetation is not diverse, with a dense woody canopy of Euphrates poplar (*Populus pruinosa*) and wild olive (*Elaeagnus angustifolia*). Willow (*Salix wilhelmsiana*), tamarisk (*Tamarix sp.*), and smaller shrubs form an impenetrable thicket below (Walter and Box 1983:95–97). The woods have little economic significance but are important for retaining the water. Some of the wood could be burned as fuel. The fauna include boar, Bukhara deer, Turan tiger, swamp lynx, rabbits, water rats, mice, and many birds, amphibians, and reptiles (Suslov 1961:509).

The natural marshes and *tugai* forest make simple occupation of the delta difficult. Canals have to be cut for the delta to be used for farming, and the canals must be maintained or they quickly become clogged by thicket. Marshes and *tugai* thicket are commonly found around abandoned canals in the modern oasis of the Murgab delta today.

Similar natural deltaic environments are found in Iran and Baluchistan near the sites of Shahr-i Sokhta and Khurab, for example (Nyerges 1982), and along the deserts of Central Asia from the Kopet Dag eastward to Xinjiang. By clearing the thicket and cutting canals, these deltaic environments could all be transformed into oases such as Margiana, and may hold archaeological materials documenting their use as agricultural oases in a vast network of desert oasis culture similar to Margiana.

Clayey Basins (*Takyr*)

Surrounding the irrigated oasis areas are barren stretches of clay pans (called *takyr*, pl. *takyri*) formed by earlier periods of standing water. Clay and gypsum deposits from the *takyr* were previously economically important. *Takyri* become vegetated when inundated from the runoff of spring rains. A zone of *takyri* is located outside of the Tedzhen and Murgab River deltas, along the Amu Dar'ya and Syr Dar'ya, and around the oases of northern Bactria. These basins serve as seasonal (springtime) storage places for water where temporary wells are dug. They have a distinctive flora and fauna that attracts grazing animals and predators, and they provide important seasonal plants and animals in the desert for caravans and herders.

Deserts

The desert itself is a mosaic of moving barchan dunes, stable dunes, scattered *takyri*, salt flats, and isolated wells stretching out from the foothill plains of the Kopet Dag and Paropamisus mountains (fig. 1.5). White saxaul (*Halaxyon persicum*), ephedra (*Ephedra strobilacea*), and *Eremosparton* are shrubby tree species found in the desert. Traditionally, the desert saxaul is collected for firewood from stands hundreds of kilometers from the oasis.

The desert, except for the barchan dunes, is covered by spring vegetation following the slightest precipitation. The thin growth of annual vegetation provides fodder for herders and nomads but forces a high degree of mobility. In spring, areas of the Kara Kum may appear carpeted with red with blossoms of the annual poppy (*Papaveraceae*), which has been collected for its medicinal properties.

Two types of dunes characterize the sandy parts of the Kara Kum: barchan ridges of moving sand dunes, and stable dunes on which vegetation can develop. The sandy ridges are oriented to the northeast, facilitating caravan movement northeast to southwest through the depressions and strongly inhibiting travel across the ridges (Suslov 1961:455). The ridges between the dunes form natural corridors between the eastern Kopet Dag foothill zone and the region of Margiana during the Bronze Age (fig. 1.6). This access bears directly on these two regions, which were in contact via the desert. Rather than being a barrier, the dunes facilitated travel in one direction.

Rivers

The flow from rivers bordering the desert areas varies widely throughout the year. The Amu Dar'ya and the Syr Dar'ya from the Pamirs are large snow- and rain-

Figure 1.5
The Kara Kum desert north of Margiana.

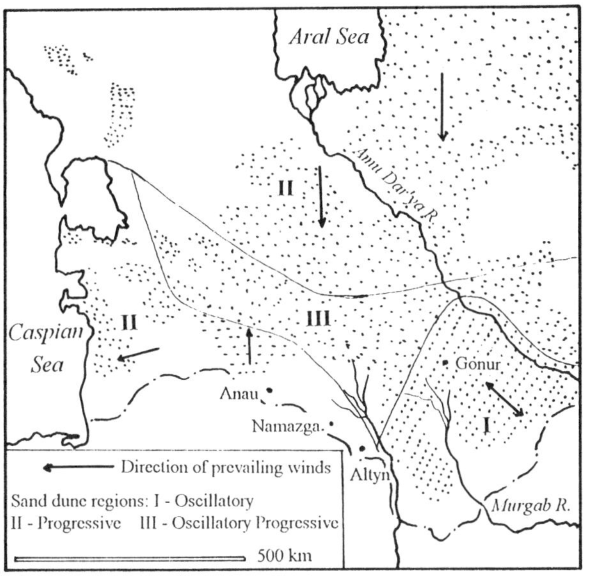

Figure 1.6
Distribution of regions of sand dune types (modified from Suslov 1961, map 14-I). In region I, stable linear dunes and troughs form natural routes between the eastern foothill plains and Margiana.

fed rivers that have stable year-round flow, carrying rich loess deposits that are good for farming. These deposits are deeply downcut, however, and required large canals for irrigation. The rivers flowing from the Kopet Dag are small and rain-fed; thus their flow is very small compared with the Amu Dar'ya and Syr Dar'ya, but more constant throughout the year. These rivers are easily diverted for watering fields and the early village settlements in the foothills of the Kopet Dag clustered along these rivers. These rivers are too small to permit large-scale irrigation.

The Murgab receives water from snow runoff in the Paropamisus mountains of Afghanistan. The watershed is between 1,400 to 3,800 m in elevation; thus the discharge is uneven, with flooding in May and June when the snow melts. The Murgab River drains 46,900 sq km and thus has a large, but highly seasonal discharge (Kirsta 1980). The upstream Murgab River bed is deeply downcut through barren sandy desert. Bronze Age burials similar to those found in the oasis cultures have recently been found at the base of the mountains where the Murgab River enters the Kara Kum desert (Udemuradov 1989). The deeply downcut areas could not support irrigation agriculture, and the occurrence of these burials suggests that the river served as a communication route despite the lack of surrounding settlements.

Foothill Plains and Mountains

The transitional landscape from the desert to the mountains forms sloping plains referred to as the foothill zone. There are discontinuous sloping plains and valleys at the base of both the Paropamisus and Kopet Dag mountains (fig. 1.7). The soils of these regions are very distinctive and fertile.

The vegetation of the foothill regions consists primarily of meadow grass (*Poa bulbosa vivipara*), sedges (*Carex* spp.), and stands of juniper and oak trees (Suslov 1961:491–492). Pistachio, oak, pine, ephedra, and juniper are found abundantly in the mountains above. Mountain goat, boar, jackal, leopard, and lion as well as a wide variety of small mammals, birds, and reptiles are found in the foothills above 1,000 m and in the mountains surrounding the deserts. Images of the mountain animals are found in some Central Asian Bronze Age designs and figurines. They are most commonly found in the north Bactrian sites, to the south of the Hissar range.

Rivers served as communication and transportation routes connecting the desert, foothill, and mountain areas. The mountains bordering the Iranian plateau remain largely unexplored today, although this must have been an important resource area for both the cultures of Central Asia and of Iran. The Kopet Dag mountains, formed of upraised sedimentary and metamorphic rock, have outcrops along the foothill zone of sandstone, schist, and limestone with nodules of flint. Alabaster, steatite, and semiprecious stones such as amethyst and onyx are also found there (*Encyclopedia of Turkmenistan* 1984:21). Archaeological finds of stone, metal ores, and other raw materials from the mountains and Iranian plateau are made in the foothill valleys and oasis settlements representing all time periods

In other areas, the Hissar range of the Eastern Pamirs is a resource area for copper, tin, silver, and gold (Grishin 1980). To the south and east, the Kungitag and Paropamisus ranges yield ferrous deposits, silver, and copper, as well as limestone, alabaster, amethyst and onyx (*Encyclopedia of Turkmenistan* 1984:19). Carnelian, lapis, and some forms of agate can be found in Badakhshan to the east and to the south in Afghanistan (Wolfart and Wittekindt

Figure 1.7
The Kopet Dag mountains near Ashgabat.

1980:62). The desert region lacks any of these mineral resources, and settlement in the desert oasis areas always required adaptation to a severe environment.

PALEOCLIMATE

Whether climate has changed in the last ten thousand years has been a topic of interest in Central Asian archaeology for nearly one hundred years, starting with the work of Pumpelly and Huntington at Anau (Pumpelly 1908). The possibility of significant climatic change remains an important unresolved question. Up until the mid-twentieth century, the boundary between desert and fields irrigated by the Murgab was far to the southwest of the ancient oasis (fig. 1.8). The modern (1990s) desert/oasis boundary has been expanded to the north by irrigation waters from the Kara Kum canal. The Bronze Age Margiana sites extended far into the dry desert. The Bronze Age sites in the desert are associated with dry riverbeds and irrigation canals indicating the position of the ancient Murgab River delta.

Lisitsyna (1978) and Gerasimov (1978) consider that the arid desert environment has been stable over the last ten to fifteen thousand years. Gerasimov attributes the abandonment of the Bronze Age Margiana sites to shifts in the river systems. According to this view, the instability of the river channels was caused by tectonic uplifts and other geomorphic processes. There is considerable evidence of tectonic instability in the area, and the Murgab delta oasis is exactly along a major fault line. In addition, the course of the Murgab was unstable because of the gradual buildup of alluvial debris and blockage of the channels. The Murgab flows above the plain on an aggraded river course as it approaches the deltaic area (Suslov 1961:468–469), and dramatic shifts in the river channel are historically attested (Davis 1905:55).

On the other hand, Dolukhanov has argued for a desiccation of the environment during the last four thousand years (1988). Large tracts of *takyr* stretching along the foothills suggest greater discharge for the rivers in the past than today.

In either case, the oasis-desert relationship of the Bronze Age oasis was similar to that of the modern oasis of the Murgab delta, 75 km to the south, independent of whether the environment was wetter during the Bronze Age. Preliminary ethnobotanical data from the Bronze Age settlements (Lisitsyna 1968; Yaneshevich 1977; Miller 1993) include xerophytic and halophytic plants similar to the modern flora surrounding the oasis rather than to a different type of environment (steppe, or forested). The lessening of rainfall may have been important for dry farming along the foothills, but it was not a major factor in the ability of the oasis to support a settlement. The present relationship of the regions to each other is thus a justifiable analogy for the Bronze Age. If environmental change is considered to be a factor that contributed to the end of occupation in Bronze Age Margiana, the archaeological evidence would suggest (chap. 7), if anything, a catastrophic, rather than a gradual, change.

CULTURAL GEOGRAPHY

Margiana

The Murgab River is associated with the cities and settlements of its delta: modern Mari (or Mary), medieval Merv, and classical Margiana (Margiane [the region] or Margus [the river]). To the north of the medieval and classical oasis is the former delta, which is today covered by the sands of the Kara Kum desert. This is the area of Bronze Age settlement typically called "Bronze Age Margiana." It is located in

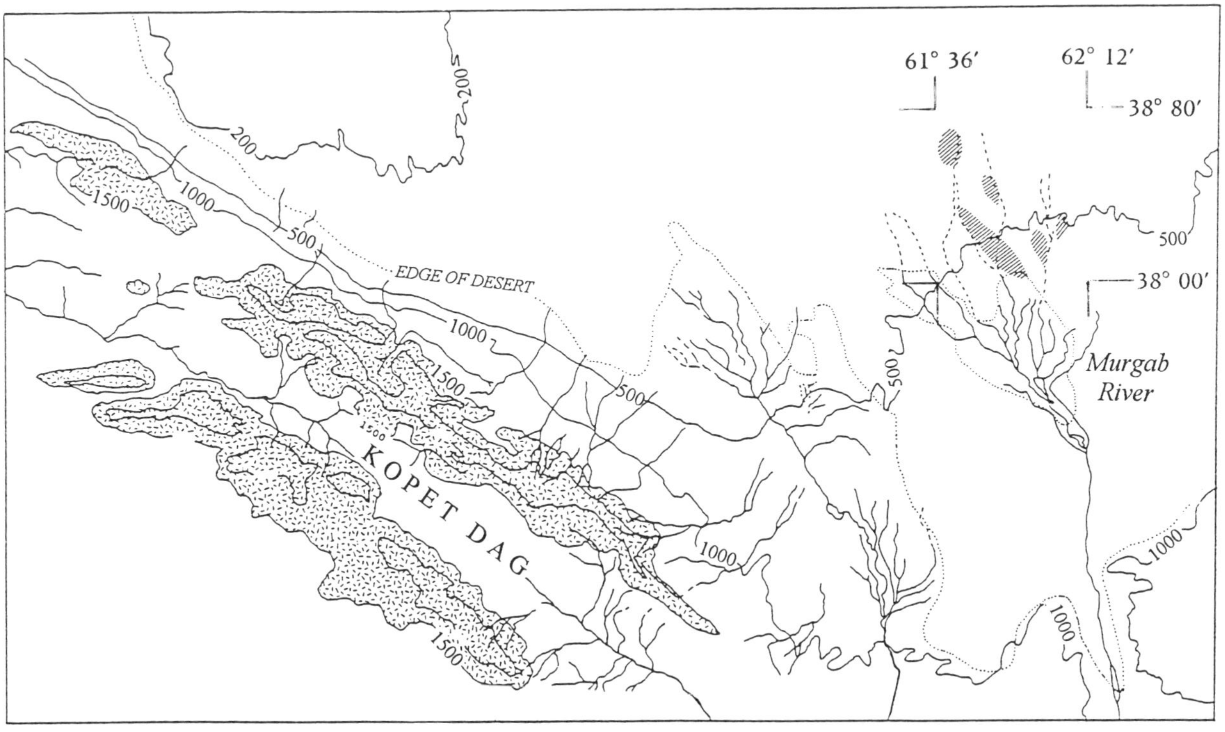

Figure 1.8
The Kopet Dag mountain region and Margiana. Areas above 1,500 m are hatched. Dry farming foothill sites are located along the rivers at the 1,000 m level. The dotted line indicates the desert edge prior to the construction of the Kara Kum canal. Dashed lines indicate the modern extension of canals. Diagonal lines indicate the area of Bronze Age settlement in Margiana.

an area 38° 00′ south, 38° 80′ north, by 61° 36′ east, 62° 12′ west; that is, 100 km north-south by 50 km east-west at its largest and widest point. It is almost five times larger than the medieval and classical oasis to the south. Although there is occupational continuity between the Bronze Age and the classical period in the Murgab delta oasis, the use of the name "Margiana" does not imply linguistic or cultural continuity from the Bronze Age to the classical period. No identification of this area in the Mesopotamian texts has yet been made.

The basic element of the name is found in Old Avestan "Moury-," in Old Persian "Marghu," Middle Persian "Marv," and Arabic "Marwazi" (*Encyclopedia of Islam* 1988). Although it has commonly been affirmed that Margiana is listed on the seventh-century B.C. Behistun inscription of Darius, this is not the case. In 1938, W. W. Tarn noted that the name "Margus" did not occur in any of Darius's lists of provinces (1951, 2d ed.:88, n. 6). The name "Margiane," according to Tarn, is later in date, probably from the Seleucid eparchy around A.D. 100. It is possible that the name of the river originally came from elsewhere, possibly related to the "Marhashi" of Elam, which Steinkeller has convincingly argued should be located in eastern Iran, south of Iranian Khorasan (Steinkeller 1989). The Bronze Age Central Asia cultures are considered to be protohistoric, having no written documents at a time when neighboring cultures to the south did have writing.

Oases Settlements

Margiana, in the Murgab River delta, is actually quite isolated from the other Central Asian oases. Four other oases areas are known to have had contemporary late Bronze Age settlements (fig. 1.9). Southern Bactria is located along the ancient delta of the Balkhab River in northern Afghanistan, where the sites form two clusters referred to as the Dashli and Farukabad oases. Northern Bactria is the deltaic oasis of the Sherabad River, north of the Amu Dar'ya in Uzbekistan, the location of the sites of Dzharkutan and Sapalli. Eastern Bactria is a group of Bronze Age sites located in an oasislike area on the southeastern border of Central Asia. Here, at the site of Shortughai, late Bronze Age Central Asian levels overlie the remains of a mature Harappan outpost. The Zamanbaba deltaic fan of the Zerafshan River ends in an oasis where the poorly explored Bronze Age Zamanbaba sites are located. These areas are divided by formidable tracts of sandy desert, and the rivers of the oases come from vastly different mountain areas; yet they shared strong cultural traditions during the late Bronze Age.

Foothill Settlements

The band of small river valleys along the northern foothill of the Kopet Dag mountains is referred to by various synonymous names: the foothill plain (Masson 1988), "piedmont region" (Kohl 1984), and sometimes, simply "southwestern Turkmenistan" (Gupta 1979). The foothill plain of the Kopet Dag mountains forms three Bronze Age cultural areas: the western foothill plain, including the important archaeological sites of Anau and Ak depe; the central Kopet Dag foothill plain, including the sites of Namazga depe and Shor depe; and the eastern foothill plain, including the sites of Ulug depe and Altyn depe (Kohl 1984). All of the sites in these regions are located at or around 1,000 m, the optimum elevation for dry farming. Between the river valley agricultural settlements, ridges and desert plains form natural barriers to communication and exchange.

The Geoksyur oasis forms a fourth "foothill plain." This region is contiguous with the eastern Kopet Dag foothill plain, but the sites are located out in the delta of the Tedzhen River rather than at an elevation of 1,000 m along the foothill plain.

Mountain Valley Settlements

Several Central Asian Bronze Age settlements contemporary with Margiana are located in valleys above 1,000 m. These are found in the upper Zerafshan valley, the Ferghana valley in Uzbekistan, and the Sumbar valley in western Turkmenistan.

Sarazm, in the upper Zerafshan valley, has late eneolithic and early Bronze Age finds strikingly similar to those from the foothill plain of southern Turkmenistan. The Bronze Age of the Ferghana valley is practically unexplored, and it may have had important links to Xinjiang during the Bronze Age.

Figure 1.9
Bronze Age sites of Central Asia, the Iranian plateau, and the Indus valley.

Contact Areas Outside of Central Asia

Areas to the southeast of the Kopet Dag are also important to place in geographic perspective. People and objects passed between the Indus valley and Central Asia through natural passes such as the Bolan Pass in Baluchistan. At the sites of Mehrgarh, Nausharo, and Sibri, objects morphologically identical to those of the BMAC document the direct interaction between the cultures of the greater Indus valley and Central Asia (Jarrige 1988). Although the Indus civilization extended to the mountain edge of modern Afghanistan at Shortughai (Francfort 1989), most contacts with the Central Asian oasis cultures occurred via the Kachi plain to the southern Indus valley sites.

The Iranian plateau and Central Asia have separate cultural traditions that date to before the Bronze Age. Through time these cultures maintained their own identity despite contact with each other through trade or other forms of exchange. Khorasan borders the Iranian plateau south of the Kopet Dag. The Gorgan plain is linked to Turkmenistan via a narrow corridor near to the Caspian. Farther south, Bronze Age sites in Seistan and Kerman also had connections with Central Asian cultures.

CHAPTER TWO

Bronze Age Sites of Margiana

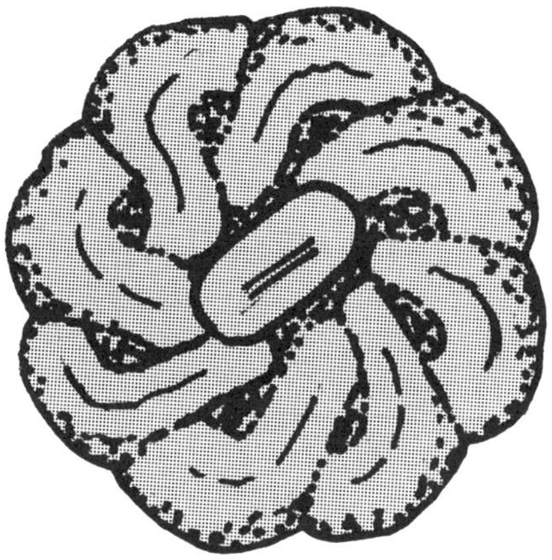

EXPLORATIONS OF THE AREA OF BRONZE AGE MARGIANA began at the end of the nineteenth century. A Russian architect, V. A. Zhukovskii, in a vast survey of the architecture and archaeological remains in the Murgab delta oasis, first noted the existence of Bronze Age remains to the north of the classical sites of Margiana (Zhukovskii 1894). In the beginning of the twentieth century, an American archaeological expedition led by Raphael Pumpelly mapped the archaeological sites of the Murgab oasis. Pumpelly surveyed the sites, which he called "kurgans," far north into the desert beyond the present-day delta oasis of the Murgab River. His maps include Uch depe at the southern part of the Bronze Age oasis and some of the Bronze Age Togolok sites (Pumpelly 1908).

Pumpelly's chronology, based on rates of soil deposition familiar to him from around the pyramids of Egypt, was not accepted by the following generation of archaeologists (Peake and Flure 1927). No further Western research followed in Central Asia because of the debate on the antiquity of the area and the closing of the area to Western researchers following the creation of the USSR.

Major archaeological study of the Bronze Age sites began in the mid-1950s, with the discovery of, and excavations at, the sites of Auchin depe and Takhirbai depe 3 (Masson 1956, 1959; Sarianidi 1957). The majority of the Bronze Age sites to the north and to the west of Auchin depe remained unknown, and none of the unique oasis architecture was excavated during this phase. This first stage of archaeological research provided a chronological framework and documented the strong cultural affinities of the Bronze Age Margiana sites with the Kopet Dag foothill sites, based on comparisons with the stratigraphic soundings at the eneolithic through late Bronze Age site of Namazga depe (Masson 1956).

Masson originally proposed two complexes of Bronze Age material from Margiana based on one season of excavation. Finds from Auchin depe were said to be parallel to the transition from Namazga V to Namazga VI, and finds from Takhirbai 3 were paralleled with Namazga VI (Masson 1959:12–28). Several burials were excavated at Auchin depe, and the excavations at Takhirbai 3 uncovered rooms from a building complex. Although the 1959 excavations were small compared with the large horizontal exposures conducted today, the ceramic chronology established at these sites has served as the chronological framework up to the present time.

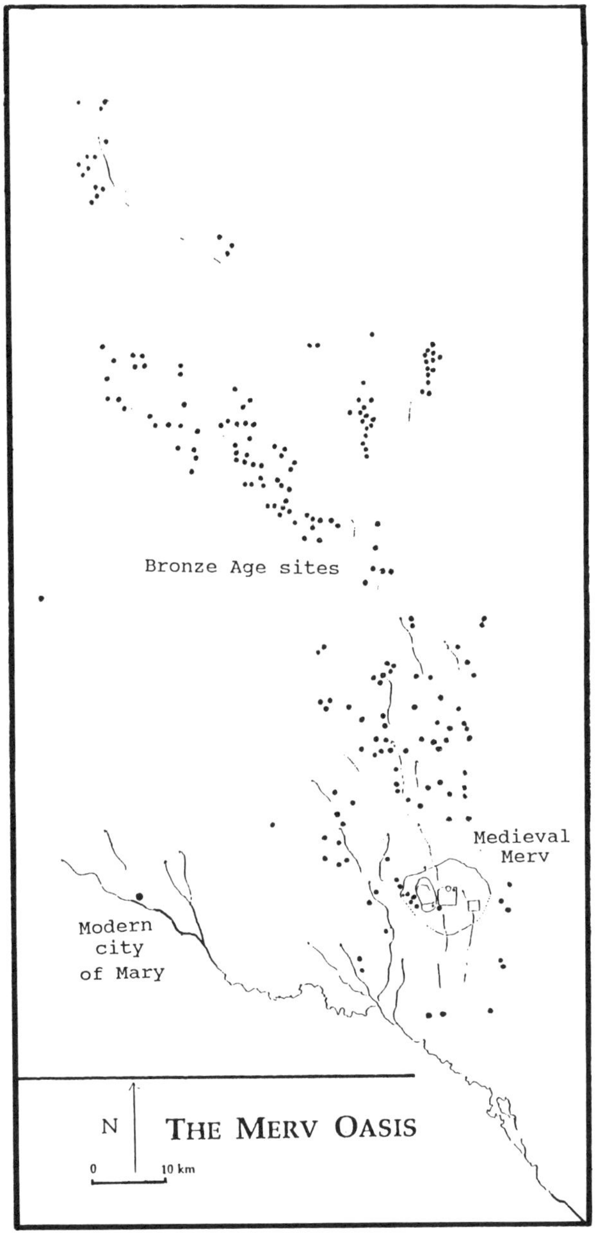

Figure 2.1
Archaeological sites of the Murgab oasis. Based on MAE surveys (1974–1981) (Sarianidi 1990, fig. 1) and survey of classical and medieval sites (Hiebert 1992a, fig. 5).

The second phase of archaeological research began in 1972, with the organization of the Margiana Archaeological Expedition (MAE) (Sarianidi 1990). Originally a collaborative effort between the Institute of History in Turkmenistan, and the Institute of Archaeology in Moscow, the project was conceived to expand the excavations begun at Auchin and Takhirbai 3. In the course of the new excavations at Auchin depe and Takhirbai, many new Bronze Age sites were discovered to the north and to the west, including Gonur depe 1 in 1974. The MAE began a nonsystematic topographic survey of sites (Lyapin 1975), in which more than one hundred Bronze Age sites were located in the ancient Murgab delta (fig. 2.1).

The sites discovered during surveys were named after local wells and nomad encampments, and the mounded sites were numbered in sequence as they were found. Nine groups of sites have been found, named Kelleli, Adzhi Kui, Adam Basan, Egri Bogaz, Taip, Gonur, Auchin, Togolok, and Takhirbai (fig. 2.2). These are Turkmen Turkish terms for the areas; for example, *Gonur* (brown) was named by the local nomads and seasonal herders.

Although nonsystematic, the MAE survey included more than forty months of fieldwork (1974–1985) in which the relatively featureless area was widely crossed. Due to shifting sands, sites in the area are

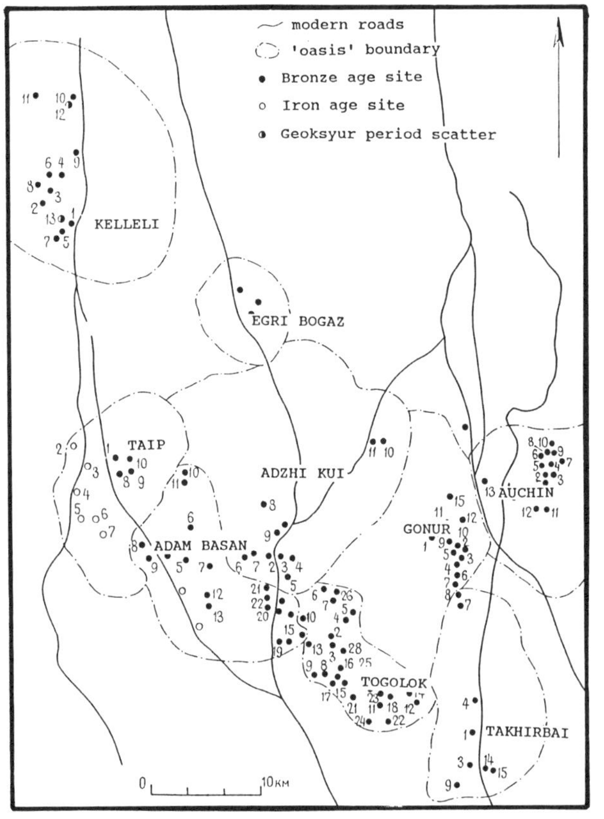

Figure 2.2
Bronze Age sites of Margiana (adapted from Sarianidi 1990, fig. 1).

still being discovered, although the general pattern of settlement has been established. These sites have been grouped into "oases" or "micro-oases" (Masimov 1978; Sarianidi 1981a). Groups of sites, however, are not isolated one from another but form long, linear patterns—three branches north, south, and east, probably following the ancient canal and riverbeds.

In 1978 the MAE divided into two teams: E. Masimov (Academy of Sciences, Turkmenistan) began excavations in the northern sites at Kelleli, Taip, Adam Basan, and Adzhi Kui (Masimov and Lyapin 1977:552) and Egri Bogaz was excavated by Udemuradov; V. I. Sarianidi (Institute of Archaeology, Moscow, and Ministry of Culture, Turkmenistan) began excavations at southern and eastern sites, around Togolok and Gonur (Sarianidi 1990).

In the Bronze Age desert oasis of Margiana, the typical site is a mosaic of dispersed buildings and features and the limits of a single site are often difficult to define. Today the Bronze Age sites form low mounds of eroded mud brick with dense scatters of wind-eroded ceramics. The lack of recent occupation and the deflation of the sites result in an unusual richness of surface finds: fragments of bronze, terracotta, softstone, and semiprecious stone are frequently found on the site surfaces.

The lack of tell formation on the Bronze Age sites of Margiana allows the use of wide-scale horizontal excavation to reveal entire building complexes. This technique is well suited to the shallow archaeological sites in Margiana, with the walls often visible at the surface. The deposits are rarely or never screened during horizontal excavation, however.

During the early 1970s there was an emphasis on ecology and scientific methods in Soviet archaeology. Central Asian archaeology, especially research at foothill sites such as Altyn depe and Shor depe, included detailed statistical analysis of ceramics and brief faunal, paleobotanical, and metallurgical analyses. These reports were primarily published in the now defunct journal *Karakumskie Drevnosti*. There has been an explicit shift from these methods to more generalized recovery and description (Kohl 1984). One justification for this shift from studies of chronology, typology, or paleoecology in Central Asia to the study of general aspects of the archaeological record is that the goal shifted to the analysis of the ideology of the culture (Masson, pers. comm.).

My approach to the study of Margiana is to combine fine-scale excavation with observations on the wide-scale excavation techniques of my Russian and Turkmen colleagues. Several sites excavated by Russian and Turkmen archaeologists were used as comparative sites for the excavations I conducted at Gonur depe. Kelleli 4, Togolok 1, and Togolok 21 provide important assemblages of artifacts and architecture that characterize the Bronze Age oasis settlements of Margiana. These examples, together with the detailed descriptions from Gonur, represent the major types of archaeological remains in Bronze Age Margiana.

NORTHERN SITES

Kelleli sites were investigated from 1979 to 1984 in the northernmost area of the Margiana oasis. Twelve sites stretching in a generally linear pattern were investigated from 1979 to 1984 by E. Masimov. Excavation of the first Kelleli site (Kelleli 1, now destroyed) was a rescue operation, and several of the sites were found during land reclamation. Kelleli 3 and 4 are sites with single architectural phases; they yielded late Namazga V type ceramics similar to those from the uppermost levels at Altyn depe (Udemuradov 1989). The excavations at Kelleli 3 and 4 have given the name "Kelleli phase" to the first major occupation in Margiana.

Not all Kelleli sites are Kelleli phase. Farthest to the north were several scatters of Namazga III/IV (Geoksyur type) ceramics (Masimov 1979b). No architecture was found, and the sites have been described as seasonal campsites (Masson 1989). At least one site in the area of Kelleli (Kelleli 6) has later, Togolok type ceramics.

To the southeast, the sites of Egri Bogaz—investigated by Udemuradov—are generally small, low sites with late Bronze Age ceramics. The sites around Kelleli appear to be discontinuous from Ergi Bogaz and the sites to the south. However, sites between Egri Bogaz and Kelleli were observed on several occasions during trips to Kelleli from Gonur and are presently under study (Masimov, pers. comm.).

Kelleli 4

Kelleli 4 was excavated in 1980 and 1981. The site was a low mound with a single architectural level close to the surface. Wide-scale horizontal excavation uncovered a square building (29.5 m x 29.5 m), with only ephemeral architecture outside of the enclosing wall (fig. 2.3). Like many sites in Margiana, only 10 to 30 cm of the wall bases were preserved. The architecture of Kelleli 4 was constructed of unbaked mud brick. The only baked brick comes from kilns and burned areas.

Masimov has described the building at Kelleli 4 as a domestic structure, with interior rooms forming several apartments and a courtyard (Masimov 1984). The building is considered unfortified, based on the relatively thin exterior wall (fig. 2.4). However, the exterior wall is paralleled by interior walls of the domestic structures, these forming narrow corridor rooms surrounding the living quarters. The result is equivalent to the effect of a thick defensive wall (often found in fortified architecture of mud brick forts from later periods in Margiana). Corridors within exterior walls are also found at other buildings in Margiana, such as at Kelleli 3 and Gonur north. Kelleli 4 has five square towers 5.5 to 7 m wide—one in the middle of each side and two on the south side on either side of the entrance to the building. On the north side is a square platform of the same size as a tower; this may have been the base of another tower.

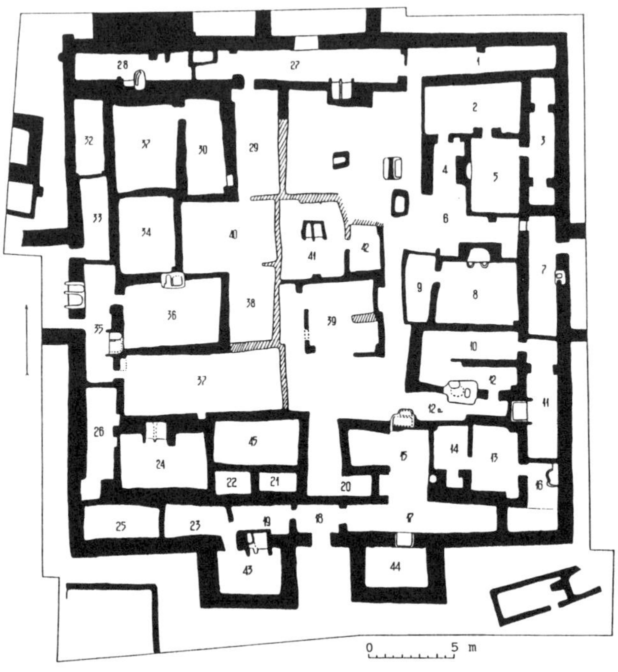

Figure 2.3
Kelleli 4 (adapted from Masimov 1984, fig. 1).

Figure 2.4
East wall (view south) of Kelleli 4. Photo: Courtesy of E. Masimov.

The finds included: many *khomi* (large storage vessels); terracotta objects including many figurines; small stone objects such as alabaster bowls and beads; large stone objects such as grinding stones; and enigmatic miniature columns and maceheads. Metal seals and tools were also found (Masimov 1984).

Kelleli 3

Wide-scale horizontal excavations at the large site of Kelleli 3 in 1979 and from 1983 to 1988 were carried out by a small expedition from the Academy of Sciences of Turkmenistan, led by Masimov with the assistance of Udemuradov.

Kelleli 3 is a single-phase architectural complex surrounded by a large square enclosing wall. The deposit was shallow, similar to Kelleli 4, ranging from 10 to 50 cm deep. An area roughly 2,800 sq m was excavated in the southeast and northwest corners (fig. 2.5). The exterior wall is doubled, forming a 4-m-wide surrounding wall, 109 m on a side. The building appears to be well planned, with six towers on each side and an entrance in the middle of each side. The entrance on the east side has an open drain running out of the door, with a mud brick cover at the doorway. Recent unpublished excavations suggest that the interior architecture from the southeast corner forms several "micro-complexes" (Masimov, pers. comm.),

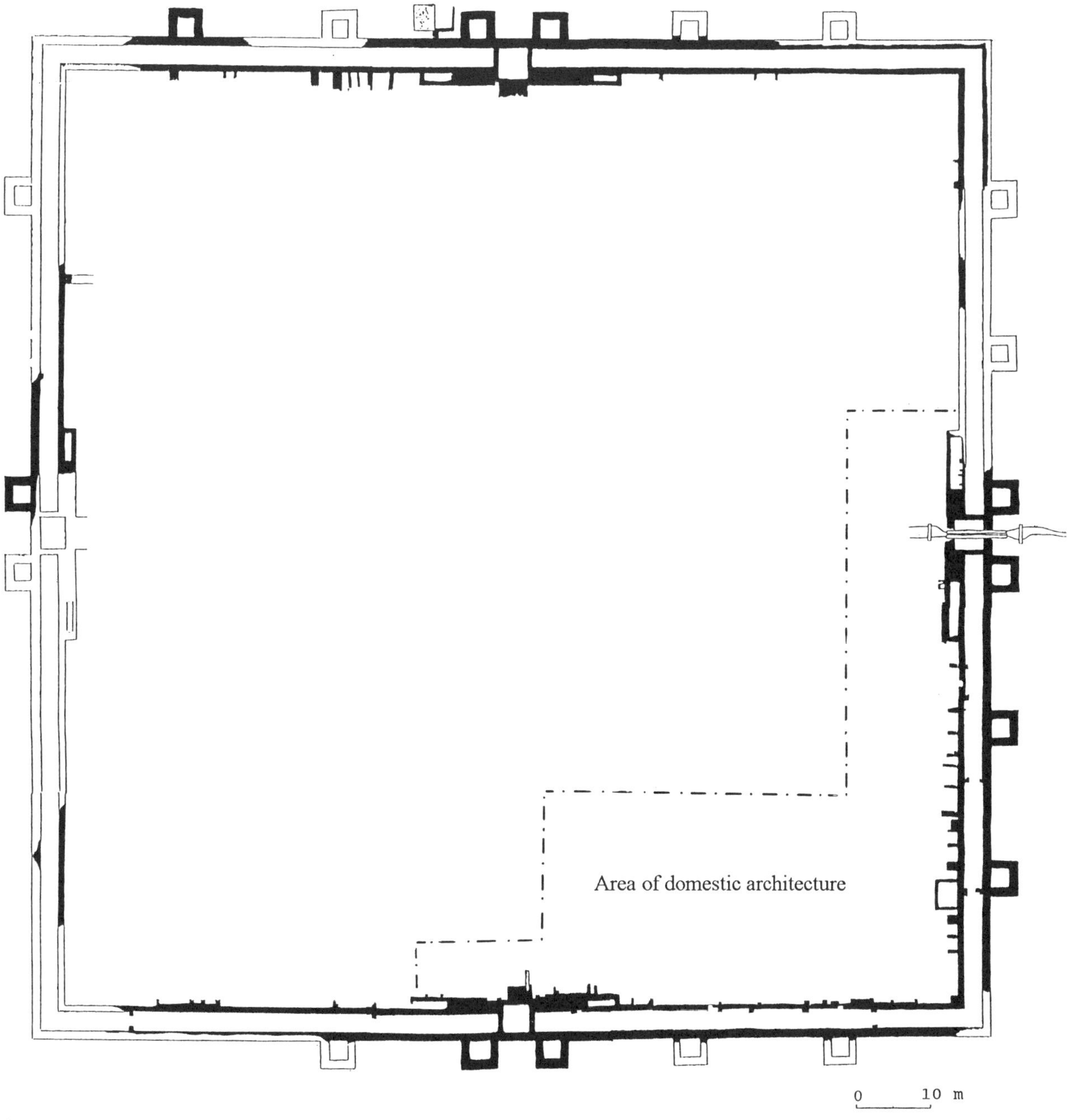

Figure 2.5
Kelleli 3 (adapted from Masimov 1986, fig. 2).

which can be interpreted as domestic units or apartments similar to those at Kelleli 4. The domestic areas at Kelleli 3 may be connected to an interior courtyard (here, unexcavated) similar to the central courtyard at Kelleli 4.

SOUTHERN SITES

The sites around the modern wells of Taip, Adam Basan, Adzhi Kui and Togolok lie in a northwest-southeast line. Of these, the Togolok sites are at the southernmost end, near to the Takhirbai sites. Excavations at Togolok 21 have revealed a large, single-period fortified building complex. This site has given its name to the second period in Margiana: the Togolok period. The artifacts from Togolok 21 are so similar to the artifacts from excavations at Dashli in southern Bactria and Sapalli and Dzharkutan in northern Bactria that the term "Bactrian-Margiana Archaeological Complex" (BMAC) was first coined on the basis of finds from Togolok (Sarianidi 1987b).

Togolok 21

The site of Togolok 21 is the largest of a series of small sites that are aligned in a northwestern direction. A small production area with kilns and ceramic slag is located 250 m to the north. The Togolok 21 site is located on a small natural rise and is located 600 m to the south of the site of Togolok 1. Thus the small mounds of Togolok 21 and Togolok 1 form an almost contiguous series of sites.

The building complex covers 1 ha and was completely excavated in several seasons (Sarianidi 1990). No architecture was found outside of the outer perimeter wall (fig. 2.6). A gully runs through the middle of the site, and the archaeological deposit

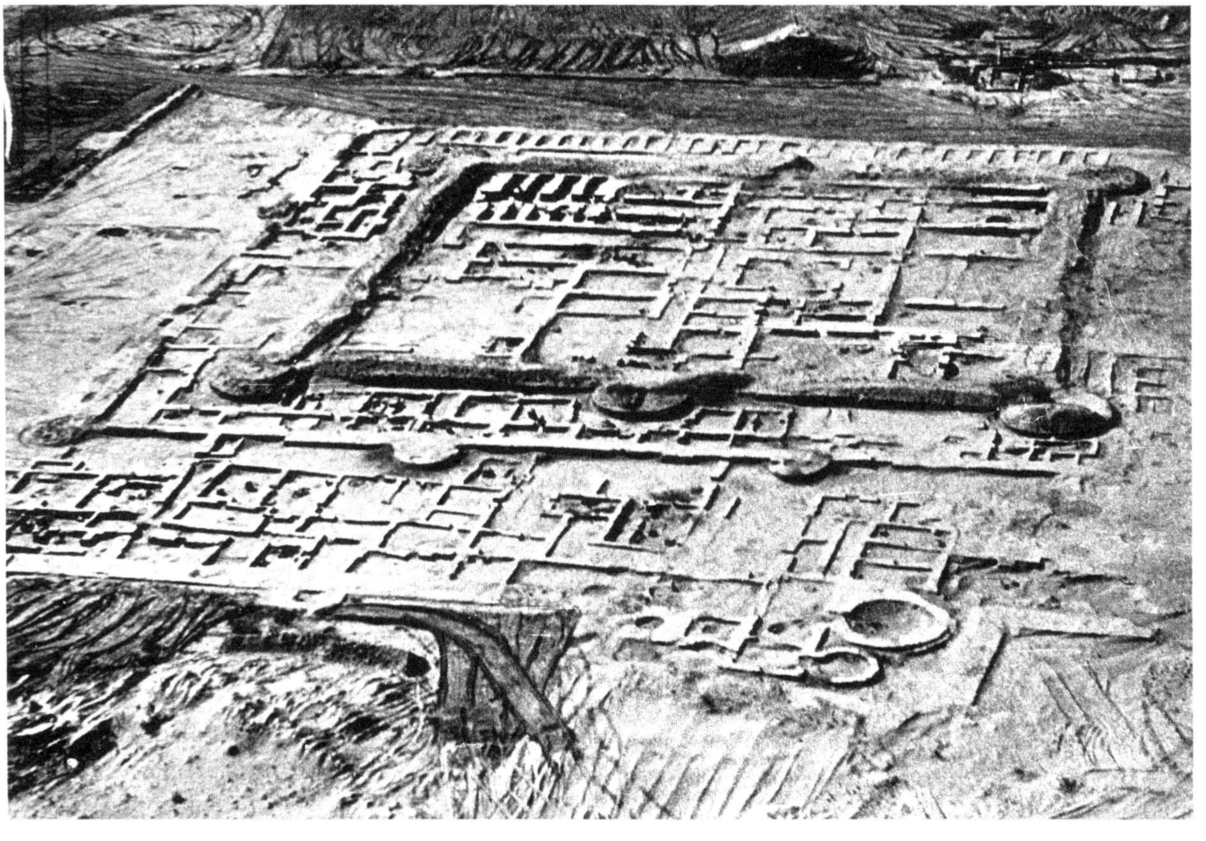

Figure 2.6
Aerial view of Togolok 21. Photo: Courtesy of V. Sarianidi.

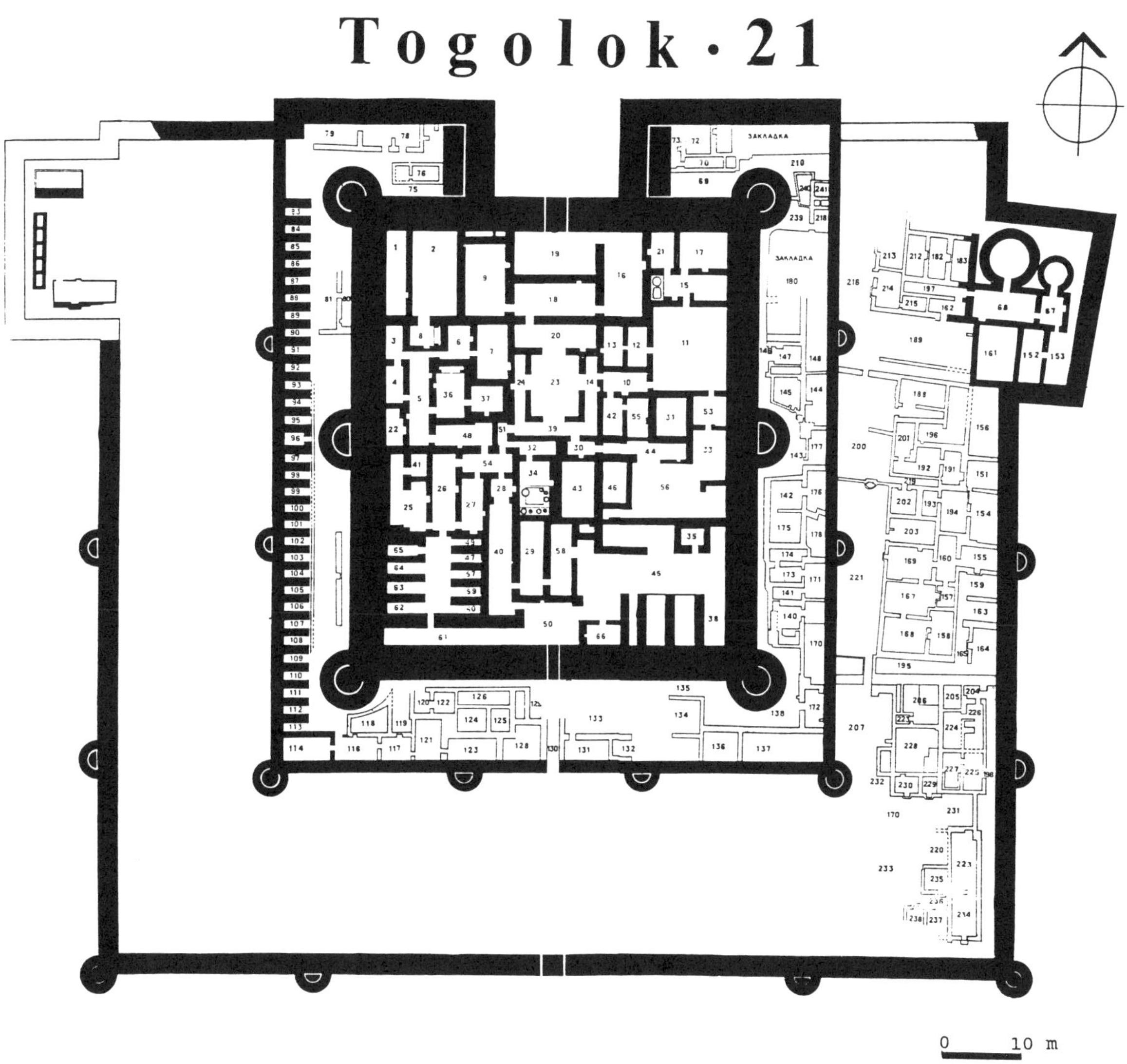

Figure 2.7
Togolok 21. Solid walls = Phase 1, open walls = Phase 2 (adapted from Sarianidi 1990, fig. 25).

inside of the building was differentially preserved. The building complex at Togolok 21 has a single basic plan. Two concentric rectangular walls surround a central building with dimensions of 53 x 62 m. The surrounding walls are 2 to 3 m thick, with towers along the sides and at the corners. The central building has 4.5-m-wide walls with towers and a large entrance to the north (fig. 2.7). The building reveals two phases of construction: the original building was constructed on sterile soil (phase 1); later occupation reused the Central Building with some modification and new floors, and many rooms were built within the enclosing walls (phase 2). A third "phase" consists of burials dug into the deposit and the floors of the building (fig. 2.8).

The distinctive miniature stone columns, steatite, alabaster fragments, and stone cylinder and bronze compartmented seals found in the rooms are very similar to those found in northern and southern Bactria (Sarianidi 1986c). The small finds and the ceramics were not excavated separately by phase. Phase 2 architectural modifications were found in the main building, in particular from Room 23, and the ceramics from the central building include both phase 1 and phase 2 ceramics. However, the assemblages from the outer perimeter area (primarily phase 2 architecture) differ very little in terms of types from the ceramics and small finds from the main building.

The burials were dug into deposits in disused rooms along the east side. The ceramics from the burials were analyzed separately from the architecture, and there are no differences in form between ceramics found in rooms and in the burials (P'yankova 1989), although frequencies of forms may differ and types may differ. This suggests that parts of the building were contemporaneous with the burials and that the entire occupation of the building occurred within a relatively short period of time.

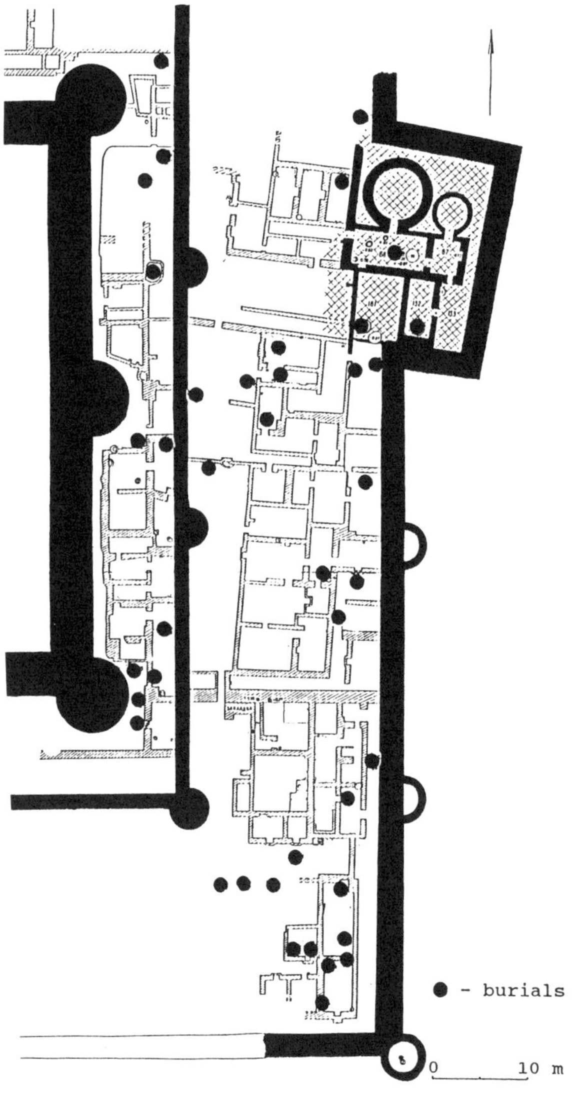

Figure 2.8
Togolok 21. Location of burials in the architectural complex (adapted from Sarianidi 1990, fig. 31).

Togolok 1

Togolok 1 consists of a small (3.5 m high) northern mound and a larger, lower rectangular mound. A large architectural complex was excavated on the low rectangular mound in 1987–1988 (fig. 2.9). Sarianidi considers the building a smaller version of Togolok 21 in both its room organization and its fortification (fig. 2.10) (Sarianidi 1994). Togolok 1, like Togolok 21, had two architectural phases, with burials intrusive to the earlier-phase architecture. These burials were found primarily on the east side, including the largest and most richly furnished burial so far found in Margiana (fig. 2.11) (Sarianidi 1990).

Ceramics from the wide-scale horizontal excavations are typologically similar to those from Togolok 21 (P'yankova 1989), and the small find assemblage also includes miniature stone columns, seals, soft-stone fragments, and bronze fragments typical of the Bactrian-Margiana Archaeological Complex.

A stratigraphic sounding was made on the north edge of the mound in which seven 0.5-m levels were excavated (Sarianidi 1987a). In the lower levels, ceramics and small finds typical of the finds from Kel-

Figure 2.9
Aerial view of Togolok 1. Photo: Courtesy of V. Sarianidi.

Figure 2.10
Togolok 1. Plan of the building complex (adapted from Sarianidi 1991, fig. 37).

leli 3 and 4 were identified; the upper layers contained ceramics similar to those from Togolok 21.

Togolok 24

Cenotaphs and burials are also found outside of buildings, in cemeteries. In 1985 a series of tombs (Togolok 24) was salvaged after being located during a desert reclamation program, located about 2 km to the northwest of Togolok 21 (Sarianidi 1986a). These burials had ceramics of similar form to Togolok 21 and Togolok 1 (the latest phase). They were different from the burials found in the architecture in that they were constructed with rectangular mud brick tombs (fig. 2.12). The tombs typically were divided into two parts by a brick partition. The body was placed on a brick floor on the left side of the partition, and on the other side many vessels and food offerings were provided (ibid.). Many of the small finds are similar to the small finds found in the architecture of Togolok 21 and Togolok 1. They are also similar to small finds from the tombs at Dashli in southern Bactria and the robbed tombs and both architectural and tomb context at Sapalli and Dzharkutan in northern Bactria.

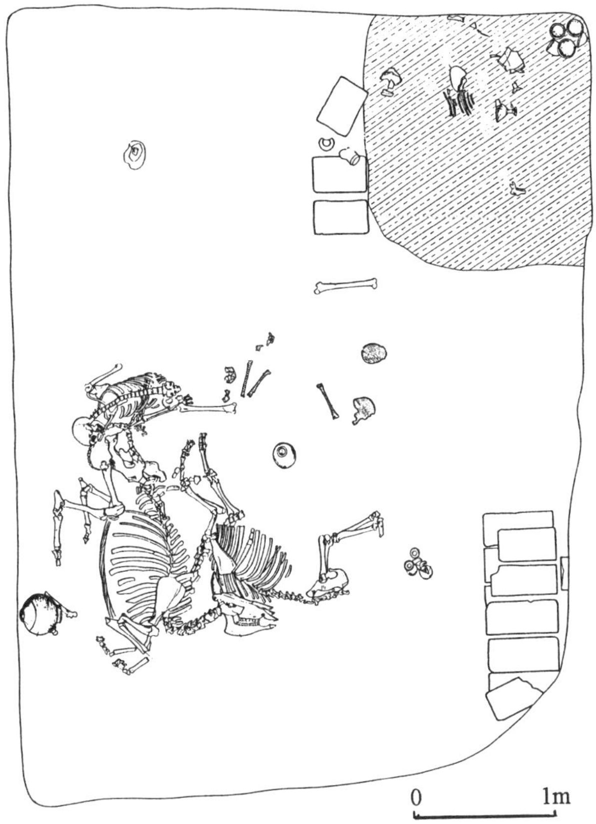

Figure 2.11
Togolok 1, plundered burial. Large pit burial, contemporary with the building complex. It contained at least two human and two bovid skeletons. Mud brick stairs give access to the pit in the southeast corner. In the northeast corner was a large cache (100+) of thin-walled open pedestal-base vessels (type 2.A.2) (adapted from Sarianidi 1991, fig. 37).

EASTERN SITES

The easternmost group of sites around the wells of Auchin, Gonur, and Takhirbai stretch in a line northward and follow a generally linear pattern. Excavations at Auchin depe documented a large architectural complex at one area and a series of isolated tombs in another. The finds published from Auchin included ceramics and small finds similar in form and manufacture to those from the southern sites of Togolok 1, 21, and 24 (the BMAC). The unexcavated architec-

Figure 2.12
Togolok 24. View of excavated burials. Photo: Courtesy of V. Sarianidi.

tural complex at Auchin is similar in form and size to Togolok 21, and I would expect an array of features—such as a monumental exterior wall, towers, regular interior architecture, interior kilns, and burials— similar to those seen at the Togolok sites. The excavations at Takhirbai 3 appear to be located within a large fortified building complex, although the small finds and ceramics were different from Auchin or the Togolok sites in diversity and manufacture.

Gonur depe

The largest of the eastern sites is Gonur depe 1 (simply called "Gonur depe"). Gonur depe is itself a series of low-lying mounds, the raised surface of which cover an area of 22 ha. Unlike the other sites, Gonur has superimposed layers of occupational debris with several stratified occupation levels and architectural phases.

The area of ceramic scatter extends 50 to 100 m beyond the mounded area of the site, including both areas of deflated architecture and areas where archaeological materials had been disturbed from their original context by wind and erosion (fig. 2.14).

In the mounded area of the site, sherd densities are quite high. For example, sherds in several squares 1 x 1 m were picked up. On the south mound, one pickup of every sherd greater than 2 cm on a side yielded a density of 218 per sq m.

There are clear differences in artifact assemblages found over the surface of the site. On the north mound, among the ceramics, figurines of the early period of the Bronze Age Murgab delta sites were found along with fragments of bronze, stone vessels, and other small finds. On the south mound among the ceramics we found amulets made of semiprecious stone and steatite and small bronze objects.

The northern mound rises to over 5 m above the plain, making it the highest Bronze Age mound

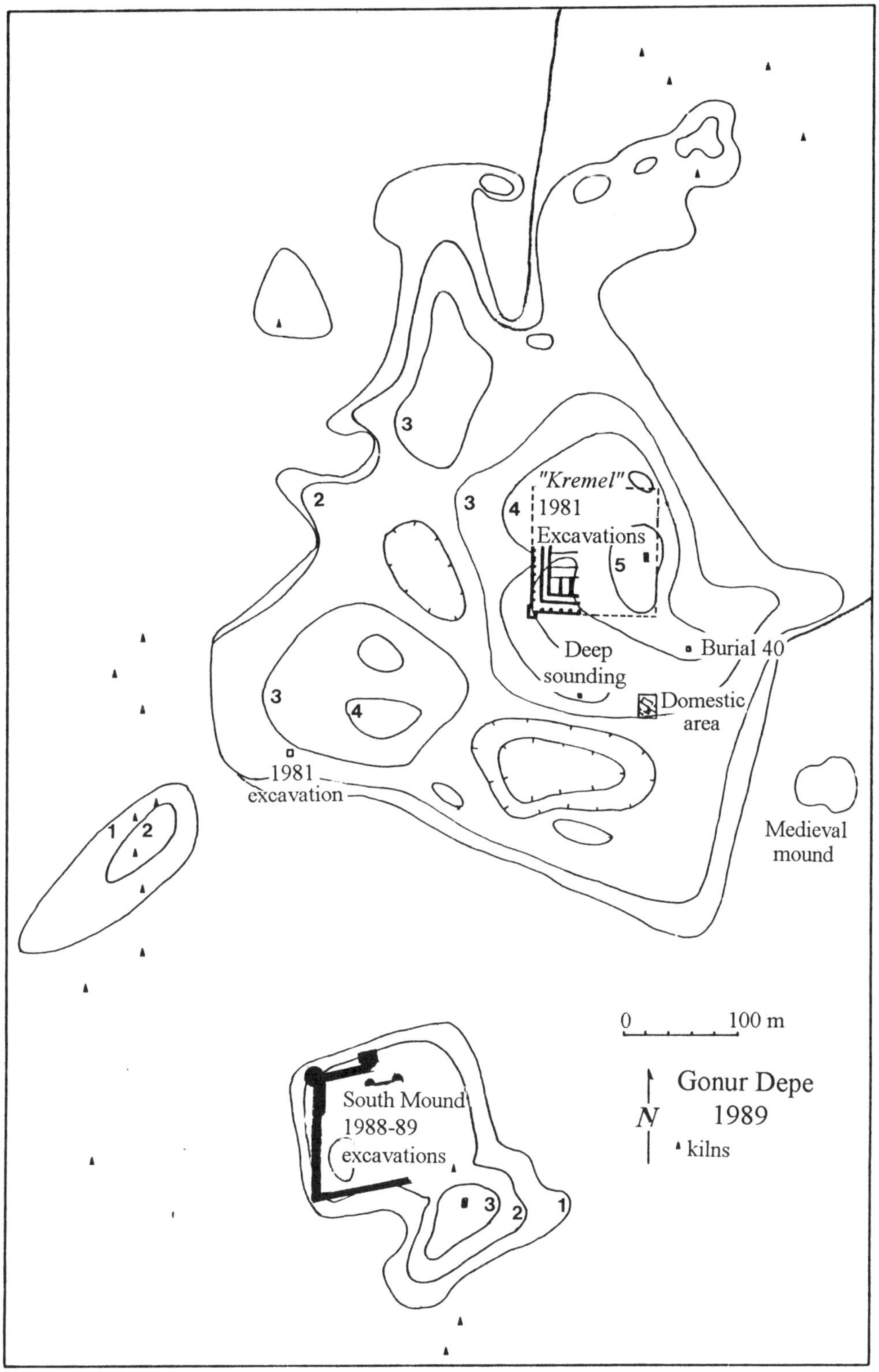

Figure 2.13
Gonur depe. Topographic map.

Figure 2.14
Excavations at the south mound at Gonur. View of stratified architectural phases as revealed in the recent excavations of V. Sarianidi.

known in Margiana. It is an irregularly shaped mound with a large central area, typical of the Margiana sites. Within the region of site buildup, site occupation was apparently continuous.

Gonur depe was the arena for collaborative investigations in 1988–1989. Sarianidi allowed me to conduct excavations, to observe his ongoing excavations, and to study the materials from these excavation.

Excavations are ongoing at Gonur depe, and various areas of the sites had been excavated by the end of 1989. A large building on the north mound was partially excavated in 1981–1983 (discussed in chap. 6). This building, referred to as the *kremel*, has fortified exterior walls and planned, straight inside rooms. Surrounding the *kremel* is an area with deep midden deposits where I excavated a sounding (hereafter called "the deep sounding"). Outside of the monumental architecture and the middens, the north mound has widespread architectural remains with areas of burials and cenotaphs. An architectural area was chosen for excavation outside of the monumental areas in order to compare the monumental and nonmonumental occupations (called "the domestic architecture").

To the west sits a small mound separated from the rest of the site by a modern road that heads north and cuts through the deposit. Estimates of the size of the settlement at Gonur must take the modern destruction of the site into consideration. Still further to the west, a cemetery of deep chamber tombs has been recently uncovered during the construction of an irrigation canal. This important cemetery is presently being investigated by an Italian team in collaboration with V. Sarianidi (Salvatori 1993).

To the east of the north mound is a small mound composed of a crumbled mud brick structure that dates to the medieval period. This building appears to have been a *kishlik*, or small rest house, similar to others found in the desert on a route from the medieval center of the oasis (Sultan Qala) to the medieval oasis of Urgench, south of the Aral Sea. Glazed ceramics and small artifacts of bronze and silver have been found both on this mound and scattered in among the Bronze Age materials on the north mound.

The north mound and the south mound are located 200 m apart. The area between the mounds has a scatter of small windblown sherds, with those above 2 cm on a side being rare (less than 25 per sq m), and appears to be without any occupational levels.

The south mound is not as large as the north mound (140 x 140 m). Rectangular-shaped and flat, it represents the remains of a single building complex with a large (4.5 m wide) wall on the four sides, and with outside dimensions of 120 x 130 m. This is the area of intensive wide-scale excavation from 1988 to 1993 (fig. 2.14). I participated in and observed these excavations (discussed in chap. 7). The building complex has several architectural phases, with earlier pits beneath the architecture and later constructions on the mound. Caches of ceramics and small finds (cenotaphs), burials, and production areas are found on the south mound.

To the south of the south mound is a small hillock, composed entirely of ashy midden. It most likely represents midden from the uppermost levels of the building complex on the south mound.

Surrounding the site to the north, south, and west of the mounded areas, sherd scatters tend to cluster in patches. Some of these patches have kiln bricks eroding out of the central area of the sherd scatter. These kiln bricks are baked red to vitrified green, with the vitrification dripping down on the surface of the bricks that line the inside of the kiln (fig. 2.15).

Sherds from a single vessel frequently are found grouped together on the surface. These often cannot be associated with architecture and are usually considered to be part of deflated cenotaphs, burials, or isolated pottery caches.

Within a kilometer of the site of Gonur, a large nomad station was found being exposed from under a large sand dune (fig. 2.16). No living surface was found in a small test excavation on the site, although sherds from more than fifty handmade nomad-style vessels were recovered. The extent of the visible scatter of sherds was 30 x 20 m. Large fragments of fired brick were found in this scatter, although no kilns exist at this site. Most likely these brick fragments were brought in from kilns at Gonur to be used as hearthstones. Four pieces of ground stone, but no chipped stone, bone, or metal were found. Both nomadic ceramics and typical Bronze Age wheel-made ceramics were found together, and although not an in situ deposit, this site appears to have been occupied during the time of the south mound at Gonur. The shifting sands around the edges of the small modern *takyri* hide sites, and other sites in the immediate area of Gonur may be found in the future.

Figure 2.15
Surface remains of a pottery kiln west of Gonur.

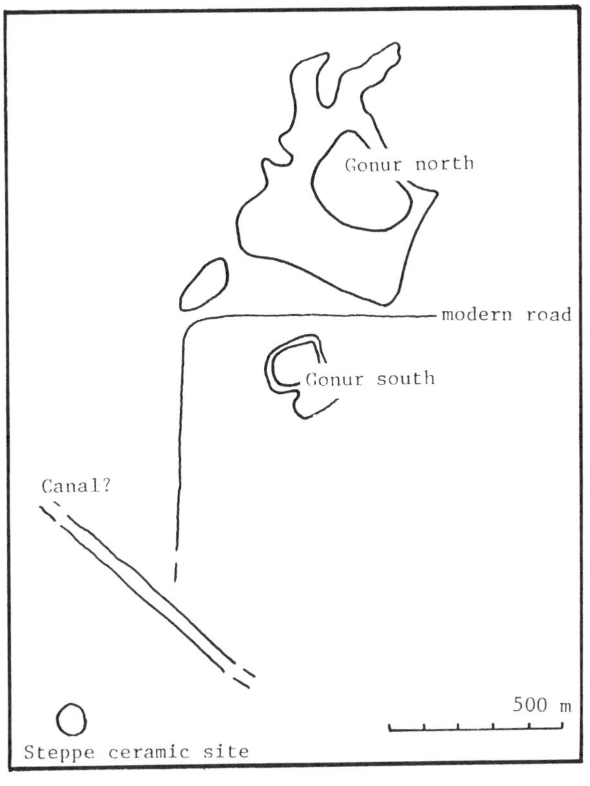

Figure 2.16
Location of probable canal and nomad site near Gonur.

SITE DISTRIBUTION

The Bronze Age building complexes of Margiana are dispersed across the landscape rather than being clustered or agglomerated settlements such as those found in the foothill plain of the Kopet Dag. The sites are isolated from each other in bands with no obvious nucleus. The Bronze Age oases both of Margiana and of southern Bactria have similar dispersed settlements along what may have been ancient riverbeds and canals (fig. 2.17).

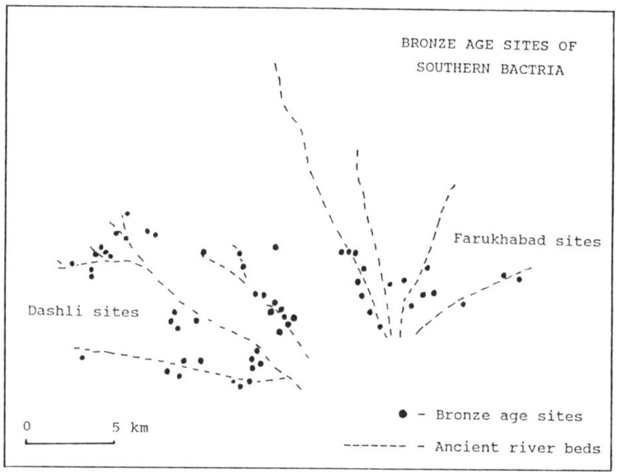

Figure 2.17
Bronze Age settlement pattern from the Dashli and Farukhabad oases of southern Bactria (adapted from Sarianidi 1977).

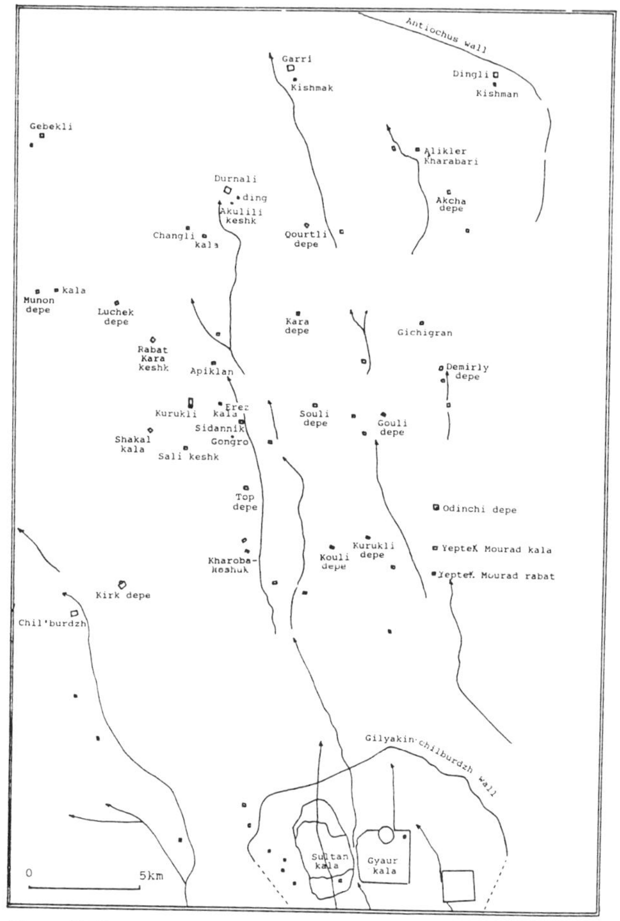

Figure 2.18
The medieval Merv Oasis settlement pattern (adapted from Hiebert 1992a, fig. 5) .

The architecture of the traditional Central Asian oasis consists of isolated buildings, and small and large fortified settlements with agricultural fields between them (smaller ones are called *keskhs*; larger ones, *qala*) (Pugachenkova 1958; Szabo and Barfield 1991). If we compare the Bronze Age oasis settlement types with that of the traditional desert oasis in Central Asia (fig. 2.18), the pattern is remarkably similar: dispersed fortified buildings, rather than a simple urban center. This type of settlement is different from the Near Eastern city (Childe 1953) or the classical and medieval Near Eastern urban center (*sharistan*) characterized by a densely occupied, internally differentiated large settlement with a surrounding rural hinterland. The only evidence found for an urban/rural dichotomy in Margiana represented brief periods of intense long-distance trade, during the third and second centuries B.C. and the eleventh and twelfth centuries A.D. (Al'khamova 1953; Hiebert 1992a). The non-urban oasis settlement pattern is typical not only of Margiana (during many periods) but of the oases around Bukhara, Khiva, and Bactria during the medieval period. In the Central Asian oases, the individual building complexes and canals may reflect traditional social and economic organization based on the segmentary lineage (Lamberg-Karlovsky 1994b). This Central Asian pattern appears to have been established in Margiana in its first widespread occupation during the Bronze Age.

CHAPTER THREE

Stratigraphic Excavations at Gonur

MOST OF THE BRONZE AGE SITES OF MARGIANA ARE SINGLE period sites so that their relative chronological relationship is difficult to determine. Gonur north is one of the exceptions to this situation as indicated by the depth of the deposit. In addition, the surface collections include materials typical of the Bactrian-Margiana Archaeological Complex and the distinctively different materials from Kelleli 3 and 4. The excavations at Gonur north from 1981–83 indicated a stratigraphic relationship of these complexes, but the excavations in the monumental building at Gonur north yielded little material inside the walls. Sarianidi suggested that the building had been cleaned out after its major period of occupation, and its materials deposited nearby.

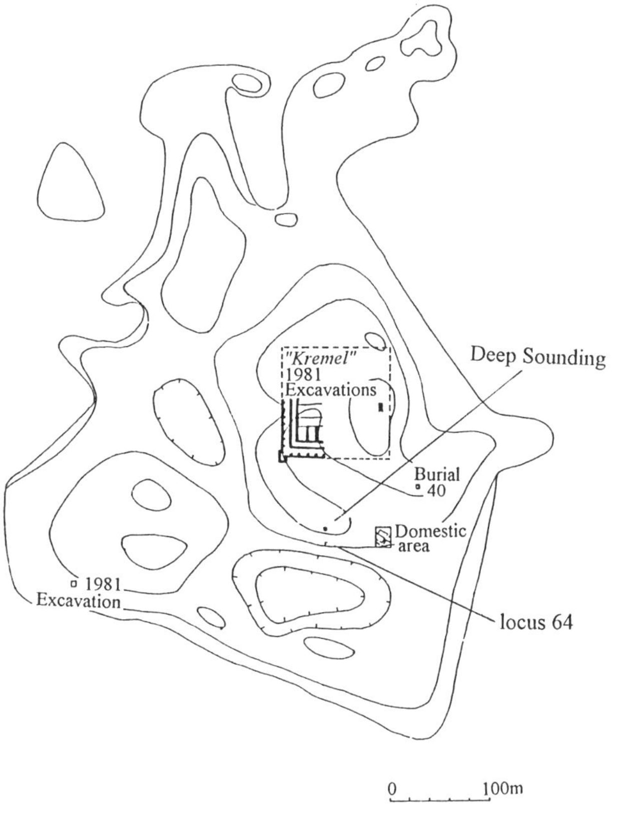

Figure 3.1
Location of the deep sounding on the north mound at Gonur.

DEEP SOUNDING ON GONUR NORTH

As part of my participation in the 1989 spring excavations at Gonur depe, a deep sounding was stratigraphically excavated on the side of the north mound 4 m above the surrounding plain (fig. 3.1). This area was outside the area of monumental architecture, 100 m southeast of the 1981–83 excavations. It was an area of finely stratified midden, which provided a rich assemblage of ceramics and charcoal for dating, and deposits of seeds and bone.

The deep sounding was excavated to sterile sand. It is possible, however, that earlier periods are elsewhere at Gonur or buried beneath the alluvium, although no sherds of distinctive Namazga III or IV painted ceramics have been found during extensive surface surveys around Gonur.

Description of the Excavation and Deposits

The excavation area was 6 x 6 m, divided into four units of 3 x 3 m. Below 1.5 m, the excavation area was reduced to 3 x 6 m, and excavated another 1.2 m. The last 80 cm were excavated in an area 1 x 1 m at the bottom of the deep sounding. Sterile soil was reached at 3.5 m below the surface (fig. 3.2).

A horizontal living surface and associated brick fall were found on the sterile sand in the first layer. Above it lay 3 m of very soft midden that sloped strongly to the northwest.

The stratigraphy of the midden is well preserved, with very little natural mixing between the layers (fig. 3.3). A few rodent holes ran through the deposit, but they did not affect the study of the ceramic sherds. The layers contain charcoal, ash, and sandy soil. The fine lenses of unsorted material are layered in the

Figure 3.2
Gonur north, deep sounding, view to the southeast.

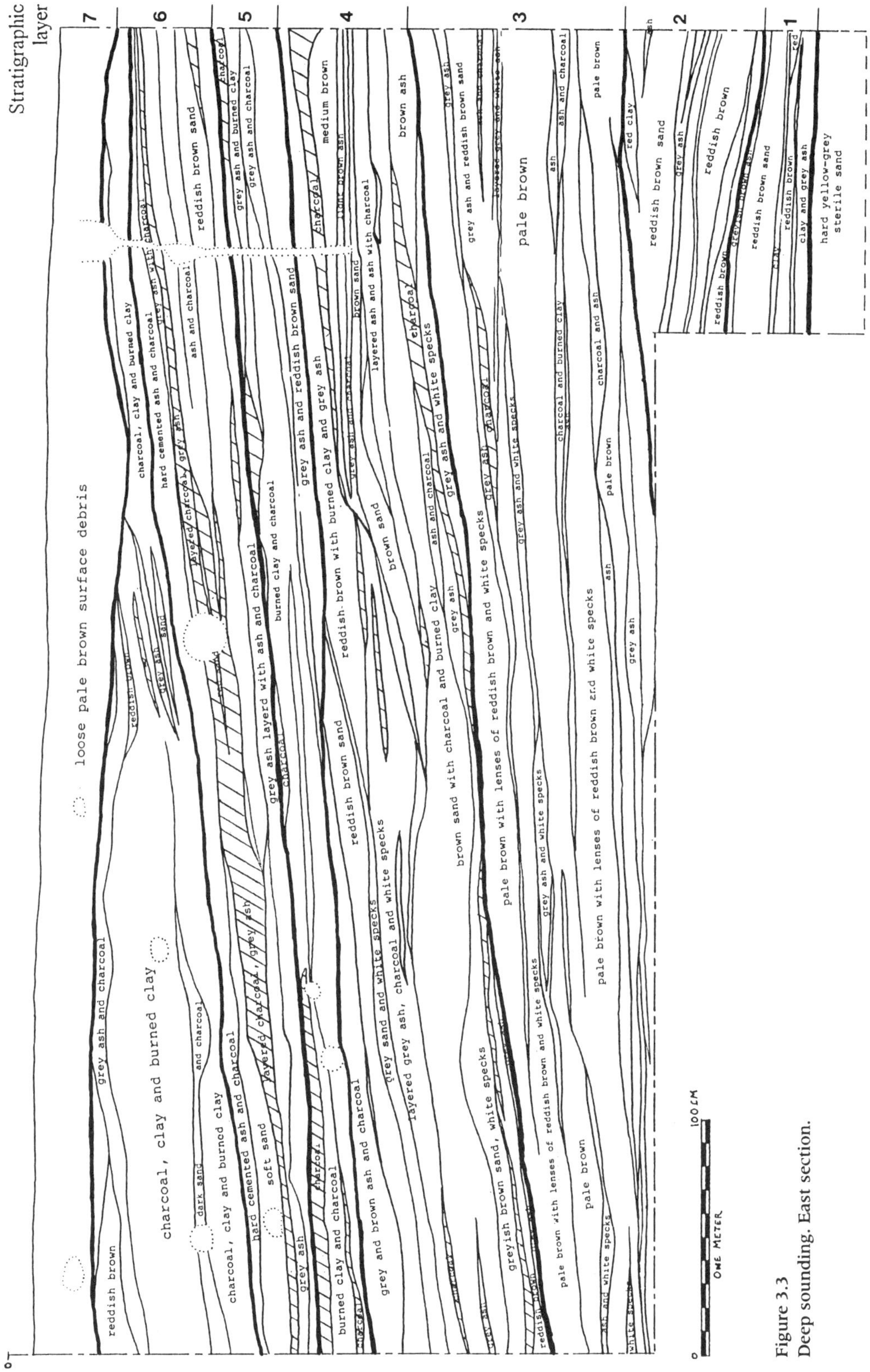

Figure 3.3
Deep sounding. East section.

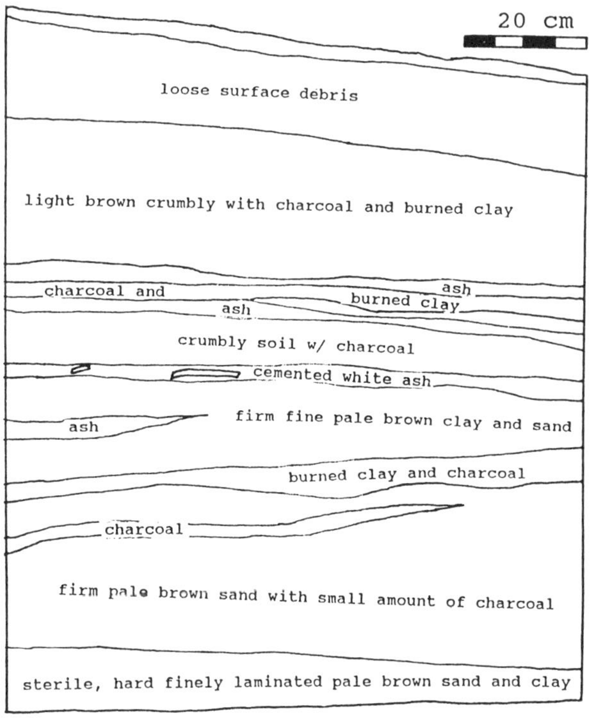

Figure 3.4
Locus 64. East section.

position in which they were thrown out, practically basket by basket, and there was no postdepositional mixing such as pits, or trenches for foundation walls. The analysis of the plant remains indicates that the middens most often originated from sweepings from floors of buildings. This suggests that the material represents the refuse of daily life, unlikely to contain older material from the surface of settlement.

The midden identified in the deep sounding is fairly widespread over this area. Locus 64 is a small sounding (1 x 1 m) located 17 m to the south. It contained similar stratified layers of ashy midden, soil, and sands, and had a high density of ceramics (fig. 3.4). The strata of the test sounding were practically horizontal and 1.2 m deep to sterile sand.

It is important to point out that materials from the latest occupation at Gonur depe are not represented in the deep sounding. These ceramics are similar to the ceramics from Takhirbai 3, located to the south of Gonur. The Takhirbai sites have long been considered transitional between the major Bronze Age and Iron Age settlements of Margiana (Masson 1959). The discovery of these materials in the uppermost levels of the south mound building (phase 5), and our radiocarbon dates associated with these levels collected in 1990 (see chap. 5) suggest that this assemblage directly continues the occupational history documented in the deep sounding.

Thus the deep sounding provides a refined ceramic chronology associated with fine-sieve samples for the major Bronze Age occupation of Gonur and Margiana. It does not exclude the possibility of earlier occupation, nor does it cover the transition to Iron Age occupation in Margiana.

Method of Excavation

The smallest unit of analysis is the *locus*, which is the excavation unit. These loci are grouped into *layers*, which are stratigraphically defined units. The layers are grouped into *periods* on the basis of the ceramics and small finds.

The sounding was excavated using 3 x 3 m squares dug in 20-cm units (locus units). This permitted us to excavate units that came from single layers, despite the marked slope of the deposit (fig. 3.5).

All sherds from each locus unit were counted, thus providing estimates of ceramic density. All pottery rims and bases were collected and drawn. The original goal was to screen all of the deposits with 1/4-inch screen, but despite several months of searching, this screen could not be found in the Soviet Union. Recovery of ceramics and small finds by eye was regularly checked with a hand sieve, and I noted that few sherds larger than 2 cm ended up in the backdirt. I consider that the percentages of diagnostic types and wares are representative of the actual deposit. The statistics that I present on the ceramics, however, should be considered with this methodology in mind. Table 3.1 presents the data on sherd density, recorded by ware and by type of ceramic (base, body, rim). I use the density of archaeological material from the deep sounding (number of sherds greater than 2 cm on a side) as an indicator of the original context.

Several fine-screened (1/16-inch mesh) botanical samples were taken in each of the stratigraphic layers (fig. 3.6). Identification of the constituent parts of the deposits (such as charcoal, plant parts, and dung) allowed me to suggest the origins of the dump deposits based on the inferences developed by Hillman (Hillman 1984).

PERIOD 2

Loc	Vol	Coarseware Rim	Base	Body	Tot	M F C Rim	Base	Body	Tot	Other	Total	Density
2	8.3	0	0	7	7	69	28	584	681	1 stamp	688	82.9
9	1.8	1	0	0	1	19	3	189	211	----	212	117.8
13	2.3	0	0	1	1	29	10	252	291	----	292	127.0
17	1.8	1	0	0	1	22	3	203	228	----	229	127.2

PERIOD 1

Loc	Vol	Coarseware Rim	Base	Body	Tot	M F C Rim	Base	Body	Tot	Other	Total	Density
24	2.3	0	0	9	9	34	26	208	404	2 Redware	415	90.2
25	1.8	2	1	0	3	15	9	172	196	2 pod-stavki	199	110.5
26	1.8	0	0	0	0	16	9	115	140	----	140	77.8
27	1.8	0	0	2	2	21	14	167	202	----	204	113.3
28	1.8	0	0	0	0	22	15	165	202	----	202	112.2
29	1.8	2	0	1	3	25	15	151	191	----	194	107.8
30	1.8	0	0	0	0	28	15	175	218	----	218	121.1
31	0.4	0	0	0	0	2	4	34	40	----	40	100.0
32	0.3	0	0	1	1	5	2	44	51	----	52	173.0
33	0.4	0	0	3	3	6	4	66	76	----	79	197.5
34	0.4	0	0	0	0	1	1	14	16	----	16	40.0

Table 3.1
Density of ceramic sherds in the volume of excavated deposit: coarseware, MFC = medium-fine chaff (wheelmade wares). Density per cubic meter.

THE STRATIGRAPHY

The stratigraphy lies naturally in seven distinct layers above sterile sand.

Sterile sand and clay are found 0.5 m above the surrounding *takyr*, which formed a small, naturally deposited, dunelike hillock. Fine sieving of this yellowish grey sand in the final 1 x 1 m probe at the bottom of the excavation showed that it contains no ceramics, stone, bone, or charcoal. This same sandy layer (*materik*) is found throughout the area of the site. It does not contain any alluvial or waterlaid deposits. Such a base layer may indicate that the site of Gonur was outside of the natural area of alluvial deposit of the Murgab River.

Period	Stratigraphic layers in the sounding	Excavation units in the sounding
	7 Surface	00, 0
PERIOD 2	6	1,2,9,13,17
PERIOD 2	6+5	8,10
	6+5+4	3,4,5,6,12,14
	5+4	16,18,20,22
PERIOD 1 Fill	4	7,11,15,19
PERIOD 1 Fill	4+3	23,24,25,26
PERIOD 1 Fill	3	27,28,29,30
	3+2	31
PERIOD 1 Architecture	2	32
PERIOD 1 Architecture	1	33,34
	Sterile sand	

Figure 3.5
Correlation of excavated loci and stratigraphic layers.

Layers 1 and 2

The earliest two layers are primary deposits from occupation in the area; these were excavated only in the 1 x 1 m probe at the base of the deep sounding.

Layer 1 (loci 33, 34), 20 cm thick, is the first archaeological deposit on the sterile sand. The cultural material comes from layered ash, reddish and reddish-brown sand, and a thick compact layer of cemented ash and tamped clay. Ceramics, bone, and ash lie directly on the tamped clay surface. On the surface at the edge of the excavation is a circular hearthlike feature. Wood charcoal and charred sheep/goat dung, burned and unburned bone, and charred seeds came from the hearth. In the small area excavated, it appears that this surface follows the slope of the natural mound, unlike the later midden deposits.

The second layer (locus 32) is reddish brown, sandy sediment 20 to 30 cm thick that slopes to the south with the natural slope of the mound. It is a dark-colored layer containing charred twigs and sticks, burned daub, burned and unburned bone and a high density of ceramics (above 100 sherds/m^3). This layer is fill and debris most likely associated with the collapse of a mud brick structure from layer 1. Only future excavations of these occupational layers will reveal the nature of the initial settlement in this area.

Layers 3 and 4

Layers 3 and 4 represent two different periods of fairly rapid dumping, with individual lenses remaining discrete. These deposits are most likely from the *kremel,* which Sarianidi reports had been kept clear of debris during its occupation and had clean sand on the floors (Sarianidi 1990). This clearing is a common feature in the occupational history of large buildings (such as large Roman buildings) and is an obvious source for the middens of layers 3 and 4.

Layer 3 (loci 27, 28, 29, and 30) was excavated over 3 x 6 m. It is 50 to 80 cm thick across the trench and consists of pale brown sandy sediment, with many thin lenses of ash and charcoal sloping to the northeast. Because this midden probably had been deposited quite rapidly, the deposit was not eroded or wind sorted.

Layer 4 (loci 7, 11, 15, and 19), 60 cm of sloping midden also probably from the monumental building, is more completely sorted suggesting that it was deposited over a longer time period than layers 1 through 3. Each individual lens was larger in area than in layer 3, and some were separated by layers of windblown sediment. Dumping of trash in this area was apparently less frequent during this time. The midden seems to have come from a variety of deposits and includes some fragments of highly fired daub from a kiln or baking oven. Some of the lenses have a high percentage of charred plant remains that proba-

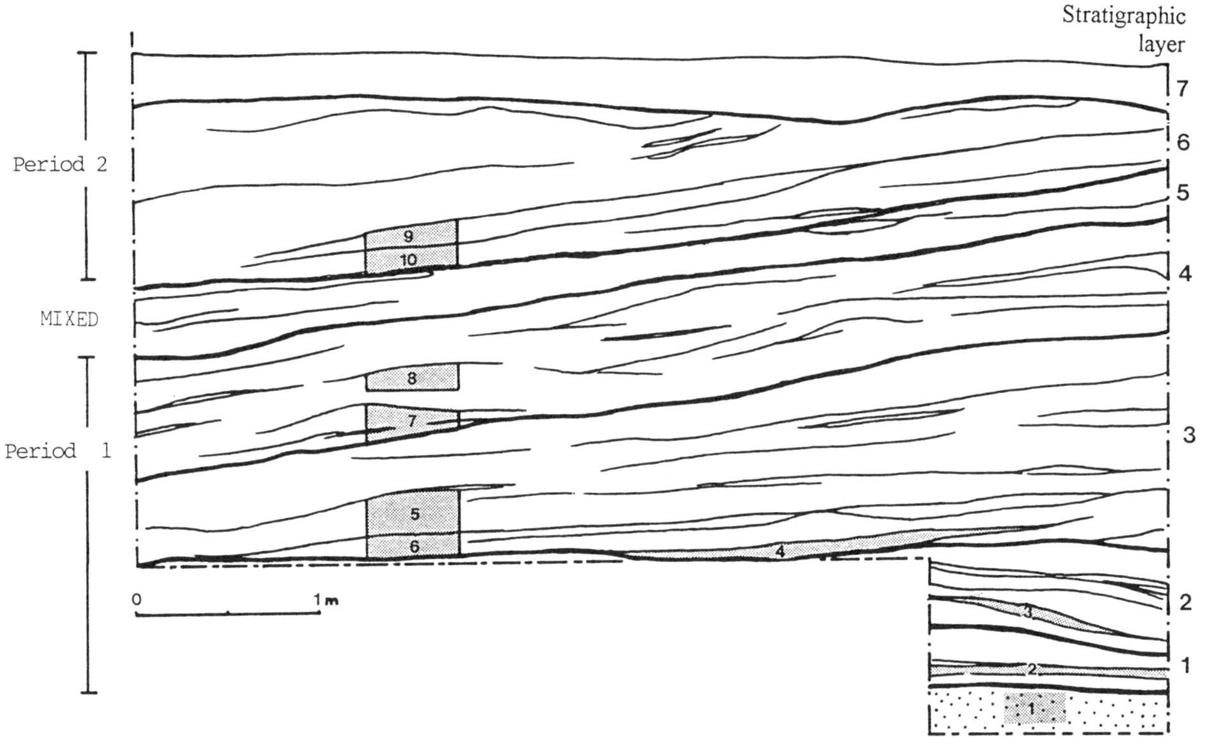

Figure 3.6
Location of the 10 soil samples from the deep sounding.

bly come from an area where storage and processing of grains took place.

Layer 5

Layer 5 (loci 3, 4, 5, 6, 12, and 14), a sloping 25- to 30-cm-thick layer, consists of reddish brown soil in fine lenses and some very thick, unsorted lenses heavy in charcoal. This layer was rapidly deposited, and the debris in the deposit suggests its origin was large ovens or kilns rather than household occupation. Layer 5 contains materials from both layers 4 and 6 due to the many pits and the slope of the deposit, but the profile indicates no hiatus in site use.

Layer 6

Layer 6 (loci 1, 2, 9, 13, and 17) contains thick lenses of dumped material with a change in the type of ceramics and small finds.

Layer 6 is divided from layer 5 by a thick charcoal layer that cuts across the entire trench. Above the widespread charcoal level is a hard layer of cemented ash and charcoal. This deposit is very similar to that found in the bottom of local ceramic kilns. These thick layers of charcoal and burned clay also had a high density of sherds, including wasters and other domestic debris.

Layer 7: Surface

The seventh layer (loci 0 and 00), the uppermost 30 cm of the excavation, is a soft or dusty pale brown soil of mixed debris. It includes ceramics and small finds of several periods. The modern surface has a firm crust 3 to 5 cm thick representing periods of wind deflation and is strewn with small finds and ceramics of both Bronze Age periods. The small objects lying on the surface are not in their original position but were windblown from other areas of the site. Thus systematic collections of surface finds at a multiperiod site such as Gonur depe will not necessarily indicate the age or nature of the specific small areas of the site. Even though different parts of the site were occupied at different times, surface finds do not accurately reflect the changing settlement.

CERAMICS AND SMALL FINDS

Period 1

Layers 1 and 2 (in situ occupational levels) and layers 3 and 4 (midden, most likely from the monumental architecture) contain ceramics similar in form to the ceramics from Kelleli 3 and Kelleli 4 and to the artifacts from the floors of the *kremel* architecture and nearby domestic architecture. No differences between the ceramics from the upper and lower layers were noted (see Hiebert 1992b for a full description of ceramics from this excavation). The ceramics and small finds belong to the earliest widespread occupation at Gonur, which I call Period 1. The ceramics (layers 1 through 4) do not have the range of forms recorded from the wide-scale excavations of architecture at Gonur 1 or from the domestic architecture. However, these ceramics do provide an idea of the frequency of the forms that were broken and discarded (fig. 3.7).

The most distinctive small finds are the terracotta human figurines: three fragments come from good context associated with the Period 1 ceramics (fig. 3.8:1, 2, 6). Overall, there is a great deal of variation in the form of the human figurines found with the Period 1 ceramics, including the typical "foothill" Namazga V crowned figurines and seated figurines more typical of earlier periods. Two fragments of ceramics have distinctive applied figures and incised trees (figs. 3.8:7). Whorls or wheels (fig. 3.8:4), animal figurines (fig. 3.8:3), and steatite vessels (fig. 3.8:5) also came from good contexts. The overall assemblage of ceramics and small finds (especially the terracotta human figurines) appears to be similar to the few artifacts from the nearby building at Gonur north (*kremel*), to the finds from domestic architecture of Gonur north, and to the materials from Kelleli 3 and Kelleli 4.

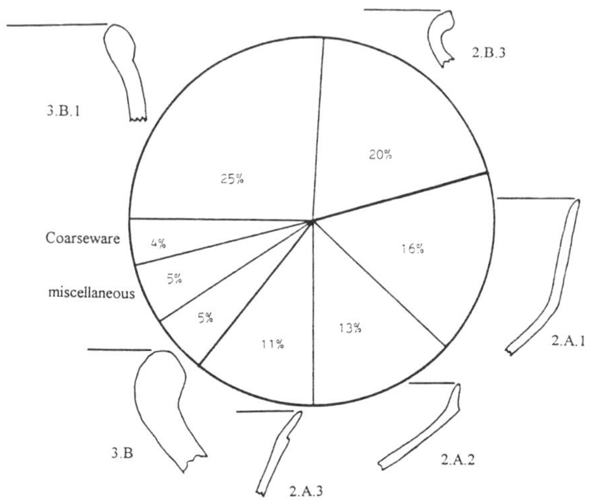

Figure 3.7
Percentages of ceramics from Period 1 (layers 1–4) of the deep sounding (n=112). Numbers below sherd illustrations refer to the ceramic typology in chap. 4.

Period 2

Layer 6 contains a limited assemblage of ceramics, clearly different from layers 1 through 4. Ceramic forms are similar to those from the monumental architecture at Gonur south, from the architecture and burials at Togolok 21, and from burials with BMAC artifacts at Togolok 24 (fig. 3.9). Specifically, finely made globular pots with triangular rims (and incised decoration), tall-necked storage jars, and goblets are characteristic of this Period 2 ceramic assemblage in the deep sounding. Deeply burnished greyware imports (fig. 3.10:2), incised geometric designs on ceramics (fig. 3.10:1), and stamp seal impression on the ceramics (fig. 3.10:3) were also found. Coarse, nomadic ware may be present, but was noted only from small body sherds.

A flint arrow point (fig. 3.10:5) and a crudely modeled animal figurine were found in layer 6. Although layer 6 contains ceramics similar to BMAC ceramics from architectural contexts at Gonur south, Togolok 1, and Togolok 21, it does not include the rich assemblage of small finds usually found in monumental architecture or burials. Given the ceramic wasters and lack of small finds in the midden, the overall context of the midden appears to have been oriented to production.

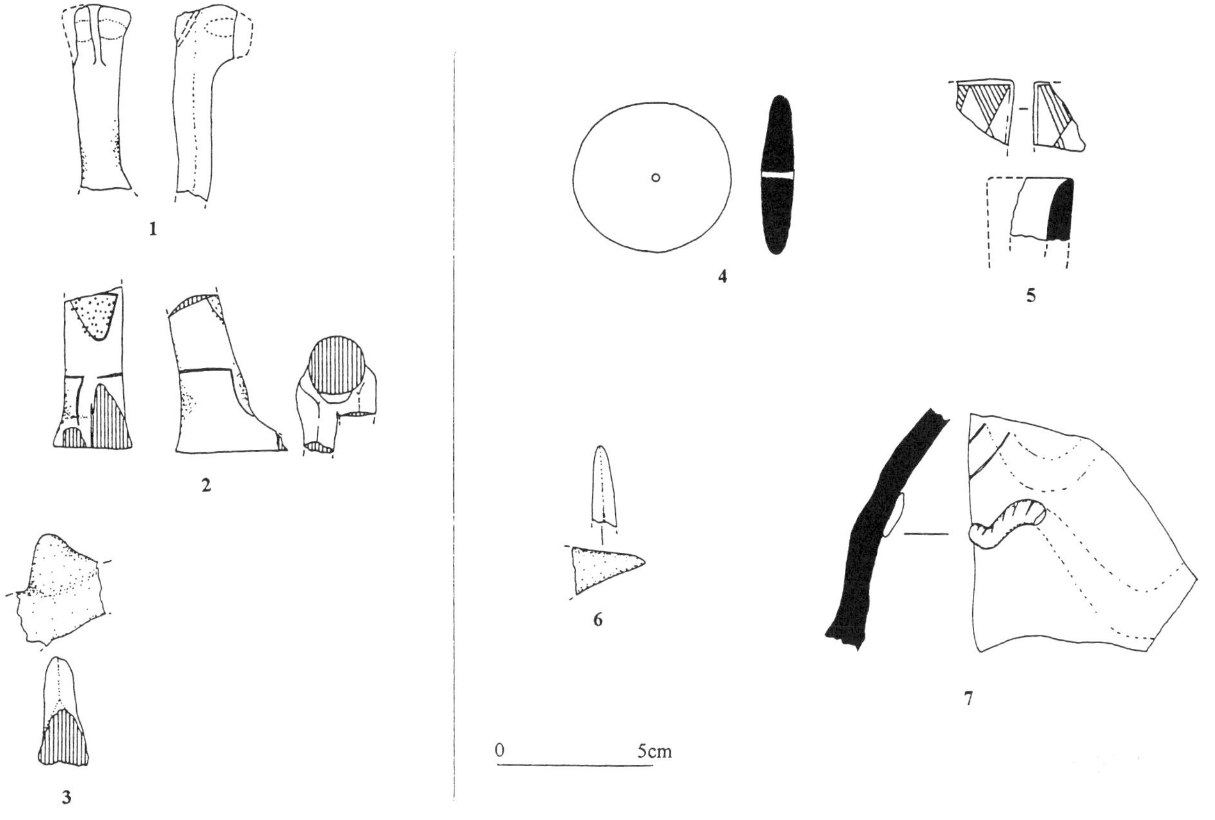

Figure 3.8
Period 1 small finds from the deep sounding.
1) Terracotta figurine, red core, buff exterior, chaff temper, hand molded, applied eyes (popped off). Locus 18; 2) Terracotta figurine, reddish-buff, chaff temper, incised decoration. Locus 20; 3) Terracotta animal figurine, red blackened, chaff and coarse temper. Locus 22; 4) Ceramic wheel or whorl, buff, fine chaff temper, smoothed exterior. Locus 15; 5) Fragment of a grey steatite dish. Locus 19; 6) Terracotta figurine fragment (arm), reddish-buff, chaff temper. Locus 30; 7) Ceramic sherd with applied decoration (snake?), buffware, medium fine chaff. Locus 7.

To summarize the stratigraphy of the deep sounding at Gonur in the context of the site, we found two phases of Period 1, an architectural level and building collapse (layers 1 and 2) built on the original hillock, and debris from the cleaning out of an architectural area (layers 3 and 4), most likely the monumental architecture 100 m to the north. Both phases have ceramics and small finds forming a very homogenous group that are similar to finds from the *kremel* and from the domestic architecture on the north mound. The other excavated architecture on the north mound have Period 1 ceramics. In the 1981 excavation and around Burial 40, architecture with small finds and ceramics similar to Period 1 of the deep sounding was found just below the surface. The Period 1 domestic architecture (described in chap. 6) was most likely contemporary with layers 3 and 4 of the sounding, since it was also built above earlier layers.

Thus, during Period 1, the entire north mound was not occupied all at one time. There were areas of dumping, areas of domestic architecture, and a monumental building dominating the central part of the mound. Although most of the Period 1 occupation is found on the north mound, several isolated pits with Period 1 ceramics and small finds have been found beneath the architecture on the south mound.

The upper layer of the deep sounding, layer 6, contained an assemblage of BMAC-type ceramics and small finds. The Gonur deep sounding is a clear example of the stratigraphic superposition of these two assemblages. Materials in Layer 6 may have come from the production areas rather than from the small,

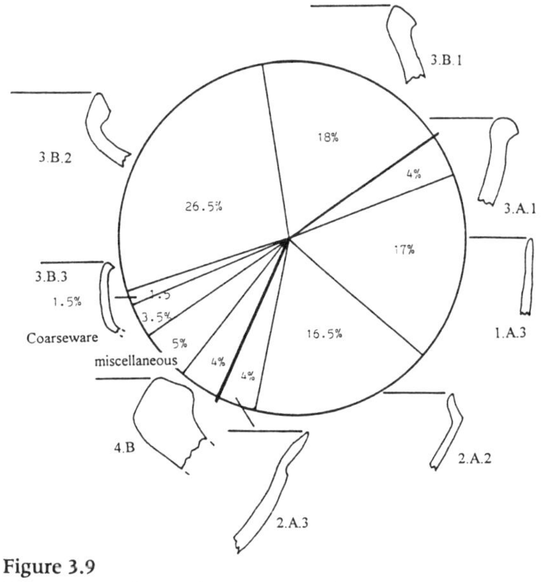

Figure 3.9
Percentages of ceramics from Period 2 (layer 6) of the deep sounding (n=139). Numbers below sherd illustrations refer to the ceramic typology in Chapter 4.

Period 2 occupation found in the upper levels of the *kremel*. The south mound building complex, entirely excavated by 1993, contains ceramics and small finds very similar to Period 2 of the sounding, with several architectural phases (Sarianidi 1993; also see Preface, this volume).

A chronological framework that integrates ceramics, small finds, and radiocarbon data allows us to evaluate the development of Margiana in a regional perspective with Bactria and the Kopet Dag foothill plain. Within this stratigraphic framework from the deep sounding, analyses of botanical and faunal remains offer preliminary indications of the ancient economy of the Margiana oasis.

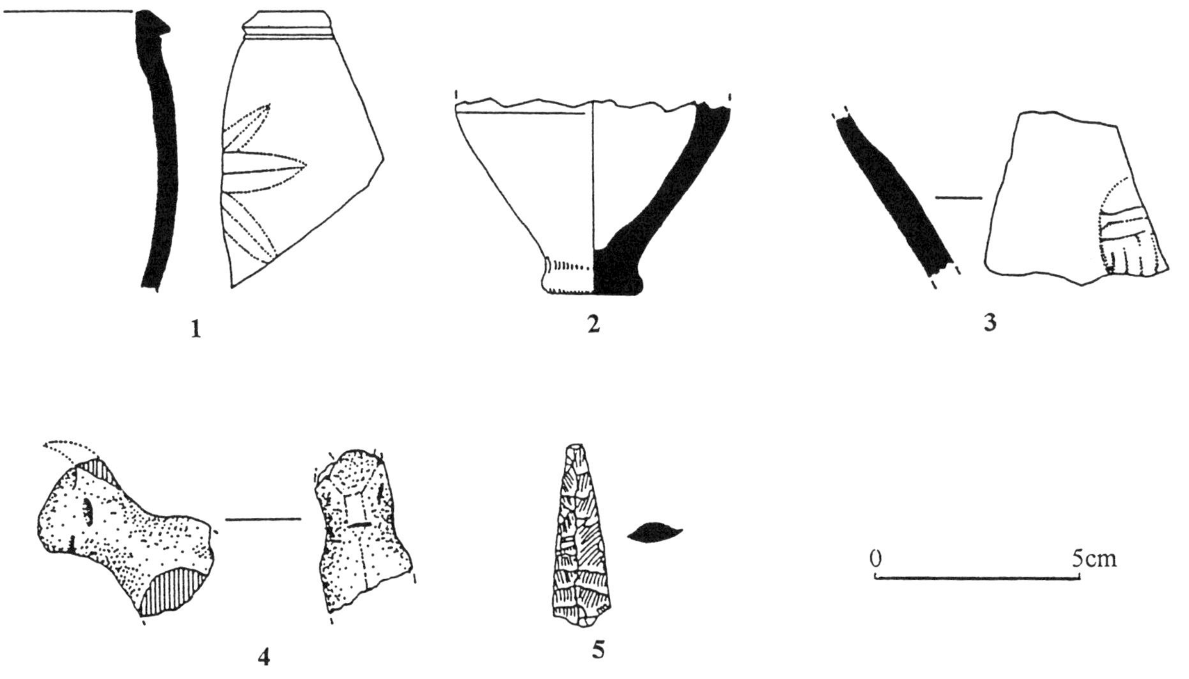

Figure 3.10
Small finds from the deep sounding, Period 2.
1) Sherd with incised flower or geometric design, buffware, medium mineral temper. Locus 2; 2) Imported ceramic, burnished very dark grey exterior, fine mica tempered greyware. Locus 17; 3) Stamp-impressed sherd, buffware, medium-fine chaff. Locus 1; 4) Terracotta figurine, red, blackened by fire, poorly hand-modeled, coarse temper. Locus 2; 5) Stone arrow point or drill, greyish white chert. Locus 2.

CHAPTER FOUR

Relative Chronology and Ceramics of Margiana

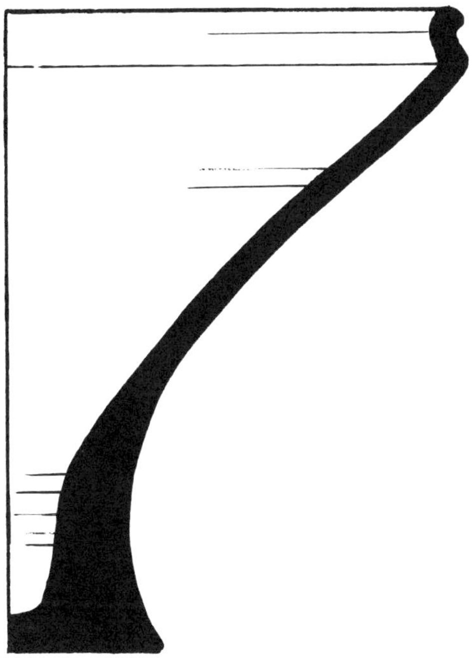

Initially, the study of ceramics in the former Soviet Union had a long tradition separate from that in the West. As early as the 1920s, statistical approaches to ceramic typology were employed by Soviet scholars to study the functions of the ceramics and ceramic assemblages, aspects of exchange, and pottery chronology (Gorodtsov 1927). However, during the 1930s and 1940s these innovations in archaeological methodology were abandoned, in part because of the replacement of one generation of archaeologists by a new generation that considered ceramic typology "bourgeois archaeology" (Mongait 1951). Under the influence of N. Marr, typology was officially abandoned because of its ideological connection to Western archaeology, and this resulted in the development of a more interpretive approach to archaeological data (Miller 1956:91). Despite the difficult conditions during the Stalin period, the basic ceramic sequences were first established in Central Asia using excavations of deeply stratified sites such as Altyn depe and Namazga depe (Litvinskii 1952; Kuftin 1956; Masson 1956).

During the late 1960s, in the then Leningrad branch of the Institute of Archaeology, statistical studies of Central Asian ceramics were revived (Shchetenko 1970; Masimov 1976; Udemuradov 1989). For example, at Altyn depe, Kircho defined ceramic assemblages based on sherds instead of whole vessels (1972). Elemental analysis and microscopic study of the paste provided information about the technology of ceramic manufacture and paste composition (Saiko 1984).

Most recently, however, methods of studying the ceramics have reverted to the use of whole ceramic forms as "index" types. This has been made possible by methods of large-scale horizontal exposure of architecture developed by Russian and Turkmen archaeologists. These typologies based on whole forms require both a large number of complete vessels and the assumption that large areas of excavation be contemporaneous. The "whole pot" typologies attempt to resolve chronological problems by identifying changing categories of ceramics (cups, bowls, and so on), which, however, given the functional nature of most of the ceramics in Margiana, tend to be stable categories through time.

In Margiana, the ceramic chronology currently in use is based on key ceramics and artifacts from each group of sites (micro-oases) as a unit (Masimov 1981; Udemuradov 1987; P'yankova 1989, 1993; Sarianidi

1990). Sarianidi and P'yankova have proposed a three-period chronology for the Bronze Age of Margiana. They suggest that these three periods are subdivisions of Namazga VI: Kelleli (comprising sites in the Kelleli, Auchin, and Egri Bogaz micro-oases); Gonur (Gonur micro-oasis); and Togolok (Togolok, Taip, Adam Basan, and Adzhi Kui micro-oases). These ceramic periods are based primarily on their geographic location, with the oldest micro-oases located in the northeast, and progressively younger micro-oases to the southwest (fig. 4.1). Masimov and Udemuradov propose that the Kelleli sites compare best to late Namazga V, the Togolok/Taip sites are dated to the Namazga VI period, and Egri Bogaz is transitional between them. They consider that the northernmost sites of Kelleli may represent an earlier settlement based on Kelleli 12, a small scatter of Geoksyur type painted ceramics in the desert, and thus propose

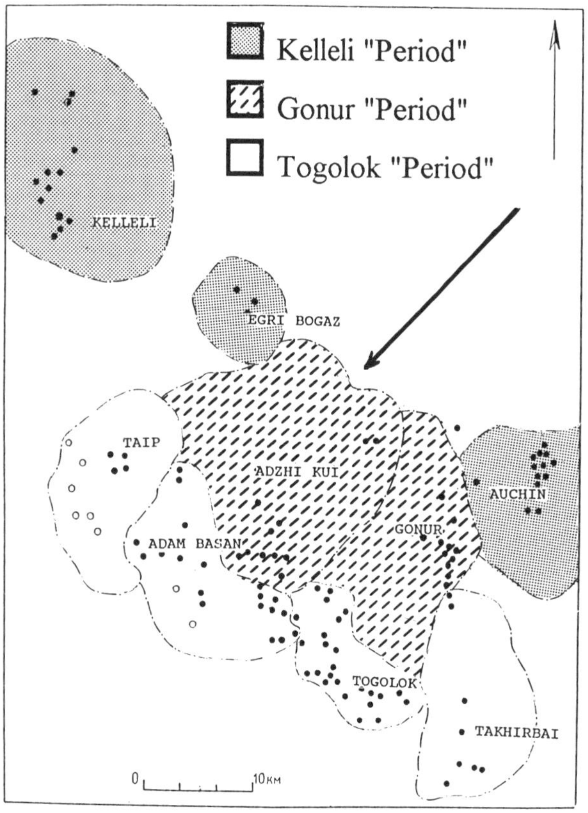

Figure 4.1
The chronological paradigm for Bronze Age Margiana during the 1970s and 1980s.

long-term occupation prior to the late Namazga V period, although this is unlikely.

Several Western scholars have reviewed the chronologies and have offered alternative sequences. Kohl (1984) follows Sarianidi's grouping of micro-oases, but makes parallels with the earlier Namazga V assemblage rather than the Namazga VI assemblages. Francfort (1989) divides the chronology into three periods (also called Kelleli, Gonur, and Togolok) based on Sarianidi (1981a), but the micro-oases that he includes in each period are not the same as those grouped together by Sarianidi or Kohl, and thus the materials grouped together in each "period" are different. Both Kohl (1979, 1984, 1992) and Francfort (1989, 1994) accept the evidence of pre-Namazga V occupation of Margiana.

The problem with the micro-oasis as the unit of analysis, however, is that there appear to be sites of various periods in each micro-oasis area. The only way we can actually define a regional chronology is to classify the ceramics on a stratigraphic basis, such as from the Gonur deep sounding. To compare the previously excavated ceramics from Margiana with the fragmentary ceramic sherds from the Gonur deep sounding, a new ceramic typology is presented here. The present classification is based on local wheel-finished or wheelmade ceramics and is a reorganization of the older "whole pot" typology, ranked by characteristics of ware, size, rim profile, and other features. By ranking the characteristics, the "whole pot" type can be determined on the basis of the sherds.

The individual levels from the Gonur deep sounding yielded enough sherds to allow for the definition of the ceramic assemblage for Period 1 and Period 2. The range of types and type variants described here is derived from the wide-scale horizontal excavations at the individual sites of Kelleli 3, Kelleli 4, Togolok 21, and Togolok 1. Comparative ceramic data from these sites are recorded in unpublished field reports (*otcheti* and *opisi*) located in archives in Moscow and in Ashgabat. *Otcheti*, records of the excavations from each field season, represent the basic level of data collection from Soviet excavations. They include plans of the excavated architecture, lists of the major finds of the season and their contexts, and the objectives of the excavations. *Opisi* are lists of ceramics and individual finds from the excavations. They provide the provenience of individual finds and include the drawings of small finds and of ceramics with descriptions of ware, temper, color, and so on. These field documents, stored at the Institutes of Archaeology in Russia and in the Central Asian Republics, form an important database for collaborative research not often used by outside researchers. Study collections of ceramics from some Bronze Age Margiana sites are stored at the Institute of History and Archaeology in Ashgabat, and in the Margiana regional museum in Bayram-Ali. Materials relating to the Takhirbai ceramic group were described from two excavations at Takhirbai 3: excavation 1, dug in 1955 (Masson 1959); and excavation 2, dug in 1972 (Sarianidi 1990).

CLASSIFICATION OF MARGIANA CERAMICS

The wheelmade ceramics from Gonur consist of a medium-fine paste with fine, horizontally oriented chaff holes. Period 1 ceramics have no sand in the temper, whereas well-sorted fine quartz grains are visible in a small percentage of Period 2 ceramics under low magnification. Sherds from the deep sounding Period 1 or Period 2 could not be assigned to period on the basis of the temper or ware alone. The overall homogeneity of the alluvial deposits of the Murgab River delta suggests that there would be very little compositional difference in the ceramics produced throughout Margiana. No differences could be visibly detected between the paste of the ceramics from Gonur, Togolok, Kelleli, or the other micro-oases of Margiana.

The Margiana wheelmade ceramics range from reddish buff to light red. In general, Period 2 ceramics are slightly redder than the earlier ceramic group. Greyish or greenish misfired ceramics are found in the Period 1 and 2 domestic middens, indicating that some improperly fired ceramics were used despite their discoloration or deformations. Ceramics from Takhirbai (Period 3) are coarser, reddish wares that occasionally have actual buff or red slipped exteriors, unlike ceramics from Period 1 or 2, which do not have slipped exteriors.

Each ceramic type is given a three- or four-digit code separated by decimal points. The first number refers to vessel size and wall thickness. Following this is a letter, indicating general form (A = open, B = closed) of the vessel. The next number indicates the rim form within each size and form category. An additional decimal number is provided to distinguish distinctive designs, holes, spouts, pedestals, feet, and so on, found on the types.

1. Small Vessels

Small vessels have rim diameters less than 15 cm and include cups, small bowls, bottles, and miniature vessels. Within this size category, cups, goblets, and bowls are defined by the slant of the wall profile. The widest variety of small vessels occurs in Period 2, including distinctive spouted vessels and goblets. The Period 2 (BMAC) small and miniature vessels appear to have contained liquids, and in some cases the appearance of carbonized fatty residues adhering to the inside indicates that they may have contained perfumes or oils. (See fig. 4.2).

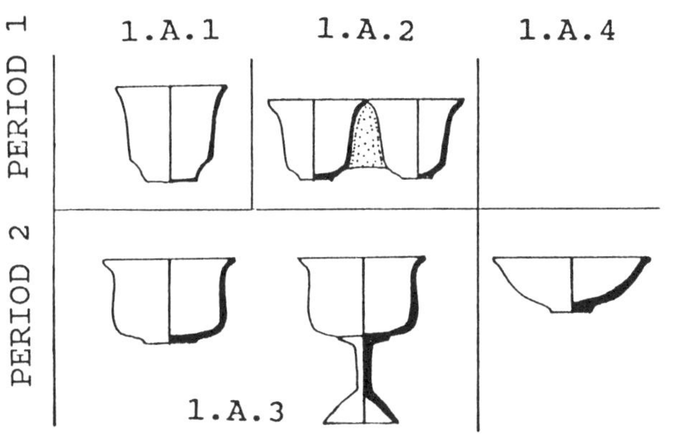

Figure 4.2
Small open vessels 1.A.

1.A.1 Slightly Open Vessels (Cups); Period 1

Cups (*piali*) have slightly open body profiles (90 to 100 degrees), slightly flaring rims, and often a slight carination at the base or a flat string-cut base. These are found in architectural contexts but rarely in burials.

This form is found only in Period 1, in layers 1 through 4 of the Gonur deep sounding. The examples have quite standardized rim diameters. Whole forms are recorded from Kelleli 4, and are analogous to cups from Altyn depe, layers 0 through 2.

This vessel type is not found in Period 2 assemblages. Functionally, this type was replaced in Period 2 by a closed version of the drinking cup (1.B.4) and goblets (1.A.3). In cases such as this, entirely different forms of small vessels clearly fulfill the same function, rather than forms evolving from one period to the next.

1.A.2 Doubled Vessels, Periods 1 and 2

Doubled vessels are composed of two cups joined together before firing. The diagnostic bridges between the two vessels occur in both periods in Margiana as well as in northern Bactria. Some sherds of small open cups from the deep sounding may have been from doubled vessels, but no doubled vessel connecting pieces were found.

Complete doubled vessels are found at Kelleli 4 and at Altyn depe levels 0 through 2 (Udemuradov 1986, 1988). These appear to be imitations of stone counterparts that have a long tradition in Central Asia (Masson 1981a). This form is also similar to alabaster doubled vases from the Indus valley (Dales and Kenoyer 1986). Doubled vessels are found in Period 2 in Margiana and Bactria, both in ceramic and in stone (Sarianidi 1977). No doubled vessels have yet been found from Takhirbai period sites.

1.A.3 Open Small Vessels, Periods 2 and 3

Small open vessels, *kubkami* (goblets), generally have two forms: with footed (hollow pedestal) bases and with simple flat bases. Goblets are larger than cups and wider (12 to 15 cm diameter), with a body profile slanting at 100 to 110 degrees. They have a distinctive flaring rim and usually have a carination just above the base. Footed goblets often do not have as sharp a body carination and are more rounded in profile than the flat-based variant.

Goblet rims are found in layer 6 (Period 2) of the Gonur sounding, although it is not known what kind of base they had. Flat-based goblets and foot-based goblets are found both in the burials and in contexts related to architecture at Togolok 1, Togolok 21 (P'yankova 1989), and Gonur south (Sarianidi 1993). Footed goblets are very common in burials and cenotaphs from Bactria and Margiana and from BMAC assemblages outside of Central Asia such as from Khurab, Shahdad (Hiebert and Lamberg-Karlovsky 1992), Sibri, Quetta, and Mehrgarh (Jarrige 1989; Santoni 1984).

Footed goblets continue in the Takhirbai levels (see fig. 4.40). A new rim form, which has a ridge below the rim, is distinctive in the Takhirbai period (Masson 1959, pl. 9:3; Sarianidi 1990, pl. 62:3, 4), and is similar in form and color to Molali period goblets from northern Bactria (Askarov and Abdullaev 1983).

1.A.4 Small Plain Plates, Periods 2 and 3

The profiles of plates have angles ranging from 135 to 170 degrees. The rim shapes vary from rounded (like cups and goblets) to sharply triangular. The base is usually flat and sometimes is string cut. Plates, cups, and bowls are commonly found together in Period 2 burials and in architecture. Several examples of this form with signs inscribed inside were found in cenotaph 41 at Gonur south (fig. 4.3). Small plain plates are commonly found in the eastern rooms of Togolok 21 (P'yankova 1989), and in burials at Takhirbai (Masson 1959).

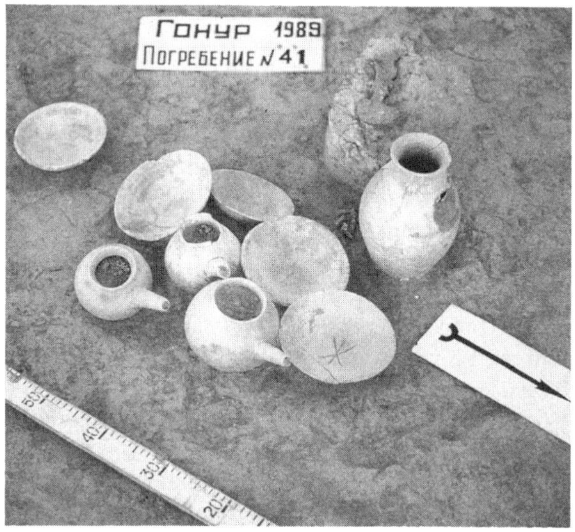

Figure 4.3
Cenotaph 41, Gonur south. Burial deposit including spouted vessels, cups, and plates with incised decoration.

1.B.1 Miniature Jars, Periods 1 and 2

Miniature jars are found in Margiana both at Period 1 and at Period 2 sites. The various forms are similar to larger counterparts, such as storage jars. The miniature vessels from Kelleli 4 (Masimov 1981) are similar to miniature vessels from late Namazga V at Altyn depe (levels 0 through 2) (Udemuradov 1987).

In Margiana Period 2 and Bactria, miniature ceramics are found together with miniature bronze tools, weapons, carts, and miniature stone columns. These have been recovered from burials where they apparently replaced full-scale items. They are found in buri-

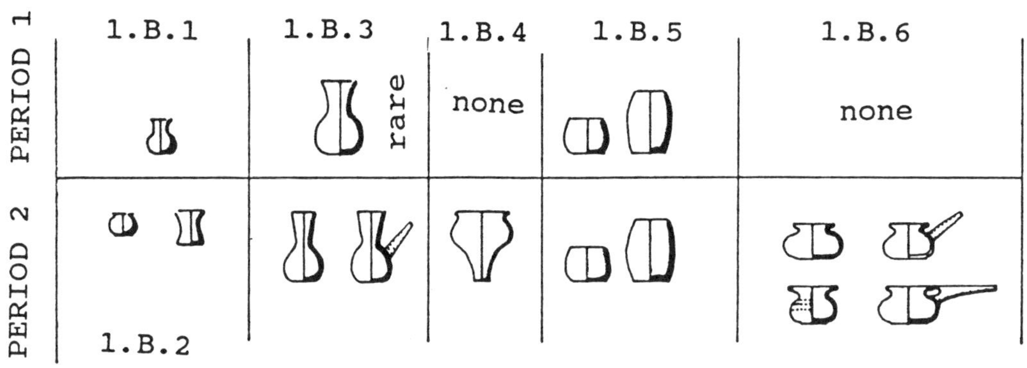

Figure 4.4
Small closed vessels 1.B.

als at Togolok 21, and similar finds in burial contexts were made at Dzharkutan and Dashli. A miniature vessel made of grey mica-tempered ware was found in layer 6 of the Gonur deep sounding. The ware of this piece is typical of Dzharkutan and was most likely an import from northern Bactria.

1.B.2 Cylindrical Vials, Period 2

In Margiana, small ceramic vessels are found only in Period 2. The wide variety of forms is similar to metal and softstone vial forms found in both Periods 1 and 2, and most likely are ceramic versions of these. Small cylindrical vials are found in architectural and burial contexts at Gonur south and Togolok 21 (fig. 4.5). Handmade versions often have incised geometric decoration. A cylindrical vial found at Togolok 21 appears to be an import from Bactria, judging from its grey ware with mica temper.

1.B.3 Tall-Necked Bottles: *Butilki*, Periods 1 and 2

These vessels have bulbous bases, long necks (total height 18 to 20 cm), rims of about 4 to 8 cm, and often have long thin spouts. This type is found in room contexts, often together with medium-sized vessels and grinding stones such as in Room 84 of Gonur south (described in chap. 7 as a food preparation area) and with others in Room 90 (fig. 4.6:top row).

This form is an element of the Namazga V foothill ceramics, but it is quite rare on Period 1 sites in Margiana. It is found very frequently in the building complexes of Period 2 at Gonur south and Togolok 21 and is a characteristic form at Dashli, Dzharkutan, and Sapalli. This type continues through the Takhirbai period. As a small sturdy vessel, it is often over-represented in the "whole pot" typologies of Margiana.

1.B.4. Bottles with Bulbous Shoulders: *Butilki*, Period 2

These bottles have a tall trumpet-shaped base with a bulbous shoulder and a wide mouth with a curved vertical-lipped rim (fig. 4.6:bottom row). The small base has distinctive string-cut marks. This form is found together with the tall-necked bottles in Period

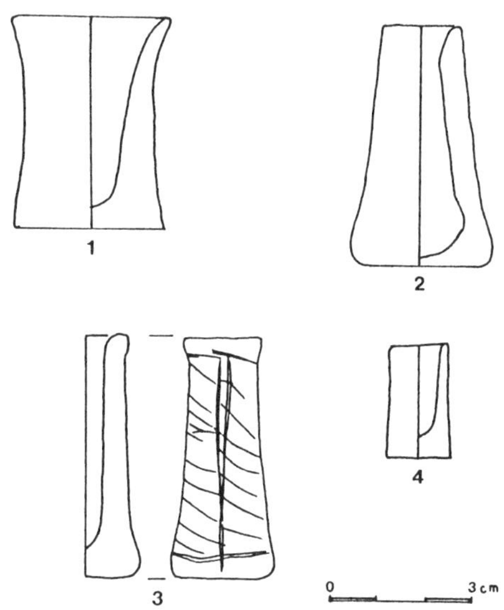

Figure 4.5
Period 2 cylindrical vials.
1) Wheelmade, medium-fine chaff buff, string-cut base. Room context, Togolok 21; 2) Wheelmade, burnished greyware, medium-fine mica temper. Room context, Togolok 21; 3) Handmade, burnished greyware. Room context, southwest corner, Togolok 21; 4) Yellow alabaster vial. Togolok 21, burial 30.

Figure 4.6
Tall-necked bottles (1.B.3). Top row, left to right, Togolok 1, Rooms 96, 97, 37, 37, 162, west tower, 94. Bottles with bulbous shoulders (1.B.4). Bottom row, left to right, Togolok 1, Rooms 37, 96.

2 settlements (Gonur, Togolok 21, Togolok 1) and from burials at Togolok 21 and from Bactria (Dzharkutan and Sapalli depe).

There are no analogous forms to these bottles in Period 1. This bottle type appears to be an innovation in Bactria and Margiana during the BMAC and does not carry into the Takhirbai period.

1.B.5. Small Closed Vessels (Cups), Periods 1 and 2

Small, slightly closed, plain-rim cups are either *banki* (tall cups) or *stakani* (short cups). These cups in medium-fine ware are found together with the exact same form in coarseware in Room 40 of Togolok 21. These examples were darkened from cooking of some kind, perhaps heating small quantities of liquids. This form is found in both periods in Margiana and in low percentages (1 to 2 percent) from the Gonur deep sounding. This form is common in the wheelmade ceramic tradition of Central Asia (Namazga IV, V, and VI, and in the Bronze Age periods in Bactria and Margiana).

1.B.6 Small Globular Pots, Periods 2 and 3

This type is a small round pot with outturned rims and flat string-cut bases. Such small globular pots occur at Altyn depe in the upper levels (with long spouts); however, they do not occur in Margiana at the same time. They are common in Margiana in Period 2 at Gonur, Togolok 21, and Togolok 1, typically found together with bottles and cups (P'yankova 1989).

Three distinctive features are found on these pots. First, several examples from Period 2 have concentric red bands painted on the upper shoulder (see fig. 4.30). The painted vessels from Margiana are superficially similar to Indus painted wares, but both postdate the band-painted Harappan wares and are locally produced on the basis of the ware.

A second feature of small globular pots is the occurrence of long thin spouts (see fig. 4.3) similar to the spouts on bottles (1.B.3). Spouted globular pots have often been found with bottles and medium-sized vessels in both architectural contexts and in burials and cenotaphs. In the Takhirbai period, this type occurs in both local reddish buff ceramic ware and in greyware, probably imported from northern Bactria.

A third feature, of particular importance, are bridge spouts (fig. 4.7) occurring only in Period 2 in Margiana and in Bactria. The spouts are generally similar to the later bridge spouts found on greyware of the

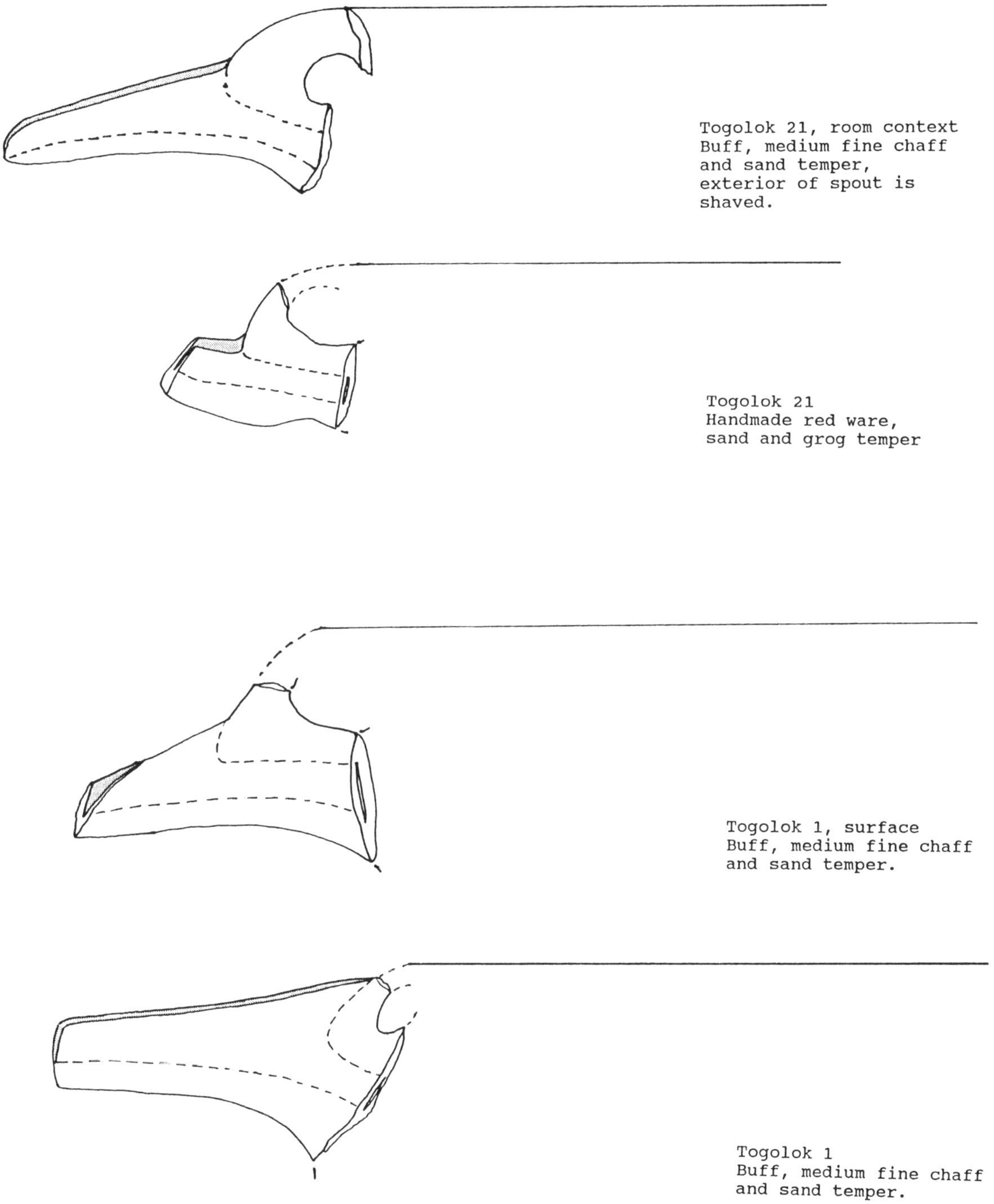

Figure 4.7
Period 2 bridge spouts from Margiana.

Early Iron Age in northern and eastern Iran (Young 1965; Dyson 1973).

1.B.7 Wide-Mouthed Small Pots, Period 3

Wide-mouthed globular pots are found only in Takhirbai levels. This form has a globular base with a more sharply defined shoulder than the earlier globular pots (1.B.6), and straight sides without an outcurved rim (see fig. 4.40). This form is found in both locally manufactured red (Masson 1959, pl. 6:15) and greywares (ibid., pl. 6:15, 17, 8:4–6).

2. Thin-Walled Vessels

Stolovaya (serving) vessels are a major category of the Margiana "whole pot" typology, and the name implies finely made or elegant forms used for food presentation. The several types included in this category are thin-shouldered vessels with rim diameters between 15 and 45 cm and upper sherd body thickness between 0.35 and 0.65 cm. From the Gonur deep sounding, thin-walled vessels account for one-third of the assemblage of both Periods 1 and 2.

Two common rim forms have traditionally been used to differentiate the Bronze Age periods in Margiana. These forms have been used as index forms based on presence or absence (Masson 1981b; Masimov 1981; Udemuradov 1987; P'yankova 1989). However, on the basis of the Gonur deep sounding, the index type of Period 1 (vessels with a vertical-lip rim [2.A.2]) is also found in Period 2 (and Period 3 from the south mound); and the index type of Period 2 (vessels with a sharply grooved rim [2.A.3]) is similarly found earlier and later. Thus the presence or absence of these traditional index forms does not differentiate between Periods 1 and 2 in Margiana.

The several types that *are* chronologically specific are rare in the ceramic assemblages. The trough spouts of the large bowls (2.A.4 and 2.B.2) are found only in Period 2, but are not common. Other rare forms include corrugated pedestal bases, which are a key diagnostic of the late Namazga V in the foothill zone (Masimov 1981), and pedestal bases with a single ridge just beneath the vessel—a form typical of Bactria, but found in Margiana Period 2 sites very rarely.

In the "whole pot" typologies, the definition of serving vessels typically focuses on the type of base—either footed or trumpet form. However, the base forms are not chronological indexes and apparently do not functionally differentiate vessels (see fig. 4.8). Footed bases are commonly found on goblets and serving vessels (1.A.3, 2.A.1, 2.A.2, 2.A.3, 2.A.4, and 2.A.5). The form of the footed bases is similar to the ceramics of South Asia, but does not necessarily indicate any specific interaction between South Asia and Margiana or Bactria. For example, footed bases first occur in the eastern and central Kopet Dag during the late Namazga IV with the beginning of wheel-fin-

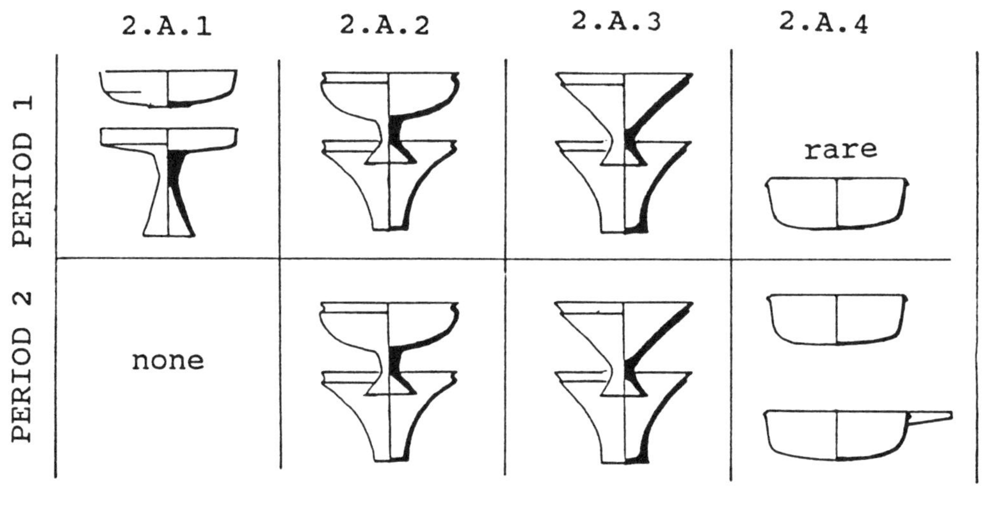

Figure 4.8
2.A Large thin-walled open vessels.

ished ceramic production. This ceramic trait appears to have been adopted from South Asia during an earlier period of wide-ranging cultural interaction.

2.A.1 Large Bowls with Simple Rims, Period 1

This distinctive type of large open bowl has a straight or slightly everted rim and upper body, a defined shoulder, and either a pedestal footed base or a flat base. In Margiana this type is not found in Period 2 or 3 and is one of the most distinctive types of Period 1. There are two size classes of these vessels, 14 to 18 cm diameter and 20 to 25 cm diameter.

This type is characteristic of both the eastern Kopet Dag late Namazga V ceramics (Altyn depe and Ulug depe) and of Period 1 in Margiana. This type comprises 8 percent of the ceramics from Period 1 architecture at Gonur and 10 percent of the ceramics from layers 1 through 4 of the deep sounding (fig. 4.9).

On the basis of the shoulder profile, it is usually possible to determine the overall form. The vessels with a sharp carination at the shoulder have a footed base on a pedestal. Those vessels with a rounded shoulder have a flat base and the smaller forms occur with both hollow pedestal bases or small solid pedestals.

2.A.2 Vertical-Rim Bowls, Periods 1, 2, and 3

These large bowls have a sharp carination at the top of the shoulder and a band rim that is deeply indented. Rim diameters of 20 to 25 cm suggest some uniform feature of production and function. Vertical rims are found with both trumpet-shaped bases, *vasobraznie konicheskie sosudi* (conical vase, type 2.A.2.1), and hollow pedestal bases (footed vase, type 2.A.2.2). As with simple rim large bowls, the base form can be deter-

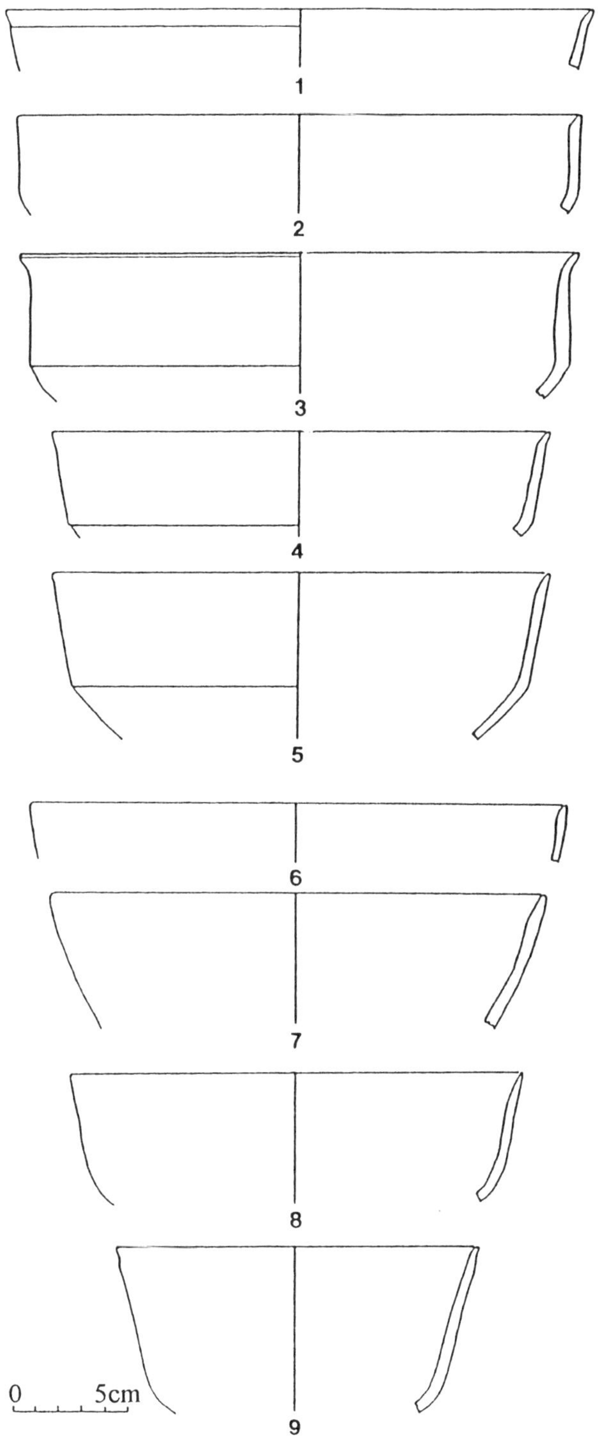

Figure 4.9
Period 1 large bowl (2.A.1) rim variants from the deep sounding.

No.	Type	Locus	Dia.	Ware and Temper
1	2.A.1	27/28	26	Buff, med.-fine chaff
2	2.A.1.2	29/30	25	Buff, med.-fine chaff, mineral?
3	2.A.1.2	32	25	Red core, buff int. and ext. at rim, med.-fine chaff
4	2.A.1.2	27/28	22	Red, med.-fine chaff
5	2.A.1.2	29/30	22	Buff, med.-fine chaff
6	2.A.1	29/30	16	Buff w/ faint red core, med. chaff, mineral?
7	2.A.1.3	29/30	22	Red, med.-fine chaff
8	2.A.1.3	29/30	20	Buff, med.-fine chaff
9	2.A.1	27/28	16	Red core and int., buff ext., med.-fine chaff

mined by the shape of the body profile (fig. 4.10). From the Period 1 domestic architecture, a small sample allows an estimate of the relative frequency of these types and variants. A few pieces have trumpet bases (2 percent of assemblage), and several were made with hollow pedestal bases (8 percent of assemblage). But in the deep sounding sample, this rim form is found more often on trumpet-shaped bases than on pedestal bases. It occurs as late as Period 3 in Margiana (Takhirbai levels at Gonur and at Takhirbai 3). This rim form is common in the foothill zone during Namazga V, and the earliest example (on a pedestal base) is from Ulug depe level 5 (excavation 3). This sample dates to late Namazga IV, the first level with wheelmade ceramics.

Figure 4.10
Vertical-rim bowls (2.A.2) from Togolok 21.

2.A.3 Sharply Grooved Rim Bowls, Periods 1, 2, and 3

These large bowls have a distinctive sharp indentation or groove 0.8 to 1.3 cm below the rim, and the lip angles out slightly above the groove (fig. 4.11). This type is also called "clipped rim" (Kohl 1984). This rim

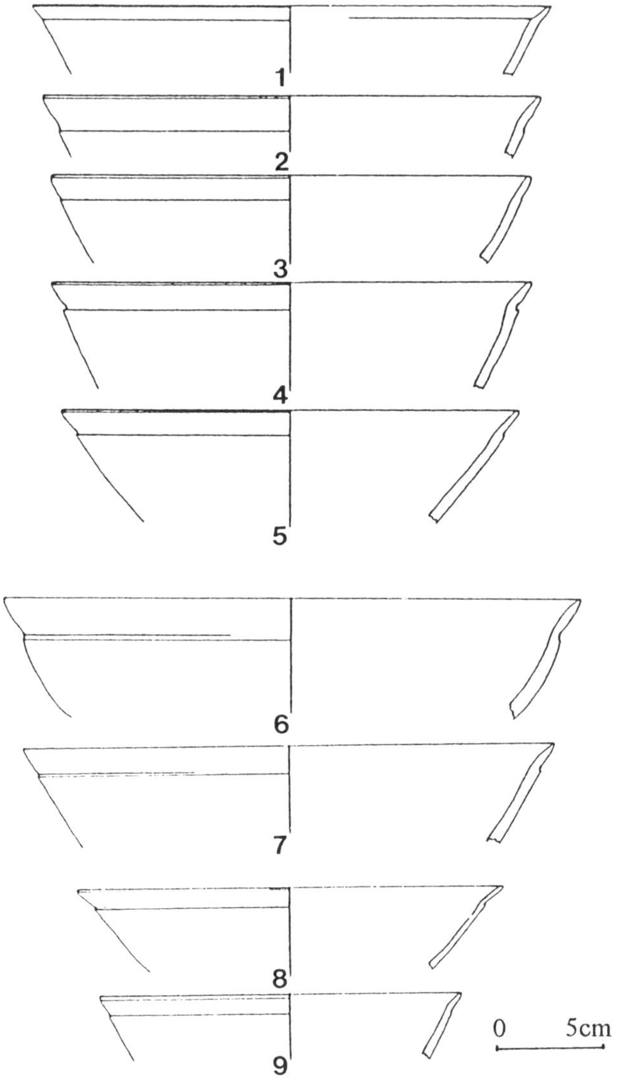

Figure 4.11
Period 1 and 2, sharply grooved rim bowls (2.A.3) rim variants from the deep sounding.

No.	Type	Locus	Dia.	Ware and Temper
1	2.A.3	29/30	24	Reddish-buff core and int., buff ext, med.-fine chaff
2.	2.A.3	27/28	23	Red core and int., buff ext., med.-fine chaff
3.	2.A.3	27/28	22	Reddish-buff core, buff int. and ext.; smoothed exterior, med.-fine chaff
4.	2.A.3	29/30	22	Reddish-buff, med.-fine chaff
5.	2.A.3	27/28	21	Buff, med.-fine chaff
6.	2.A.3	2	27	Buff, med.-fine chaff
7.	2.A.3	2	25	Red, med.-fine chaff
8.	2.A.3	2	20	Buff, med.-fine chaff, mineral
9.	2.A.3	2	17	Reddish-buff core, grey int. and ext., med.-fine chaff

is found on ceramics both with trumpet-shaped bases and with pedestal bases. For this type, it is not possible to suggest what form the base had on the basis of the shoulder profile. This type has two general size categories—~20 cm diameter and 25 cm diameter—and thus is not as standardized as the vertical-lip rim type. The vessels with the sharply grooved rims appear to be deeper than the vertical-lip vessels.

Sharply grooved rims are common in the first period at Gonur (16.5 percent of the total assemblage from the stratigraphic sounding). This rim shape is typical at all Period 1 sites in Margiana, as well as in the upper levels (0 through 2) of Altyn depe. In Period 2 of the Gonur deep sounding, it is less common (5 percent of the assemblage). It is also found on other Period 2 sites in Margiana and from Takhirbai period levels, primarily on trumpet-shaped bases. This rim form is not found in northern or southern Bactria, although Bactrian bronze vessels often have this rim shape.

2.A.4 Triangular-Rim Bowls, Periods 1 and 2

Large-diameter (15 to 35 cm), thin-bodied bowls with flat bases often have distinctive triangular rims in profile and trough spouts. This rim form is found in both Period 1 and 2 deposits from the Gonur deep sounding. This form is typically found in Period 2 sites of Margiana and in Bactria, but is rare in Period 1 sites of Margiana and is not found in the foothill zone. Bronze bowls with the same form and trough spout are also found in graves from southern Bactria. This form occurs earlier in ceramics than in the metals, suggesting that the bronze vessels were made in the form of the ceramics. This general type is also found in the later Takhirbai assemblages, but with only a plain rim.

2.A.5 Inturned-Rim Bowls, Period 3

Large thin bowls with inturned rims are found in Margiana only in post-BMAC contexts, at Takhirbai 3 and from the uppermost level at Gonur south (see fig. 4.40). This rim form is best known from northern Bactria, where it is common on large open bowls in the Dzharkutan, Kuzali, and Molali periods. At Takhirbai 3, the type varies from rounded to sharply inturned (Masson 1959, pl. 6:4, pl. 71:10). This rim form is found both with footed bases and with flat bases, and has a dark red slip that may have been an imitation of typical Bactrian ceramics.

2.A.6 Ledge-Rim Bowls, Period 3

Large thin bowls with wide horizontal (ledge) rims are an innovation in the post-BMAC ceramic assemblages of Margiana and Bactria. In Margiana this form is found only at Takhirbai sites, and in northern Bactria this form is found only in the Molali period. From Margiana, ledge-rim bowls with tall footed bases were excavated at Takhirbai 3 (Masson 1959, pl. 7:3; P'yankova 1993, fig. 4:10). (See fig. 4.40).

2.B.1 Large Jars with a Faint Rim Line, Period 1

The widest part of these closed vessels is approximately one-fourth of the way up from the base. Often referred to as "biconical jars," these vessels appear to

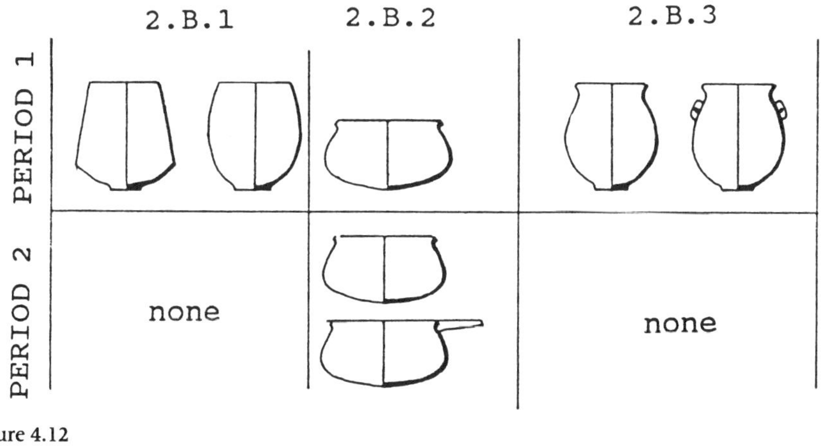

Figure 4.12
2.B Large thin-walled closed pots.

Figure 4.13
Trough-spouted bowl (2.B.2). Togolok 21, Room 42.

have been either thin versions of small storage pots (3.B.1 and 3.B.4) or large versions of the drinking cups (1.A.1 and 1.B.5). This form is found in Margiana only at Period 1 sites. It has a faint finger line or indentation 0.75 to 1 cm below the rim. The angle of the lip is sometimes slightly more upright than the angle of the wall profile.

This form is typical of the late Namazga V ceramics from Altyn depe and common in Margiana Period 1 (9 percent of the Gonur north domestic architecture assemblage). In the Kopet Dag foothill sites of Altyn depe and Ulug depe (among others), the widest part of the ceramic is evenly biconical in the early and middle Namazga V period (Masson 1981b). In the late Namazga V period, the widest part of the vessel is located in the lower quarter of the vessel (Udemuradov 1987). Thus the form provides an indication of the relative chronological position of Margiana Period 1 in the Namazga sequence.

The deep sounding at Gonur yielded individual rim sherds from vessels varying in size from small to quite large (10 to 35 cm diameter), with body profiles ranging from sharply carinated to rounded or egg shaped.

2.B.2 Large Closed Bowls with Triangular Rims, Periods 1, 2, and 3

Slightly closed bowls with flat bases and a triangular rim occur rarely in Period 1 sites of Margiana (Gonur sounding 1 percent). It occurs more frequently in Period 2, similar to open versions of the large bowls. In Period 2 this type occasionally has a trough spout (fig. 4.13).

2.B.3 Hole-Mouth Pots, Period 1

Pots of this type are deeper than they are wide, with a straight, narrowing, conical upper part. The rim is undifferentiated from the body, with distinctive vertical lugs on two sides of the vessels near the rim. The lugs are pierced with small holes. The lugs probably served to tie on lids rather than to support the thin-walled pots. The distinctive lugs have been found at Kelleli 4 (Masimov 1979) and on the surface at Gonur (P'yankova 1989); rim fragments are common in all Period 1 deposits and absent from Periods 2 and 3. Exact parallels are found in the eastern Kopet Dag late Namazga V levels at Altyn depe (Udemuradov 1993) and Ulug depe.

3. Large Vessels with Thick Shoulders

The Soviet "whole pot" typology classifies series of types as *bitovaya* (common) vessels, which are large and heavy. Serving and common vessels can be differentiated by measuring the thickness of the body profile below the rim. The common vessels have shoulder thicknesses greater than 0.7 cm and rim diameters from 15 to 45 cm. The closed forms (3.B) are primarily storage vessels, in some cases found buried in walls and beneath floors with just the mouth exposed. The large open forms (3.A) are less likely to have been intended for storage and are sometimes decorated on the outside or on the rim. The decorated vessels are found in cenotaphs, burials, and nondomestic contexts.

There is no difference between serving and common ceramics in terms of ware, the amount or type of temper, or the firing.

In Periods 1 and 2, these large vessels typically were manufactured in two parts. The base is first fashioned on a chuck or a form, and the upper part is then added on the wheel. The impressions of the chuck are often visible as mold marks and sand impressions (fig. 4.15). According to experimental reproductions, the walls are added using a slab/coil technique, and the vessel form is finished on the wheel (R. Meadow, pers. comm.). The technique of making large vessels in two parts in this way is typical of the manufacture of large wheelmade vessels from the Indus valley (Dales and Kenoyer 1986), Baluchistan (Casal 1961), and Central Asia. This technology first is found in Central Asia during the early Namazga V at Ulug depe in the eastern Kopet Dag zone, and probably originates in the

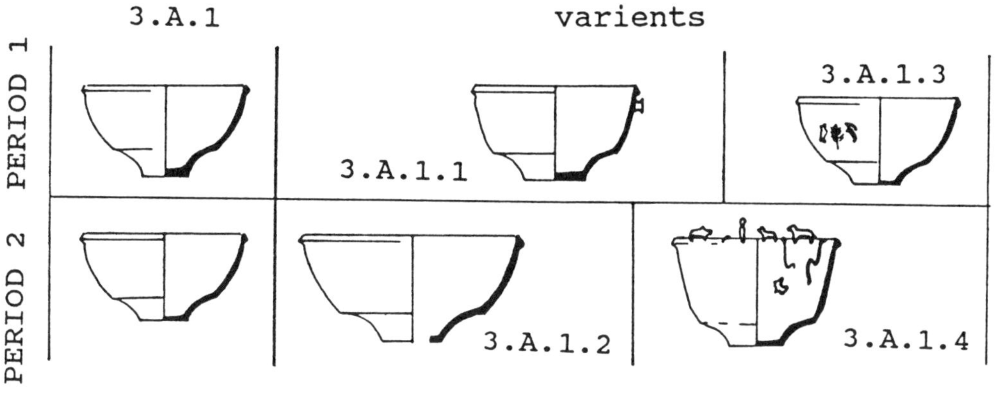

Figure 4.14
3. Large vessels with thick shoulders.

late Namazga III to early Namazga IV Geoksyur region when Geoksyur was part of a larger South Asian interaction area (Hiebert n.d.).

Common vessels constitute over half of all of the rim sherds (Period 1, 45 percent; Period 2, 54 percent). The open and closed forms of this size category (3.A.1, 3.B.3, 3.B.4) are practically indistinguishable from Period 1 to Period 2. In Period 3 they are differentiated only by changes in the base; the rim forms remain the same.

3.A.1 Large Bowls and Basins, Periods 1, 2, and 3

Large, slightly open vessels have standard sizes that are grouped into two distinct size categories: *miski* (large basins, 24 to 30 cm diameter) and *tagori* (very large basins, 35 to 45 cm diameter). The rims are rounded to triangular shaped, with no pronounced neck. These large bowls are associated with grinding stones when found in architectural context, suggesting that they functioned in household food preparation and other small-scale production (fig. 4.16). These vessels make up 6 percent of the ceramic assemblage of Period 1, from the domestic architecture from the Gonur north mound excavations and from the midden deposits of the deep sounding. Large bowls and basins are slightly more frequent in the industrial midden of Period 2 from the upper levels of the deep sounding. The basic form of the vessels remains the same over time in Margiana, but the features differ between Periods 1 and 2, as described below.

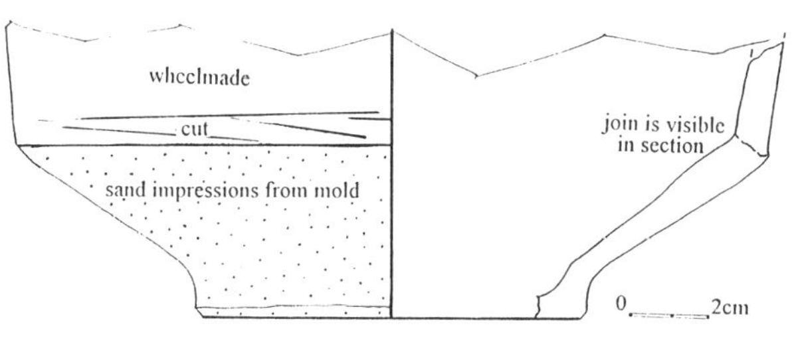

Figure 4.15
Cross-section of a moldmade base. Period 1, Gonur north, sounding beneath Room 1, domestic architecture.

3.A.1.1 Spouted Basins, Periods 1 and 2

Large basins occasionally have one or more spouts. Short round spouts on the upper shoulder of large basins are found in all periods in Margiana. Period 1 basins also have distinctive short oval spouts on the upper shoulder, similar to the eastern Kopet Dag tradition at Altyn depe and Ulug depe (Altyn depe type X, see fig. 4.37). Period 2 basins occasionally have open trough spouts on the rim, such as the complete example at Gonur south from a cenotaph deposit (see fig. 7.25).

3.A.1.2 Sidilki, Periods 2 and 3

Large bowls and basins that have a hole 3 to 5 cm in diameter in the bottom (fig. 4.17) occur in Margiana (Periods 2 and 3 and Yaz I early Iron Age), and in the Kopet Dag region at Namazga depe (upper levels) and El'ken depe (level 2) (Khlopina 1972). Some examples have grooves in the base that would allow liquids to flow out if the vessel were placed on the ground.

Figure 4.16
In situ assemblage of large basins (3.A.1) with grinding stones and smaller pots. Period 2, Gonur south, Room 84.

These vessels are thought to have been used as sieves, or *sidilki* (strainers), in conjunction with *podstavki* (potstands) (Khlopina 1981). However, *sidilki* and *podstavki* have not been found together in situ, and potstands are found in assemblages without *sidilki*, so we cannot be sure of their function. Sarianidi (1993) suggests that they were part of a ritual assemblage of ceramics used in the production of beverages including *haoma*. Sarianidi suggests that wads of coarse fiber, found in *kelli* (narrow storage rooms) at Togolok 21, would have been placed in the bottom of the vessel as a strainer.

3.A.1.3 Basins with Incised and Applied Decoration, Period 1

Basins with applied clay decoration and incised designs on the sides are found only in Period 1 sites in

Figure 4.17
Sidilka (3.A.1.2). Togolok 21, Room 169.

Margiana (fig. 4.18). The decoration, which consists of incised trees with applied clay animals (usually goats) on either side of each tree, is found on the outside of the bowl and is not visible from above (fig. 4.19). This motif is found only during Period 1 and only on large basins. There are no antecedents to this motif in the Kopet Dag region, although it reflects a generalized Mesopotamian theme of goats and trees (Kepinski 1982). The early Near Eastern motif is similar in having two animals surrounding a tree, but differs in the context of the motif on the vessels, the lack of other Mesopotamian images, and the occurrence of a wide variety of animal forms on either side of the tree. The Margiana style and technique of decoration are similar only to tree and goat motifs found on the much later (1300–1200 B.C.) Late Bronze Age to Early Iron Age ceramics of Syro-Palestine (Amiran 1969, pl. 50). Both wild and domestic animals are common

Figure 4.18
Period 1 decorated basin (3.A.1.3). Gonur north, domestic architecture, Room 3.

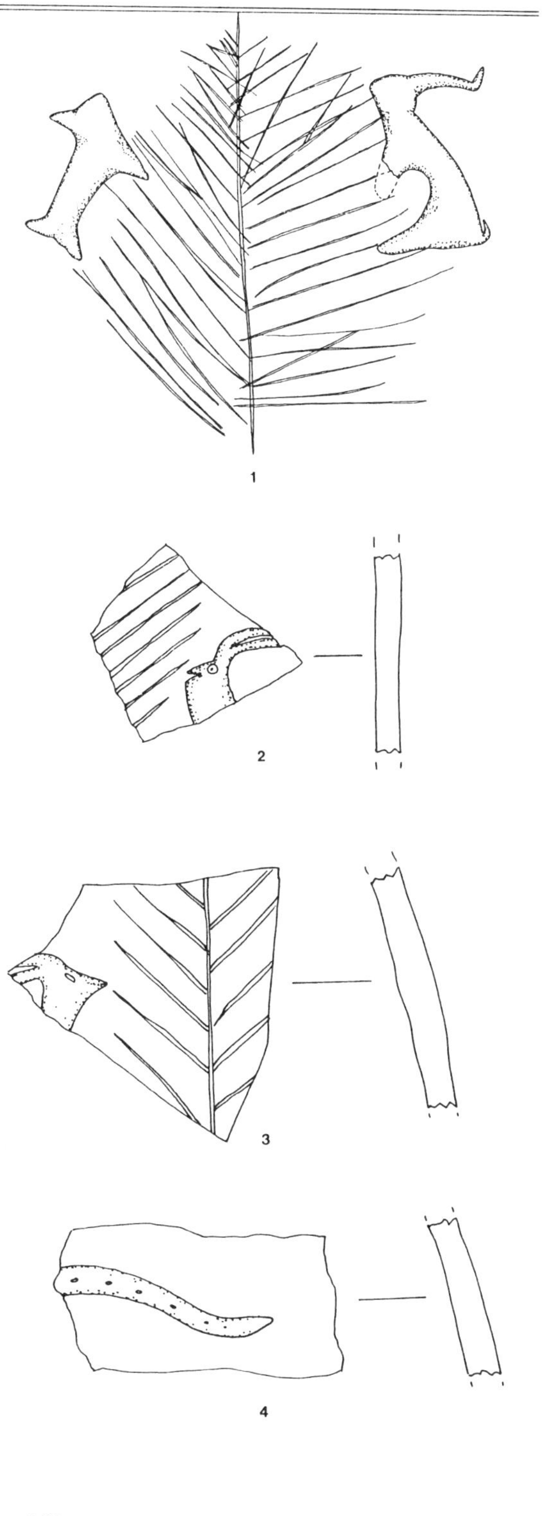

Figure 4.19
Period 1 incised trees and applied animal decoration (3.A.1.3). 1) Gonur north, domestic architecture, Room 3; 2) Egri Bogaz, surface find; 3) Kelleli oasis, surface find; 4) Kelleli oasis, surface find.

decoration in the art of the Central Asian oases such as Margiana (Moore 1993a). The Period 1 design most likely represents a local motif, inspired by the common occurrence of desert and oasis animals climbing in trees to browse.

3.A.1.4 Basins with Terracotta Rim Decoration, Period 2

A frieze of terracotta figurines applied to the rim and to the inside of large bowls and basins occurs in Period 2 in Margiana and on BMAC sites in Bactria (fig. 4.20). In well-preserved examples, the series of animals and humans on the vessel rims has a particular order, implying a narrative. Although very few whole vessels have been found, fragments of figurines from such vessels are found on all Period 2 sites in Margiana, suggesting that these bowls were widely distributed during this period.

Sarianidi has argued that this vessel type was part of the ritual assemblage of ceramics and grinding stones used in the preparation of ritual liquids for libations, such as *haoma*. This type of vessel, with different decoration (3.A.1.3), occurs in Period 1 prior to the time when the libation ritual is thought to have been introduced. The inference that these are ritual vessels comes strictly from the form and decoration; no archaeological context suggests its function.

Incised and applied decoration on basins (3.A.1.3) appears to have been replaced by this rim decoration. The fact that only this one type of ceramic vessel has distinctive decoration in both Periods 1 and 2 suggests cultural continuity, while the changes in the type of decoration from Period 1 to 2 suggests an ideological change with the beginning of Period 2 (the BMAC). The decorated variant of this type does not continue into the Takhirbai period (Period 3).

3.B.1 Large, Slightly Closed Storage Vessels, Periods 1 and 2

This type is a short (15 to 25 cm high) pot with a wide (20 to 25 cm diameter) rim opening. These can be differentiated from other medium-sized pots by the almost vertical shoulder and the outturned rim (fig. 4.21). The shape of the rim (fig. 4.22) is quite standardized and does not change from Period 1 to 2. This form is the single most common ceramic type found in the domestic architecture from the north mound at Gonur (22 percent). In the Gonur deep sounding, this form is common in Period 1 (15 percent) as well as in Period 2 (24 percent). In Period 1, these vessels are

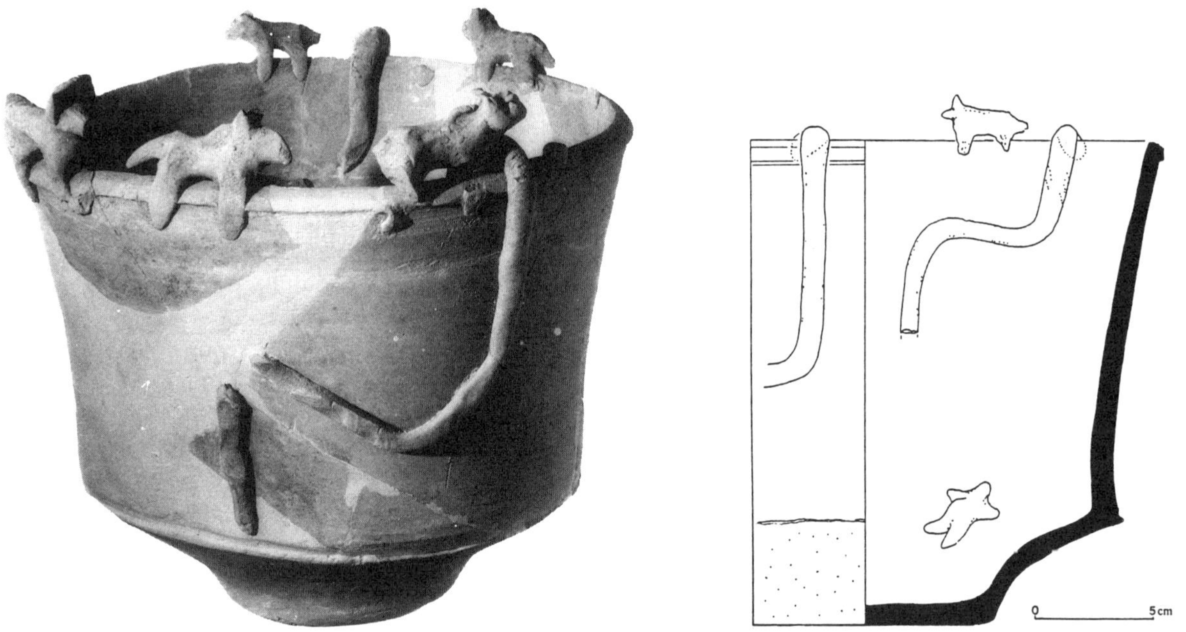

Figure 4.20
Period 2 decorated basin (3.A.1.4). Togolok 1, burial 20, found with two bronze figurative axes.

found with wide oval spouts directly below the rim in a fashion similar to that of the large basins.

3.B.2 Short-Necked Storage Pots, Periods 1, 2, and 3

These vessels, called *khomchi* (medium-sized storage vessels), have a shape similar to the larger *khomi* (storage vessels) (fig. 4.23). Short-necked storage jars have small-diameter mouths with rounded and triangular rims. This type is common in the Bronze Age pottery of Margiana and shows little change through time. The common variants of short-necked storage pots have three rim diameters (11 to 15 cm, 18 to 25 cm, and 28 plus cm) and have miniature versions (see type 1.B.1).

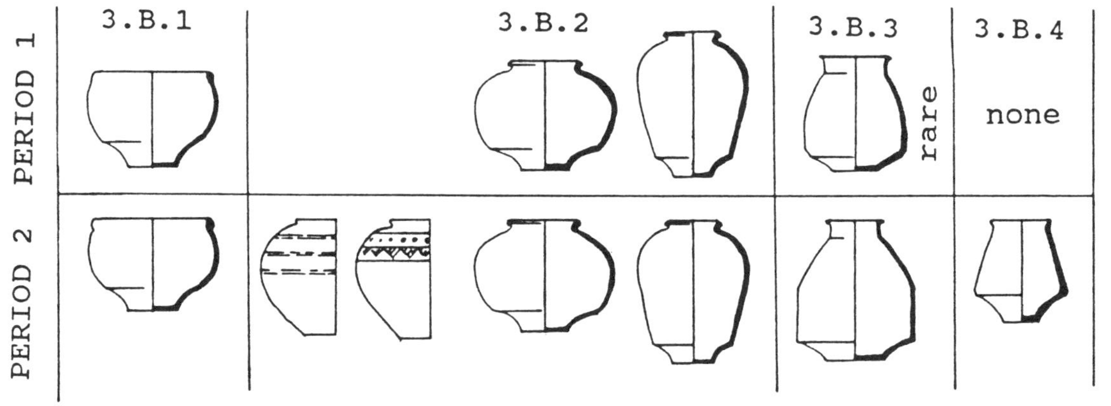

Figure 4.21
3.B Storage vessels.

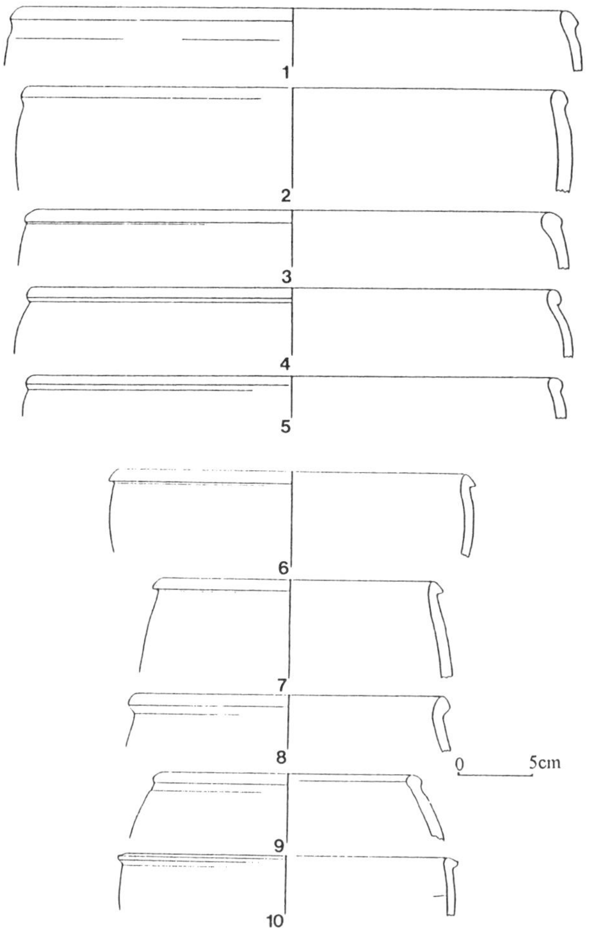

Figure 4.22
Period 1 and 2 storage vessels (3.B.1) rim variants from the deep sounding.

No.	Type	Locus	Dia.	Ware and Temper
1.	3.B.1	29/30	36	Greyish-buff, med. chaff and mineral
2.	3.B.1	29/30	35	Buff with thin red core, med.-fine chaff
3.	3.B.1	29/30	34	Red core, buff int. and ext., med.-fine chaff
4.	3.B.1	29/30	34	Red core, buff int. and ext., med.-fine chaff
5.	3.B.1	29/30	34	Reddish brown core, buff int. and ext., med.-fine chaff
6.	3.B.1	2	25	Buff, med.-fine chaff
7.	3.B.1	2	20	Buff, med.-fine chaff
8.	3.B.1	2	22	Reddish buff core and int., buff ext., med.-fine chaff
9	3.B.1	2	18	Buff core and int., greyish-buff ext., med.-fine chaff
10	3.B.1	2	23	Greyish-buff, med.-fine chaff

Figure 4.23
Short-necked storage jars (3.B.2). Togolok 21 room and burial contexts.

In Period 1 these vessels are always made in the two-part technique with molded bases; in Period 2 there are both two-part construction and entirely wheelmade variants. These pots are imitated in the coarse handmade pottery, even including the convex base hand-formed in the shape of a molded base.

Some Period 2 vessels have simple geometric incised designs and painted bands. The undecorated forms are common during Period 1 in the Gonur sounding (9 percent) and in Period 2 (15 percent).

In the Takhirbai period, none of the complete vessels of this type has two-part manufacture; they are entirely wheel made. The tradition of decoration continues with potter's marks and incised geometric designs on the upper shoulders.

3.B.3 Tall-Necked Globular Pots, Periods 2 and 3

Tall-necked pots (also described as *khomchi* in the traditional typologies) have rims that vary from sharply

Figure 4.24
Tall-necked globular pots (3.B.3). Togolok 21 room and burial contexts.

triangular to band shaped on a 2 to 4 cm vertical collar. The overall shape is similar to the short-necked pots above (3.B.2), including the wide globular bodies and molded concave bases (fig. 4.24). A single tall-necked pot was found in a well-documented Period 1 architectural context, but this form occurs frequently in Periods 2 and 3. In the deep sounding at Gonur, the tall-necked *khomchi* are relatively few in Period 1 compared with Period 2, where they are a characteristic form. This type continues in the uppermost levels at Gonur south and is found at the Takhirbai sites.

3.B.4 Short, Wide-Mouthed *Khomchi*, Periods 2 and 3

These *khomchi* are squat conical pots with thick body profiles and little differentiation of the rim. This type has a mold-made base similar to the larger *khomchi* (3.B.2 and 3.B.3). This form allows us to distinguish Period 2 assemblages from Period 1, and it continues in the Takhirbai period. While this form is an index type for Period 2, it is not very common, nor is it readily differentiated from other globular pots of this (3.B) category. (See fig. 4.28).

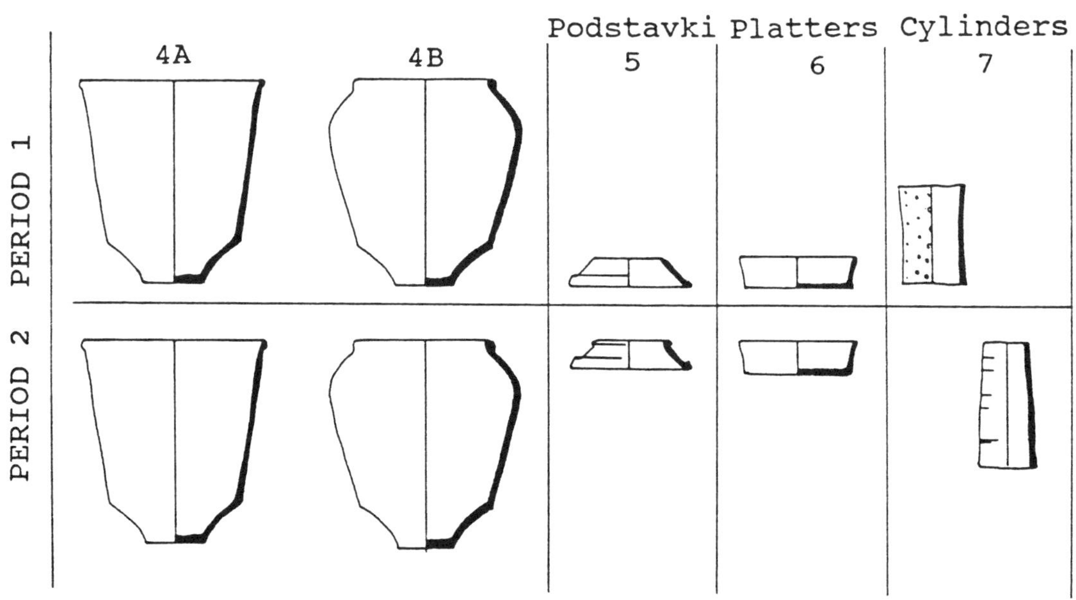

Figure 4.25
Very large vessels (4), *Podstavki* (5), Platters (6), and Cylinders (7).

4. Large Storage and Production Vessels, Periods 1, 2, and 3

Khomi (large storage jars) are large, thick- walled (1.3 cm plus), wheelmade jars (see fig. 4.25). The mold-made bases are made from the same size mold as the *khomchi* (3.A and 3.B). Unlike the *khomchi*, however, these have shoulders wider than the bases and are generally over 70 cm tall (fig. 4.26). The paste of the very heavy pots is medium in texture with fine chaff inclusions, and is only slightly coarser than the medium-fine ware typical of the smaller forms. When *khomi* and *khomchi* sherds from the Gonur deep sounding are compared (such as from loci 11 and 14), there is a clear gap in distribution of sherd thicknesses, suggesting that there are only these two sizes and not a continuum of storage-jar sizes in these deposits at Gonur.

Rim diameters of the open vessels (4.A) are generally quite large (35 cm plus), and there is no change from Period 1 to 2. Rim sherds of this category in the Gonur deep sounding constitute 2 percent (Period 1) and 4 percent (Period 2) of the ceramics.

Some closed *khomi* (4.B) were more than 1 m tall. Although few vessels of this size are preserved whole, several examples have been found spalled into thousands of fragments on floors. In the Gonur deep sounding, these pots make up 7 percent of the sherds in Period 1 and 4 percent of the sample in Period 2.

Figure 4.26
Khom **(4.B). Togolok 21, Room 27.**

5. *Podstavki*, Periods 1, 2, and 3

These are truncated-cone-shaped ceramics open at both ends. The smaller opening varies in diameter from 20 to 40 cm and the larger opening from 30 to 60 cm. The rims at both ends often have flattened flared lips.

The Russian name *podstavki* (potstand) is used, despite the unclear function of these ceramics. They appear to be used as pot supports for the typical concave molded form of base; some *podstavki* have holes for supports (strings?). However, no *khom* has yet been found in situ sitting in a potstand. In the architecture at the south mound at Gonur as well as at Togolok 21, special circular hollows have been found in floors in which storage vessels (*khomchi*) and large storage vessels (*khomi*) were found.

The principal function of the *podstavki* may have been as chucks for the production of the bases of the large molded base ceramics. *Podstavki* often have potter's marks, both on the interior and on the exterior, that were engraved prior to firing. Potter's marks molded on the base of several *khomi* found at Gonur can be matched with marks found on the inside of the *podstavki* (fig. 4.27).

Podstavki are found on all of the Bronze Age Central Asian sites, in the foothill plain of southern Turkmenistan Margiana and Bactria, from the early Namazga V period through the Takhirbai period. The earliest examples in Central Asia are from Shor depe, early Namazga V (Shchetenko 1970), and they are common in Margiana through the Bronze Age occupation into the Iron Age Yaz I ceramic assemblages.

6. Platters, Periods 1, 2, and 3

Very large diameter (35+ cm) flat plates with shallow (6 to 10 cm high) sides are found at Gonur from Periods 1 and 2 excavations and from Period 3 at Takhirbai. Join marks are visible in a section where base and wall come together, showing that a plate was constructed from two or more pieces and finished on the wheel. The paste is the same as in wheelmade ceramics.

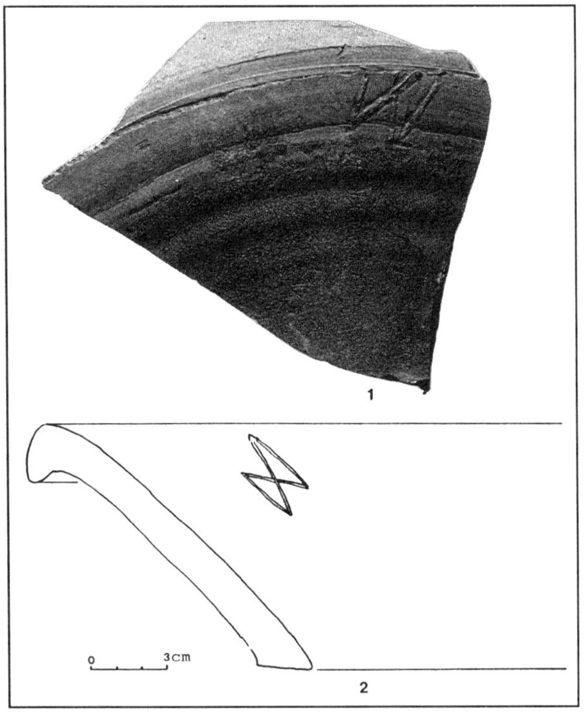

Figure 4.27
Potter's marks from *podstavki*.
1) Raised imprint of a "bow-tie" motif on the moldmade base of a storage vessel. Gonur, surface; 2) "Bow-tie" motif incised inside of a *podstavka*. Gonur south, surface.

Figure 4.28
Period 1 ceramic cylinder fragments. Gonur north, surface.

Figure 4.29
Period 2 ceramic cylinder pipe in situ. Togolok 1.

7. Cylindrical Ceramics

In Period 1 in Margiana are found cylindrical strainers 10 to 24 cm in diameter, with small (~ 5 mm) holes pierced in an even pattern through the cylinder wall. Whole examples of the vessels are rare, but all fragments appear to have come from open-ended tubes (fig. 4.28). One example from Kelleli 3 is perforated to the edge of the rim of the vessel (Masimov 1981, fig. 4:26). The vessels are locally made, with the same ware as the wheelmade ceramics. This ceramic type is not found in the Kopet Dag foothill plain. It occurs very rarely in Period 1 and has not been found on Period 2 or 3 sites in context.

Ceramic drainpipes are found in Period 2 at Togolok 1 and Togolok 21 (Sarianidi 1990) (fig. 4.29). The pipes are tapered so one pipe will fit into another. Although drainage ditches are found in Margiana in all periods, ceramic pipes are found only in Period 2. Other drainage systems also are found; for example, at Togolok 1, fragments of fired ceramic pipe were placed as a drainage pavement (Sarianidi 1991). Both of these types of cylindrical ceramic apparently can be used as local chronological indicators but, because of their rarity, are poor indices.

SURFACE TREATMENT

Decoration on the wheelmade ware occurs only in Periods 2 and 3 in Margiana. Apart from the large ritual vessels (3.A and 3.B) described above, there are three types of ceramic decoration.

Painted and Incised Designs, Periods 2 and 3

Firstly, a small percentage of painted vessels continues although the fast-wheel Central Asian ceramics during Namazga V and VI are primarily unpainted. In Period 2, reddish-brown/brown washed or painted and incised decoration is found on closed pots of various sizes. The most frequent painted design consists of several horizontal bands of reddish-brown paint around the shoulder and body of the pot (fig. 4.30). Incised designs often follow the same pattern as the painted wares, although from the Gonur deep sounding (layer 6) came a sherd decorated with an engraved design of a flower (or a flower shape). Similar designs and motifs are made with both incised and painted decoration. Large storage vessels (type 3.B.1) are found at Gonur south and Togolok 21 with engraved designs containing red pigment. The decorated vessels are found in a variety of contexts including burials, cenotaphs, floors of rooms, and middens from courtyards and domestic contexts. Thus the occurrence of decoration appears not to correlate to status or specific context, but to simply be a minor component of the Periods 2 and 3 ceramic assemblages.

Potter's Marks, Periods 2 and 3

Secondly, potter's marks are found on Period 2 and (more rarely) Period 3 ceramics. Overall these marks are not common on the ceramics of Margiana or Bactria. The designs are incised prior to firing on plates, small bowls, *khomchi,* and *podstavki* (fig. 4.31). Potter's

Figure 4.30
Period 2 band-painted ceramics. Togolok 1.

Figure 4.31
Period 2 potter's marks, range of motifs from excavated contexts.
Top: Margiana (Togolok 1, Togolok 21, Gonur south).
Bottom: Southern Bactria (Dashli).

marks are found on three areas of the vessels: on the base of the ceramics or on the bottom part; on the side or lower shoulder of vessels; and on the inside of shallow bowls. These latter probably are not potter's marks per se but have similar designs. Four designs are found in the ceramic assemblage that I studied from Togolok and Gonur: geometric cross motif, tree motif, bow-tie motif, and star formed by intersecting lines (this motif is frequently found on ceramics from burials, not only on the bottom of vessels but inside bowls). Based on the archives of the Soviet expedition to Afghanistan, six types of potter's marks were found at Dashli 3, four of which are different from Margiana. Similar potter's marks are found at Dzharkutan on cemetery vessels (Askarov and Abdullaev 1983). The occurrence of similar marks in Bactria and in Period 2 of Margiana illustrates the cultural link between the two regions at this time.

Sarianidi (1977) presents several different signs found on Bronze Age ceramics from Margiana and Bactria in summary illustrations. Most of the Bactrian ceramics with these marks are recorded from burials; however, no ceramics from the architecture were published. In Margiana they are found equally rarely in burials and in architectural context, and the contexts have not yet provided insight into the meaning of the marks.

Figure 4.32
Period 2 stamp and cylinder seal impressions on storage vessels. 1) Seal impression on shoulder stamped prior to firing. Gonur south surface; 2) Seal impression on upper body sherd stamped prior to firing, Gonur south, Row 2 courtyard (see chap. 7, fig. 7. 9); 3) Cylinder seal rolled across shoulder prior to firing. Gonur south, Phase 1 room context.

Seal Impressions, Period 2

Finally, seal impressions found on large storage jars were made prior to their being fired (fig. 4.32). Impressions of cylinder seals run across the upper side of the vessel; stamp seal impressions are found on the rim or the upper side of the vessel. Whether they were intended as simple decoration or as an administrative symbol marking the vessels is not clear.

COARSEWARE CERAMICS, PERIODS 1, 2, AND 3

Hand-formed coarseware ceramics have paste with distinctive large, coarse grog temper in addition to fine chaff and fine, well-levigated quartz grains like the rest of the locally produced ceramics. Most of these vessels are handmade, often with the slab construction clearly visible, and some are finished on the wheel. These ceramics are handmade in forms similar to the wheelmade forms, especially the closed vessels (3.B) and platters (6) (fig. 4.33). The fabric color varies from reddish buff to dark reddish grey. Well-preserved examples have bases sooted from fires and occasionally have food remains adhering to the interior, earning the ware the title *kukniya* (kitchenware).

The excavations did not reveal even distribution of coarseware. These handmade ceramics tend to be found either in situ near hearths and cooking areas or cached in storage areas. In the Gonur deep sounding middens, coarseware comprises 1.5 to 4 percent of the assemblage from domestic areas.

Several examples of textile-impressed kitchenware have also been found. Examples are found in the production-oriented midden from the Gonur deep sounding. Several examples of coarseware have the

Figure 4.33
Period 2 coarseware ceramics from rooms of the central building at Togolok 1.

Figure 4.34
Period 1 and 2 coarseware ceramics with cloth impressions. Gonur depe.

cloth impressions on the inside (fig. 4.34). Other examples from surface collections show cloth impressions on the exterior.

DISCUSSION

Period 1

Comparison of Gonur and Kelleli

Period 1, defined on the basis of comparative ceramics and small finds from the Gonur deep sounding (fig. 4.35), corresponds to the Kelleli period of the traditional micro-oasis-based chronology. Based on ceramics from excavations and from surface collections in Margiana (Sarianidi 1990), it is now clear that Period 1 ceramics and small finds are found widespread over the area of Bronze Age Margiana—from Kelleli in the north to the southernmost excavated assemblage of Period 1 found in the lowest levels of the sounding at Togolok 1 (Sarianidi 1987a). The evidence for widespread occupation of the Margiana oasis at the time of Gonur Period 1 is in sharp contrast to the isolated scatters of earlier ceramics found on the northern edge of the Kelleli area. This strongly suggests that Period 1 represents the earliest widespread occupation of the Murgab delta.

Some differences are seen between presence and absence of certain categories of forms from the Gonur deep sounding and those from Kelleli. The wide-scale excavations at the Kelleli sites provided a great variety both of intact examples of the smaller, sturdier vessels and of the rare forms from extensive areas of excavation. While the deep sounding has a less diverse assemblage, the collection of surface ceramics from Gonur north includes the full range of the Kelleli forms (P'yankova 1989, pl. 1, 2). It is not possible to differentiate Gonur Period 1 ceramics from Kelleli 3 or 4 ceramics on the basis of specific types, ware, or temper, yet ceramic kilns found on each site suggest local production during Period 1.

Comparison of Period 1 with Late Namazga V in the Foothill Plain of the Kopet Dag

A high percentage of the forms are shared between the late Namazga V of the foothill zone and the Period 1 ceramics in Margiana (fig. 4.36). Altyn depe levels 0 through 2 (Masson 1988; Udemuradov 1987) and Ulug depe (unpublished *opisi*) provide the best

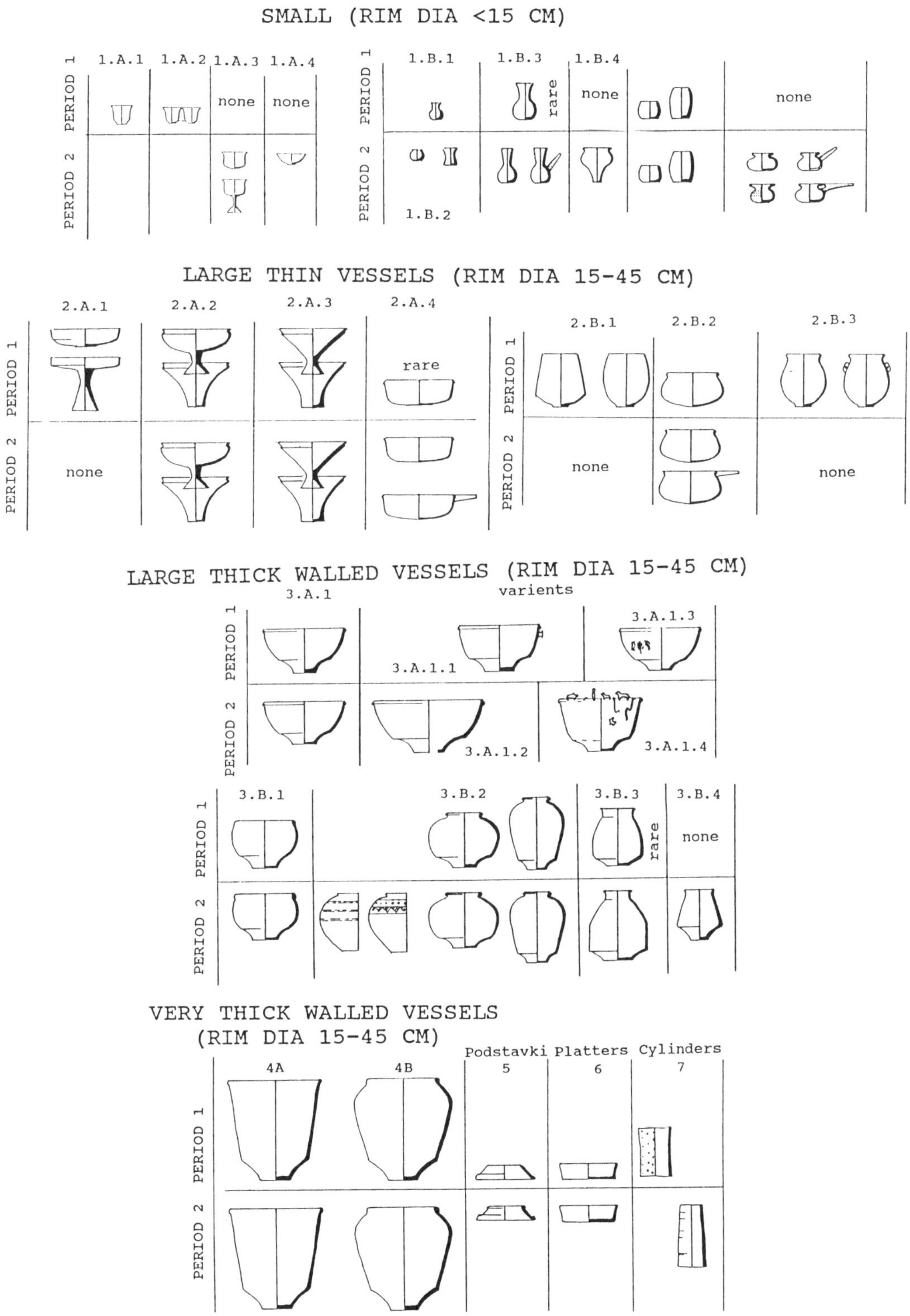

Figure 4.35
Ceramic typology of Margiana Periods 1 and 2 based on stratigraphic excavations at Gonur.

provenienced assemblages of late Namazga V ceramics from the foothill plain. It must be noted that the drawings of the ceramics from the upper levels at Namazga depe (Namazga V and VI) are too generalized to allow specific comparisons to other sites (Khlopina 1972, 1981; unpublished *opisi*).

The assemblages are not identical (table 4.1), and the foothill assemblage includes distinctive sharply carinated, biconical pots; thin-walled open vessels; and small lids with distinctive inturned rims. Margiana Period 1 has more types of footed vessels, distinctive decorated large bowls and basins (3.A), and a greater incidence of mold-made bases.

Some of the differences previously suggested are less pronounced based on the present analysis. P'yankova (1989:51) noted the lack of elongated biconical pots with flaring rims (Altyn type 2) and caldron pots (Altyn types 17 and 18) from Margiana, but these are more characteristic of early Namazga V than of late Namazga V. Several types that Udemuradov identified as being found only in the foothill region have now also been found in Margiana Period 1: One sherd of shaved buff ware is probably a hollow leg of a four-legged vessel from the Gonur north domestic architecture. In addition, a distinctive ceramic animal head found at Gonur north (fig. 4.37:1) is precisely paralleled at Altyn depe (fig. 4.37:2). The parallels between the late Namazga V ceramic assemblage and the Period 1 assemblage from Margiana are extensive and suggest the duplication of the late Namazga V entire assemblage in Margiana.

In fact, the only way to distinguish similar forms from the late Namazga V and from the early period in Margiana is on the basis of the clay sources, reflected in the ceramic ware. Preliminary descriptions of ceramic ware, based on visual inspection of ceramics, were made on comparative collections from previously excavated assemblages in Ashgabat, Saint Petersburg, and Moscow.

Late Namazga V wheelmade wares from Altyn depe have a medium-fine buff paste with fine sand and mineral temper; the Ulug depe wheelmade ceramics typically have a fine buff-to-red paste, often with white (possibly lime?) inclusions. The Ulug ceramics typically have a light colored exterior with a carefully finished exterior surface, similar in appearance to a slip. The wheelmade ceramics from Namazga depe (Periods V and VI) have a fine paste with a distinctive green color and whitish green exterior surfaces. Fre-

ALTYN NMG V	MARGIANA PERIOD 1
I......	2.B.1
II.....	close to 2.B.1
III....	2.A.2, 2.A.3
IV.....	2.A.1
V......	heavy form of 2.A
VI.....	1.A.1
VII....	1.A.3 (rare in both areas)
VIII...	large 2.A.2
IX.....	podstavki
X......	Not found in Margiana
XI & XXI....	platters
XII....	footed platters
XIII...	1.B.5 (rare)
XIV....	2.B.3
XV & XVI....	3.B.3
XVII...	large 2.A.4
XVIII..	2.A.4
XIX....	1.B.1, 1.B.2
XX.....	3.B.1
XXII...	3.B.2, 3.B.3
XXIII..	4.A & 4.B
XXIV...	Not found in Margiana

Table 4.1
Comparison of Altyn ceramic typology with Period 1 ceramic typology.

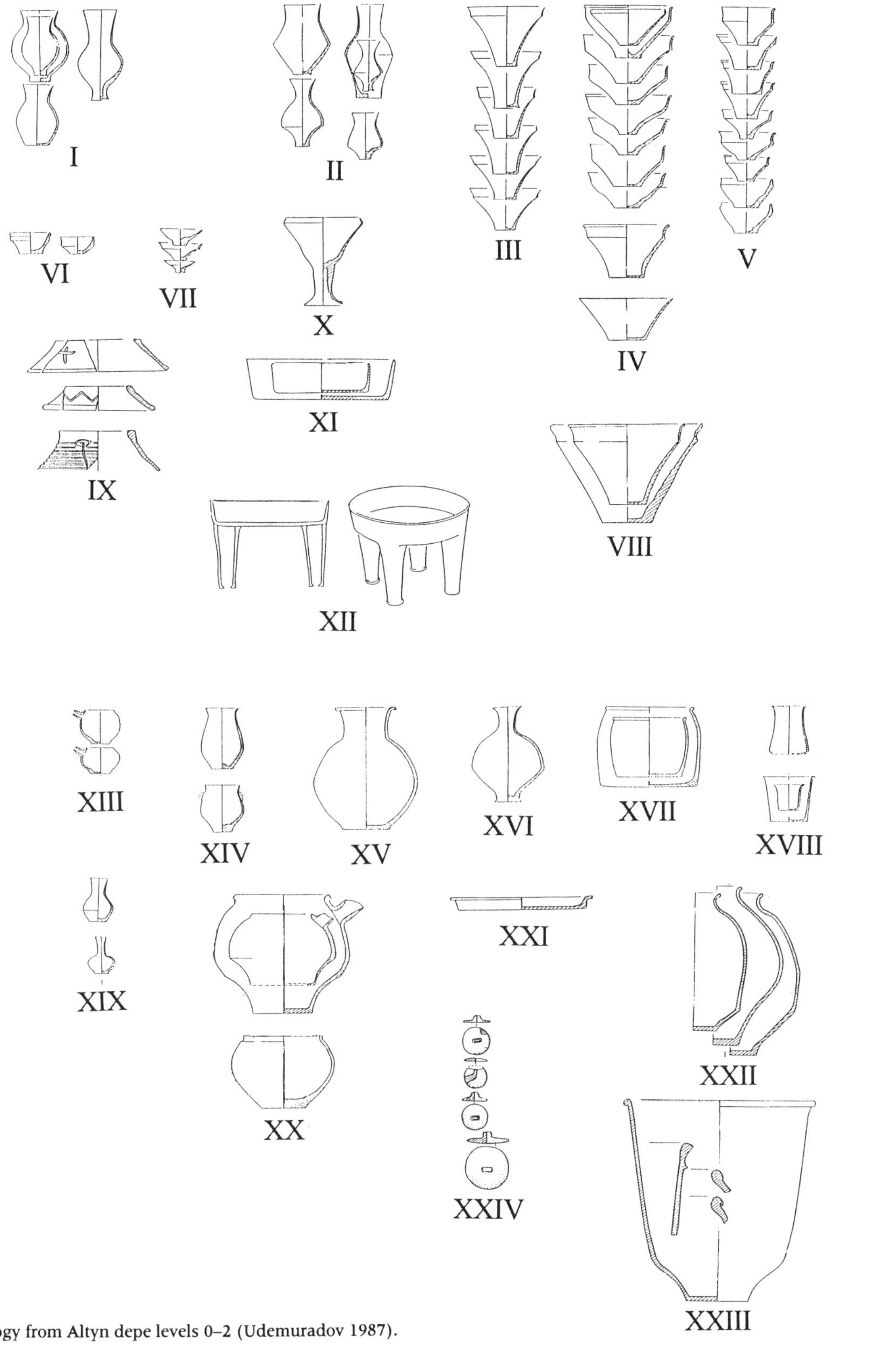

Figure 4.36
Ceramic typology from Altyn depe levels 0–2 (Udemuradov 1987).

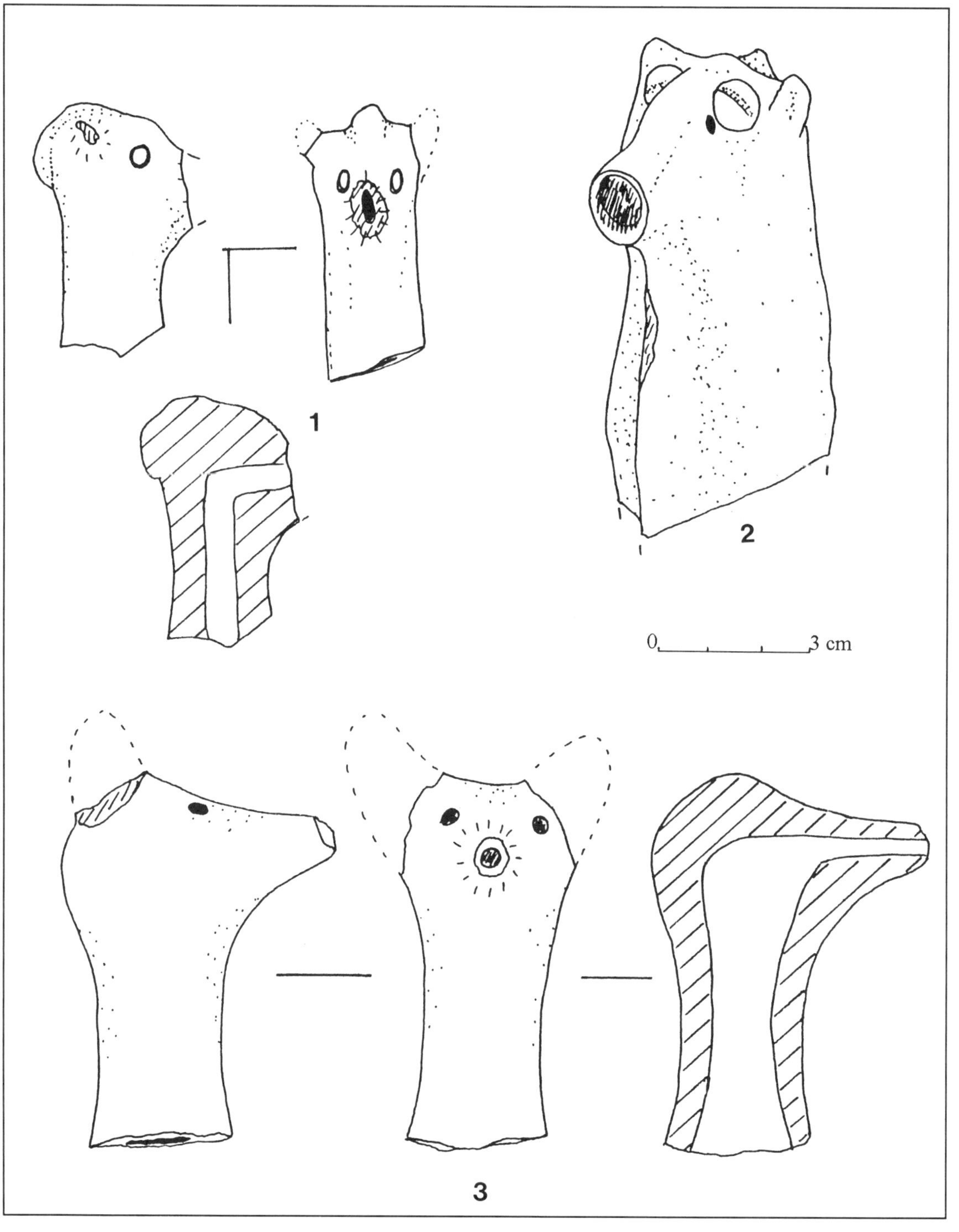

Figure 4.37
Period 1 zoomorphic ceramic head spouts.
1) Gonur north, *kremel*; 2) Altyn depe, exc. 5, street; 3) Gonur north, surface.

quently, the surface discoloration is considered to be a slip; however, low magnification clearly reveals this to be not an applied slip but a discoloration.

Imported Wares from the Gonur Deep Sounding

The Gonur deep sounding layers 1 through 4 yielded a small amount of green or greenish white ceramic made on a fast wheel with sand temper, typical of the Namazga V ceramics from Namazga depe. Other sand-tempered, medium-fine sherds may have been imported from Altyn depe; no wares similar to Ulug ceramics were recorded from the deep sounding.

All excavated first-period sites have a small amount of greyware ceramics. Greywares from the Iranian plateau (e.g., Hissar, Tureng depe) (Cleuziou 1986) and from the Indus valley (Rehman Dheri, Period 3) (Durrani 1988) do not have the same forms as those found in Margiana. Most of the Margiana grey ceramics are actually misfired pieces of the local medium-fine buff ware. These ceramics, found in the domestic debris, indicate that the vessels were used despite having been misfired. This occurrence was quantified at Gonur north, where in the domestic architecture they comprise 3 percent of the body sherds.

The Bronze Age ceramic assemblage from northern Bactria includes a true greyware that is burnished and has mica in the temper. No greyware of this type has been found in Period 1, although it is found in level 6 (Period 2) of the deep sounding at Gonur. To date there is no known occupation in northern or southern Bactria similar to the late Namazga V, although a local culture that has not been described may have existed there at that time.

Actual greyware ceramics were found at Kelleli 1 and are similar to the carinated greyware found at Ak depe near Ashgabat (Masimov 1979; Udemuradov 1986). Ak depe is known for its Namazga IV carinated greywares (Sarianidi 1976), and they have been used as the main evidence for proposing a Namazga IV date for Kelleli 1. However, most Ak depe ceramics are made of greyware, including during the Namazga III, IV, and V periods, and are not confined to the best-known Namazga IV levels at Ak depe. Greyware is found in the Namazga V levels as a small but consistent component of the ceramic assemblage in the stratified sites of the foothill zone of southwest Turkmenistan. In my examination of the Namazga V ceramics from Ulug depe, for example, greyware is 5 to 10 percent of the Namazga V assemblage, and perhaps represents local production (personal observation, Moscow).

The widespread Period 1 ceramic assemblage in Margiana relates directly to the Kopet Dag foothill late Namazga V culture. The ceramic evidence does not support proposals that the oasis populations came from Iran (first suggested by Sarianidi in 1977), nor the proposal that there must be local occupation in Margiana prior to the late Namazga V period (first suggested by Masimov in 1979). The high-quality, locally produced wheelmade ceramics duplicate the late Namazga V assemblage of the Kopet Dag foothill sites. This replication of the ceramic assemblage is also seen in the small-find assemblage of Period 1, indicating not only contemporanity of occupation but cultural affiliation as well.

Period 2

Period 2 Ceramics in Margiana

Some general trends in the wheelmade ceramics of Margiana are observed from the study of ceramics in the Gonur deep sounding. In general, the wheelmade ware is slightly coarser (less well levigated) in Period 2. Across forms, rims tend to be more triangular, and necks tend to be taller through time. There is an increase in the number of small vessels and in the occurrence of spouts. Carinations are less sharp, a trend continuing from the very sharp early Namazga V ceramics of the foothill sites. The vertical-lip form (type 2.A.2) becomes more common, and the form of this rim becomes more deeply indented. The incidence of inturned rims of this form is much higher (in Period 1, 50 percent of rims are inturned; in Period 2, over 90 percent).

The sharply grooved rim (2.A.3) is considered an indicator of Period 1, and vessels with the vertical lip (2.A.2) are considered indicative of Period 2 (Masimov 1981; Udemuradov 1989). These have been used as fossil indicators of these periods; however, the two rim forms are found together and are not exclusive to a single period (table 4.2).

Many of the diagnostic forms that distinguish the two periods are in fact quite rare in the Gonur deep sounding. Key forms for the identification of Period 1 in the deep sounding are thin-walled, plain rim bowls (2.A.1), biconical pots (2.B.1), and hole-mouth pots (2.B.3). Key forms for the identification of Period 2 in

Gonur	Sharply Grooved (2.A.3)	Vertical Lip (2.A.2)
Period 1	16%	12.5%
Period 2	4%	16.5%

Table 4.2
Occurrences of Kelleli "Period" indicator (2.A.3) and Togolok "Period" indicator (2.A.2).

the sounding are thin-walled, triangular-rimmed bowls (2.A.4), tall-necked pots (3.B.4), deeply burnished greyware imports, incised geometric designs on ceramics, and stamp seal impressions on the ceramics. Nomadic ceramics appear to be present in layer 6, but no diagnostic decoration was found on the small body sherds.

The extensive excavations at Gonur south, Togolok 1, and Togolok 21 include these ceramic types and diagnostic features of Period 2, as well as a wide variety of other ceramic forms that occur only with the Bactrian-Margiana Archaeological Complex. These chronologically distinctive forms include certain bottles, spouted vessels, footed goblets, and large decorated bowls. Most of these ceramics are poor key types because they are rare or difficult to identify.

The Togolok 1, Togolok 21, and Gonur south building complexes include elite or ritual areas with vessel types different from those from production assemblage such as from layer 6 of the Gonur deep sounding. The central part of Togolok 21, identified as a ritual or elite area, may have a specific ceramic assemblage—including bridged and open spouts, basins with terracotta figurines on the rims, and painted designs on the local ware. Only the application of fine-scale ceramic analysis will permit the characterization of functional—such as ritual, domestic, and production—assemblages in the BMAC.

Period 2 and Bactria

In northern Bactria, ceramics from the excavations of buildings and burials at Sapalli and Dzharkutan relate directly to the Margiana Period 2 ceramic assemblage. The ceramic types correspond closely with Period 2 ceramics from Margiana. The differences are primarily in the occurrence in Bactria of inturned rims, the lack of carinations on the goblets and other footed vessels, and scarcity of large open bowls and basins with a terracotta frieze. Unlike in Margiana, it is possible to clearly differentiate the early BMAC (Sapalli period) from the late BMAC (Dzharkutan period) based on both stratigraphy of buildings and burials (Askarov and Abdullaev 1983). These Bactrian periods show a development of ceramic forms, but both have BMAC type small finds.

A small amount of imported ceramics from northern Bactria was found in layer 6 of the Gonur deep sounding. Northern Bactrian ceramics are red to reddish buff with fine to heavy micaceous mineral temper that sparkles in a fresh break. Reddish greyware with micaceous inclusions and a distinctively streak-burnished exterior surface is a small (~3 percent of the assemblage) but consistent component from the sites of northern Bactria (personal observations of collections in Samarkand and Tashkent).

A large short-necked storage jar (*khomcha* type 3.B.2) from the upper levels of the Gonur *kremel* is exactly parallel to a burnished greyware vessel from Burial 89 at Sapalli (Askarov 1977, pl. 23).

From southern Bactria, whole vessels from burials are the ceramic sample available for study. At Dashli 1 or 3, ceramics were available from burials but not from the building complexes. The ceramic types from Dashli 3 burials are similar to types from Sapalli and Dzharkutan, but the ware and surface treatment are different (Sarianidi 1977; fig. 25). The common ware from the southern Bactrian site of Dashli 3 is buff redware with sand temper (ibid.). A small number of burnished reddish grey ceramics from Dashli appear to have been imported from northern Bactria (ibid., 70). Large basins with a terracotta frieze, similar to the Margiana BMAC vessels, are found in southern Bactria but not in northern Bactria (Sarianidi 1979b).

In general, the wares of northern Bactria, southern Bactria, and Margiana Period 2 ceramics are distinctively different, but the forms are very similar. Although the imported vessels attest to contemporaneity, ceramics were not an important exchange item between Margiana and Bactria.

Nomadic Pottery

Steppe nomadic ceramics from Margiana are handmade, with fine grog and sand temper, and ornamented with incised with distinctive punctate or incised decorated. The range of forms and decoration indicates a wide variety of cultural contacts. The steppe bronze nomadic ceramics are typically found on the surface, from presumed deflated nomadic encampments, rather than from architectural contexts. Handmade steppe nomadic type ceramics have been found in situ in Bronze Age Margiana buildings in rare but significant instances.

Two types of steppe nomadic ceramics have been identified from within the large Period 2 building complex of Togolok 1, on the floor of rooms 14 and 20. The first type consists of globular pots with cord-impressed decoration along the rim and upper shoulder (from room 20). P'yankova suggests that these vessels are similar stylistically to the Poltavkino and early Petrovo ceramics of the northern Caspian Sea region (Kachalova 1985), but acknowledges that the ware is more similar to Andronovo ceramics (Kuz'mina 1986). A second group of steppe nomadic ceramics from Togolok 1 includes slightly closed wide-mouth jugs with comb stamping (fig. 4.38). P'yankova attributes this ceramic type to the early stage of the Timber-Frame culture north of the Caspian Sea in the lower Volga basin (P'yankova 1993). However, the ware and designs are more similar to the Fedorovo type of early Andronovo ceramics, according to Kuz'mina (1986). Fedorovo steppe culture is identified with areas northeast of Margiana (up into the Altai) rather than to the northwest (near the Caspian Sea). Fedorovo type nomadic ceramics

Figure 4.38
Period 2 Andronovo steppe nomadic pottery. Togolok 1, Room 14.

are commonly found on BMAC sites in northern Bactria and southern Tajikistan (P'yankova 1989; Vinogradova and Kuz'mina 1986). The examples from Margiana are the first to have been found in architectural context.

A small number of other steppe ceramics have been found on Margiana sites of Period 3. In situ steppe nomadic ceramics from the excavations at Takhirbai 3 have direct parallels with the Tazabag'yab nomadic ceramics from Khorezm (Sarianidi 1975b). Although widely correlated with the BMAC (ibid.; Kuzmina and Lyapin 1984), these ceramics have been found from excavated context only from Takhirbai period sites in Margiana. The shift in the source of these later nomadic ceramics reflects a change in the orientation of nomadic contacts between Period 2 (the BMAC) and Period 3 (Takhirbai period). Incised handmade ceramics typical of the steppe nomads of stages 4 and 5 of the pre-Aral area (Vinogradov 1968) have been found in Margiana (Sarianidi 1975b), but not from excavated contexts (fig. 4.39). These can be correlated with the Tazabag'yab nomadic ceramics, which are found together in Khorezm (Itina 1977).

Nomadic ceramics, rare but ubiquitous in the oasis settlements, may be used as an estimate of the nature of nomadic contacts. In Margiana the amount of nomadic material is very limited and indicates a diversity of nomadic cultural affiliations. There is no evidence of nomadic contact prior to the BMAC. During the BMAC, the nomadic contacts appear to be associated with areas to the north and to the east, from the Aral Sea to the Altai. Later, with the decline of the BMAC, the nomadic contacts appear to be associated with the northwest, to the northern Caspian region. Steppe nomadic materials represent a much larger percentage of the typical site ceramics in northern Bactria (from BMAC and Molali period sites) than from Margiana (P'yankova 1989). In southern Bactria the steppe ceramics are known primarily from surface collections, and they include ceramics of both the Fedorovo type of the Andronovo nomadic culture and the Tazabag'yab culture, a pattern similar to Margiana (Sarianidi 1977, fig. 66; Vinogradova and Kuz'mina 1986, fig. 3).

Figure 4.39
Tazabag'yab steppe nomadic ceramics from the surface of Gonur. Incised decoration, coarse sandy temper, redware with buff exterior.

Absence of Foothill Zone Parallels to Margiana

None of the distinctive red-slipped ceramics from Namazga depe Namazga VI deposits have been found in Margiana associated with BMAC materials. The original parallels with Namazga VI and Margiana were made with the later Takhirbai ceramics (Masson 1959) and not the Togolok (here referred to as Period 2) ceramics. Khlopina's parallels between Namazga depe and Margiana rely primarily on the ceramic types characteristic of wheelmade ceramics throughout Central Asia, rather than on key chronological forms of Period 2 in Margiana (Khlopina 1981).

Other Namazga VI burial assemblages in the foothill plain, however, could be Bactrian-Margiana type burials in structure and content. The burials at Yangi kala (Ganyalin 1956) and El'ken depe (Marushchenko 1959) and the Namazga VI burials at Ulug depe have closer ceramic parallels with Period 2 of Margiana and Bactria than with Namazga depe. Finds from Ganyalin's hoards at Altyn depe have parallels with the small finds of Period 2 of Margiana (Ganyalin 1967). Farther west, the Hissar IIIC hoards may in fact be BMAC type cenotaphs without Bactrian-Margiana type ceramics, based on the observation that the small finds are typical of the BMAC. These burials and cenotaphs in the foothill plain of the Kopet Dag and northwest Iran are very similar in context to the BMAC type burials and cenotaphs from southern Iran and Baluchistan. These BMAC assemblages in Iran document the spread of the BMAC out of Margiana and Bactria (Hiebert and Lamberg-Karlovsky 1992).

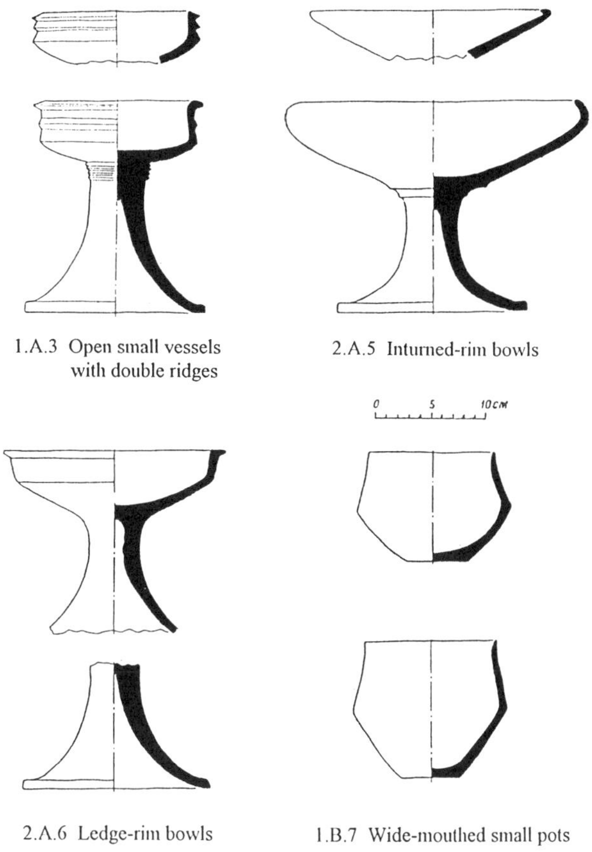

Figure 4.40
Distinctive ceramic forms from Period 3 (excavations at Takhirbai 3, Masson 1959, pls. 7–9).

Takhirbai Period

The ceramics from the uppermost level of Gonur south differ from the BMAC assemblage of the main occupation of the building complex (Period 2). This upper level, excavated for the most part after the 1989 collaborative fieldwork, is included provisionally in this study of ceramics as Period 3. The ceramics from the upper level at Gonur south appear to correspond with the ceramics from Takhirbai 3 (Masson 1959; Sarianidi 1990). Like those of Periods 1 and 2, Period 3 ceramics are widely distributed across the Margiana oasis from the Gonur and Togolok micro-oases, and extend south to the Takhirbai micro-oasis, beyond the BMAC regions. None of the distinctive small finds characteristic of the BMAC are found associated with materials of the Takhirbai period. While the ceramics and their distribution suggest occupational continuity, the BMAC culture does not continue into Period 3, the Takhirbai period.

The ceramic assemblage of Period 3 is different from the BMAC wares in the incidence of red and grey wares. Takhirbai has red-burnished redwares typical of Namazga VI from Namazga depe. The original parallels between the late Bronze Age of Margiana and the Kopet Dag foothill culture of Namazga VI were based primarily on these ceramics from Takhirbai 3 rather than on BMAC materials (Masson 1959).

Some differences in vessel form also can be outlined. Many typical BMAC ceramic forms are found in Takhirbai context, although the footed goblets of Period 3 (1.A.3) have a distinctive ridge below the rim, a distinctive cup appears (1.B.7), and some of the larger vessels have a distinctive inturned rim, similar to BMAC vessels of Bactria (fig. 4.40). In northern Bactria this period has been subdivided into the Kuzali, Molali, and Bustan phases (Askarov and Abdullaev

1983). The Takhirbai 3 pedestal vessels have swelling profiles of the feet or pedestals of the fruit stands, which most closely parallel those from Molali and cemeteries from South Tajikistan.

As noted above, nomad ceramics suggest a shift in relations with the nomadic populations from the northeast during the BMAC period to the northwest during the Takhirbai period.

Geomagnetic Dating

Independent confirmation of the relative ordering of the ceramic periods in Margiana is provided by measurements of the archaeomagnetic intensity of ceramics (paleointensity) conducted by researchers from the Institute of Physics in Moscow. Paleointensity is a relative dating technique based on measurements of the intensity of the geomagnetic field at the time of heating (thermoremanent magnetization—TRM), allowing the sample TRM intensity to be matched to a reference set of TRM intensity of known age. Unlike traditional archaeomagnetic analysis, the TRM *intensity* can be measured from movable fired objects, such as bricks or potsherds.

Samples from the Gonur deep sounding were submitted for analysis and comparison with a large series of samples of known relative age (Nachasova and Burakov 1993). The lowest levels from the Gonur deep sounding, from level 3 (field intensity value of 52.4 mcT) and level 4 (55.3 mcT), are similar to the mean values from Altyn depe (upper-level materials), Kelleli 1 ceramics, and the Kelleli 4 kilns (50.7 mcT).

Samples from level 6, Period 2, average 45.7 mcT; and the material from level 7, the surface layer, average 43.8 mcT. Four samples from Taip (Period 2) range from 35.9 to 52.7 mcT, with mean intensities from 41.7 to 48.7 mcT, and thus are similar to the upper layers at the Gonur deep sounding—consistent with the ceramic parallels. Togolok 21 has materials from two stratigraphic levels inside of the building, from outside the walls, and from kilns. TRM determinations for these ceramics cluster in the range of the Dzharkutan materials and do not include any values above 60, that is, ranges of the Iron Age. These uppermost levels compare also to the values from Dzharkutan. The paleointensity data concur with the relative dating of sites in Margiana.

CONCLUSIONS

Although the form and manufacture of Bronze Age ceramics from Margiana are tremendously conservative, two ceramic periods can be defined on the basis of the fine-scale ceramic analysis from the Gonur deep sounding: early (Kelleli 3 and 4, Gonur Period 1) and late (Togolok 1, Togolok 21, Gonur Period 2). I expected to be able to subdivide this ceramic chronology; however, I found no strong changes in the ceramics in the four stratigraphic layers of Period 1. I found no clear chronological differences between the assemblages of layer 6 of the sounding and the earliest architectural phases and the latest burial phases on sites such as Togolok 1 and Togolok 21. Both the stratigraphy and ceramics strongly suggest continuity of occupation from Period 1 to Period 2 and from Period 2 to Period 3 at Gonur, and in Margiana.

Although I found several index forms for each period, they are relatively rare finds. In addition, commonly used index forms, such as the thin-walled bowls, are not exclusive to Period 1 or to Period 2. In many cases it is not possible to distinguish archaeological deposits of these periods, because the ceramic tradition of Periods 1 and 2 are so similar. This lack of distinctiveness in ceramics contrasts with the distinctions in architecture and the small finds between these periods.

The distribution of Bronze Age sites of Margiana (Periods 1 and 2) can be estimated by comparing the previously excavated and survey materials (Sarianidi 1990). The distribution of Period 1 and 2 ceramics and their associated small finds suggests widespread occupation of the Murgab delta during both Period 1 and Period 2 (fig. 4.41), rather than a shifting of the occupation to the south within the Bronze Age occupations of Period 1 and Period 2.

The ceramics within each type at Gonur are very standardized. Although there is no evidence of mass production in Margiana, this standardization implies intensive information flow between pottery workshops (Arnold 1991). There are few differences between the ceramic assemblages from the foothill sites of the late Namazga V and Period 1 in Margiana. The ceramic parallels provide the best evidence that the initial widespread occupation in Margiana was from the foothill zone. Despite these close similarities, the occurrence of actual imported ceramics is rare. In Period 2 there are many parallels between the ceramics of Margiana and Bactria. Exchange in ceramics does not characterize either Period 1 or Period 2 of

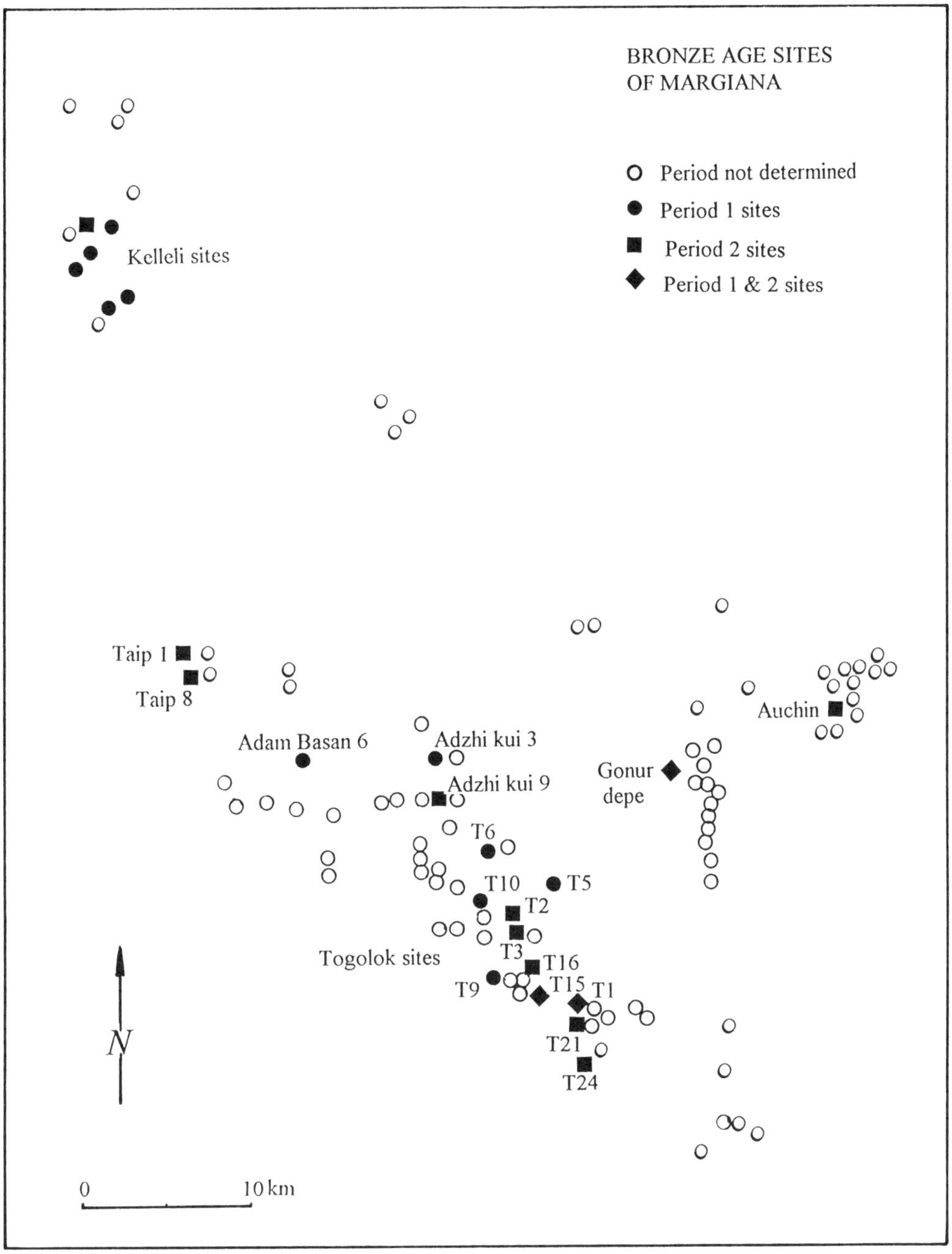

Figure 4.41
Distribution of Bronze Age Margiana Period 1 and Period 2 sites.

Margiana. The rare ceramic imports in Period 2 are important, however. The ties with Bactria, the presence of Andronovo ceramics, and the lack of parallels with the foothill settlements indicate an important shift of interaction spheres from Period 1 to Period 2 in Margiana.

CHAPTER FIVE

Absolute Chronology and Radiocarbon Dates

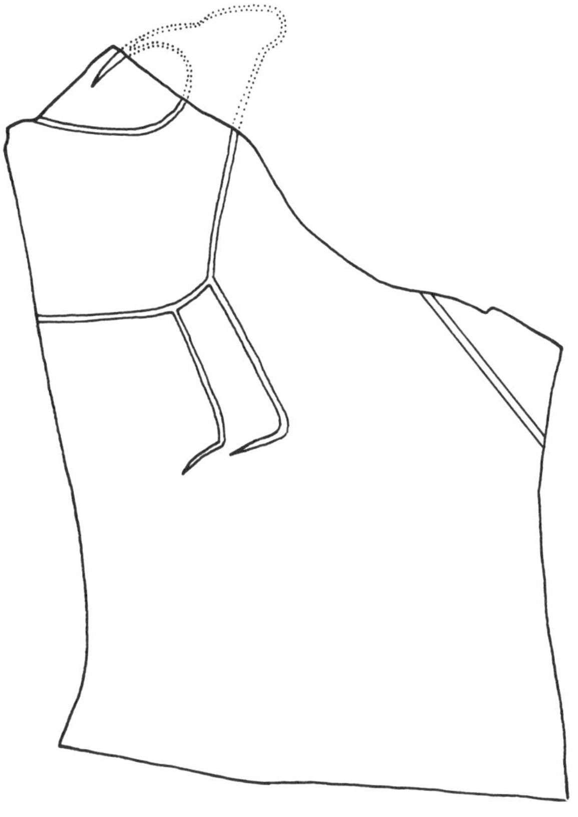

RADIOCARBON DATES FROM THE 1989–1990 EXCAVATIONS AT Gonur depe provide absolute dates for the ceramic assemblages of Periods 1, 2, and 3 of Margiana. These dates are compared with previously determined radiocarbon dates from Margiana, from other Central Asian sites, and from sites outside of Central Asia (the Indus and Iran) that include Margiana and Bactrian type objects.

Radiocarbon analysis has advanced in recent years, both in terms of interpretation of the data generated by the labs and in terms of the numbers of determinations available from excavated contexts in the region. Because the recent compilations of dates from Central Asia (Kohl 1984, 1992) and South Asia (Possehl 1989; Meadow 1991) present comparable analyses, it is possible to obtain a systematic radiocarbon chronology for the whole region.

Radiocarbon analysis was a popular technique in Soviet archaeology in the 1960s and 1970s (e.g., Ivanova, Kind, and Cherdyntsev 1963, Kurtis 1981), and samples from many Bronze Age Central Asian sites were analyzed. However, for any one archaeological assemblage or culture, coherent clusters of radiocarbon dates did not emerge, leading many researchers simply to pick and choose dates that best fit their preferred chronology based on cross-dated artifacts. In addition, the use of radiocarbon dates that were not calibrated led to the formation of two sets of radiocarbon chronologies for Central Asia—a younger, uncalibrated chronology and an older, calibrated chronology. Many scholars chose to avoid radiocarbon data altogether.

One primary goal of the collaborative field project at Gonur was the collection of radiocarbon samples from contexts directly associated with each of the ceramic periods. New radiocarbon analyses were made on samples collected by the author from recently excavated deposits containing clearly differentiated assemblages of ceramics of Periods 1 through 3. These samples were analyzed at the Beta Analytic Laboratory in Florida and at the Helsinki Radiocarbon Laboratory. Radiocarbon samples taken from the deep sounding and from the domestic architecture (Gonur north), and from the on-going excavations at Gonur south are directly correlated with the ceramics presented in chapter 4 and the fine-screen samples in chapter 8. Further charcoal samples were collected from the current excavations at Dzharkutan in northern Bactria.

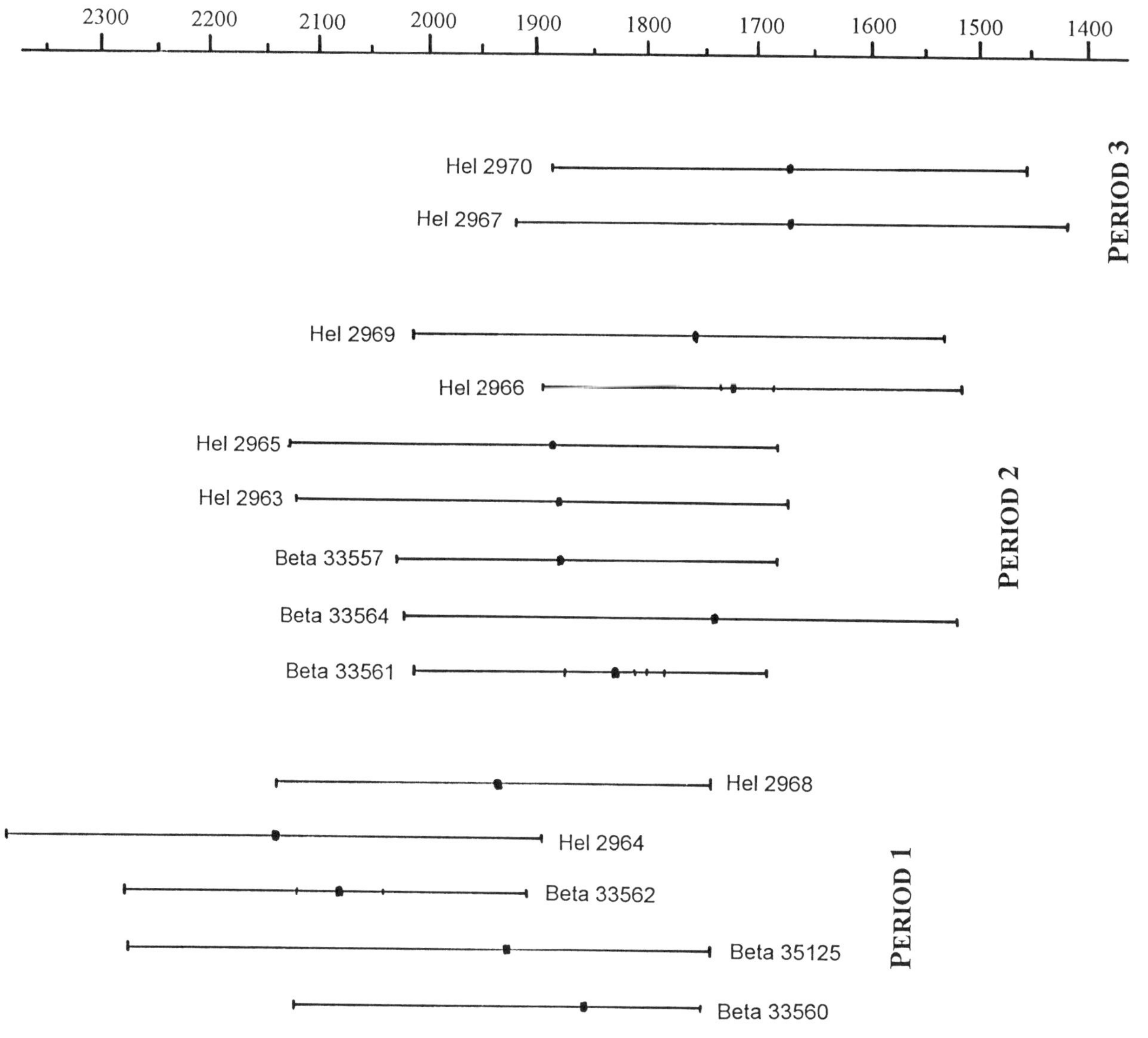

Figure 5.1
Radiocarbon dates from Margiana.

Previous radiocarbon determinations from Margiana are incorporated into this analysis only where the laboratory conditions could be taken into consideration and where the associated ceramics, sample location, and type of deposit could be determined. Most Margiana determinations up to now were made at the laboratory in Saint Petersburg (lab code is LE—Leningrad). The Leningrad laboratory participated in comparative tests on samples from Gonur depe, which were analyzed in Helsinki to estimate the variation between laboratories (H. Jungner, pers. comm.). When calibrated, many of the previously analyzed radiocarbon dates from Central Asia cluster in a coherent manner with the new dates, as well as with related sites in the neighboring areas of the Indus and Iran.

All of the dates were calibrated with the CALIB 3.0.3 computer program (Stuiver and Reimer 1993). The calibrated range (a standard deviation of 2 sigma) of the dates provides an estimate of the single date and not of the duration of the period. In the current version of the calibration, Bronze Age radiocarbon dates have ranges no smaller than two hundred years, and the range may often be broader, depending on the amount of carbon in the sample, its condition, and laboratory conditions under which it was analyzed (fig. 5.1).

NEW RADIOCARBON DATES

Period 1

Only deposits clearly associated with Period 1 ceramics and small finds were sampled for radiocarbon analysis (table 5.1). A large sample of charcoal (no. 1 in the list below) from layer 3 of the Gonur deep sounding from a large charcoal-rich lens of oven sweepings is associated with Period 1 ceramics. Another Gonur north sample (no. 2) was from the excavations of Period 1 domestic architecture, sealed between two floor levels. Several samples (nos. 3, 4, 5) come from pits sealed beneath the architectural complex on the south mound at Gonur. Although no architectural levels have been found beneath the main south mound architecture that dates to Period 2, the pits located there include ceramics and small finds (such as terracotta figurines) that are similar to the Period 1 materials from the lower levels of the deep sounding on the north mound. These well-provenienced dates cluster around 2100 to 1900 B.C., with a 95-percent chance that the dates belong in the range from 2285 to 1785 B.C.

In the field, I documented the stratigraphic position and associated ceramic assemblage of some of the previously analyzed radiocarbon samples (Sarianidi 1990). Two samples (nos. 6, 7) from the floor of the Gonur north monumental building (*Kremel*) room 5, and the bottom layer of the initial sounding, are associated with ceramics and small finds similar to Period 1 of the nearby deep sounding.

Period 2

Radiocarbon samples associated with Period 2 ceramics and the small finds of the Bactrian-Margiana Archaeological Complex were taken from several excavations in Margiana and Bactria (table 5.2). Sample no. 8 came from the deep sounding at Gonur, layer 6, a large charcoal-filled lens of oven sweepings. I was able to collect a sample (no. 9) at Togolok 21 from a dense layer of charcoal sealed beneath a secondary floor at the altar complex (*Bolshoi altar*) in the northeast corner. A third sample (no. 10) came from the northern Bactrian site of Dzharkutan, from the recently excavated temple (courtesy of A. Askarov). This sample, from the central hearth, is associated with typical Bactrian-Margiana finds such as bone tubes, bronze seals, and stone stamp seals, all of which are almost identical to those found at Togolok 21 (Askarov et al. 1988). Four further analyses (nos. 11 through 14) came from hearths in the best-preserved deposits from the southwest corner at Gonur south (Sarianidi 1993). Taken together, these dates associated with Period 2 ceramics cluster around 1900 to 1750 B.C., and there is a 95-percent chance that Period 2 (BMAC) dates belong in the range from 2042 to 1680 B.C.

Three of six previously analyzed samples from Togolok 21 correspond to Period 2 of the Gonur deep sounding. The dates (nos. 15 through 17) cluster around a midpoint of 1800 B.C.. The other dates are too early for any ceramic comparisons and do not form a cluster. The early dates from the previously taken samples at both Togolok 21 and Gonur north may indicate some systematic type of contamination,

CONTEXT	5568 B.P.	Calibrated Date B.C.	Calibrated Range (2 sigma)
1. Gonur north, deep sounding, layer 3 (RC #2) From sloping midden in the sounding 2.60 meters below surface. Beta-33560	3580+/-60	1911 B.C.	2042–1745 B.C.
2. Gonur north Domestic architecture From sealed context just below the floor of Room 2. Beta-35125	3630+/-90	1973 B.C.	2204–1742 B.C.
3. Gonur south Pit beneath Room 48 A large charcoal-filled pit beneath the walls of the main architecture. From before the building was built. Beta-33562	3700+/-60	2084 B.C.	2208–1905 B.C.
4. Gonur south Room 65 Pit beneath BMAC Architecture HEL-2964	3750+/-90	2140 B.C.	2457–1890 B.C.
5. Gonur south Room 134 Pit beneath architecture HEL-2968	3600+/-80	1936 B.C.	2143–1739 B.C.
6. Gonur north, *Kremel,* Room 5 LE 2408	3510+/-40	1811 B.C.	1717–1695 B.C.
7. Gonur north *Kremel*, Layer 1 LE 1207	3560+/-70	1887 B.C.	2042–1733 B.C.

Table 5.1
Margiana Period 1 radiocarbon dates.

CONTEXT	5568 B.P.	Calibrated Date B.C.	Calibrated Range (2 sigma)
8. Gonur north Deep sounding, layer 6, (RC #4) Sloping midden. Beta-33561	3520+/-60	1818 B.C.	1978–1682 B.C.
9. Togolok 21 Bolshoi altar, sealed under secondary floor. Beta-33564	3470+/-100	1748 B.C.	1990–1520 B.C.
10. Djarkutan khram Bolshoi altar. Beta-33557	3540+/-70	1881 B.C.	2035–1682 B.C.
11. Gonur south Room 200, fireplace Phase 1 original construction of building. HEL-2963	3540+/-80	1881 B.C.	2042–1676 B.C.
12. Gonur south Room 226A, hearth Original construction (Phase 1) Near south court complex. HEL-2965	3550+/-80	1884 B.C.	2045–1679 B.C.
13. Gonur south Room 226B Original construction (Phase 1) Near south court complex. HEL-2966	3410+/-80	1728 B.C.	1896–1515 B.C.
14. Gonur south Room 208, chimney Original construction (Phase 1) Narrow room with bullae. HEL-2969	3480+/-90	1758 B.C.	1986–1527 B.C.
15. Togolok 21 Room 60 LE 2678	3270+/-40	1520 B.C.	1628–1433 B.C.
16. Togolok 21 Room 64 LE 2683	3540+/-40	1881 B.C.	1970–1744 B.C.
17. Togolok 21 Room 47 LE 2685	3540+/-40	1881 B.C.	1970–1744 B.C.

Table 5.2
Margiana Period 2 radiocarbon dates.

such as the use of old wood from the surface of the desert.

Period 3

The 1990 excavations of the upper level (Phase 5) at Gonur south revealed poorly preserved architecture associated with a post-BMAC ceramic assemblage very similar to that found at Takhirbai 3. A number of intact hearths provided adequately sized samples, although they came from deposits close to the surface. Both analyses date to 1677 B.C., and the actual date ranges between 1859 and 1520 B.C. (table 5.3).

CONTEXT	5568 B.P.	Calibrated Date B.C.	Calibrated Range (2 sigma)
18. Gonur south Room 178 Upper-level floor near kiln (Phase 5, Takhirbai ceramics). HEL-2967	3380+/-110	1677 B.C.	1937–1419 B.C.
19. Gonur south Room 266 Upper-level room deposit, Central building (Phase 5). HEL-2970	3380+/-90	1677 B.C.	1888–1442 B.C.

Table 5.3
Margiana Period 3 (Takhirbai Period) radiocarbon dates.

These preliminary dates are the first absolute dates for the Takhirbai period in Margiana.

Data not used

Several of the new radiocarbon samples were discarded for specific reasons. The first discarded date (Beta 33559 3300+/-80) is from a hearth deposit located on the first occupational level above the sterile sand in the Gonur deep sounding. The sample contained too little carbon for a determination after processing in the lab.

The second discarded analysis (Beta 33563 3470+/-100) had a heavy 13/12 C ratio, unusual for this region. This indicates a problem with the sample after it was excavated, because no source of isotopically enriched carbon would have been available in the vegetation in this area. The sample was reanalyzed to insure that a processing error had not occurred; it is unclear what might have contaminated this sample.

A third discarded analysis (Beta 33558 4330+/-70) was from a good sample, but the date did not correspond to the cluster of other dates associated with the Period 1 ceramics. This sample, recovered from a hearth on the floor, may have been mixed with older carbon such as coal or bitumen, or may have been old wood that had been found on the desert surface.

Interpretation

When calibrated, the radiocarbon dates for the Bronze Age periods cover a time period from the late third millennium to the mid-second millennium (see fig. 5.1). Gonur depe Period 1, the late Namazga V ceramic complex, dates to circa 2200–1900 B.C. Period 2, as dated from Gonur depe and Togolok 21, dates to circa 2000–1750 B.C. Period 3, preliminarily dated from the upper levels at Gonur, dates to circa 1800–1500 B.C. Although the distributions of radiocarbon dates overlap, the midpoints of each group of samples associated with specific ceramic types are: 2100 B.C. for Period 1, 1850 B.C. for Period 2 and 1650 B.C. for Period 3. Only when the radiocarbon dates are associated with ceramic assemblages can they provide a framework in terms of actual time for the chronology of this Central Asian Bronze Age oasis of Margiana.

PARALLELS

Calibrated radiocarbon results from sites with comparable archaeological material in Iran, the foothill zone of southern Turkmenistan, Bactria, and the Indus valley are presented in the following tables. The tables present the standard deviation range (2 sigma) of the calibrated dates.

The Foothill Zone

Radiocarbon dates from the foothill zone for the Namazga V and Namazga VI periods have been included here from the sites of Altyn depe and Ulug depe (table 5.4).

A series of seven dates from Altyn depe are from general contexts associated with Namazga V ceramics, and five samples are from early Namazga V context—Altyn level 3 (Masson 1970). The dates from any single period at Altyn have no significant mode, and thus cannot be used as a secure basis for dating the Namazga V of the foothill zone.

A series of radiocarbon samples were taken from a test excavation conducted by Shchetenko at Namazga depe tower or citadel (Dolukhanov, Shchetenko, and Tosi 1985). Samples were taken from more than 5.5 m of excavated deposits that span the Namazga V and Namazga VI periods. The Namazga VI levels (the upper 4 m) include a component later than the BMAC period and perhaps even later than the Takhirbai period. The upper Namazga VI architecture at Namazga depe had four dates centering around 1400 B.C. The lower Namazga VI architecture had three dates: one that appears to have been contaminated (too late), one which appears to be from the Namazga V–VI transition, around 1884 B.C., and one around 1477 B.C. Aside from the upper architecture of the Namazga VI levels, the Namazga depe dates, like those from Altyn depe, do not cluster around any mode. Three radiocarbon dates from test excavations of architectural levels at Ulug depe are associated with the mid-Namazga V, late Namazga V, and Namazga VI ceramic assemblages. Only the Namazga VI date from Ulug depe corresponds to the Namazga VI radiocarbon dates from Namazga depe.

None of the other radiocarbon sequences form clusters associated with their respective ceramic assemblages. Future research on Kopet Dag foothill sites will include systematic sampling for radiocarbon data, but the present data do not permit specific comparisons of assemblages with other regions.

Northern and Southern Bactria

Unlike the foothill zone, the desert oases of northern and southern Bactria have provided radiocarbon dates that strongly cluster around a midpoint. When calibrated, the radiocarbon dates from Bactria fit well with the radiocarbon dates for parallel materials from Margiana (table 5.5). Unfortunately, the size and exact provenience of the samples are unknown. It is important to note, however, that these uncalibrated dates have been used to suggest a chronology almost five hundred years later than that indicated by the calibrated dates (Sarianidi 1977). Two radiocarbon dates were analyzed from Sapalli depe, which includes BMAC materials (Askarov 1977). These together with the dates from the southern Bactrian sites of Dashli 1, 2, and 3 (Sarianidi 1977), when calibrated, generally fall into the first half of the second millennium B.C. Most of the radiocarbon samples are from architectural contexts; one is associated with the ceramic corpus from a tomb. These dates support an early second to late third millennium date for the BMAC.

Eastern Bactria: Shortughai

Periodization problems have plagued excavators at Shortughai, because the site had complex stratigraphy and was extensively pitted. Divisions of the site into four discrete time periods (Desse 1989) are unmerited. Two periods (1–2 and 3–4) are defined on the basis of both the stratigraphy and the materials recovered (Francfort 1989) and a large number of radiocarbon analyses were made on these materials (table 5.6).

Period 1–2 at Shortughai is well known for its Harappan connections. These materials grant it the title of the northernmost Harappan site of the Bronze Age (Francfort 1984). The radiocarbon dates from Period 1–2 come from Butte A (rooms 1, 2, and 3). Butte A is a habitation deposit with many pits and later intrusive holes. Several of the radiocarbon samples that came from pits (NY 429, and MC 1727 in particular) deviate strongly from the dates of the

CONTEXT	5568 B.P.	Calibrated Date B.C.	Calibrated Range (2 sigma)
Altyn depe, exc 7 Namazga V (early) LE 767	3140+/-60	1410 B.C.	1519–1261 B.C.
Altyn depe, exc 7 Namazga V (early) LE 769	3260+/-60	1518 B.C.	1678–1408 B.C.
Altyn depe, exc 7 Namazga V (early) BLN 717	4025+/-100	2527 B.C.	2879–2208 B.C.
Altyn depe, exc 5, Room 29 Namazga V (early) LE 770	4660+/-50	3467 B.C.	3620–3342 B.C.
Altyn depe (early NMG V) BLN 716	4120+/-100	2655 B.C.	2913–2409 B.C.
Altyn depe (late NMG V) LE 1097	3540+/-80	1881 B.C.	2122–1676 B.C.
Altyn depe (late NMG V) LE 1048	3770+/-50	2160 B.C.	2330–1988 B.C.
Namazga depe (NMG VI) Upper Architecture R-1297	2870+/-50	1009 B.C.	1199–905 B.C.
Namazga depe (NMG VI) Upper Architecture R-1298	3130+/-40	1405 B.C.	1498–1269 B.C.
Namazga depe (NMG VI) Upper Architecture R-1299	3240+/-50	1513 B.C.	1621–1408 B.C.
Namazga depe (NMG VI) Upper Architecture R-1300	3050+/-50.	1306 B.C.	1416–1128 B.C.
Namazga depe (NMG VI) Upper Architecture R-1300a	2880+/-60	1022 B.C.	1257–901 B.C.
Namazga depe (NMG VI) Upper Architecture R-1301	2960+/-50	1145 B.C.	1372–1003 B.C.
Namazga depe (NMG VI) Lower Architecture R-1302	3220+/-90	1477 B.C.	1684–1267 B.C.
Namazga depe (NMG VI) Lower Architecture R-1303	2680+/-95	818 B.C.	1010–546 B.C.
Namazga depe (NMG VI) Lower Architecture R-1304	3550+/-50	1884 B.C.	2021–1742 B.C.

Table 5.4
Namazga V and VI periods, radiocarbon dates from the foothill zone **(continued on page 83).**

Table 5.4 (continued)

Namazga depe (NMG V) R-1305	3380+/-140	1677 B.C.	2026–1328 B.C.
Namazga depe (NMG V) R-1306	3760+/-50	2166 B.C.	2319–1984 B.C.
Namazga depe (NMG V) R-1306a	4080+/-50	2586 B.C.	2869–2468 B.C.
Namazga depe (NMG V) R-1307	3860+/-40	2315 B.C.	2460–2147 B.C.
Namazga depe (NMG V) R-1308	3770+/-40	2160 B.C.	2296–2037 B.C.
Namazga depe (NMG V) R-1309	3550+/-40	1884 B.C.	1974–1747 B.C.
Ulug depe (NMG V) LE 1098	3910+/-50.	2423 B.C.	2554–2203 B.C.
Ulug depe (NMG V) LE 1096	3500+/-50	1843 B.C.	1938–1682 B.C.
Ulug depe, exc 2, upper level Namazga VI LE 980	3280+/-95	1522 B.C.	1749–1324 B.C.

CONTEXT	5568 B.P.	Calibrated Date B.C.	Calibrated Range (2 sigma)
Sapalli depe BMAC Period LE 916	3640+/-90	2009 B.C.	2277–1745 B.C.
Sapalli depe BMAC Period LE 1078	3450+/-50	1742 B.C.	1885–1624 B.C.
Dashli 1, Room 18 BMAC Period? LE 976	3200+/-45	1443 B.C..	1526–1395 B.C.
Dashli 1, Room 24 BMAC Period? LE 975	3520+/-45	1818 B.C.	1946–1695 B.C.
Dashli 2, pit BMAC Period? LE 977	3340+/-40	1619 B.C.	1735–1517 B.C.
Dashli 3, burial BMAC Period LE 978	3440+/-50	1740 B.C.	1882–1617 B.C.
Dashli 3, 'palace' BMAC Period LE 1252	3670+/-50	1991 B.C.	2191–1889 B.C.

Table 5.5
Radiocarbon dates from northern and southern Bactria, BMAC period.

CONTEXT	5568 B.P.	Calibrated Date B.C.	Calibrated Range (2 sigma)
Shortughai, Butte A, Room P1 C59, just above virgin soil Period 1 MC 2447	3725+/-80	2073 B.C..	2395–1988 B.C.
Shortughai, Butte A Level 6, Room P1 Period 1 MC 2446	3890+/-80	2379 B.C.	2573–2058 B.C.
Shortughai, Butte A Room P2, beneath Floor 9 Period 1 MC 1726	3875+/-95	2389 B.C.	2580–2036 B.C.
Shortughai, Butte A Room P2, Hearth 2 on Floor 9 Period 1 or 2 NY 425	4040+/-100	2519 B.C.	2882–2284 B.C.
Shortughai, Butte A Room P2, Floor 8 (AI) Period 1 NY 430	4075+/-95	2584 B.C.	2887–2341 B.C.
Shortughai, Butte A Level 3, Room 1 Period 2 MC 2445	3890+/-80	2379 B.C.	2573–2058 B.C.
Shortughai, Butte A Room 2–3, Floor 6 Period 2 NY 428	4190+/-125	2715 B.C.	3086–2459 B.C.
Shortughai, Butte B Level 3, beneath Room 17 Period 3 MC 1729	3620+/-105	1957 B.C.	2281–1686 B.C.
Shortughai, Butte B Level 4, Room 14 Period 4 NY 421	3535+/-165	1831 B.C.	2322–1446 B.C.
Shortughai, Butte B Level 1, Hearth #2 P5 Period 4 MC-1730	3640+/-95	2009 B.C.	2281–1742 B.C.

Table 5.6
Radiocarbon dates from eastern Bactria.

other samples, and should not be included in determining the general radiocarbon chronology. If the samples taken from pits are discounted as well (NY 422, NY 424, NY 427 and MC 1728), the midpoints of the samples for Period 1–2 fall between 2600 and 2200 B.C.

On the basis of the small finds, parallels, and ceramics from the Indus valley, Francfort argues that Shortughai Period 1–2 is contemporary with late mature Harappan, dated to circa 2200–1700 B.C., whereas Jarrige suggests that an earlier, 2500–2200 B.C. range is more appropriate. The radiocarbon dates support Jarrige's view.

All the Period 3–4 architecture was excavated on Butte B. Period 3–4 has ceramic and small find parallels with the BMAC (Period 2 in Margiana) (Francfort 1981). Several radiocarbon dates from indeterminate contexts on Butte B are unusually young, and a sample from a pit (MC 1728) is aberrantly old. The radiocarbon samples from good context (MC 1729, NY 421, and MC 1730) cluster at the beginning of the second millennium, similar to the dates of the parallel materials from Margiana.

The absolute chronology of Shortughai is a key to understanding the chronology of Indus valley-Central Asian interaction: The Harappan outpost of Shortughai 1–2, predates the desert oases of northern and southern Bactria and Margiana. Indus type artifacts are found in early/mid-Namazga V levels at Altyn depe, but none have *so far* been found in the Period 1 levels in Margiana. By Period 3–4, Shortughai no longer had Harappan type archaeological materials, but had artifacts and ceramics similar to Margiana Period 2 and the BMAC small finds. It may be that there is no occupational continuity at Shortughai from Period 1–2 to Period 3–4. The strategic location of the site of Shortughai would have made it an obvious place to reoccupy had it been abandoned at the end of Period 1–2.

South Asia

Shortughai Period 1–2 is contemporary with the urban or mature Harappan phase (table 5.7), based on a cluster of dates from Mohenjo daro and from Harappa (Possehl 1989). More than 20 well provenienced radiocarbon dates from the mature or urban phase at Harappa (Meadow 1991:42–56) confirm this dating. This clearly shows that the BMAC *is not* contemporary with the urban phase (Harappa IIIa–b), despite the identification of several isolated BMAC type artifacts in the Indus valley. For example, a stepped diamond-shaped steatite amulet bearing the image of an eagle has been commonly illustrated as an Indus valley object (Childe 1953); however, this object is *typical* of the BMAC and comes from the uppermost level at Harappa, most likely from late mature Harappan levels (Harappa period IIIc). There are many stylistic parallels between small finds from the Jhukar (Late Harappan) levels at Mohenjo daro (Marshall 1931) and at the site of Chanhu daro (Mackay 1943). The parallels may, in fact, be BMAC imports into the Indus valley. There is only a single Jhukar period radiocarbon date (from Mohenjo daro—TF-75), which matches with the Central Asian area of Margiana and Bactria.

Iranian Plateau

BMAC-related artifacts, or actual imports from Central Asia, are found throughout the Iranian plateau and have been used to cross-date the Central Asia material. Greyware ceramics similar to those from the upper levels of Tureng tepe have been found in Period 2 Margiana and Bactria (Sarianidi 1990). Margiana Period 2 (BMAC) type artifacts have been found both at Tureng tepe and at Hissar IIIC. These artifacts are generally found in burials and in caches of artifacts called hoards similar to the cenotaphs of Period 2 in Margiana and Bactria. Radiocarbon data from both Tureng tepe IIIC2 and Hissar IIIC cluster in the early second millennium, which reconfirms an early-second-millennium date for the BMAC complex (table 5.8).

CONCLUSIONS

The radiocarbon data from Margiana provide an excellent absolute date for the Bronze Age oasis occupation. The Margiana cluster of dates for Period 1 (2100 B.C.), Period 2 (1850 B.C.), and Period 3 (1650 B.C.) can be compared to other dates from Central Asia and to dates from related occupations on the Iranian plateau and in South Asia. Within the absolute range so established, a refined chronology must still rely on style and forms of ceramics and small finds.

CONTEXT	5568 B.P.	Calibrated Date B.C.	Calibrated Range (2 sigma)
Mohenjo daro mature or urban phase P 1177	3985+/-64	2469 B.C.	2842–2299 B.C.
Mohenjo daro mature or urban phase P 1179	3913+/-64	2420 B.C.	2569–2149 B.C.
Mohenjo daro mature or urban phase P 1180	3828+/-61	2212 B.C.	2462–2043 B.C.
Mohenjo daro mature or urban phase P 1178A	3802+/-59	2201 B.C.	2455–2035 B.C.
Mohenjo daro mature or urban phase P 1176	3801+/-59	2201 B.C.	2455–2035 B.C.
Mohenjo daro mature or urban phase P 1182A	3702+/-63	2083 B.C.	2281–1898 B.C.
Harappa mature or urban phase WIS-2219	3910+/-65	2423 B.C.	2568–2147 B.C.
Harappa mature or urban phase QL-4484	3730+/-30	2071 B.C.	2198–1987 B.C.
Harappa mature or urban phase QL-4483	3784+/-30	2152 B.C.	2288–2048 B.C.
Harappa mature or urban phase WIS-2220	3815+/-60	2243 B.C.	2459–2039 B.C.
Harappa mature or urban phase WIS-2221	3940+/-120	2459 B.C.	2869–2041 B.C.
Harappa mature or urban phase QL-4488	3750+/-40	2140 B.C.	2282–2030 B.C.
Harappa mature or urban phase QL-4487	3816+/-25	2237 B.C.	2329–2143 B.C.
Mohenjo daro Late Harappan or Jhukhar Period TF 75	3600+/-110	1936 B.C.	2277–1676 B.C.

Table 5.7
Representative radiocarbon dates from the Indus valley.

CONTEXT	5568 B.P.	Calibrated Date B.C.	Calibrated nge (2 sigma)
Tepe Hissar, main mound, upper strata Hissar IIIC P 2620	3610+/-70	1944 B.C.	2140–1748 B.C.
Tepe Hissar, Treasure Hill below top two building levels Hissar IIIC TUNC 20	3480+/-60	1758 B.C.	1938–1631 B.C.
Tureng tepe Period IIIC2 LY 1147	3580+/-130	1911 B.C.	2285–1538 B.C.
Tureng tepe Period IIIC LY 2302	3690+/-130	2089 B.C.	2462–1699 B.C.
Tureng tepe Period IIIC LY 2301	3620+/-130	1957 B.C.	2393–1634 B.C.
Tureng tepe Period IIIC TUNC 42	3520+/-70	1836 B.C.	2027–1676 B.C.

Table 5.8
Radiocarbon dates from northern Iran.

CHAPTER SIX

The Earliest Architecture at Gonur Depe

HUNDREDS OF ROOMS IN MANY BUILDINGS IN MARGIANA have been mapped by Soviet archaeologists, yet little information about room contents or associations of artifacts with rooms has been reported. The goal of the architectural analysis in this study was to record detailed contextual information from a small sample of rooms, allowing us to suggest functional contexts for an assemblage of artifacts that have been found in a wide geographic area. The results of this fine-grained study are a tool to apply to the large body of excavated rooms in Margiana (including those from Gonur depe).

This study of the architecture from Gonur is based on fieldwork I conducted in 1989 while participating in excavations there. I used three approaches in evaluating the architecture at Gonur: (1) my own excava-

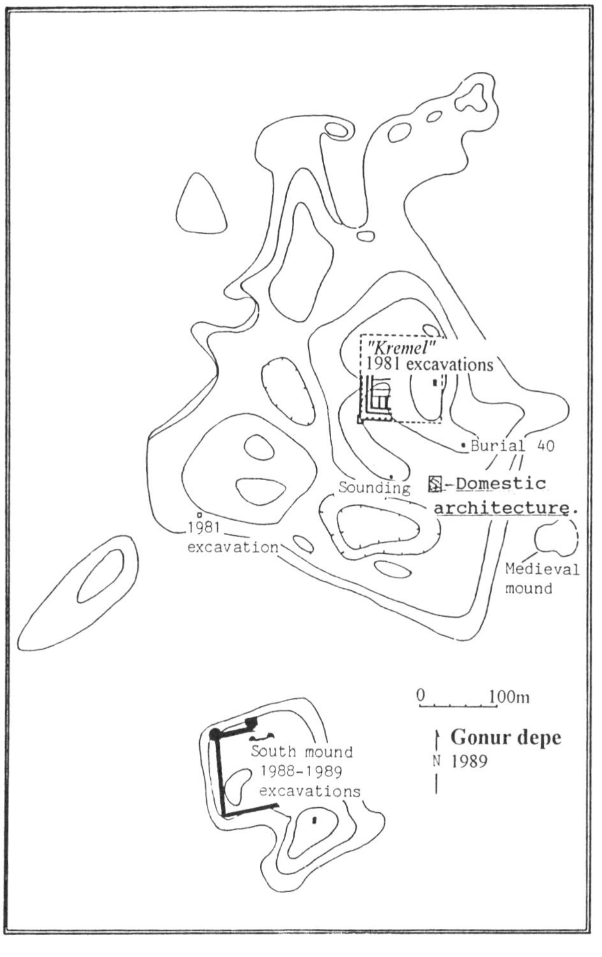

Figure 6.1
Gonur north: location of the domestic architecture, excavations of 1989.

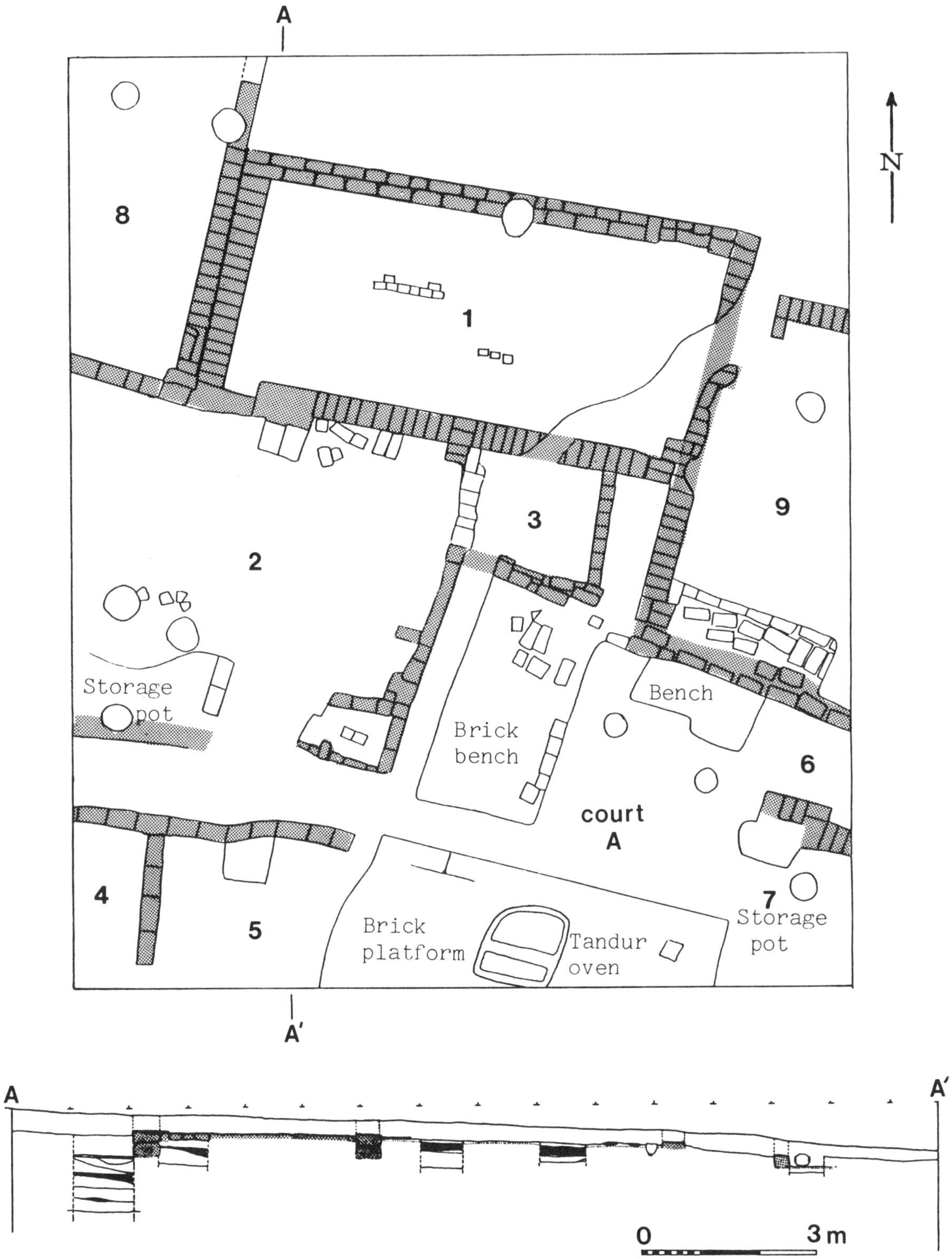

Figure 6.2
Domestic architecture. Shaded areas are wall foundations. Brick pattern indicates overall brick floor or platform.

tions of Bronze Age oasis domestic architecture; (2) observations and detailed descriptions of the monumental architecture on the north mound that had been dug from 1978 to 1981; and (3) participation in the ongoing excavations of monumental architecture from the south mound.

BRONZE AGE HOUSE

Fifty meters to the east of the 1989 deep sounding was an area where the ceramic scatter was dense and several isolated artifacts lay on the surface (fig. 6.1). A small test pit (Locus 44) in this area revealed architecture 30 to 35 cm below the surface, overlaying earlier stratified occupational debris. I excavated the upper architecture in an area of 13 x 17 m and conducted several soundings beneath the architecture.

The architecture in this excavation is composed of large rooms connected by courtyards and alleyways (fig. 6.2). Three rooms (1 through 3) form a single apartment or household, with an east-west running alleyway opening onto a courtyard. A series of rooms (4 through 9) appears to be part of a different domestic complex unconnected to the main apartment.

The excavation methods used here differed from the deep sounding in that separate locus numbers were given to units that could be room fill material from the floors, test probes, or separately excavated features. These locus numbers (36 through 55) follow sequentially those employed in the deep sounding.

Phases are based on architectural modifications such as rebuilt floors and walls. Brick size can be used as an indicator of phase based on size and form.

Materials from on and near the surface were systematically collected. The top 25 to 30 cm consisted of laminated, hard, thin sediments mixed with soft dusty deposit. This deposit, like the surface layer in the deep sounding, contains windblown artifacts layered in sand. It was removed down to a firm undisturbed deposit using a blade attached to a tractor. This intact surface was brushed thoroughly, and the area was excavated by removing 15 to 20 cm of upper fill until wall lines became visible and rooms could be defined. The depth of deposit in the rooms is between 15 and 35 cm above the floor and below the preserved tops of the walls. This indicates heavy deflation over time in the area, a phenomenon typical of Bronze Age Margiana sites with architecture.

Rooms 1 and 2 of the main apartment have two floors. The upper floor was entirely excavated, but the lower floor was exposed only in subfloor soundings (fig. 6.3). These tests also show that the whole complex was built on sloping midden, with the walls following the slope of the mound. The mud bricks were generally of standard size (20 x 45 x 15 cm) with 1 to 3 cm of light brown mud mortar between them.

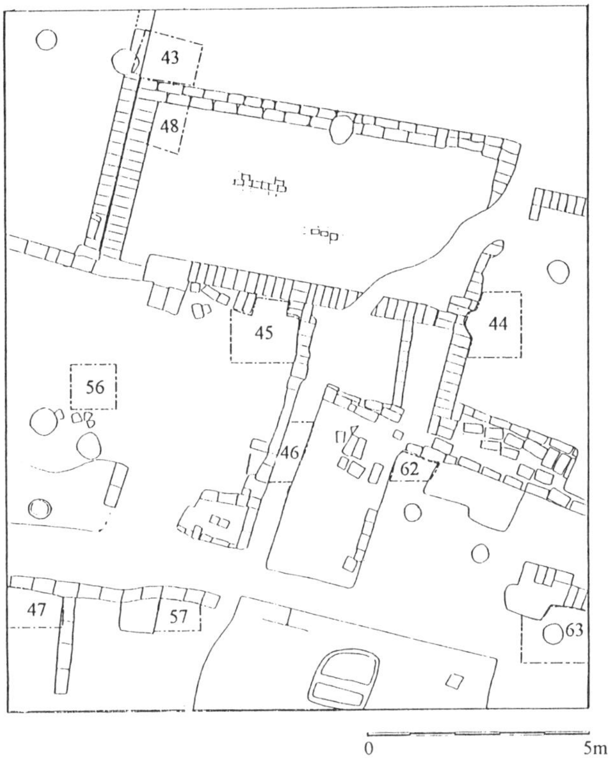

Figure 6.3
Location of soundings beneath floors of the architecture (numbered by locus unit).

Room 1

The central room of the main apartment, Room 1, measures 7.75 m x 3.3 m (25.6 sq m). Several features of this room set it apart from the other rooms. Most important, it has a brick floor, with 14 x 14 x 20 cm brick pieces (half bricks) separated by wide (3 to 4 cm) bands of mortar. The brick floor is a *zakladka*, (fig. 6.4) previously found only in the monumental architecture at Togolok 21 and Togolok 1, where it is brick fill above an existing floor. In the Togolok buildings, *zakladka* (Russian for "filling") apparently were not

Figure 6.4
Room 1 *zakladka*-type upper floor.

used as flooring but as fill to seal off a room. Here it was clearly used as a floor, since ceramics were in place on it and there was a burned area around the hearth in the north wall.

The hearth in Room 1 is 55 cm in diameter and partially built into the wall. It was preserved only at floor level, but is similar to the type of wall hearths better preserved in Bactria at Dashli 1 (Sarianidi 1977:32, photo), Sapalli (Askarov 1977), and Kelleli 4 Room 30 (Masimov 1984:16), and at Tepe Yahya in Iran (trench B, room B/C, Period IVA). An erosional feature runs through the southeast corner of Room 1, but the entire floor of the room was originally bricked. The four walls of Room 1 are each 40 cm thick; the bricks were laid using the header and stretcher construction technique. In contrast, the walls of Rooms 2 and 3 are only one brick thick (20 to 40 cm).

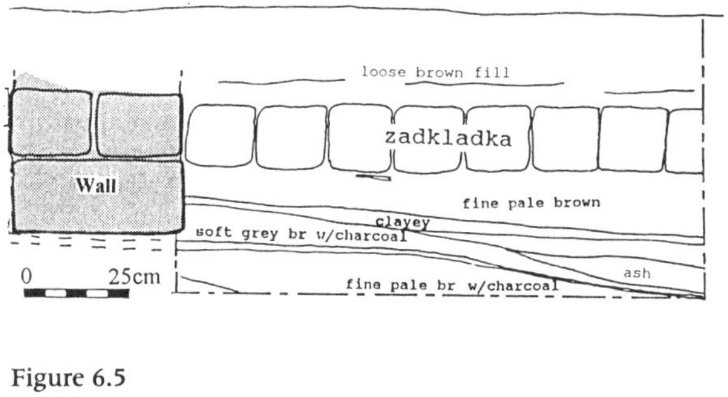

Figure 6.5
East section of Room 1 (locus 48).

Room 1 is connected to Room 2 by a raised doorsill formed by a narrow series of mud bricks across the doorway. Many rooms at Togolok 1, Togolok 21, and Kelleli 3 and 4 have raised doorsills rather than openings flush with the floor. Raised doorsills are still seen in the traditional mud brick architecture of Central Asia where doorways lead to covered rooms. A small mud plaster threshold is in front of the doorsill in Room 2. Similar doorsills are found at Hissar in the Burned Room, including a compressed mud threshold leading into the room (Dyson and Remsen 1989:93). The relatively thick walls, the raised doorsill, the hearth built into the wall, and the brick floor all suggest that Room 1 was roofed.

A test beneath the floor of Room 1 (locus 48) showed that the *zakladka* bricks are 18 cm deep and irregularly broken off (fig. 6.5). The brick layer lies on soft greyish brown sediment and ash, containing sherds and charcoal. This soft deposit itself lies on the original floor of the room composed of very fine grey clay. Sherds were found directly on this floor, which laps up against the edge of the brick of the wall on the north. Along the west wall of Room 1, *zakladka* bricks lie against a fire-reddened section of the wall. This floor lies on the sloping, soft greyish brown soil

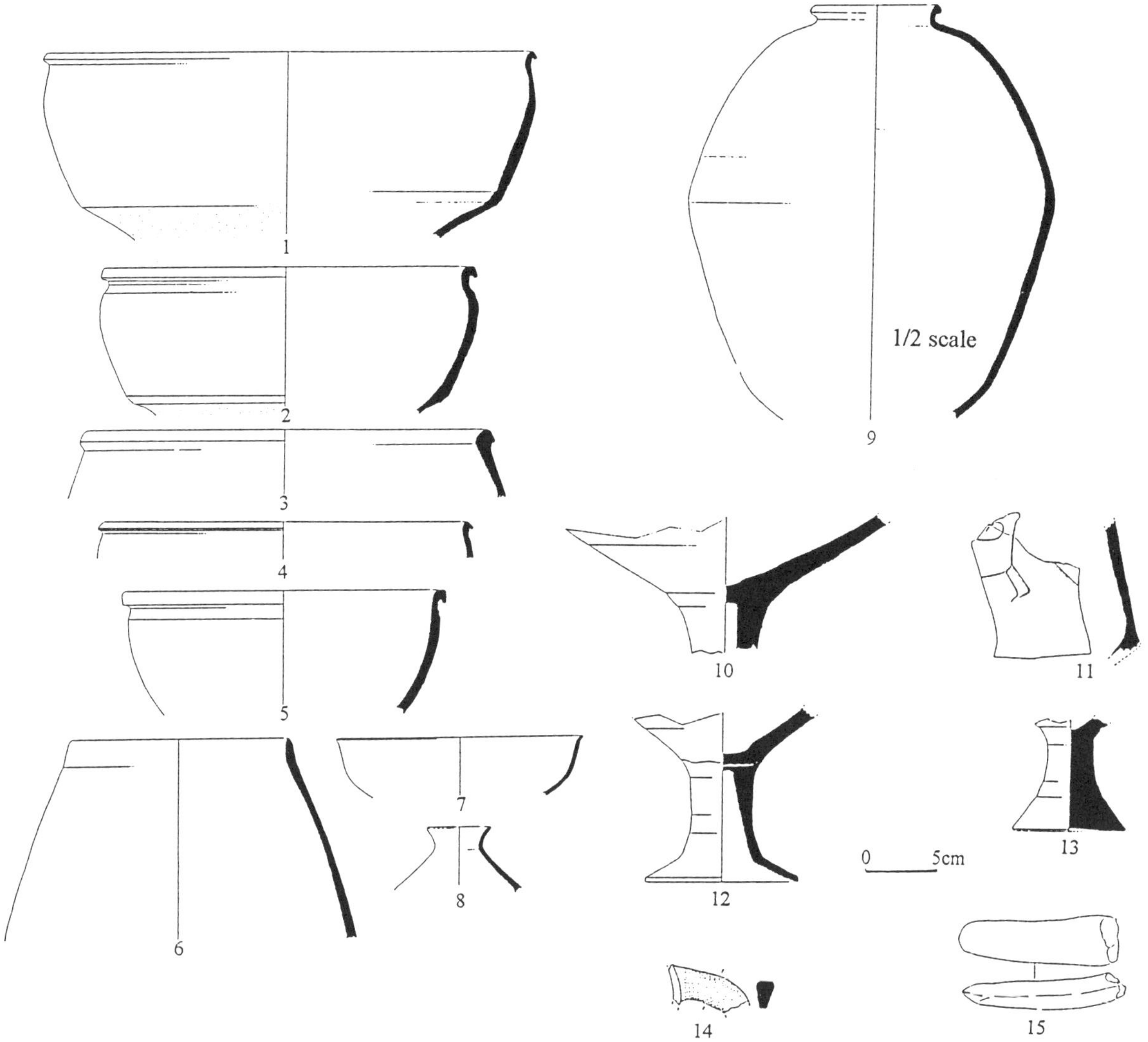

Figure 6.6
Finds from the floors of Rooms 1 and 2.
1) Locus 49, type 3.A.1, reddish buff, med.-fine chaff; 2) Locus 49, type 3.A.1, red, med.-fine chaff; 3) Locus 49, type 3.B.1, buff, med.-fine chaff; 4) Locus 42, type 2.B.2, reddish buff, med.-fine chaff; 5) Locus 37, type 3.A.1, red, med.-fine chaff; 6) Locus 37, type 2.B.1, buff, red core, med.-fine chaff; 7) Locus 37, type 2.A.1, buff, med.-fine chaff; 8) Locus 58, type 1.B.3, red, buff int. and ext., med.-fine chaff; 9) Locus 58, type 3.B.2, reddish buff, med.-fine chaff; 10) Locus 53, type 2.A, buff, med.-fine chaff; 11) Locus 37, type 3.A.1.3, buff, med.-fine chaff; 12) Locus 37, type 2.A, buff, med.-fine chaff; 13) Locus 37, type 2.A, buff, med.-fine chaff; 14) Locus 37, handle, red, coarse grog temper, handmade; 15) Locus 37, grey crystalline smoothing stone.

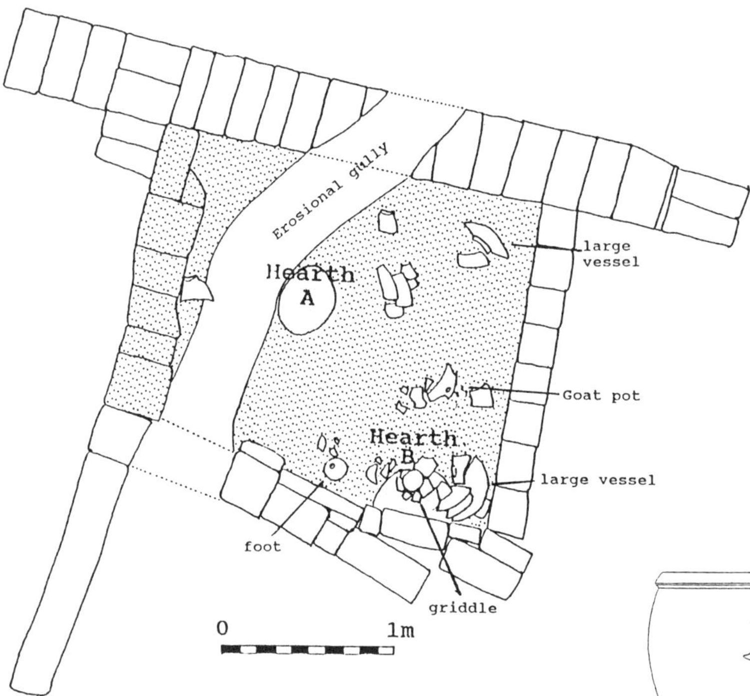

Figure 6.7
Room 3, domestic architecture, Gonur north.

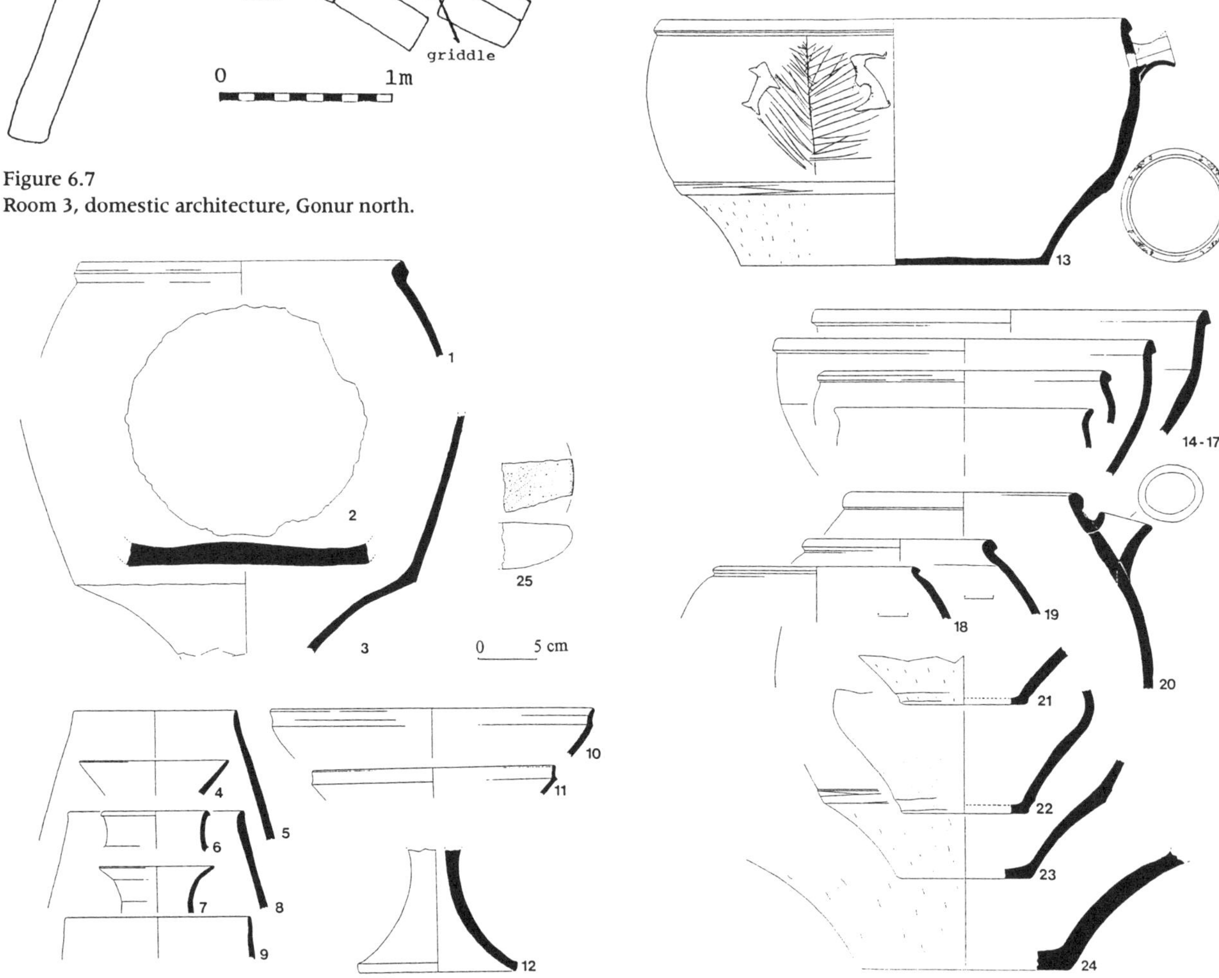

Figure 6.8
Finds from Room 3. 1–3) Handmade coarseware; 4–24) wheelmade ceramics; 25) grinding stone fragment.

containing sherds and charcoal found beneath the entire area of excavation.

Room 2

Room 2 is large, 5 m by at least 7.5 m. The open entrance has no threshold and leads to the alleyway. The east wall of room 2 is partially eroded by the gully, but appears to have originally been no more than 20 to 40 cm wide. In the southwest corner, the floor contains brick fragments in an irregular pattern. The rest of the floor in room 2 is made of tamped earth.

An upside-down storage jar (*khom*) was found buried along the base of the south wall. The base of this jar had been broken off at floor level and was covered with a large sherd. Pots embedded in walls and under floors are found in many other areas at Gonur and at Togolok 21. The upturned vessel with its base broken off may have been used for storage of dry materials. Its location under the floor at the base of the wall would have provided a cool and dry storage area.

Two shallow basins in the floor near the south wall were used as hearths. These hearths, 46 and 50 cm in diameter, are rich in charcoal, ash, and burned bone. Hearth 1 is particularly rich in charcoal, and flotation samples were taken from this installation. Hearth 2 is full of burned bone of medium-sized mammals (sheep/goat), charcoal, and burned fragments of daub (Moore 1993a).

The large size of the room, the hearths on the floor, and the thinness of the walls suggest that this room was not roofed. The ceramics found in Rooms 1 and 2 consisted of large storage and processing vessels and large-diameter thin-walled vessels (fig. 6.6). Artifacts found on the floor include a sherd of the lower part of a large open pot with an incised depiction of an animal, a handle from a handmade, coarse kitchenware vessel, and a small, very smooth rubbing stone.

The floor of room 2 consists of brick fragments in a tamped earth matrix but, unlike Room 1, shows no discernible brick pattern in the floor. An earlier floor lies 15 to 20 cm below the upper floor and the fill between the floors contains dark charcoal-laden deposits. A radiocarbon sample (Beta 35125) was taken from the sealed context between the two floors at locus 45. Below this reddened ashy clay floor, soft midden deposits were found which sloped downhill to the south.

Room 3

The floor of room 2 continues underneath a section of the east wall toward Room 3. The wall separating Room 3 from Room 2 was built as a later architectural addition.

Room 3 (1.5 x 2 m) has a specially prepared floor made of firm yellowish brown clay with white plaster specks (fig. 6.7). Most of the ceramics lie on top of a thin layer of windblown sand that covered the original floor as if the sand had purposely been laid during the room's use. A slightly raised hearth (hearth A) of tamped earth contains fragments of burned brick and burned grasses (no bone or charcoal).

The ceramics in Room 3 appear to have been in situ, having a functional relationship to each other (fig. 6.8) Several vessels were stacked one on another. A pottery sherd chipped into a disk (20 cm diameter) had been used as a griddle and lay on a prepared base of coarseware sherds that in turn lay on a soft black film of burned chaff and stems (hearth B). Near this assemblage was a handmade grog-tempered storage vessel (*khom*). Its form exactly duplicates the wheelmade wares, including the characteristic incurving base of the large wheelmade *khomcha* and *khomi*. A cluster of ceramics that included a finely made foot for a tall-footed vessel also was found. On the north side of the room, a fragment of a grinding stone lay among another cluster of sherds. In the corner to the east was part of a basin with a large oval spout similar to spouted vessels from Kelleli 3 (Masimov 1981:201, figs. 4, 8). Another large spouted basin was found on the floor. It had two sets of incised tree motifs on its side, with animal figures applied to each side of the tree as if they were climbing the tree. It is likely that there were originally four sets of motifs. These animal figures were hand modeled and then pressed into the side of the vessel after the tree had been incised.

It has been suggested that in traditional pre-Islamic Central Asia, each household had a shrine (Grenet 1987). This is a Zoroastrian tradition thought to have come from a pre-Zoroastrian Central Asian pattern (Boyce 1975). Room 3 could be interpreted as a early example of the Central Asian household shrine. The well-made floor of Room 3, the unusual hearth, and the distinctive ceramics set it apart from the other rooms of the domestic architecture. A similar area at Kelleli 4 (on a platform) is also considered a small shrine or ritual area. The occurrence of shrines at a household level would be consistent with the widespread discovery of ritual objects such as figurines at sites throughout Margiana, rather than clustered around temples.

Other household shrines dating to the Bronze Age have been identified in neighboring regions. A similar room (Room 10) at Altyn depe excavation 10 is thought to be a household shrine (Masimov 1973). The Burned Building at Hissar also has a household shrine that may be compared to Gonur Room 3 in terms of construction and artifacts (Schmidt 1937:164; Dyson and Remsen 1989:96–97).

Court A

To the south of Room 2 leading to Court A is an alleyway with a sloping surface of compacted dirt, 1.10 m wide. Court A has raised brick benches and a platform on three of its sides. Two circular hearths each about 45 to 50 cm in diameter dot the reddened dirt surface of the courtyard (fig. 6.9).

Two benches on the northern part of Court A were preserved to 20 cm above the floor surface of the court and have brick fall from the nearby walls above them. The face of the benches was coated with mud plaster. Bricks laid end to end form the perimeter of the benches, while the center parts have irregularly laid bricks and brick fragments placed in a mud matrix. The west bench is cut off from the west wall by the erosional gully.

The brick platform on the south side of the excavation is cut on its west side by the erosional gully but was originally about 6.5 m wide. Like the other benches in the courtyard, this platform has a line of bricks running around it and a composite of brick fragments inside. The base of an oven with two chambers, one small and one large, was found on the surface of this platform (fig. 6.10). Its plastered sides were burned, and it had a hard layer of grey ash at the bottom, similar to the ash found at the bottom of ceramic kilns. This two-chamber oven is similar to a communal *tandur* oven, still in use in Turkmenistan. In modern ovens, the deep chamber is the fire chamber and the shallow broad chamber is for cooking meat or bread. Similar ovens from the Bronze Age are found in the courtyard of Kelleli 4 (Masimov 1984, fig 1); Dashli 3 (Sarianidi 1977); Altyn depe (excavations 9,10) (Masson 1981a, fig. 12), Shortughai (Room P21, Period 3) (Francfort 1989, pl. 8); and Susa (Gasche 1986).

The ceramics from Court A (fig. 6.11) are similar to those from Rooms 1 and 2 of the house and include a complete trumpet-shaped vessel on the floor of the court next to the southern platform. A fragment of a vessel on legs made of the local ware provides a close parallel to similar legged vessels from Altyn depe levels 0 through 2.

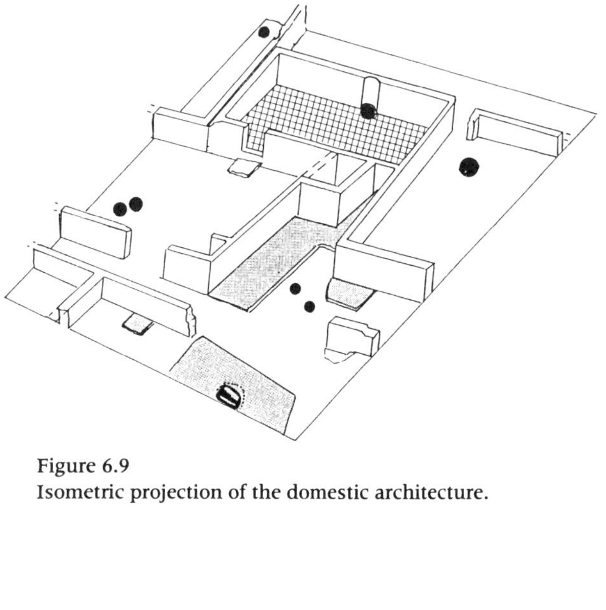

Figure 6.9
Isometric projection of the domestic architecture.

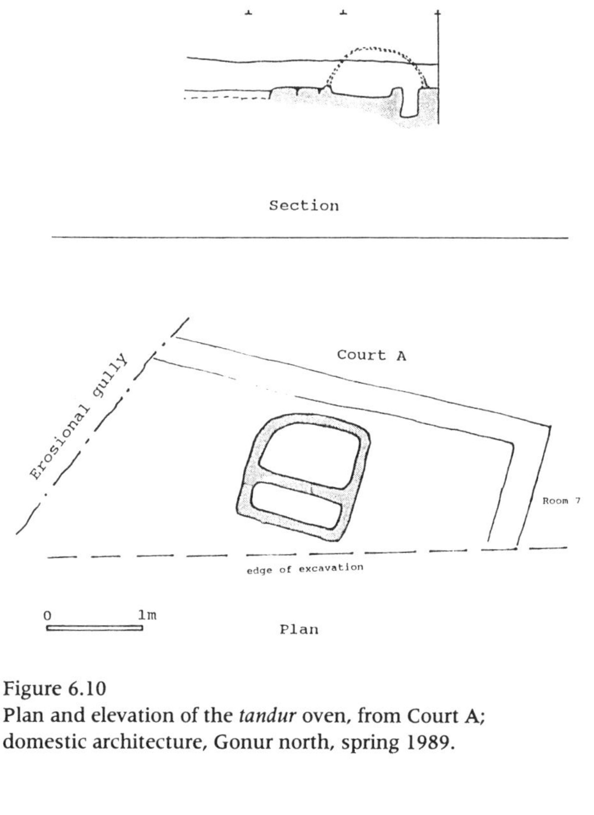

Figure 6.10
Plan and elevation of the *tandur* oven, from Court A; domestic architecture, Gonur north, spring 1989.

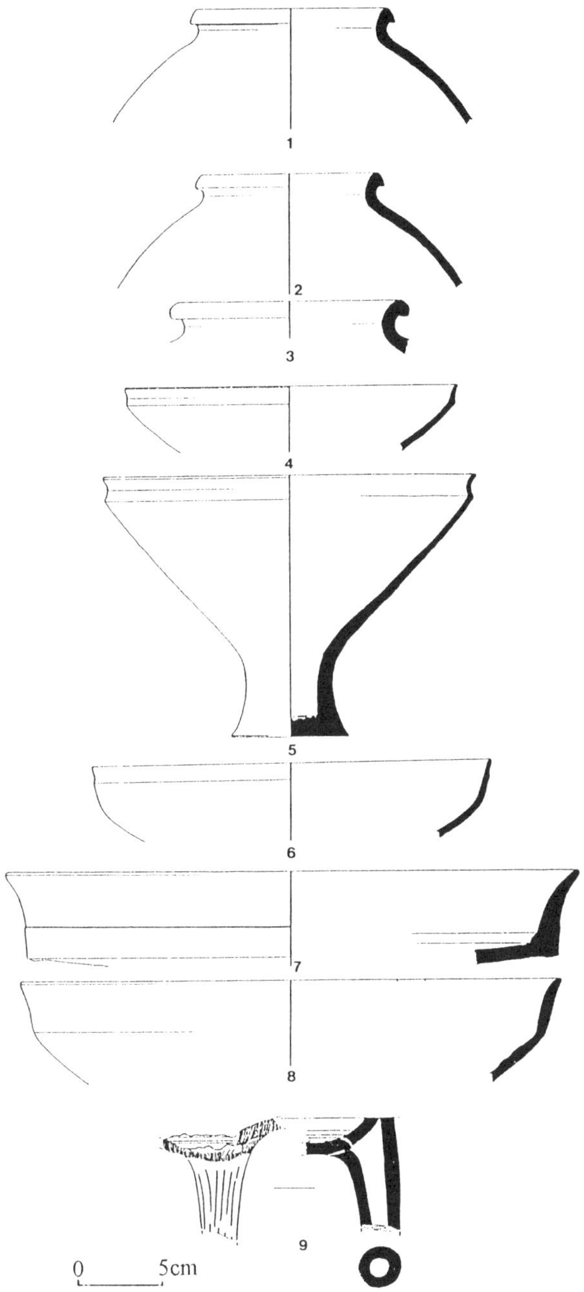

Figure 6.11
Ceramics from the floor of Court A.
1. Locus 41, type 3.B.2, red, med.-fine chaff.
2. Locus 41, type 3.B.2, reddish buff, med.-fine chaff.
3. Locus 42, type 3.B.2, misfire, red, grey core, med.-fine chaff.
4. Locus 49, type 2.A.2, reddish buff, med.-fine chaff.
5. Locus 50, type 2.A.2, buff rim, red base, med.-fine chaff.
6. Locus 49, type 2.A.1, reddish buff, med.-fine chaff.
7. Locus 49, type 2.A.1, red, med.-fine chaff.
8. Locus 49, type 2.A.1, buff, med.-fine chaff.
9. Locus 51, import, greyish buff, fine, shaved exterior.

SURROUNDING ROOMS

All of the rooms outside of Rooms 1, 2, and 3 appear to be parts of other domestic units. If this main apartment was indeed one household, then the courtyard was probably shared by several households similar in structure. These houses were adjacent to each other, shared walls, and were connected by alleyways.

To the southeast of Court A was a room (Room 7) probably belonging to a different house separated by a continuation of the alleyway ("Room" 6). A large storage vessel was set in a depression 25 cm below the floor of Room 7. The circular depression in the floor provided a stable support for the small bases of the storage jars.

Rooms 4 and 5

Rooms 4 and 5 appear to have been large open rooms (similar to Room 2) or yards, which are set apart from the main apartment by an alleyway. A 1-m sounding in Room 4 (locus 47) revealed a tamped mud floor or living surface 12 to 15 cm below the preserved top of the wall. The alleyway wall is only 20 cm thick at its base with the bricks laid end to end. Examples of well-preserved walls of this thickness are found in Bronze Age architecture either as fences for open areas or as interior walls.

A small mud brick workbench 80 x 80 cm, was excavated in Room 5. Ceramics and a piece of a grinding stone were found on this platform (fig. 6.12:1). The gully cutting across the excavation eroded the wall between Room 5 and the bench in Court A.

Room 8

Room 8 shares its southern wall with Room 2, and its east wall was built up against the west wall of Room 1. It has a poorly preserved upper floor on which a terracotta human figurine was found (fig. 6.12:6). Several centimeters below the upper floor is a very firm dirt floor with two hearths. One hearth was built into the wall and probably had a chimney. This type of hearth may indicate that this room, like Room 1, was covered.

Room 9

Room 9, to the east of Room 1, has an open doorway to the north, apparently unconnected to the main apartment. The fill of the room contained finely stratified mud brick collapse and ash, lying on greyish brown floor deposit. The floor was hard tamped earth with the remains of a hearth in a small depression. The floor was built on sloping midden similar to that found in other subfloor soundings, and there was no other floor in this room. Room 9 has hearths in the middle of the room and an open entranceway similar to Room 2 of the main apartment. Along the southern wall of Room 9 was found the base of a bench with mud plaster on the northern edge.

Artifacts from Room 9 include ceramics, a single piece of stone inlay made of white limestone, and a fragment of a schist rod with an original diameter of 3 to 4 cm (fig. 6.12:3, 5). These latter two fragments are from larger objects. Stone inlay has been found in elite burials from Namazga V contexts at Altyn (Masson 1981b) and Ulug depe (unpublished *opisi*), and the schist fragment is similar to stone staffs found in burials of Namazga V and in BMAC burials, such as at Sibri. So far, no other examples of schist staffs have been found in Margiana.

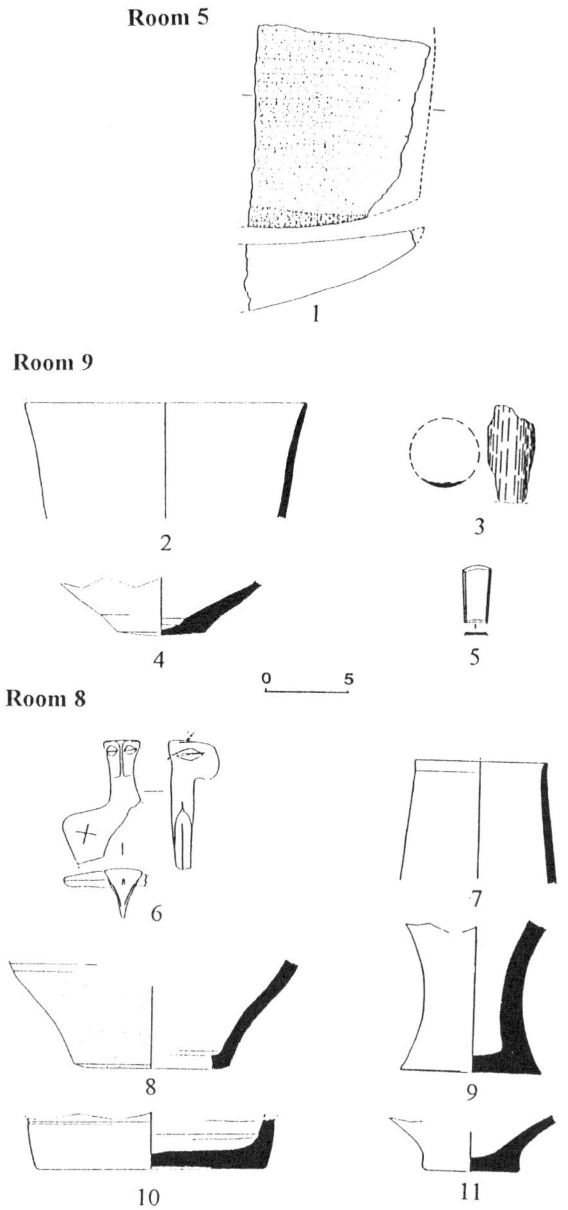

Figure 6.12
Finds from the floors of Rooms 5–9.
1) Grinding stone; 2) Ceramic (type 1.A.1) local ware; 3) Fragment of a cylindrical rod, schist; 4) Ceramic (2.A.4 or 2.B base) local ware; 5) White stone inlay; 6) Terracotta figurine, applied eyes, incised sign on shoulder; 7) Ceramic (type 2.B.1) local ware; 8) Ceramic (type 3 base) local ware; 9) Ceramic (type 2.A base) local ware; 10) Ceramic, flat-bottomed base, local ware; 11) Ceramic, string-cut base, local ware.

CERAMICS

The ceramics from the domestic architecture are similar to those from layers 1 through 4 of the deep sounding, 50 m to the west. These types of ceramics form the first widespread horizon of ceramics in Margiana (Period 1) and represent the earliest *period* of Bronze Age occupation, although not the first occupation. Here, as in the deep sounding, the Period 1 ceramics and small finds are found in several architectural levels.

Closed pots and jars and closed cylindrical basins (*khomchi*) are very common, comprising almost half of all of the identifiable rim sherds from the floors (fig. 6.13). Other common forms are the large storage vessels (*khomi*) (including vessels buried under walls), biconical jars of various sizes, deep open bowls with simple rims, vases with a deep foot and a carination at the shoulder, and wide open basins with molded bases. In this domestic assemblage, open carinated-rim vessels are rare. Small fragments of greyware

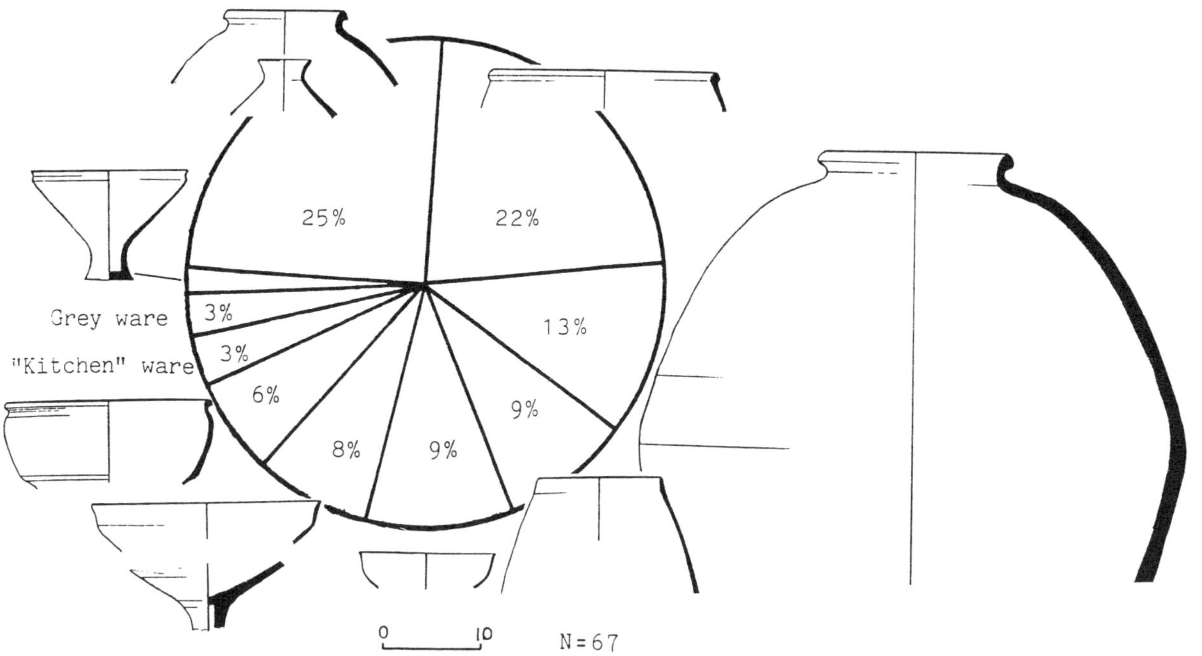

Figure 6.13
Ceramics from the floor of the domestic architecture, Gonur north.

found in the upper fill of Rooms 1 and 2 are similar in ware and color to greyware from the Iranian plateau. The proportion of open (25 percent) versus closed (75 percent) vessels is typical of household assemblages in other areas of the world (Fry 1980). It is interesting to note that exotic small finds occur just as frequently in the domestic architecture as they do in the monumental architecture (described below).

STRATIGRAPHY BELOW ARCHITECTURE

Despite the early type of ceramic assemblage found in the rooms, it does not represent the first occupation in this area. A 1.2 x 1 m sounding to sterile sand, excavated to the north of Room 1 (locus 43), contains ceramics and associated occupational surfaces stratified beneath the domestic architecture (fig. 6.14). This area is outside of the building and contains no floor surface. The top 20 to 25 cm of deposit contains wall fall of broken bricks and laminated mud layers with ceramics scattered throughout it. These lie on a compact brown and grey ashy layer—the ancient surface at the time of occupation of the apartment complex.

One meter of cultural material, in four stratigraphic layers, had built up before the architectural complex described here was constructed. These deposits lie on the natural mound composed of yellowish grey sands (*materik*). The lowest 40 cm is light greyish brown soil with no cultural material. The second layer

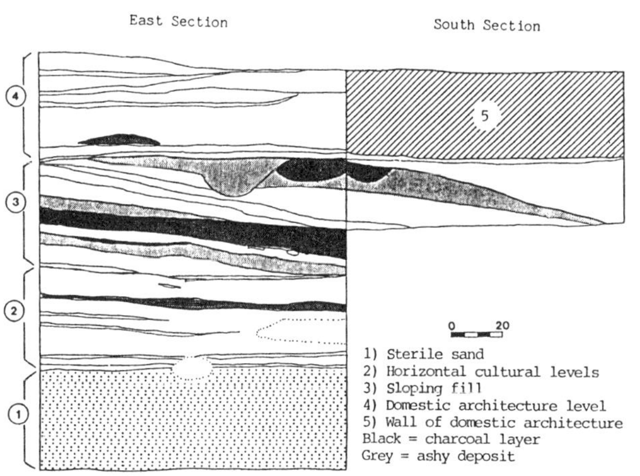

Figure 6.14
Sounding beneath the domestic architecture (locus 43).

consists of four horizontal hard grey clay surfaces with many sherds as well as a charcoal-rich hearth. Layer 3, above this, consists of 25 cm of sloping ashy midden deposits with charcoal and ceramics. The fourth layer consists of a separate level of sloping ashy midden. Deposits similar to this were found just beneath the architecture in all of the soundings.

Occupational levels were found on sterile soil in the deep sounding and in this small probe, giving the impression of widespread occupation directly on the original mound. The ceramics from this small sounding are indistinguishable in form or in ware from the ceramics from the architecture above (fig. 6.15). The stratigraphy of Period 1 layers here is similar to the deposits of Period 1 in the deep sounding, suggesting that the domestic architecture was contemporary with the monumental building, but not the initial occupation of the northern mound.

OTHER ARCHITECTURE ON THE NORTH MOUND

Surface finds from the domestic area described above are similar to those on the surface of the north mound around the *kremel* to the south, west, and north. Two excavations confirmed that the architecture of these areas is similar to the domestic architecture.

In 1981, A. F. Ganyalin excavated an area of architecture 5.5 x 3 m on the west side of the mounded area of the north mound. He was hoping to find a large city wall but did not locate this in his trench. In 1989 we cleaned Ganyalin's excavation and mapped the architecture (fig. 6.16). Ceramics and small finds from the fill clearly indicate that this was a Period 1 construction.

Floors of two rooms were found 35 cm below the surface. The walls are made of bricks with dimensions of 15 x 20 x 45 cm, similar to the brick sizes from the

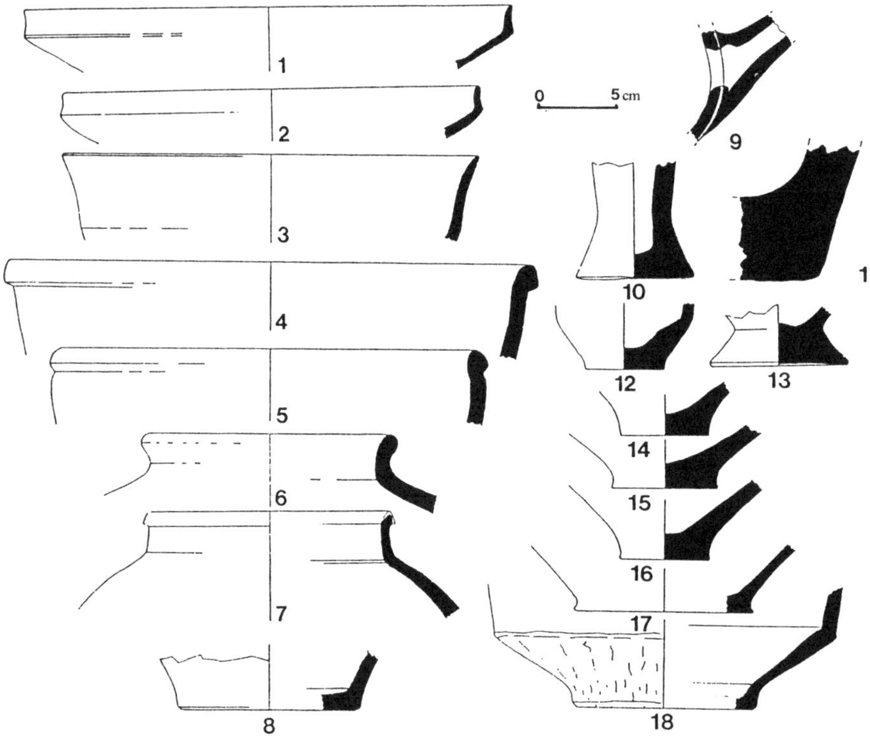

Figure 6.15
Ceramics from the lowest cultural levels of the domestic architecture sounding (locus 43).
1) Type 2.A.2; 2) type 2.A.2; 3) type 2.A.1; 4) type 3.A.1; 5) type 3.B.1; 6) type 3.B.2; 7) type 3.B.3; 8) type 3, moldmade base; 9) vertical spout, local ware; 10) type 2.A base; 11) type 6; 12) type 1.B.3; 13) type 2.A base; 14) type 2, wheelmade base; 15) type 2, wheelmade base; 16) type 2, wheelmade base; 17) type 3, moldmade base; 18) type 3, moldmade base.

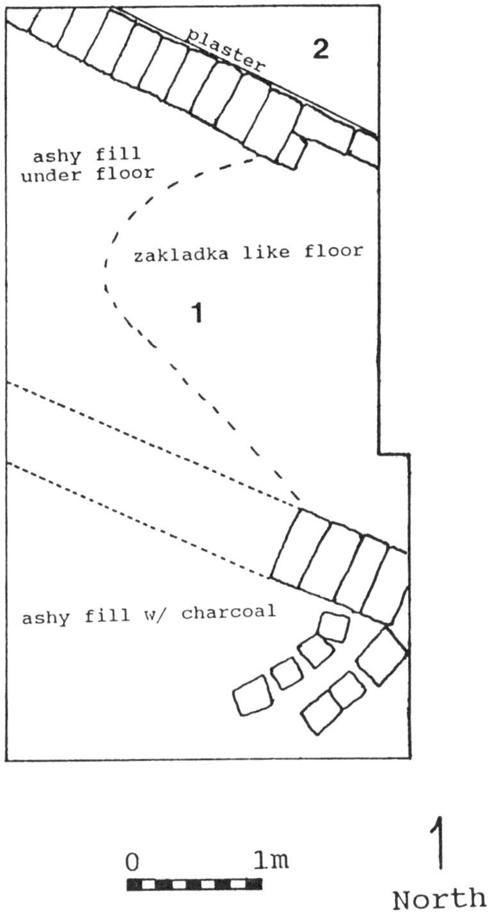

Figure 6.16
Plan of the 1981 excavation on Gonur north, based on 1989 cleaning. Period 1. Rooms 1 and 2 are part of an architectural complex similar to the domestic architecture.

1989 domestic architecture. Room 1 is 2.3 m wide and more than 5.5 m long. The room has a *zakladka* type brick floor. A threshold, similar to the threshold in the 1989 domestic architecture, leads from Room 1 to Room 2. Room 2 has a poorly preserved tamped earth floor, and white gypsum plaster coated the wall face—an unusual feature at Gonur.

On the west side of the north mound, several later burials and cenotaphs were excavated in 1989. Burial 40 intruded into earlier walls and a floor associated with Period 1 type ceramics (fig. 6.17). This architecture was less deflated than that of the 1981 excavation, and a floor was found 45 to 50 cm below the surface. The northern wall belongs to an unexcavated building to the north. On the east side, a wall fragment forms an oblique area with a tamped earth surface on which ceramics lie. The bottom half of a large storage jar was built into the wall and under the surface, very similar to the storage jar found in Room 2 of the 1989 domestic architecture except that it was upright.

These areas are similar to the domestic architecture in that the rooms are large, interior rooms have brick floors and thresholds built into the wall, the walls follow the slope of the mound, and storage jars are built into the architecture. In general, the size of the bricks, wall construction, and associated ceramics suggest occupation contemporary with the excavated domestic architecture. The uniformity in the pattern of surface finds, which stretch in a wide band around the depression south of the deep sounding and to the east, suggests a continuous living area of households and courtyards.

ARCHITECTURAL COMPARISONS

Gonur's domestic architecture is different from that of the contemporary late Namazga V urban sites of the Kopet Dag foothill plain. At Altyn depe, the rooms in the domestic architecture of excavation 10 are smaller than the rooms at Gonur and more complex than at Gonur, Kelleli 4, and Togolok 21, and more

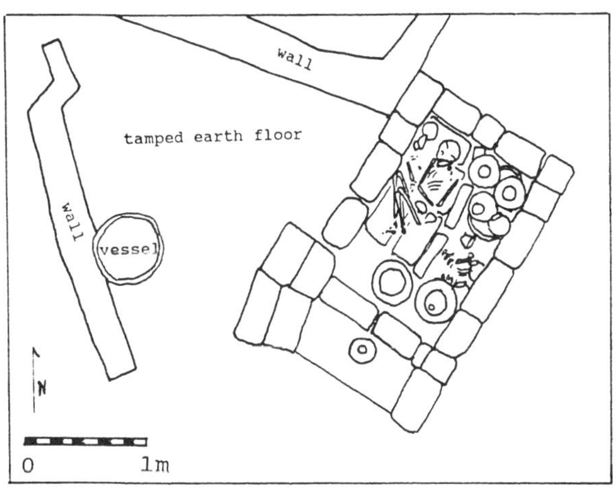

Figure 6.17
Plan of the architecture which was excavated during the uncovering of Burial 40. Burial 40 is Period 2, while the two walls and associated floor is Period 1, similar to the domestic architecture.

complexly interconnected, with many doors and corridors.

In contrast, the household architecture of Gonur is similar to that of other Period 1 sites of Margiana. Room size, number of hearths per complex, and the number of rooms connected by doorways at Kelleli 3 and 4 are very similar to Gonur domestic architecture. Unlike Gonur, however, these domestic units are isolated from other architecture by an enclosing set of walls and towers.

The domestic architecture at Gonur is similar to patterns of household units at Kelleli 4. For example, Rooms 2 through 6 at Kelleli 4 appear to form one unit (fig. 6.18). Room 5 at Kelleli 4 is comparable to Room 1 at Gonur, with a hearth in the wall. Room 2 at Kelleli 4 and Room 2 at Gonur are both large rooms opening onto an alleyway (as at Gonur) or onto a short corridor and alley (Rooms 4 and 6 at Kelleli 4). The alleyway at Kelleli (Room 6) leads to a common courtyard where four large ovens are located; this is a clear parallel to the organization of the domestic architecture at Gonur. There were a total of six apartments at Kelleli 4, each composed of three or four rooms with an associated large oven and several hearths built into the walls.

At Kelleli 4, the doubled exterior walls form a corridor, which is divided into long narrow rooms that are connected to the interior rooms. These rooms typically contain many storage jars but no hearths or other habitation debris. The double exterior walls and towers at these sites appear to have been for defense and are similar in plan to casemate walls found in later fortress architecture from which artillery was fired. Casemate rooms are also known from Early Iron Age Syro-Palestinian fortresses. Casemate walls are generally filled with rubble in Syro-Palestinian forts, but in some instances the walls were not filled and were used for storage and, possibly, habitation (Mazar 1990:388).

Other Period 1 settlements are also fortified domestic compounds. For example, Kelleli 3 has six towers on each side and a gateway to the exterior in the middle of each side (briefly described in chap. 2). The interior of the building complex was not excavated, but seven micro-complexes were identified along the southeast corner (Masimov, pers. comm.). These are

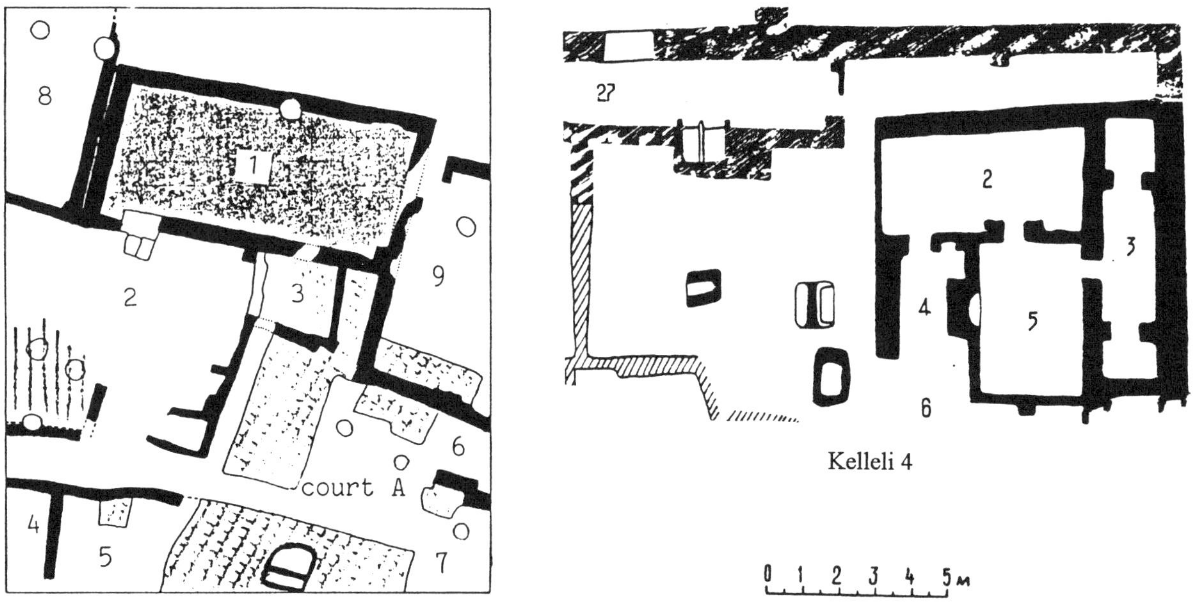

Gonur north, domestic architecture

Kelleli 4

Figure 6.18
Comparison of Gonur domestic architecture and part of Kelleli 4.

large three- or four-room apartments, most probably for single households, each appearing to have individual court areas in addition to a shared interior courtyard.

Features of Kelleli 3 and 4 are more evocative of the architecture of traditional Central Asian agricultural oases than of Mesopotamian palaces or of Kopet Dag foothill cities. The form of the enclosed building complexes in Margiana is similar to that of the *qala,* a traditional building found in oasis areas of Central Asia and Afghanistan (Pugachenkova 1958; Szabo and Barfield 1991). The fortified buildings, or *qala,* are found for the first time in Central Asia during this period.

At Gonur, the households were part of a large village agglomeration surrounding the monumental building of the north mound. Similar village-level architecture is likely to be found on all of the smaller sites of the Gonur oasis dating to the initial period of widespread occupation of Margiana.

EARLIEST MONUMENTAL ARCHITECTURE AT GONUR

When Gonur depe was discovered in 1974, wide walls oriented north-south in a rectangle covering 120 x 130 m could be traced on the surface of the central part of the north mound. Excavations (50 x 60 m) carried out within the southwest corner of this area from 1978 to 1981 (fig. 6.19) revealed part of a very well preserved large building with a double exterior wall, corner towers, and large straight interior walls: the *kremel* (Sarianidi 1990:17–33).

I reexamined this architecture in 1989 to compare it with the domestic architecture and with the later monumental architecture of Period 2. The walls were preserved to a maximum height of 2 m. Approximately one-sixth of the building complex was excavated in 1981 and V. Sarianidi is presently continuing these excavations. The building has a single general plan (fig. 6.20) but with several phases of architectural modification, clearly seen in the brick sizes and wall joins. Preservation of architecture to this height has

Figure 6.19
Aerial view of excavations at Gonur north; 1981 monumental building, *kremel*, and 1989 deep sounding.

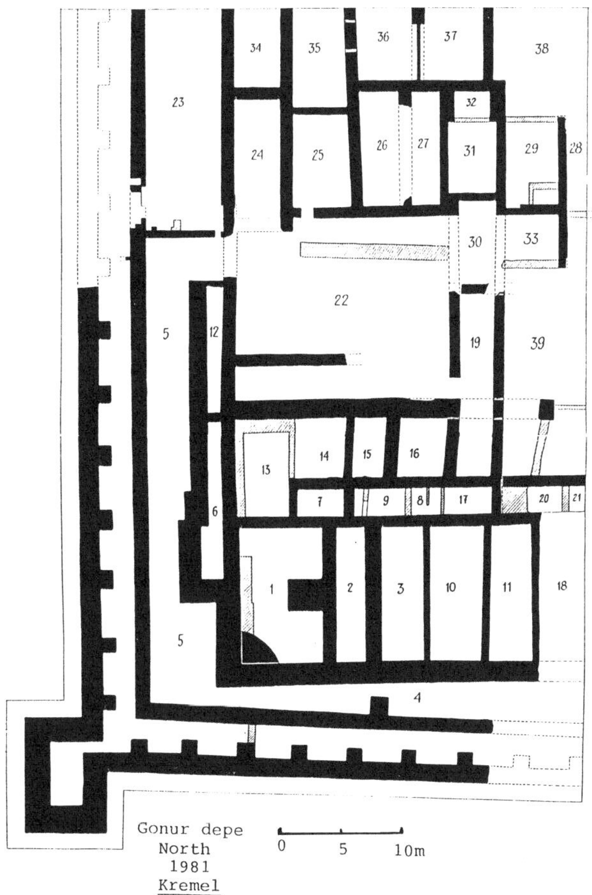

Figure 6.20
Plan of the north mound monumental building, *kremel*, 1981 excavations, based upon Sarianidi (1991).

not been found elsewhere in Margiana or at any other Bronze Age site in Central Asia. This architecture provides insight into details of the typical Bronze Age Margiana architecture, which usually is preserved only to the bases of the walls.

As in the domestic architecture, the bricks in the walls are laid in header and stretcher rows. Benches, which I found preserved only to ground level in the domestic architecture, must have been similar to the 40-cm-tall bench found in Room 1. Doorways have raised doorsills that are preserved to a height of 8 to 12 cm. All walls are preserved to a height of 1.5 to 2 m no matter what their thickness; walls 25 cm thick at the base (Rooms 8 and 17), 40 to 45 cm thick (Rooms 3, 10, 11, and 18), and as much as 2 m thick (Room 1) are equally well preserved. The building was fortified with thick exterior walls and towers, but no windows or arrow slits. Parthian and Sasanian mud brick fortresses in Margiana, which have similarly thick exterior walls, stand 10 to 15 m high without any window openings (Pugachenkova 1958). The Bronze Age architecture must have been comparably large.

Stratigraphy and Phasing

The architecture of the *kremel* was built on a sterile, yellowish sandy deposit similar to the *materik* found in the deep sounding. In most rooms, sand covered the lowest floors, which had been found mostly cleared of debris (Sarianidi 1990:24). However, several areas of in situ materials were found, for example in Room 4, described below. During Sarianidi's excavations, several radiocarbon samples were taken that, when calibrated, correspond with those from the lower levels in the deep sounding and the domestic architecture.

The second phase of use is indicated by architectural modification using bricks of a different size. The bricks of the original construction are generally of the dimensions 45 x 20 x 15 cm, the same size as those used in the domestic architecture. The second phase bricks are distinctly shorter and taller, 35 x 30 x 16 cm on average, and have little, if any, mud mortar between them (fig. 6.21). During the second phase of occupation, many rooms, such as 7 through 9 and 13

Figure 6.21
Gonur north monumental architecture, *kremel*, Rooms 22 and 24.

through 17, were closed off. These rooms appear to have changed function. Corridors were divided into small doorless rooms, probably for storage, and large court areas were subdivided into rooms. However, the building appears to have maintained the fortifications as well as the overall organization of courts, corridors, and rooms.

A third phase of occupation or reuse occurred after the building had been abandoned and 1 m of fill had accumulated. Doorways were cut through the upper parts of walls, and in the northern balk, hearths, and features could be seen eroding from a level almost 1 m above the original floors. Ceramics illustrated that came from the building (fig. 6.22) most likely are associated with this phase. They are similar to those from layer 6 of the deep sounding (Period 2) and have close parallels to the ceramics of Togolok 21 and to

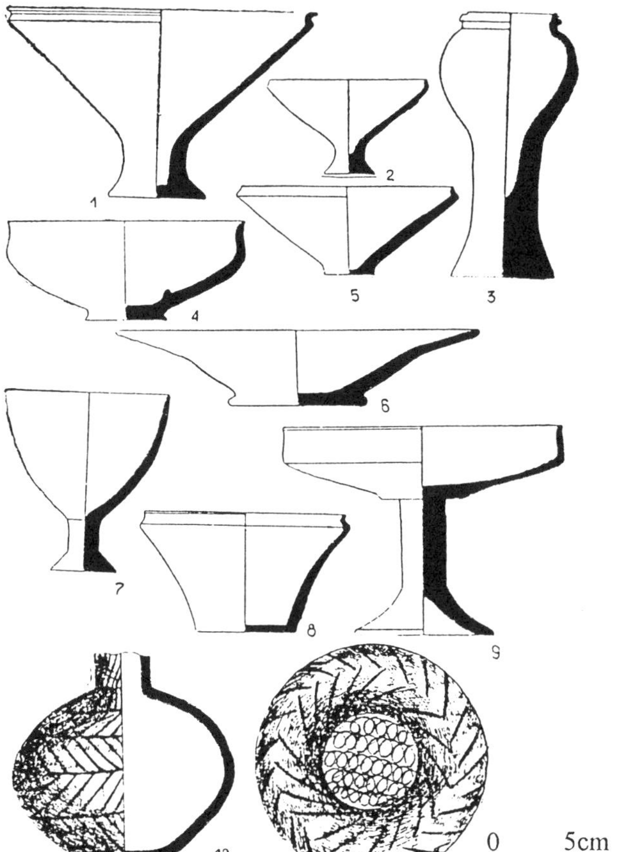

Figure 6.22
Ceramics typical of Margiana Period 2 (BMAC), found in the upper levels at the *kremel* (adapted from Sarianidi 1990, fig. 13).

Bactria. These contrast with the small finds on the floor of Room 4, which correspond to layers 1 through 4 of the sounding (Period 1).

A final use (latest phase) of the building was as an area for burials in the upper layers of the deposit. These burials were simply placed in shallow pits with a small assortment of Period 2 type grave goods and are similar to the burials in the eastern part of Togolok 21 or at Togolok 1. These are contemporary with the burials surrounding the area of the *kremel,* which have rectangular graves constructed of brick and many grave goods.

Exterior Corridor

The exterior wall of the south side is 1.25 m thick, with an interior parallel wall forming a large corridor. Interior pilasters strengthen the wall and may have supported a roof. The fill in this corridor contains ashy midden, apparently from the upper levels (Sarianidi 1990:19). This corridor is similar to the exterior wall and corridors at Kelleli 3 and 4, except that it is much larger. The doubled exterior wall most likely supported a raised walkway around the top and functioned as a double or casemate wall for defense.

Interior Corridor

Rooms 4 and 5 form an interior corridor. In the eastern end of Room 4, an ashy hearth deposit (1.0 x 0.4 m) on the floor was found that included the bones of *Bos* and *Ovis/Capra*, a compartmented seal of the geometric type, a small bone needle, and three human figurines of Namazga V type (fig. 6.23). This feature was considered a sacrificial place (Sarianidi 1990:19) but is similar to the hearths and associated artifacts in the domestic architecture of Rooms 1 and 8. In addition, the assemblage is similar to the figurines, bone needles, and bones from the lower levels of the deep sounding, which came from a domestic midden possibly originating from this building. This corridor continues north (Room 5). A radiocarbon sample from a similar hearth (LE 2408) falls generally in the range of the early second to late third millennium (see chap. 5).

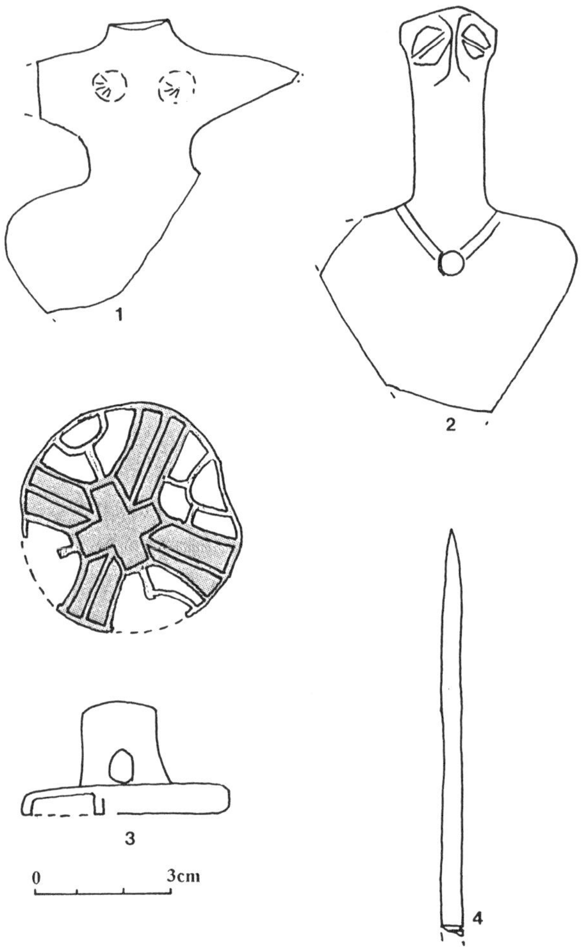

Figure 6.23
Finds from the monumental building (*kremel*, Room 4, floor, near a hearth). 1,2) Terracotta figurines; 3) bronze compartmented seal; 4) bone needle, tip reddened.

Of particular interest are Rooms 6 and 12. These long narrow rooms are completely closed without any doors and with their surrounding walls preserved to a height of 2 m. There is a deep plastered cistern for water, or a well, in Room 6. Most likely these were covered, with access from a floor above. Long narrow rooms continue to be typical in the desert oasis architecture from Period 2 at Gonur, at Togolok 21, and in Bactria. Traditional *qala* architecture often has storage in the walls next to the exterior wall (Szabo and Barfield 1991:195). Such rooms are not found in the foothill plain of the Kopet Dag or mountain regions of Central Asia and may be an adaptation to the desert/oasis environment.

Courtyard and Adjacent Rooms (13 through 38)

The interior corridor, Rooms 4 and 5, leads to a large courtyard (Room 22). The courtyard originally had small parallel walls in its south part that apparently were razed during a later phase of occupation. Several floor levels were found superimposed in the courtyard. In the fill of the courtyard, several small finds, including an alabaster footed cup, came from apparent floor contexts (Sarianidi 1990, fig. 24:2).

Rooms to the north of the courtyard were occupied and modified during all three architectural phases. Some walls were preserved only at the base (dotted walls:fig. 6.20), and often had floors covering them.

During Period 2, new walls were built (hatched walls:fig. 6.20) and some rooms (Rooms 31 and 32) were closed off. A marked floor level is seen in the north balk section at 1 m above the original Period 1 floor. Ceramics found in Room 32 are similar to the ceramics found in Period 1 levels of the deep sounding.

The whole vessels published from this building appear to have come from the upper level (Period 2), and a glazed tile from Room 24, typical of the medieval Islamic period, is clearly intrusive (ibid., pl. 13).

To the south of the courtyard, Rooms 13 through 21 appear to be two east-west corridors. Many small objects from the first phase were found here, including bone needles, *série récente* steatite vessel fragments, and terracotta figurines (ibid., 20–21). These corridors were later divided with small secondary walls.

The south wall of Room 8 is reddened near the top from secondary reuse during the third phase. Ceramics similar to the upper level of the deep sounding (Period 2) were found in Room 14, in Room 17, and in the surface layer. The grey burnished ware (fig. 6.22:10) is probably from Dzharkutan (Dzharkutan period), and the red burnished ware (fig. 6.22:7) has a distinctive form, as does the bowl (fig. 6.22:4). The latter two have precise analogies at Dashli 3 (Sarianidi 1977).

Rooms 1 through 18

The rooms in the area just north of the corridor (Room 4) are 10 m long. Rooms 2 through 18 are unusual in that they had no doors in the first or second phases. These rooms had sand on their original floors and had almost no artifacts on them or in the fill just above the floors.

Room 1 is a large rectangular room with very thick walls. On the basis of brick size, I suggest that it was entered via Rooms 13 through 16, which were blocked up during the second phase. On the east wall is a large solid pilaster as tall as the preserved walls. A 1-m-tall curved platform or bench in the southwest corner was built with the original construction of the building; its bricks interfingered with the wall. A 40-cm-tall bench was built against the west wall. Curved platforms or benches are found in mud brick architecture supporting arches and domes. An analogy from late medieval Anau illustrates this feature (fig. 6.24). At the corners of the first floor are squinches to support the ceiling, and under them are semicircular platforms. In the third phase (Period 2), a floor was constructed more than 1 m above the original floor.

Room 2, a corridorlike room with no door or entrance, has a double-chambered oven and a chimney (in which ashes remain) in the southwest corner. The walls dividing Rooms 3, 10, and 11 were built against the north and south walls. Although the bricks are similar in size to those of the original structure, the walls appear to be a late addition. Rooms 3, 10, and 11 originally formed one large room or court, and a doorway from Room 11 to 18 was blocked off when the secondary walls were built.

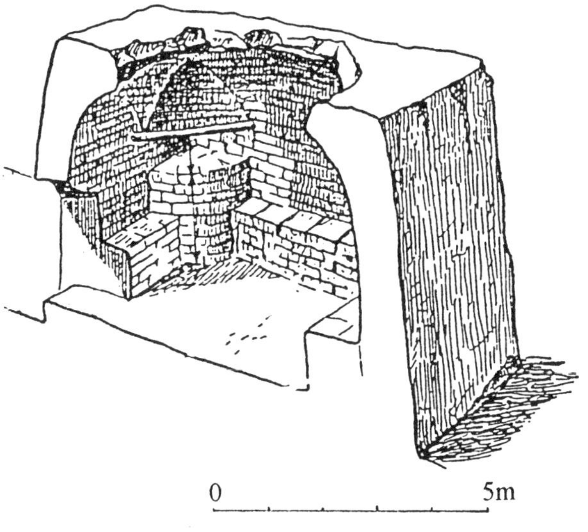

Figure 6.24
Late medieval domestic architecture from Anau, Turkmenistan. Note round platform beneath arch in the corner (Pugachenkova 1958).

ARCHITECTURAL PARALLELS

In comparison with Kelleli 3 and 4, the walls of the *kremel* at Gonur are much larger and more regularly laid out. The *kremel* has regularly planned series of rooms and courts unlike the domestic units of three or four rooms. The *kremel* has few of the wall hearths and ovens found in the domestic architecture. The monumental nature of the interior architecture is represented only in the southwest corner of the walled complex. The monumental nature of the southwest corner of the *kremel* suggests that it served as a citadel among the surrounding domestic quarters.

During the initial occupation of the oasis there already appears to be differentiation of domestic architecture and monumental architecture. The center of historically documented elite architecture of the desert oases of Central Asia (e.g., Merv, Bactria, Khiva, Bukhara) is the ark or citadel (Hiebert 1992a). Traditionally, an ark is part of the enclosed fortified settlement, unlike the elite architecture of the Kopet Dag foothill sites or sites in the greater Near East.

CONCLUSIONS

The common features of the earliest oasis architecture may be summarized as follows. The rooms are large (compared with the foothill region), and there appear to be three or four rooms per household. There is the common use of below-ground storage areas for water or grain. The initial occupation is characterized by enclosed planned living compounds (*qala*), which have defensive towers and casemate walls. The monumental architecture appears to be the source of the Central Asian fortified citadel or ark. Altogether, this demonstrates that the first Bronze Age occupation of the desert oasis of Margiana resulted in an architectural style unique in the greater Near East at that time. This distinctive type of fortified building complex appears for the first time in Margiana Period 1 and spread to the other oasis areas of northern and southern Bactria by the time of the Bactrian-Margiana Archaeological Complex.

CHAPTER SEVEN

The Period 2 (BMAC) Architecture

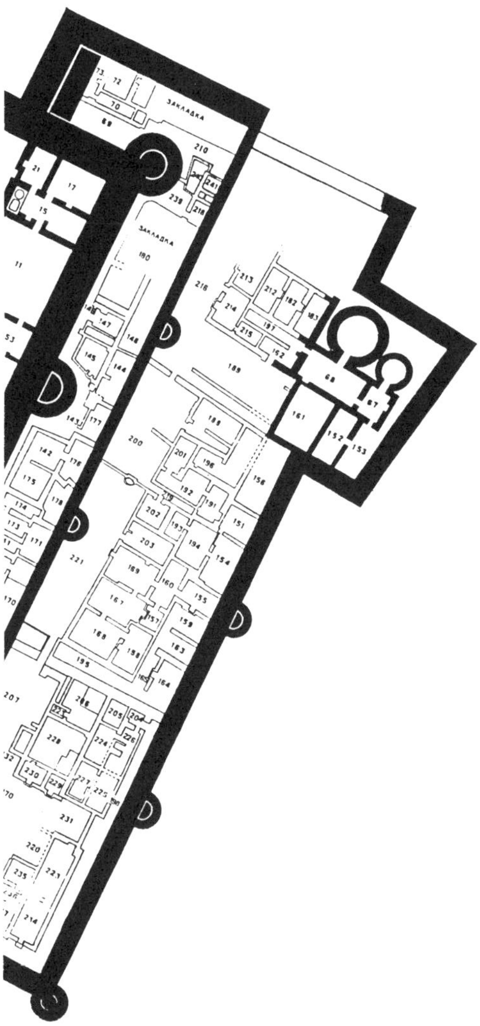

EXCAVATIONS AT THE SOUTH MOUND AT GONUR HAVE revealed a large single building complex that is later in date than the domestic architecture or the *kremel* on the north mound. The south mound rises 1.5 to 2 m above the plain and is wholly composed of the building complex enclosed by a massive wall that outlines a parallelogram 115 m on a side. No building remains occur beyond the walled area, and no occupational levels were found in soundings made off of the mound to the south and to the west.

The south mound is currently being investigated using wide-scale horizontal excavations (fig. 7.1). Although the entire plan is not yet known, many features of this large building complex are typical of the architecture of Period 2 in Margiana and related sites of the BMAC in northern and southern Bactria. The building at Gonur south is particularly interesting because its deep stratigraphy is better preserved than the Togolok or the Bactrian sites. The ceramics and small finds from the main complex at Gonur south are similar to Period 2 from the deep sounding at Gonur north.

METHODS OF EXCAVATION

At Gonur south, horizontal excavations have exposed large areas of room complexes within the building. The goal is 100-percent clearance of the building architecture. The methods of excavation described below are similar to the methods that were employed at Togolok 1, Togolok 21, Kelleli 4, and the sites of northern and southern Bactria.

The excavation rows are 6 and 8 m wide, with 7-meter balks between them. As of the spring of 1989, eight rows had been begun, with Row 1 at the north and Row 8 at the south wall. Excavations within each row are carried out in the following fashion: the soft surface layer is removed with flat shovels, or scraped with the blade on a small tractor, just to the point that harder intact deposits are exposed. This is done over the width of the row, for a distance of several meters at a time.

When the in situ layers are exposed, a sharpened flat shovel is skimmed over the surface and the difference between mud bricks (from walls) and collapse becomes clearly visible. Thus the preserved tops of the walls are revealed across an extensive area (fig. 7.2). If no walls are noted in the skimming, another sever-

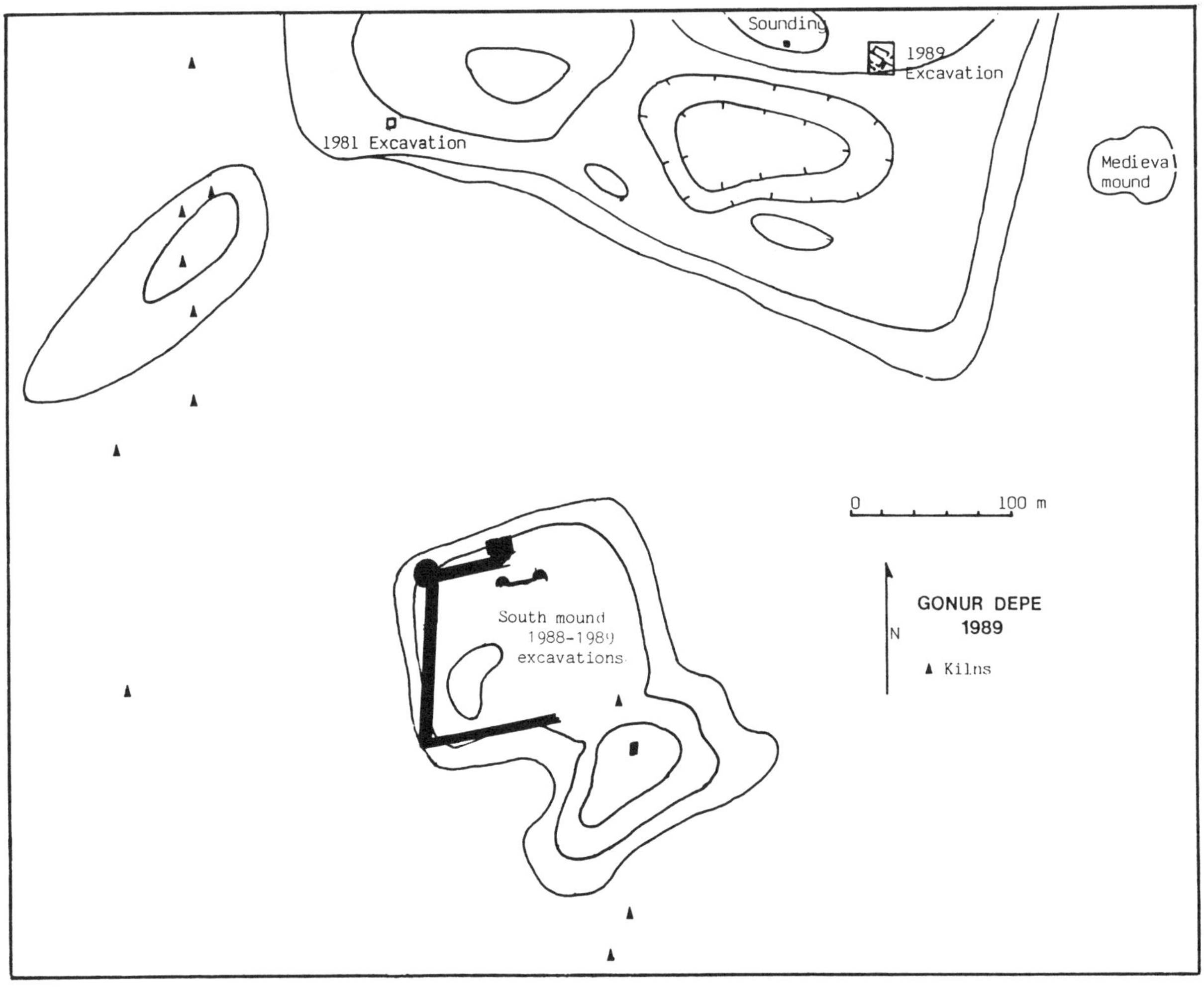

Figure 7.1
Location of monumental building of Gonur south.

al centimeters are skimmed off the wide surface. This is repeated until walls or floors are located. The system of walls as located on the surface is then outlined and individual rooms are designated. Each area enclosed by walls is considered a room and is given a number. When rooms of the upper architecture are cleared out, the walls are left standing and excavation continues within the confines of the pedestalled walls. Other features, such as pots or baskets, are sometimes also left in place. Normally the rooms are excavated to the floor or sterile soil. Small finds and special ceramics are described in *opisi*, field records that list the significant finds by room number and describe the artifacts. Bulk artifacts, such as ceramics, bones, and grinding stones, are placed in sherd yards by room number, which allows for further study by specialists.

Several sources were used for the following summary of the 1989 season of work: observations of the previous excavations and analysis of finds from the "field museum" (the sherd yard); collaborative excavations of one row (Row 2); and fine-scale excavations of several types of rooms (domestic room, *kelli*, storage area, cenotaph, and a burial). In the spring of 1989, no site plan had yet been made for the ongoing excavations on the south mound. I made a tape and compass architectural plan (fig. 7.3) and assigned phases to the architectural levels. The summary of work provided here presents only the observations

Figure 7.2
O. Rosenthal cleaning upper layers to expose walls at Gonur south, 1989.

made on the architecture through the spring 1989 season.

The excavations I directed were integrated with the ongoing Soviet excavations, and I used a system of *loci*, *phases*, and *periods* to interpret the ongoing excavations. The upper room numbers act as loci, and I excavated the floor levels and plotted artifacts on floors. My goal was to examine separate contexts from each phase of occupation. Samples for radiocarbon analysis, ceramics, and animal bones were recovered as well. Architectural phases are defined in terms of superimposed floor levels and changes in the architectural layout through time. They thus differ from the chronological periods as defined by ceramics and small finds such as in the Gonur deep sounding. Gonur's south mound had multiple phases of architecture, as did the Togolok sites and Gonur north. The superposition of the architectural phases is best seen in the pedestalled upper walls, which form small stratigraphic sections wherever upper architecture was encountered. Walls of the various phases were traced from one excavation row to another, providing a preliminary history of occupation of the building complex. Burials and cenotaphs are found throughout the architectural remains. We do not currently have the stratigraphic or stylistic proof to determine the architectural phase of an individual burial or cenotaph. Thus burials and cenotaphs are grouped as a separate phase.

STRATIGRAPHY

The foundations of the building are below the surface of the local *takyr*, rather than on a hillock as on the north mound or at Togolok 21. The interior architecture was built in a depression, which may have been created by mining *takyr* mud for building the exterior wall. These interior walls lie on yellowish grey sand

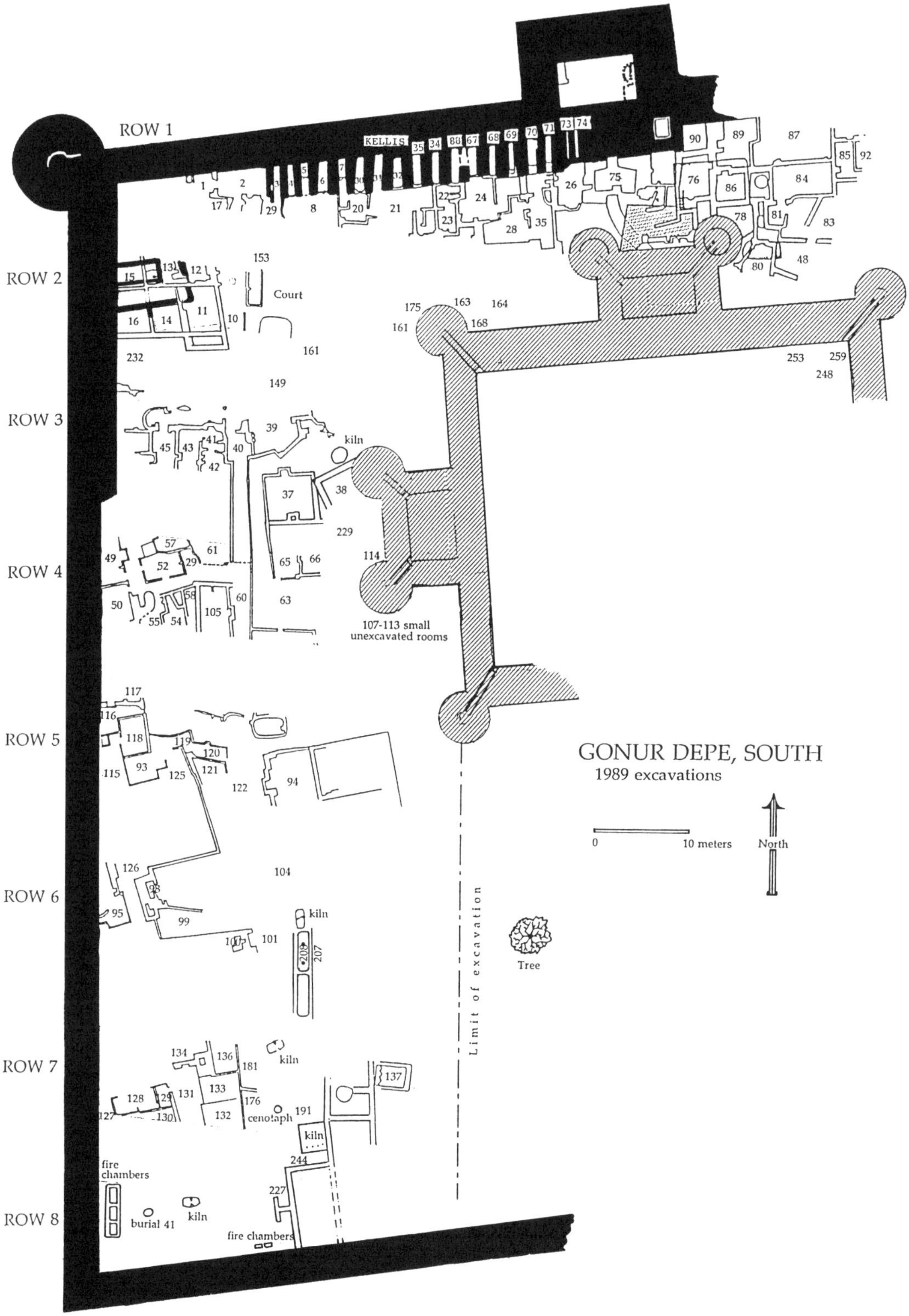

Figure 7.3
Preliminary tape and compass map of the building complex at Gonur south, excavations of 1988–89.

and clay located in subfloor probes in Row 1 (Rooms 24, 30, and 68); Row 2 (Room 11); Row 3 (Room 37); Row 7 (Room 176); and 20 m to the west of the building complex in a test probe.

A series of large pits containing Period 1 type ceramics and small finds were excavated along the north side under Rooms 48, 66, and 76, and along the west side in Row 4 (Rooms 66 and 67), and in Rows 7 and 8. These pits appear to have existed before the south mound building complex was built. Although it is possible that an earlier building existed somewhere on the south mound, the ceramics and small finds are so rare and fragmented that an earlier occupation of the south mound is not thought to have been intensive. Possibly the pits were dug by people from the north mound exploiting the clay of the *takyr* in this area. These Period 1 features do not appear to have been widespread and are exceptions to the pattern of walls and floors built on sterile pale brown sand or the yellowish grey *takyr* clays.

The First Architectural Phase: The Original Construction

In general, the exterior wall of the entire building complex and the interior walls were constructed as a single unit. During 1989, however, the first phase had been exposed only in the northwest corner. The original building was surrounded by a monumental wall, 5 m wide along the west side and 4 m wide on the north side. Inside the wall was a system of straight and regular walls, usually 50 cm wide (approximately two bricks). The row of long narrow rooms, *kelli*, also is part of the original building complex. The ongoing excavations have begun to reveal a large area of Phase 1 rooms along the south side (to the east of the limit of excavation, fig. 7.3). The entire building appears to have been originally laid out at one time on a single plan.

Phase 2

The second architectural phase was constructed on top of the razed remains of the interior walls of Phase 1 and is built in a slightly different orientation. Most of the interior walls of Phase 1 were razed, but the exterior walls and the areas on the northern side were not razed and remained in use throughout the occupation of the building. This occupational phase appears to have been longer than the initial occupation, although the layout of interior architecture is less regular and less well planned.

Phase 3

Phase 3 walls and floors lay on 20 to 50 cm of deposit above the Phase 2 floors. In many places these walls subdivided Phase 2 rooms, reusing many older walls. In other places the Phase 3 walls were superimposed on the remains of Phase 2 rooms. This upper phase of architecture is just below the modern surface. Deflated and eroded vessels lying on Phase 3 floors were often covered only by the broken surface crust and windblown sediment.

Phase 4: BMAC Burials and Cenotaphs

Cenotaphs, burials, and caches of ceramics are intrusive features in the midden levels of the rooms. The burials and cenotaphs found in the building complex at Gonur south are labeled as Phase 4, although their ceramics and small finds are identical to the surrounding middens and are roughly contemporary with Phases 1 through 3 of occupation in the building. Burials and cenotaphs are also found stratigraphically beneath the foundation of the central building along the north side. These include burials in the middens of Rooms 80 and 84, and cenotaphs in Rooms 27 and 84. The occurrence of burials and cenotaphs in abandoned rooms adjacent to occupied rooms is a pattern also found at Togolok 1 and Togolok 21.

Phase 5: Central Building

The central building on the south mound is the latest occupational phase at Gonur south and is associated with Takhirbai ceramics (Period 3 at Gonur north). The architectural remains consist of the foundations of a structure with 3-m-wide walls and towers and some of the interior architecture of a large fortified building.

The central building was constructed sometime after the third phase of occupation in the main building complex: Phase 3 walls of the courtyard in Row 3 (Room 36) run under the central building; along the north side, Phase 3 room fill is stratified below the foundation of the central building in Rooms 77, 78, and 80. However, it is possible that there were other buildings outside of the central building of the Takhirbai period.

Relative dating

Ceramics of Period 2 at Gonur are associated with architectural Phases 1 through 4: the construction of the main building complex and the burials and cenotaphs. The individual phases cannot be distinguished by ceramics at this time, but are all part of the Bactrian-Margiana Archaeological Complex ceramic tradition (fig. 7.4). The central building (Phase 5), excavated in 1990, contained little material on the floors but appears to be post-BMAC, with ceramics similar to the later Takhirbai materials.

The small finds from Gonur south include a wide variety of metal and stone seals, other stone and metal objects, and terracotta objects of the BMAC style similar to those found at Togolok 21. Most of the finds from the horizontal excavations cannot be placed into a particular architectural phase, because rooms as originally defined on the surface had more than one phase. However, it is important to note that the small finds and ceramics known to have come from floors of Phases 1 through 3, as well as from the burials and cenotaphs (Phase 4), are all BMAC style.

THE EXTERIOR WALL

The exterior wall of Gonur south is 3 to 5 m wide. Because the building complexes at Kelleli 3, Kelleli 4, and Gonur north (*kremel*) had doubled exterior walls, there is in fact very little difference in thickness of the exterior defenses of the building complexes in Periods 1 and 2. BMAC buildings, such as Togolok 1, Togolok 21, and the Dzharkutan temple, have thick exterior

Figure 7.4
Ceramics from 1988–89 excavations at Gonur south, from Phases 1–4.

walls and round towers similar to Gonur south. Massive exterior walls made of mud brick are typical of the later (Parthian, Sasanian, and medieval) architecture of the Margiana oasis (Pugachenkova 1958) and can be used as an analogy for the deflated remains of massive exterior walls in Bronze Age Margiana to suggest that these walls functioned both for defense and for insulation against summer heat and winter sandstorms.

In traditional Central Asian *pakhsa* and mud brick construction, the earth usually is taken from immediately outside the planned building, forming a drainage ditch and giving the appearance of a taller building (Szabo and Barfield 1991:143). This appears to have occurred at Togolok 21, for example. At Gonur south, however, the interior had been excavated out, apparently to make the bricks or filling for the exterior walls. Along the north wall, near Room 80, the interior floors lay 80 cm below the exterior surface; and outside of the exterior wall along Row 2 on the west side, the floors lay 25 to 30 cm below the surface outside of the main wall (fig. 7.5). In a harsh environment, a semisubterranean building would act to moderate the heat (Fitch and Branch 1960).

At Gonur south, only the base or foundation of the exterior wall is preserved. The entire excavated surface of the wall is made of regularly laid bricks about 25 x 40 cm in surface dimensions. The wall is eroded, sloping to the outside where it stands no more than 20 cm tall. Thin interior walls stand taller, filled with midden and brick fall.

Such extreme erosion of the main wall is not typical of a solid mud brick wall, which should have been better preserved. There does not appear to be adequate debris mounded on this exterior wall to suggest that it was a solid 4 m wide to a significant height. There are several possible explanations. First, the exterior walls could have been looted of bricks or brick fall for the later construction of the central building. Second, the base of the wall may have

Figure 7.5
North side of Gonur south. View east.

formed a platform for a thinner exterior wall. An analogy for this is found in the monumental mud brick building complexes of West Africa, where buildings are surrounded by several-meter-wide platforms that serve as a foundation and walkway (Bourgeois 1989). Third, it is possible that the solid wide-wall bases provided the foundation for doubled exterior walls, similar to those found in Period 1, and found in the BMAC architecture of Bactria (Dashli, Sapalli). The tower foundation at Gonur south, 10 m in diameter, is solid, and the tower probably had a room in it.

Round corner towers are typical of Margiana Period 2 architecture and are found at Togolok 1, Togolok 21, and Gonur south. At Gonur south itself, both square and round towers are found. In Bactria, buildings associated with the BMAC do not always have towers or have long narrow rooms that act as towers.

The central north wall tower is square, is very shallowly preserved, and has a large room (8 x 5 m) inside. Interior modifications, evidently on a floor, were visible in the form of brick alignments and the base of a brick bench.

COLLABORATIVE EXCAVATIONS AT ROW 2

Row 2 provides an example of the occupational history of these large buildings. Here, three phases of architecture were found: lower (Phase 1), middle (Phase 2), and upper floors (Phase 3). The upper walls define the excavation units of eight rooms and a courtyard (fig. 7.6).

The typical room fill consists of hard mud brick fall. Ceramic sherds are scattered throughout the deposit but are concentrated around hearths, in niches, or along the edges of rooms. Grinding stones, bone tools, and whole ceramics are found clustered in certain rooms and niches where they appear to have been placed in storage before the space was abandoned.

Floors are made of clay with flakes of white gypsum. Clayey floors with varying amounts of gypsum flakes are found throughout the south mound building complex and were often remade and repaired. The floors lap against the wall bases—that is, the walls

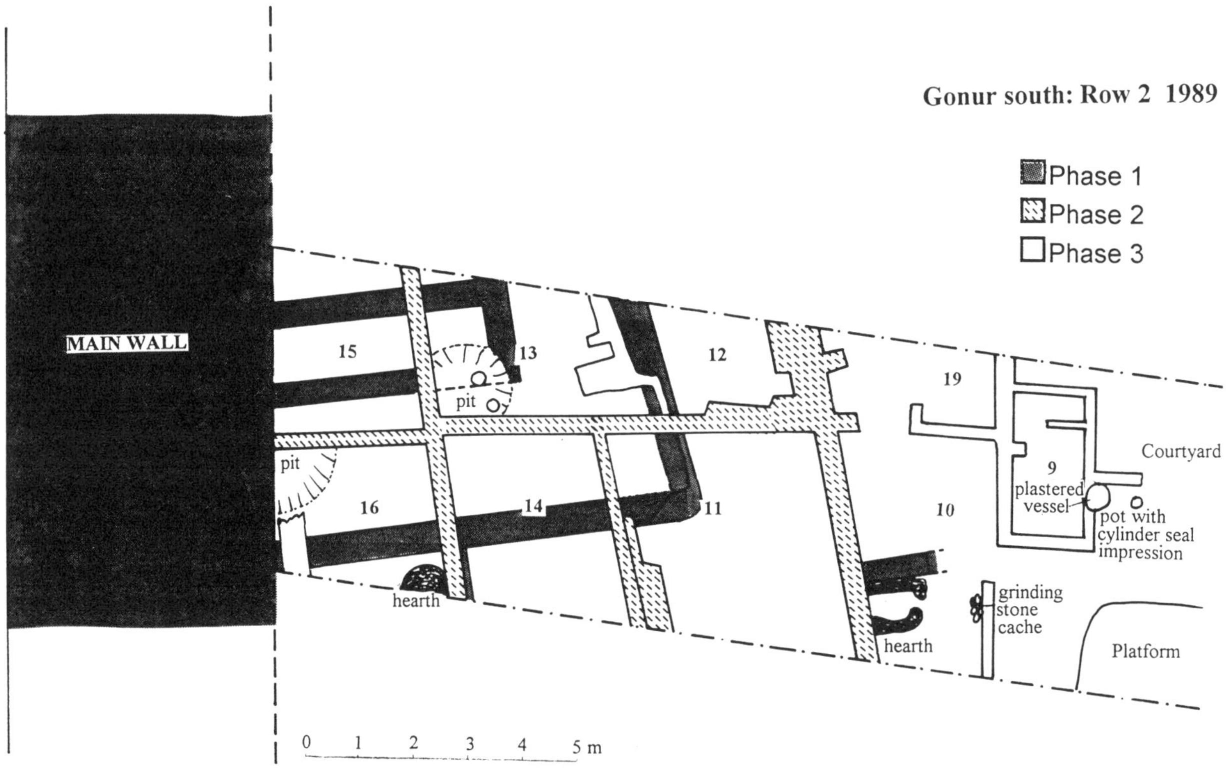

Figure 7.6
Gonur south, Row 2, plan of 1989 collaborative excavations.

were not set in foundation trenches—but the floors were constructed after the walls were built. The absolute elevation of floors differs between adjacent rooms (such as Rooms 14 and 16) of the same phase.

Phase 1: Domestic Architecture

The first architectural phase was traced in all of the rooms of this row (Rooms 9 through 16) and in the courtyard (fig. 7.7). The floors were poorly preserved, but ceramics were found in situ on them.

The original floor was well made with gypsum and lapped against the exterior wall. The bricks of the interior walls of the first phase were interlocked with the bricks of the exterior wall at the base. The interior walls were 50 cm wide and oriented with the north main wall rather than the nearby west main wall. In Room 16, a hearth with ceramics around it lay next to the original wall. In Room 10 was a reddened circular hearth built next to the wall, with a cache of eight grinding slabs and a bone tube nearby. The courtyard had a tamped earth surface with several whole pots in situ. The ensemble of rooms from Row 2 gives the impression of a domestic area, similar to the Period 1 household architecture.

A micromorphological analysis of a soil sample from this type of room deposit included many phytoliths from grasses, many holes from straw, yet very little charcoal or other burnt material. It included a great amount of gypsum, probably from fallen construction material (P. Goldberg, pers. comm.). Possible sources for this material include a threshing floor or bedding for animals.

Phases 2 and 3

The Phase 1 interior architecture was razed, and an entirely different room organization was built during

Figure 7.7
Excavations at Row 2.

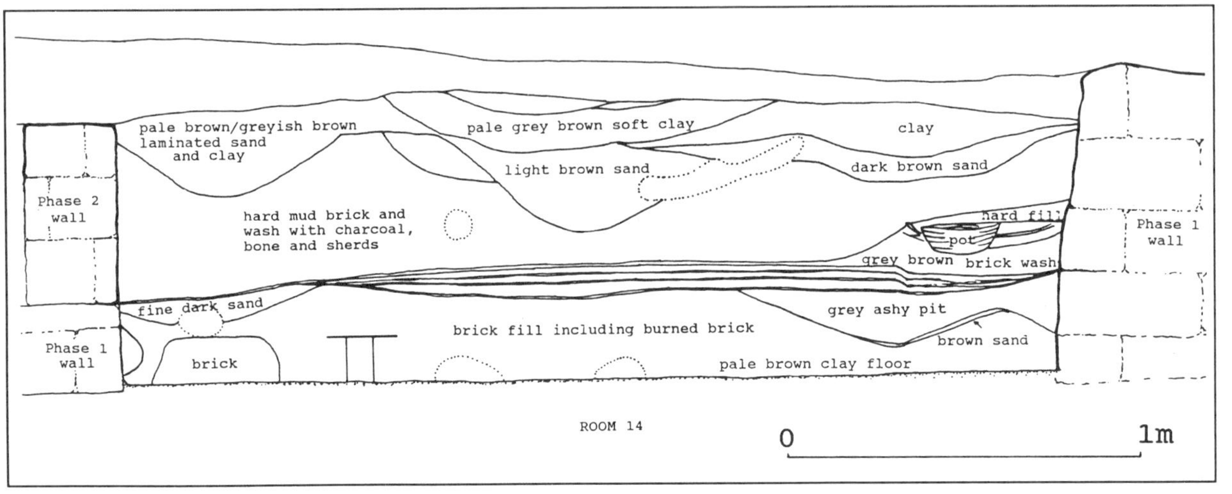

Figure 7.8
Stratigraphic section of Room 14, Row 2, south section.

Figure 7.9
Row 2 courtyard, excavation of storage vessel with cylinder seal impression.

Phase 2. Even the court area appears to have been leveled. The Phase 2 interior walls are thinner and were built on a well-made gypsum-specked floor (fig. 7.8). Multiple floors were found in some areas (such as Room 14), and typical domestic debris of ceramics, bones, and ashy hearths was found on them.

Many of the rooms, filled with pits and midden, appear to have fallen into disuse by Phase 3. Others, however, have upper floors, and a few rooms were divided by small ephemeral walls, clearly reusing some of the Phase 2 walls.

Unlike the room architecture, courtyards do not have seem to have changed their function from Phase 1 to Phase 3. As in Phase 1, the courtyard on the eastern side of Row 2 contains large storage jars. One of the jars in Phase 2 context in the courtyard of Row 2 (fig. 7.9) was impressed with a distinctive BMAC cylinder seal impression (see chap. 4, fig. 4.35).

In each phase at Gonur south, there is a mosaic of occupied and abandoned domestic rooms. Abandoned rooms have lenses of soft charcoally midden, such as in the upper fill of Room 14. Occasionally, whole storage pots are found in these deposits. Burials, cenotaphs, and storage caches of ceramics, tools, and so on are found in these types of deposits throughout the building.

NORTH SIDE

Kelli

The narrow rooms (0.8 x 3.5 m) found in rows along the northern wall at Gonur are called *kelli*. There are *kelli* at Togolok 21 and Gonur, but at both sites their function has been enigmatic.

The Russian term *kelli* means long narrow room or cell. The word's original use was for an element of monastic architecture—long narrow cells inhabited by monks. The first set of prehistoric *kelli* was defined at Togolok 21, where the rooms were found in long rows. These *kelli* were more regular than those at Gonur but less well preserved; the walls of the *kelli* at Togolok are 5 to 10 cm high, whereas the walls of the Gonur *kelli* are 50 to 80 cm high. Little more than the floor plan was known about this type of room until the excavations at Gonur. The literal interpretation of these narrow rooms as monastic cells is evident in some of Sarianidi's writings (e.g., Sarianidi 1987a), but as more is known about them, the idea that they were actually occupied is no longer current. The name is still used, however.

Excavation of a *kelli*

Kelli 68 (fig. 7.10) is 310 x 90 cm. The original floor is preserved 50 cm beneath the present-day natural surface outside of the main wall. Excavations beneath the original floor in the south half of the room revealed that the walls and floors of the room were built on at least 10 to 15 cm of sterile grey clay similar to the grey clay deposit found in other subfloor tests (fig. 7.11).

The *kelli*'s original (Phase 1) floor is compact brown dirt with an ashy grey surface; no material was found lying on the floor itself.

The Phase 2 floor is a compact brown dirt surface 3 to 4 cm thick with chaff and white gypsum specks; it was plastered up against and along the sides of the *kelli*. A whole handmade *khomcha* blackened by use lies several cm above the floor, and only a few sherds lie directly on this surface.

The walls of the *kelli* are preserved 60 to 65 cm above this second floor. The east and west walls are poorly preserved in the southern half of the room, where they may have been disturbed by a later pit. The *kelli* is blocked off to the south by a later wall (Phase 3) 15 to 20 cm thick, barely one brick wide. Soft bricky midden filled the *kelli* before it was blocked off. The upper levels were disturbed by rodent burrowing.

Some of the better-preserved *kelli* on the eastern side, such as 69, 70, and 71, have low arched doorways (fig. 7.12). *Kelli* 34, 35, and 36 appear to have never had access doorways. The easternmost *kelli*, 73 and 74, are much narrower than the rest, have no doorways, and do not appear to have ever been used for storage. Many of the *kelli* were later reused and incorporated into domestic areas. I suggest that the *kelli* were originally part of a substructure on which upper architecture rested. The *kelli* were open to the interior courtyard by short doorways, no more than 50 cm tall. They all have unusually thick walls for simply architectural purposes. On the basis of the plan of the *kelli*, Dietrich Huff (pers. comm.) has suggested that the *kelli* were substructures for a ramp,

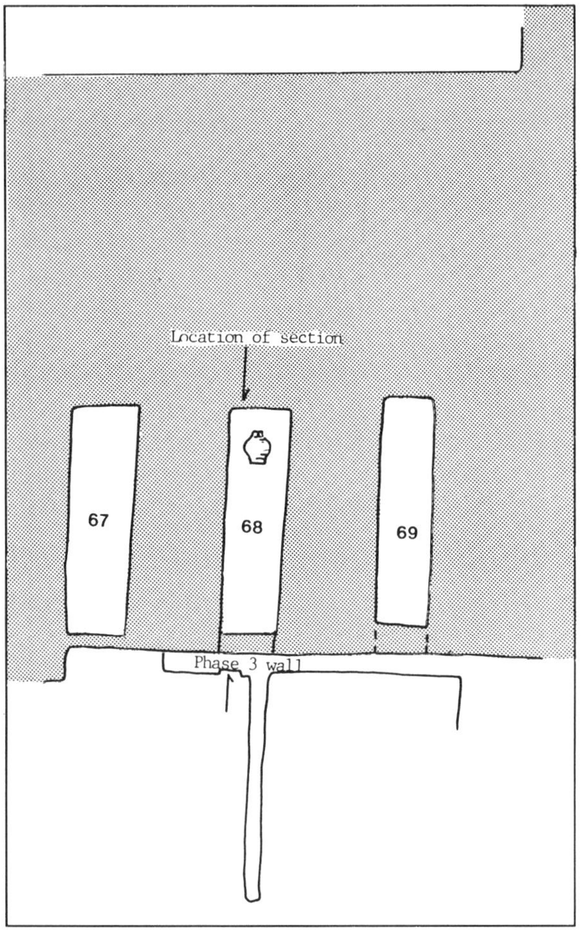

Figure 7.10
Kelli 68.

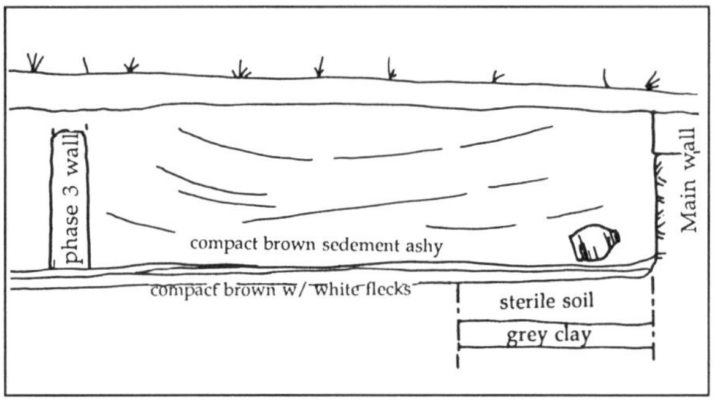

Figure 7.11
Kelli 68, east section.

allowing access to the top of the monumental exterior wall in a fashion similar to Roman forts (fig. 7.13). Such a ramp would have smaller *kelli* near the base end, similar to the easternmost *kelli* at Gonur. The ramp would have led up to the tower on the northwest corner or to the wall. In the case of Togolok 21, the *kelli* would have supported an even longer ramp, leading up to the northwestern central pylon. At Togolok 21, it can be envisioned that Room 114 would have served as a gatehouse or entrance for the ramp.

Architecture South of the *Kelli*

During Phases 1 and 2, most of the *kelli* were open to the south toward a large courtyard (fig. 7.14:A). During Phase 3, domestic structures were built in the courtyard area and several of the *kelli* were modified for other uses (fig. 7.14:B). The floors of the Phase 3 architecture (Rooms 8 through 28) lie on 25 to 50 cm of bricky fill above the former courtyard area. Rooms 8, 20, and 21 form a typical three- to four-room unit built up against eight *kelli*. Most of the *kelli* entrances were closed off except for one in each room. *Kelli* 7 and 31 contain storage jars, and functioned like long narrow rooms. *Kelli* 5 was transformed into a kiln or oven for Room 8. It appears that, by Phase 3, the superstructure or floor above some of the *kelli* had been destroyed.

NORTHEAST SIDE

Phase 2 architecture is built against the exterior north wall and runs underneath the later Central Building (Phase 5). The Phase 2 architecture consists of a series of large rooms connected to courtyards.

Phase 2: Domestic Architecture

Room 84 is a large domestic room that appears to have been roofed; it has 40-cm-wide header/stretcher wall construction, a well-built plastered floor, and a doorway with a 20-cm raised sill. The doorway leads to two smaller Rooms (81 and 82) with open doorways leading to a courtyard area (Room 83). The two smaller rooms had tamped earth floors and probably were not roofed.

The floor of Room 84 had been replastered once, with smooth grey mud with flakes of gypsum. The floor was well preserved over the entire room and

Figure 7.12
Arched entrances of *Kelli* 70 and 71.

Figure 7.13
Possible reconstruction of *kelli* as a foundation for a ramp.

floor was well preserved over the entire room and sloped to the north (fig. 7.15).

Three large open conical vessels (*tagora*) were found along the south side of the room. Two of the large vessels were simply lying on the floor: one had several layers of plaster on the inside up to the rim; the other had a large plaster plug in the base, with slight traces of plaster along the sides; vessel C was plastered inside and outside and may have been plastered in place. Around the large pots was a cache of grinding stones, including two prismatic hand grinding stones, eight slab grinding stones (some longer than 40 cm), and three smaller pounding stones, finer than the grinding slabs (fig. 7.16). Smaller closed vessels on the floor include small spouted bowls (type 1.B.6), egg-shaped cups (type 1.B.5), and a bottle with a wide shoulder and small base (type 1.B.4) (see chap. 4, fig. 4.18). Against the wall was a *khomcha*. All of these vessels appear to have been used together, and all

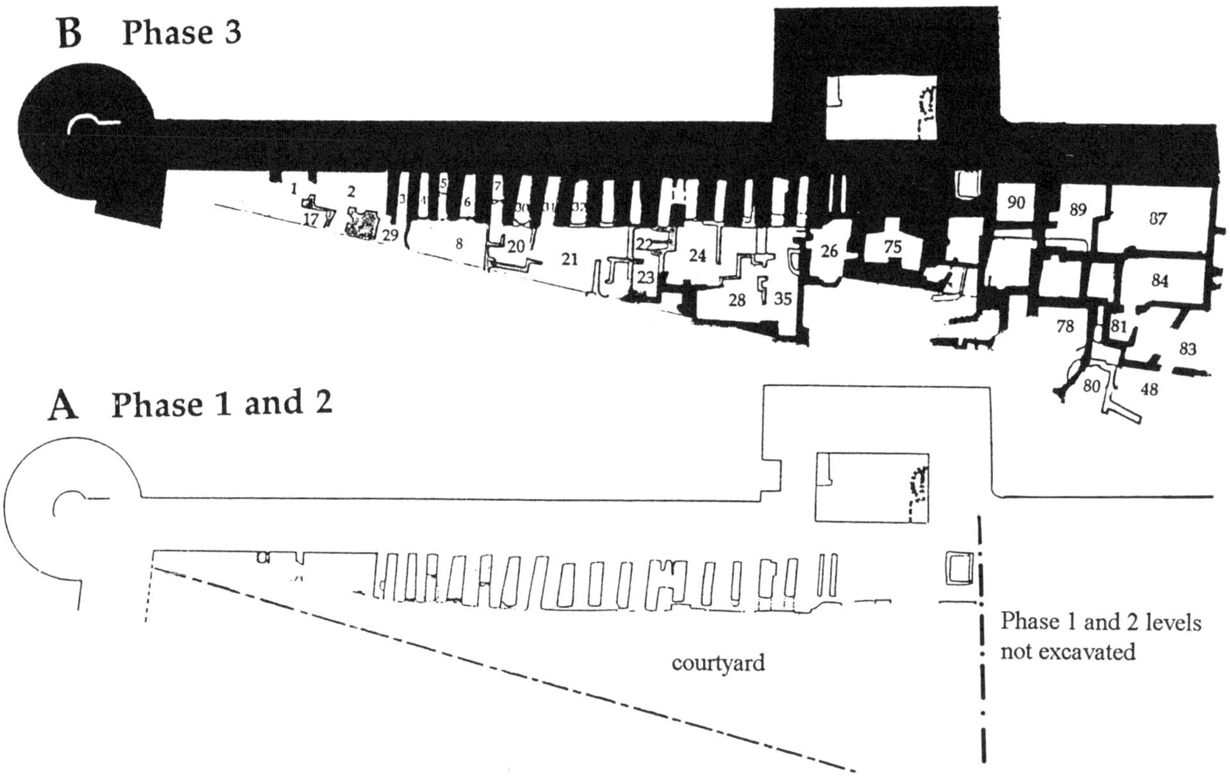

Figure 7.14
Area to the south of the *kelli*. A: Phase 1 and 2; B: Phase 3.

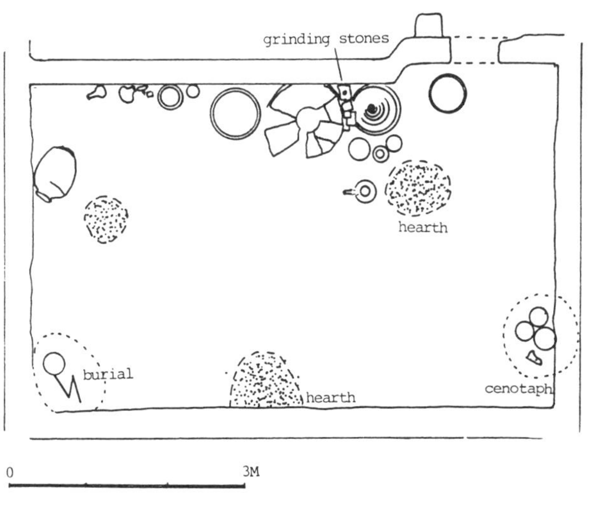

Figure 7.15
Room 84, Phase 2.

appear to have been involved in the processing that involved the *tagoras*. No such large vessels were found in the domestic architecture of Period 1 from the north mound.

The upper fill (Phase 3) is very bricky and contains crushed ceramic vessels. The room appears to have been used as a dump after it fell out of use. Some of the pots were filled with hearth and courtyard sweepings during the later dumping. In the northeast corner, an infant was buried in the Phase 3 deposit without any preserved burial objects. In the same deposit (in the northeast corner) was found a small group of pots and a worked bone object in the form of an axe. This group of objects appears to have been a small cenotaph most likely associated with the infant burial.

Figure 7.16
North side, Room 84.

Comments Concerning Domestic Architecture

We have evidence for continuity of domestic occupation at Gonur south, from its initial construction (Row 2), into its second phase (Room 84 complex), and into the upper level, Phase 3 (Room 8 complex). Although there is a shifting of function and construction within the building complex, the overall function of the building appears to have included domestic residences throughout its occupation. A similar mosaic of occupation may have also occurred at the other BMAC sites of Togolok 1 and Togolok 21, where occupational deposits, middens, and burials were found within the building complex.

WEST SIDE, ROWS 3 THROUGH 8

During the first period of occupation in Margiana (Gonur north, Kelleli 3, and Kelleli 4), production appears to have been limited to domestic scale; there is no evidence that it was carried out in large scale, as in the contemporary foothill sites.

In the architecture of Period 2 in Margiana (Gonur south, Togolok 1, and Togolok 21), large-scale storage and production occurred within the building complex in special rooms and areas, and new architectural forms reflect this. These include communal spaces dedicated to storage or production and specialized features such as heavily plastered vessels, kilns, and firepits.

At Gonur south these features are best documented on the west side, where both domestic areas and large-scale production/storage areas are found.

Phase 1

It is possible to trace several interconnected rooms leading to courts and alleyways in a pattern similar to that of Phase 1 architecture in Row 2 (fig. 7.17). For example, Room 37 (Row 3) is a large room with a hearth, and has a large storage vessel buried under the wall near the west wall, and a plastered reed basket on the floor. It appears to have been a room of a domestic area. This room is connected by a doorway with a doorsill to Courtyard 36. A straight alleyway connects two courtyards (Room 36 in Row 3 and Room 63 in Row 4). Courtyard areas have tamped earth floors with ashy midden deposits. In Phase 2 of this courtyard (Room 36) were large fragments of several *podstavki* (potstands).

Phase 1 rooms are poorly preserved along the western side of the building complex. The original walls were razed by later occupants. Well-preserved rooms were uncovered in the subsequent seasons (1990–1993) along the east side of Rows 5, 6, and 7, which were part of the original building complex (phase 1). These rooms include some of the most distinctive finds including bullae, in situ vessels, and intact architecture (fig. 7.18). Sarianidi (1994) interprets the architecture of this part of Gonur south to be dedicated to ritual and administrative activities.

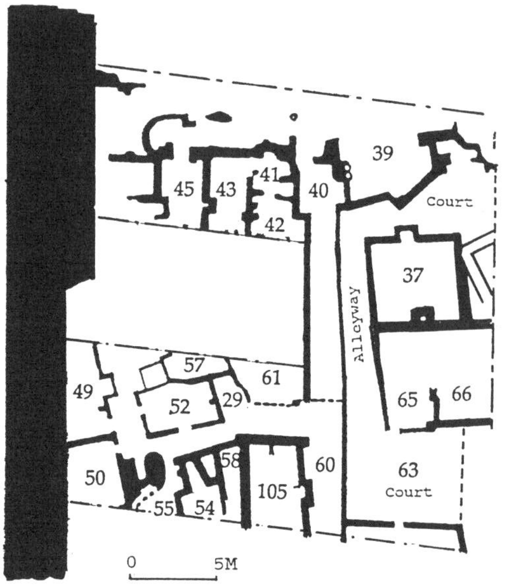

Figure 7.17
Rows 3–4.

Phases 2 and 3

Most of the preserved architecture on the west side is Phase 2 with Phase 3 modifications. Like the Phase 1 architecture, these phases are characterized by courtyards, room groups, and alleyways.

Khom khana: Room 52

Room 52 (Row 2) is isolated from the rest of the architecture of Phase 2 in this area in that it is not part of a multiroom complex (fig. 7.19). Its function appears to have been a communal storage area not associated with one particular household. It is surrounded on two sides by an alleyway, and the room opens through two doorways with doorsills 15 to 20 cm tall on the west and the south sides. A platform to the north of the room seems to have been a later (Phase 3) feature. The room may have been part of an earlier ground plan, but we did not find an earlier floor. The 25- to 30-cm (one-brick-wide) walls were built together with the other Phase 2 walls. The room had a pilaster to support a roof, and 80 cm of room fill consisting mostly of brick fall.

On the east side of the room is a platform, 15 to 20 cm above the floor, containing two or three rows of circular shallow pits lined with clay. These held a few

Figure 7.18
Gonur south, south side, Room 208, Row 6.

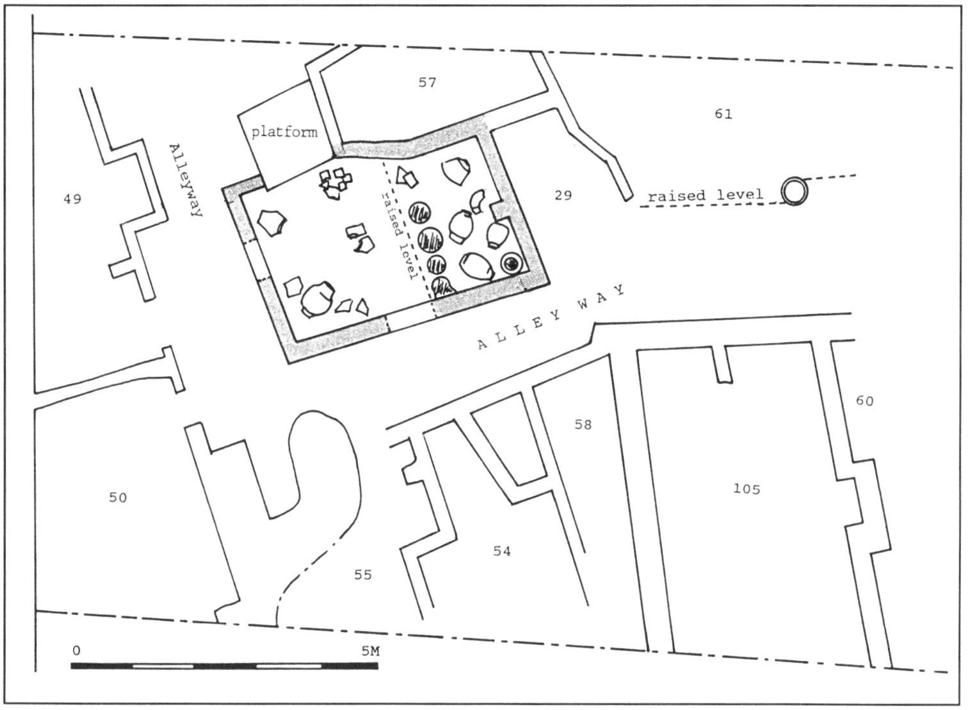

Figure 7.19
Row 4, Room 52, Phase 2, *khom khana*.

sherds and brick fragments. Six large storage jars, *khoms,* sat on or above the platform bench (fig. 7.20). On the west side of the room were some large broken fragments of *khoms* that were sitting on, or just above, the floor.

Rooms with benches and *khom* storage areas or *khom khanas* can be compared to Room 34 at Togolok 21, the "*haoma* production area." This room is an example of a production/storage facility within the architectural complex not found in the earlier period in the Margiana oases.

Figure 7.20
Pots plastered in place in Room 52.

Plastered Baskets and Vessels

Khoms and baskets plastered with white gypsum were found in many rooms (Rooms 2, 13, 37, and 137, among others) along the west and north sides and are known from all phases. For example, a plastered basket was found at Gonur south on the floor in Room 37 (Phase 1). It is an open basket estimated to be 1 m in diameter and 50 cm deep, lying on its side and slightly folded over on itself. The plaster is thick inside and out and thickly covers the rim. Seven layers of replastering could be seen.

The baskets were covered with plaster, apparently to make them waterproof. With the abundant and well-made ceramics from Gonur, it was surprising to find plaster-covered reed baskets. Equally surprising was to find many white-plastered ceramic vessels, such as two pots in Room 8 coated inside and out with white plaster (fig. 7.21).

The plastered baskets and vessels may be for specialized storage or production. Plastered reed baskets are also found at contemporary sites in southern Bactria where they were excavated at Dashli 3 (Sarianidi, pers. comm.). At Gonur, plaster-coated vessels are found in domestic areas (Room 37), and in rooms used for large-scale production or storage (Room 137).

Rooms such as Room 137 containing plastered vessels appear to have been for specialized production (fig. 7.22). Room 137 has 40-cm-thick walls and a well-preserved floor, suggesting that it was roofed, although no doorsills were located. The floor was plastered with white gypsum and sloped to the west toward three thickly plastered vessel bases beneath the floor. This arrangement is similar to architecture from southern Iraq and the Arabian Gulf area, where dates were laid in specially plastered rooms and the date juice dripped into basins at one end of the room (Rougeulle 1982). Although there is no evidence for dates in Margiana (Miller 1993), Room 137 appears to have been used for a similar type of production.

Figure 7.21
Plastered vessel, Room 9, Row 2.

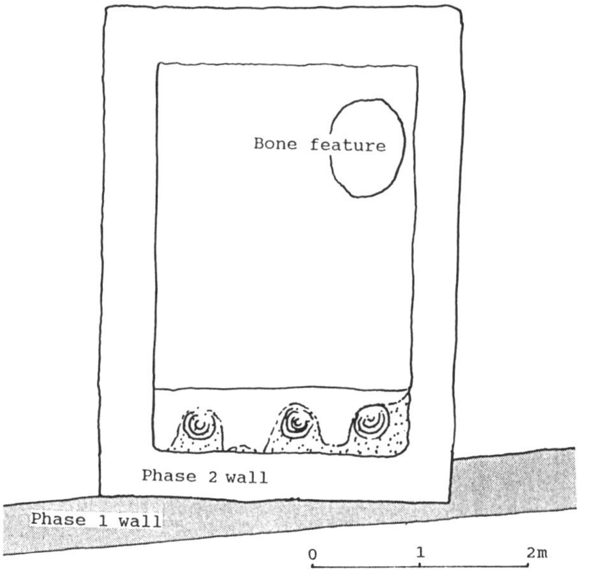

Figure 7.22
Row 7, Room 137. Room 137 has a slightly sloping plastered floor with three plastered vessels set into the floor at the low end.

Plaster

White gypsum plaster is a common construction material incorporated into the standard floors. Several rooms, such as Room 105 (Row 4)(see fig. 7.19), had white-plastered floors (as opposed to fragments of plaster in the flooring).

Many rooms of the northwest quarter of the central building at Togolok 21 have white plastered floors. The difference between the plastered floors and the clayey earth floors has been suggested to reflect the difference between ceremonial (*paradnii*) and domestic areas. At Gonur, plastered floors are found in domestic room complexes, in production/storage areas, and in ceremonial areas.

A sample of the white plaster from Gonur was analyzed. It is composed of calcium sulphate ($CaSO_4$), indicating that the sample was a gypsum plaster (R. Tykot, pers. comm.). Gypsum is a naturally forming mineral common in water-lain pans such as *takyri* (Dietrich and Skinner 1979). Gypsum would have been an abundant local resource surrounding the Murgab delta. The production of gypsum plaster requires firing at a low temperature (150° to 200°C) and can be produced in an open pit (Kingerly, Vandiver, and Prickett 1988). The excavated Period 2 sites in Margiana and Bactria have many plastered floors and vessels; however, kilns for producing the plaster have not yet been identified.

Kilns

Ceramics kilns are found in the building complex of Gonur south along the west and south side. Most of the kilns are intrusive into Phase 1 and 2 architectural deposits. For example, kilns in Rows 6 and 7 that are associated with Phase 3 architecture are dug into the earlier room fill.

The kiln in Row 6 (near Room 206) is a small, rectangular, two-chambered oven, typical of the late Bronze Age of the foothill zone and of Margiana (Sarianidi 1957; Masimov 1976). It was set 1.5 m into the earlier deposit with burned brick scattered on the surface (fig. 7.23). Typical of ceramic production in Margiana, no misfired ceramics were found around the kiln. Room 206 immediately to the north had a series of unbaked bowl fragments preserved on the floor, apparently ready to be fired at the time they were abandoned.

Kiln areas are found in several other areas on the west and south side of the building complex. Surrounding the site of Gonur to the west and to the north are scatters of similar kilns dated to Period 1 or Period 2, based on the associated ceramics.

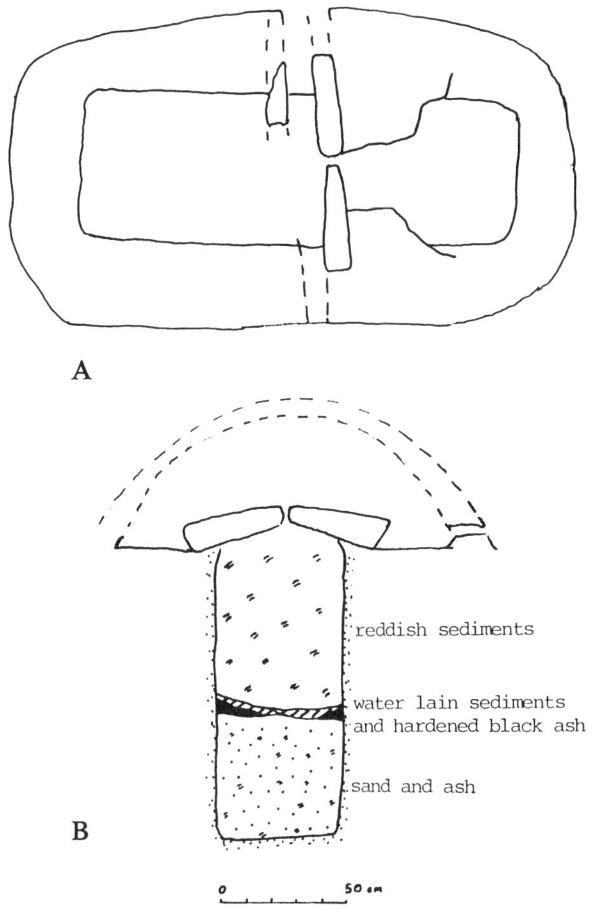

Figure 7.23
Row 6, ceramic kiln. A: top plan; B: section.

Fire Pits

Other highly fired features are found along the south side of Gonur south. Fire pits are rectangular brick-lined chambers built beneath the floor surface (fig. 7.24). They occur in rows from two to five chambers long and have indications of very intense heat. Fire pits are found along the west exterior wall and along the south exterior wall (Row 8). It is unclear during what phase of occupation these pits were constructed and used. Similar fire pits (a row of five chambers) were found at Togolok 21 along the northwest exterior wall. In both cases they appear to be located apart from the room complexes, in open areas. No analogous features are found in the earlier Margiana architecture or in the architecture of the foothill zone. Similar chambers from the Dzharkutan temple, a contemporary site in northern Bactria, are associated with metal production (Askarov et al. 1988:35–37). However, the purpose of the fire pits at Gonur or Togolok is unclear since no slag, burned debris, or unfinished materials were found in or near them.

The location of the fire pits at Togolok 21 in the northwest corner wing of the building complex, opposite another ritual area, suggests to Sarianidi that they had ritual function (Sarianidi 1989a), with strong architectural parallels to altar rooms located in the corner wings of later (classical period) Bactrian temples, such as the Oxus temple (Sarianidi 1990).

Semifinished Artifacts

There appears to have been some stoneworking at Gonur south on the southwest side. A large partially worked steatite block with a depression pecked into it was found along the south exterior wall. Although unfinished pieces of steatite have yet to be found together with debitage and tools for working the stone at Gonur south, rooms with similar partly fin-

Figure 7.24
Row 8, fire chambers.

ished steatite and tools have been found at Togolok 21 (such as Room 148).

At Gonur, fragments of melted copper and a copper-alloy ingot come from Room 185, in the room complex along the east side of Rows 5, 6, and 7 excavated in 1990.

It is possible that metal casting, plaster production, and stoneworking occurred within the Period 2 building complexes of Gonur south, Togolok 1, and Togolok 21. Ceramic production is documented within the building complex at least in the later phases of occupation.

Burials and Cenotaphs (Phase 4)

The building complexes of Period 2 such as Togolok 1, Togolok 21, and Gonur south include abandoned areas that served for dumping and for burials. The burials and cenotaphs are contemporary with Phases 1 through 3 in the south mound building complex.

Cenotaphs are groups of ceramics and small artifacts that serve as burial offerings without any human remains. I suggest that in Margiana they occur together with a nearby burial. At Gonur there are several instances of burials with cenotaphs 5 to 15 m away. For example, from Room 84 (north side), both an infant burial and a cenotaph were interred. This pattern appears to be found in other BMAC burials in northern Bactria (Dzharkutan); BMAC burials outside of Central Asia, such as at Shahdad, Khurab, Sibri, Mehrgarh VIII, and the Quetta hoard also follow this pattern of burials with nearby cenotaphs.

Two types of Period 2 burials are found at Gonur: burials with tombs made of mud brick containing ten to twenty vessels, elite artifacts, and food offerings; and burials of individuals without constructed graves, usually with few, if any, burial goods. Both appear to have cenotaphs associated with them.

By 1989 more than forty burials and cenotaphs had been excavated from Gonur. Most of the cenotaphs from midden contexts in the building complex at Gonur south did not contain exotic goods. The cenotaph in Room 84 had a copy of an axe, made out of the bone of a large mammal. From Row 8, a cenotaph consisted of a spouted ritual vessel and the remains of an upper fore- and hindlimb of a cow or bull (fig. 7.25). These cenotaphs were found in the vicinity of graves of individuals that were shallowly dug into room midden in the south mound building complex.

A rich cenotaph was found on the south side of the building complex, in the courtyard near the three fire pits. No burial has been found near it. This cenotaph contained eight small pots, some with incised pottery marks inside (see chap. 4, fig. 4.5). A bronze axehead in a zoomorphic shape with a (poorly preserved) wooden handle and wrapped in woolen cloth was found near the ceramics. While the cenotaph was located in the courtyard, the objects could not have been buried long after that particular area was occupied, based on a comparison of the ceramics with those from the occupational levels in the building.

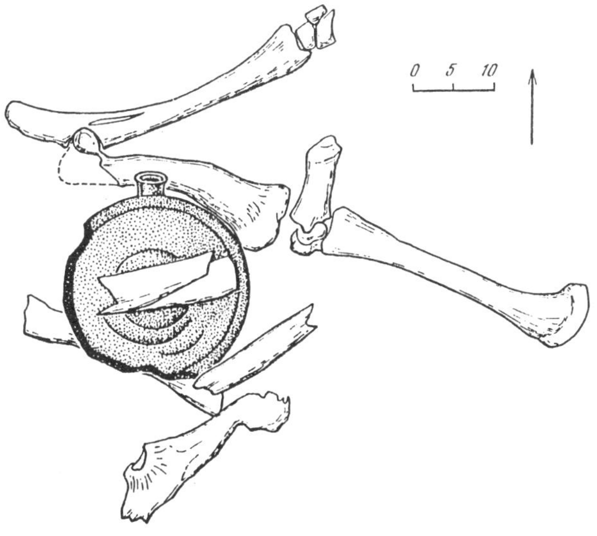

Figure 7.25
Row 8, cenotaph with cattle bone and ceramics near surface of southern mound of Gonur depe.

CONCLUSIONS

Fortified self-contained settlements are first found in the initial widespread occupation of Margiana, that is, at Kelleli 3 and 4 and the *kremel* at Gonur north. The architecture developed in the second period, where the complexes are completely self-contained, including production within the building complex itself.

When the monumental buildings of the BMAC were first excavated (Sarianidi 1977; Askarov 1977), well-planned enclosed building complexes were unknown from Bronze Age Central Asia. These buildings were unlike any Bronze Age architecture of the Kopet Dag foothill zone and were originally interpreted as temples or ritual architecture (Sarianidi 1977; Askarov 1977).

It is now clear that these are typical of, rather than the exception to, Margiana and Bactrian architecture. For example, the Dzharkutan temple has an alleyway, courtyard, multiroom complex, wall hearths with chimneys, and *zakladka* courtyard. Surrounded by the massive wall, this building appears to be a typical BMAC occupation compound rather than a building dedicated to ritual.

The features characteristic of Period 2 described from Gonur south are found at all of the contemporary settlements of Margiana and Bactria. The Bactrian sites of Sapalli, Dashli 1, and Dashli 3 have doubled exterior walls; Gonur south and Togolok 21 may have these as well. They all have domestic areas, communal production/storage areas, and abandoned areas with middens and burials.

The exception to the architectural pattern in Bactria and Margiana is Togolok 21, which has many features of habitation and production similar to Gonur south but has some important contrasts as well. The main building has domestic architecture only in its northeast corner, the other areas have apparently roofed interconnected rooms and almost no hearths built into the walls and thus do not appear to be domestic. Although our interpretation of Togolok 21 is limited by the excavation methods used, the central building at Togolok 21 appears to have been an elite area, such as a large citadel or ark, similar to the huge Parthian period citadel Gyuar kala in Margiana.

At Gonur south, the building complex appears to have been abandoned suddenly at the end of the BMAC. Valuable grinding stones are found in the upper levels, unbaked ceramics lay near pottery kilns, and storage areas have large *khoms* still in place. Similar situations appear to be the case at Togolok 1 and Togolok 21, where there is no occupation following the Period 2 (BMAC) occupations.

It is unclear whether there is continuity of population from the Bronze Age of Margiana to the later classical and medieval occupations in Margiana. However, a strong environmental factor appears to dictate the type of economy and thus the kinds of architectural forms found in the oasis. This has led to a relatively conservative form of settlement, which, once established, has remained stable from its origin through the development of the traditional *qala*.

Continuity of the Margiana architectural pattern of the fortified isolated building complex or *qala* is seen in Iron Age oasis architecture, for example, from Tillya tepe in Afghanistan and at the site of Garri Kyariz I from the desert north of the Kopet Dag mountains in the region of Ashgabat (Pilipko 1984). At Gonur south, the central building (Phase 5), built on the abandoned BMAC building complex, also follows the *qala* pattern.

The influence of Central Asian *qala* architecture on large Parthian fortified buildings stretched from classical Bactria to the Persian Gulf. Later *qala* buildings were transformed into entrepôts for trade known as caravansari. The caravansari form of architecture was not borrowed from the Romans or Syrians; rather it was an adaptation of the typical oasis architecture first developed in Bronze Age Central Asia.

CHAPTER EIGHT

The Domestic Economy of Gonur Depe

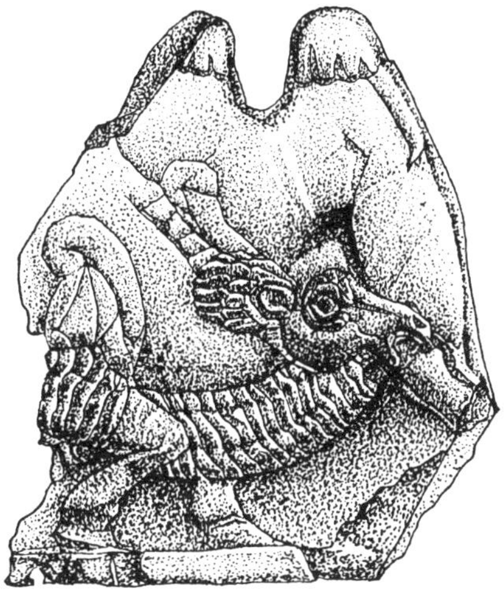

ONE OF THE MOST DRAMATIC DIFFERENCES BETWEEN THE foothill zone and the desert oases of Central Asia is in the natural ecology of the two areas. The seasons of flooding of the rivers between the two areas are reversed, and the natural delta of the Murgab must have been cleared of the *tugai* thicket and drained with canals before it could have been farmed. The resources of the oasis environment, once it was cleared of the natural thickets, allowed for greatly expanded agricultural potential but also placed constraints on the agricultural economy and herding. The importation of many raw materials for construction and manufacture led to new demands on animal transport as well. An entirely different ecological environment—that of the man-made oasis—is documented from the new excavations at Gonur.

THE PALEOETHNOBOTANICAL RECORD

The analysis of preserved plant remains, mostly from charred food remains and hearth sweepings, sheds light on the types of plants available in the environment and how they were used. These paleoethnobotanical remains were collected during the 1989 season at Gonur (Hiebert and Moore 1993) and have been published (Miller 1993, Moore et al. 1994).

Our initial research plan called for flotation of remains from the deep sounding and other contexts from the Murgab delta sites. For the most part, our plan to float samples in the field was thwarted by strong winds, but we did float several inside a tent on calm days. These few flotation samples allowed us to judge what information we were missing by not having carried out a complete program of water separation. Instead, samples were sieved with a fine (2 mm) screen. Hearth deposits and pot contents were sampled, and a series of samples was taken from the midden deposits of the deep sounding on the north mound at Gonur (see fig. 3.6).

The amounts and types of plants and plant parts preserved (Hillman 1984) indicate the original source of midden deposits. For example, the high amount of plant parts versus seeds and charcoal, may indicate plant processing debris typical of the courtyards. This contrasts with a sample from a hearth from the Period 1 domestic architecture (Room 2). It contained mostly charcoal and seeds, presumably from cooking;

a second hearth (hearth 2) was filled with burned bone fragments.

Cultivated Plants

Cultivated crops included barley, wheat, and pulses. Several forms of wheat and barley have been identified from the Gonur samples. Barley is the common cultigen and is found in all of the samples. The barleys (*Hordeum vulgare hexastistichum*) are all six-row and include naked and hulled forms. Both seeds and stem fragments of the barley have been identified (Miller 1993). Larger samples that include more measurable seeds could show other forms of barley as well, since barley is native to the foothills of Turkmenistan and a variety of types are found in Central Asia (Yaneshevich 1977). Free-threshing bread wheat (*Triticum aestivum*) is the most common wheat. Miller notes that the grain size is small, more similar to club wheat (*T. compactum*). Only a few of the small-sized wheat (*T. sphaerococcum*) and a few remains of emmer wheat (*T. dioccum*) were recovered. This diversity of grain cultigen types perhaps represents the attempts of ancient farmers to hedge their bets against the possibility that one type might fail.

The presence of dwarf or shot wheat (*T. sphaerococcum*) in the upper levels of the deep sounding (Period 2) is potentially significant because dwarf wheat is considered to be a South Asian variety (Costantini 1977a). Caution must be used in overemphasizing this identification, however, because the small wheat grains may be *T. compactum*, and the size of the puffed seeds was difficult to measure. The dwarf wheat is particularly draught resistant and thus would be a successful crop in this environment (Vishnu-Mittre and Savithri 1982). It must be noted, however, that the South Asian cultigens associated with the second agricultural revolution of double cropping, including sorghum, rice, and millet (Vishnu-Mittre 1977), have not been found in the Bronze Age sites of the Murgab delta (Moore et al. 1994).

Other cultigens found in the Gonur samples are several pulses (lentils, chickpeas, and peas) that were recovered in small number. Both grape (*Vitis vinifera*) pips and stems were found in the Gonur samples. Grapes are very well adapted to the oasis environment and bear fruit with renowned flavor and sweetness. Remains of other fruits, such as possible apples and plums, may indicate that the Bronze Age inhabitants tended permanent orchards or gardens.

Field Weeds

The wide diversity of weedy plants from the archaeological levels indicates the utilization of environmental zones with distinctive flora. Field weeds such as *Rumex* (dock) are typical of fairly moist irrigated fields (Miller 1993). Sedges (Cyperaceae) are typical of the salty marshes that surround the edges of the delta branches and are found along the canal edges. The herbaceous species and annuals that were identified, such as the Cruciferae, as well as *Adonis, Salsola, Suaeda, Seteria,* and *Phalaris,* are typical of the Central Asian shrub desert steppe (Walter and Box 1983:200). The most ubiquitous wild plant is camelthorn (*Alhagi*), which would have been found outside of the cultivated areas, between and beyond the fields as well as in overgrazed areas immediately around the site. Camelthorn, a thorny plant that inhibits grazing, is usually found where overgrazing has occurred. The presence of camelthorn seeds in sheep dung probably indicates that the sheep have been browsing on the oasis edge and in the desert.

Fuel

Some of the seeds from the deep sounding likely originated in dung fuel that was preserved by only partial burning. Other plant material appears to have been burned as a whole stalk, given that the seeds and pods were intact. In particular, stalks of some members of the mustard family (Cruciferae) were burned in quantity. This ephemeral wild plant, which propagates both by seeds and vegetatively, would not have been useful for fuel because it has no woody parts. However, it could have been harvested as bedding or fodder and subsequently burned.

Charred wood was abundant in the hearth samples. Analysis of the Gonur charcoal is pending the collection of comparative material from the oasis and desert areas surrounding the modern area of Gonur. Common trees of the oasis environment and the surrounding desert, such as poplar and tamarisk, were typical fuels at Bronze Age Shahr-i Sokhta (Costantini 1977a, 1977b). We expect to find use of *Haloxylon* (saxaul), the desert shrub wood famous for its high burning temperatures and long-burning coals. Based on observations in Bayram-Ali and the farms of the modern oasis, wood charcoal would come from desert shrubs, old wooden implements, fruit trees, and vines. Access to wood resources in the Margiana oasis would have been important because there appears to have been considerable use of fuel for ceramic, metal, and gypsum plaster production.

FAUNAL REMAINS

The sample of animal bones from the Gonur deep sounding was compared with bones from the fine-sieved samples to ensure that the recovery of bone was adequate for a preliminary assessment of the prehistoric animal use (Moore 1993a, table 1). Bones were collected for systematic study from the north mound domestic architecture, the deep sounding, and several of the early rooms at Gonur south (Moore 1993a, Moore et al. 1994). Additional material was collected by R. Meadow from several room contexts from the south mound (Meadow 1993).

Wild Animal Exploitation

Wild boar, gazelle, onager, hare, and birds were hunted and eaten as a small complement to the domestic animals. Wild animal remains in the deposits never exceeded 5 percent of the identified sample but represent some of the most interesting information about the relationship of humans to the desert environment.

Wild pigs and gazelle represent two different environments used for hunting: the boar inhabits the natural *tugai* thickets along the banks of the river branches and the gazelle is typical fauna of the Kara Kum desert. Hunting of wild boar occurred primarily in Period 1, suggesting that areas of the deltaic thicket still existed. By Period 2, the frequency of wild pig is less than 1 percent, perhaps indicating that hunting had become less important as the oasis was cleared and planted. The animals that would have been found on the fringes of the fields and in the desert, such as tortoise, hedgehog, and wild rodents, were found in low numbers throughout the occupation.

Wild animals are featured more commonly than domestic animals in the local designs on metal and stone objects. Snakes, scorpions, birds, tigers, wild sheep, and other less distinctive animal depictions are found. It is typically suggested that the artistic designs must have come from outside of Central Asia (Sarianidi 1990; Masson 1989). Although Bukhara tiger, snakes, scorpions, and so on are also part of the Central Asian desert and river ecology, their remains have not yet been found in the archaeological deposits. Mountain goat designs are more common on artifacts from the related Bactrian oases, which are close to mountain resource areas. Few bird bones were found from sieved deposits, but bird motifs are common on Margiana (BMAC) stone and metal seals. These birds are usually interpreted as eagles, and in fact the bones of a small eagle were found from Gonur south, room 84.

Domestic Animals

Sheep and Goats

Domestic sheep and goat bones were the most common of all animal remains found at Gonur. Moore (1993a) finds that the herd represented by the Gonur remains contained older individuals typical of an economy emphasizing secondary products.

The herds of sheep and goat provided meat as well as secondary products such as milk and wool. Very young sheep and goat remains from Gonur indicate that some sheep and goat would have been kept near to the settlement, similar to the ethnographic situation in the traditional oasis (see below).

There is no perceptible difference in the animal composition or herd composition between Period 1 and Period 2 (throughout the Bronze Age occupation at Gonur).

Cattle

Cattle (*Bos*) are traditionally not pastured outside of the oasis area and could have been kept at Gonur in the building complexes, as is typical in the modern oasis *qala,* by providing them with forage and water.

In the excavations at Gonur, *Bos* remains were few compared with sheep and goat, probably reflecting the actual low number of these large animals. The specific type (humped vs. unhumped) of domestic cattle found in the excavations could not be determined from the bones. However, many animal figurines with humps probably were intended to be images of humpbacked cattle.

All of the cattle remains came from domestic animals, with none of the *Bos primigenious* that inhabit steppe environments. Any occurrence of *Bos primigenious* would have indicated a considerably less desertic environment than the present environmental conditions.

The *Bos* remains were found in midden deposits from domestic debris. Like sheep/goat, cattle bones are found in ritual contexts interred together with ceramic vessels in isolated cenotaphs. In one particular case, the type of meat left in the cenotaph is determinable: two hindlimbs and a forelimb were found, representing the meaty part of a mature animal. In another case, an entire bull or cow was interred in the large (although robbed) burial at Togolok 1 (see chap. 2).

Both Sarianidi and Masson have written about the prominence of cattle in the symbolism of the Bronze Age of Central Asia and about its Mesopotamian origins. Masson relates a gold bull's head from Altyn depe to bull's heads found in Mesopotamia. This parallel has been interpreted as an imported Mesopotamian "bull cult" in the foothill zone of Central Asia (Masson 1976). A similar small white stone bull's head from Togolok 21 has been interpreted as a connection between Zoroastrian bull symbolism and Central Asian Bronze Age symbolism (Sarianidi 1990). However, the Central Asian Bronze Age sites produced such a diversity of animal forms in figurines that no special significance can be attributed to the occurrence of a bull or cow figurine.

Camel

The other important large domestic animal at Gonur was the camel (*Camelus* sp.). Grab sampling revealed no remains of camels from the excavations of Period 1: not from the north mound monumental building (*kremel*), the north mound domestic architecture, or the north mound deep sounding. Faunal materials excavated in past seasons are kept together with the ceramics in the "field museums," that is, the pottery yards next to the excavations allowing a scan for characteristic camel bone features. No identifiable camel bones were found in the collections from Togolok 1 or Togolok 21 from excavations carried out between 1983 and 1986. From the 1989 season at Gonur south (Period 2), no camel bones were found in excavations of secondary buildings inside the main wall on the north and the west side. However from the latest phase of construction at Gonur south, uncovered in the 1990 field seasons, camel phalanges and limb bones were found in Rooms 231, 252, and 254, all of which are part of the later (Phase 5) central building (Meadow 1993). The significance of the late appearance of the camel bones in the Margiana oasis is not yet clear. The camel would have been a key animal for transport of the large amount of stone and metal materials imported to the desert oasis. The Bactrian (two-humped) camel is clearly shown in several figurines and amulets from Margiana and from Bactria. Camels certainly could have been present in the sites of the Murgab delta during Period 1, without their bones having been deposited in the areas we sampled.

Equids

Remains of the true horse, *Equus caballus*, have not yet been positively identified from secure contexts at the Central Asian Bronze Age sites.

Figurines of wheeled carts are found in both Periods 1 and 2 of Margiana and have been part of the Central Asian tradition since the early third millennium (Namazga IV). The animal figurines connected with the carts always have humped torsos, indicating either camel or a humped cow (Kuz'mina 1980). At Gonur, primarily onager remains have been found in the room and midden deposits. These would have been hunted in the desert along with gazelle and not used for transportation.

Meadow (1993) identified several bones of domestic donkey (*Equus asinus*) from the south mound excavations at Gonur in 1990. These remains were recovered from architectural phases 3 through 5, ranging from BMAC period to late Bronze Age and early Iron Age. Although we are not able to place them within a particular phase, it is important to note that the BMAC period has steppe nomadic ceramics (Andronovo type), and that Andronovo nomads were familiar with the domestic horse (D. Anthony, pers. comm.).

Two Types of Bronze Age Pastoralists

Herding formed an important component of the economy in Bronze Age Margiana in a pattern similar to the traditional mixed (farming and herding) economy in the oases of Central Asia (Niyazklychev 1973).

Turkmen living in the Murgab River delta (Margiana oasis) in the nineteenth century farmed and herded karakul and fat tailed sheep with some goats. Camel were herded by separate herders. Horses were widely used for herding in the nineteenth century, in contrast to the Bronze Age system. The traditional *qala* of the oasis had stables and folds for herd animals inside of the building. Typically, animals were kept in the oasis in the fall and winter, stabled in the *qala* compound at night. Stratigraphic and micromorphological evidence from several courtyards at Gonur south suggest a similar pattern for the Bronze Age.

Traditional agriculturalists in the Kopet Dag foothill plain also participated in herding, forming a network of local pastoral nomadic routes into the desert on a seasonal basis in search of fodder (fig. 8.1). The implications for the ancient oasis system are twofold. First, the desert served not as a barrier but as a bridge between regions linked by these herders. Seasonal pastoralists such as these may have been the original colonizers of the Margiana oasis, as well as being the traders between the foothill zones and the desert oases.

Finds of Andronovo materials are evidence for a second type of nomadism. These Andronovo steppe nomadic ceramics and metal objects are found in Period 2 buildings and from campsites surrounding the oasis. Interaction with distant nomadic peoples by Period 2 at Gonur is a key to understanding the interaction of the oasis of Margiana with a broader region. In the next chapter I argue that the underlying factor in the development of the BMAC was the ability of the Bronze Age inhabitants of the oasis to bring in raw materials from distant areas. If these Andronovo nomads were involved in long-distance migrations, as is suggested by the nomadic ceramic parallels from distant areas, they may have played an important role in the development of the oasis economy.

Figure 8.1
Today, herders such as this man near Gonur depe, cross the Kara Kum desert following traditional patterns of movement from foothills to the oasis.

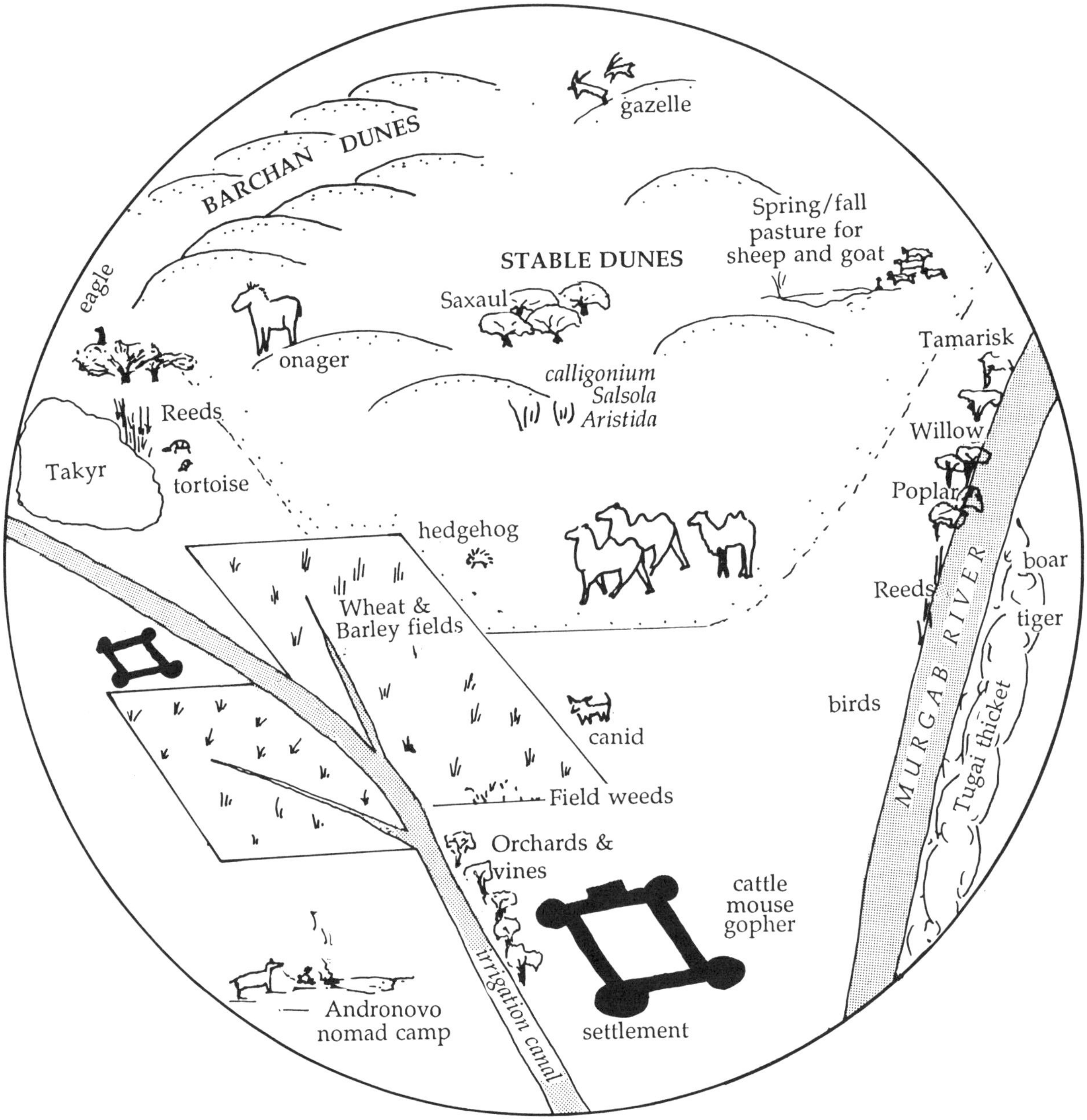

Figure 8.2
Reconstruction of the oasis environment of Bronze Age Margiana.

CONCLUSIONS

In conclusion, it is possible to sketch out a picture of the new settlements of the desert oasis that originated in Margiana (fig. 8.2). Dispersed fortified building complexes (similar to *qala*) were built on small natural rises or *takyr* flats where irrigation agriculture would not have been possible. Surrounding the building complexes were fields and orchards tended by families of the *qala*. Irrigation water and river runoff formed salt marshes and dry *takyr* with useful reeds, salt-adapted plants, and seasonal fauna. The desert edge lay at the margins of the fields and *takyr* with regions of dunes stabilized by saxaul, useful as a source of wood and as seasonal vegetation for herds. Small sites of local herders would be found in these areas, as well as camps for interaction outside of the oasis by traders and steppe nomads. Along the banks of the Murgab River, *tugai* thicket would have been exploited for wood resources as well as for boar and tiger. Beyond the immediate region of the oasis, moving dunes would have prevented travel except in north-south gullies between the dunes, which would have acted as a natural conduit to the eastern foothill zone of the Kopet Dag. The configuration of canals, orchards, and field edges is a fragile system that traditionally requires year-round attention. In the traditional oasis, when these features are not maintained, the man-made oasis environment quickly succumbs to the regrowth of reeds and *tugai* thickets, to salinization, and to the encroachment of moving dunes.

CHAPTER NINE

The Development of the Bactrian-Margiana Archaeological Complex

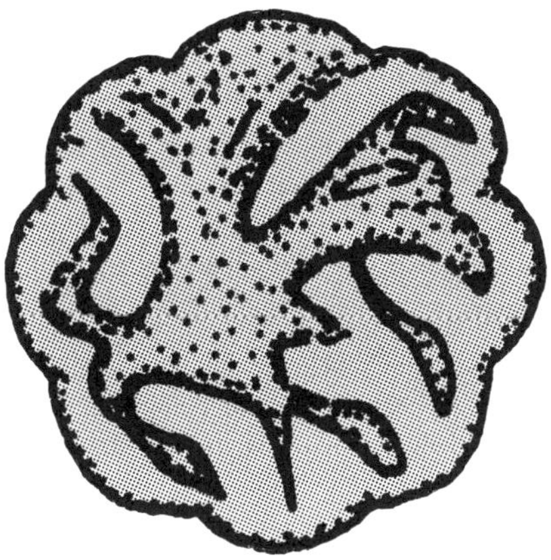

THE MOTIFS SPECIFIC TO THE BACTRIAN-MARGIANA ARCHaeological Complex include a set of images featuring human figures, isolated heads, desert animals and plants, and fantastic dragons (Sarianidi 1981b). The iconography of the BMAC is depicted on small stone objects, terracotta friezes on ceramics, bronze compartmented seals, cylinder seals, and ceremonial objects. The latter include stone staffs, miniature stone columns, amulets, and decorated maceheads and axes. Specific elements of the BMAC images appear in the later iconography and myths of Iran, South Asia, and even the eastern Mediterranean (Mitanni). This group of symbols is associated with a shared Indo-Iranian mythology reflected in both Vedic Indian myths and Avestan (Persian) myths (Sarianidi 1986b, 1990; Parpola 1988; Wilhelm 1989). In the BMAC, other iconographic precursors of later Indo-Iranian mythology and Persian religion (Zoroastrianism) are found. These include narrative scenes of power and domination, images of narcotic plants, and the use of amulets on bullae. BMAC artifacts include black/white (steatite/alabaster) symbolism evoking the structural dichotomy of good/evil and purity/pollution that emerges in later Zoroastrian ideology (Choksy 1989).

Given the chronology presented here, the BMAC is the earliest currently documented appearance of this new set of iconographic symbols. My colleagues excavating in Margiana base their chronology on stylistic parallels and have not accepted the chronology presented here (see preface, this volume). The Central Asian assemblage predates its previously suggested sources and thus the problem posed here is the source of the BMAC style.

Much research has been conducted on the interpretation of the iconography (Francfort 1993, 1994; Amiet 1986, 1990a), although this must be reconsidered with a careful review of the chronology of the occurrence of these artifacts, the production evidence for these artifacts, and the source material:

1. *Chronology.* Chronologically, the BMAC occurs only in Period 2 of Margiana; this is a later and successive stage in the occupation of the oasis, which began in Period 1. Most *categories* of small finds are present in both Periods 1 and 2. There is no important change in the use of the environment, agricultural system, or settlement between Periods 1 and 2. It is the emergence of a complex or an assemblage of objects with a specific style and attributes that characterizes the BMAC. There appears to be continuity of

PERIOD 1	PERIOD 2
Terracotta	
NMG V style human figurines	
Whorls of the Anau style	
	• Unbaked clay figurines
	• figurines from ceramics
	• terracotta amulets
animal figurines	animal figurines
cart + animal figurines	cart + animal figurines
Bone objects	
bone needles	bone needles
worked astragali	worked astragali
bone tools	bone tools
	• bone tubes
	• bone axes
textiles?	textiles
Steatite + alabaster	
steatite bowls w/triangles	steatite bowls w/triangles
steatite circle + dot motif	steatite circle + dot motif
kidney shaped bowls	• kidney shaped bowls
alabaster bowls	• alabaster bowls
alabaster cups on stands	• alabaster cups on stands
stone staffs	• stone staffs
miniature columns	• miniature columns
stone pocket bags	stone pocket bags
biconical beads	biconical beads
	• "cosmetic flasks"
	• figurative mace heads
	• amulets
	• cylinder seals
	• two-part pieces
	• multi-part figurines
	• steatite plaques
	(1) indian ocean sea shell
Bronze + other metals	
standard knifes + spears	standard knifes and spears
strainer vessels	strainer vessels
plain bronze pins	plain bronze pins
geometric bronze seals	• geometric bronze seals
bracelets	bracelets
	• figurative bronze pins, seals, and vessels
	• bronze amulets
	• ceremonial axes
	(1) curved 'nomadic' type knifes
gold and silver jewellery	• gold, silver and lead jewellery

• = BACTRIAN-MARGIANA ARCHAEOLOGICAL COMPLEX
Period 2 unstarred items are part of the general tradition in Margiana.
(1)= Imported objects not produced in Bactria or Margiana

Table 9.1
Chronology of small finds in Margiana.

settlement in Margiana from Period 2 (the BMAC) to Period 3, although only a few categories of artifacts have been found at Takhirbai 3 or in the central building at Gonur south. Most of the objects and symbols distinctive of the BMAC have disappeared although occupations continued.

2. Production. Several of the specific objects characterizing the BMAC were fabricated in Margiana. The analysis of the Period 2 architecture at Gonur (chap. 7) shows that production becomes based *within* the building complexes.

3. Raw Material Sources. Many BMAC small finds, both ceremonial and domestic objects, were produced from imported materials as well as from locally available material. The distribution of the BMAC outside of Central Asia, appearing primarily in burial contexts, is evidence for the movement of Central Asian peoples involved in acquiring raw materials, trading, or conquest.

In the following sections, I compare the small finds from Period 1 sites with those from Period 2 sites, by class of material. Small finds are made of both locally available materials and exotic materials that had to have been brought to the desert oasis. The two locally available classes of materials are clay (terracotta) and bone. Stone resources, including large utilitarian stones and semiprecious stones for ornaments, metals, and shell, were imported. The BMAC regional style was used not only on the locally available raw materials of animal bone and clay, but also in metal and on many kinds of stone.

Table 9.1 summarizes the chronology of the Margiana small finds from excavated contexts. Period 1 excavated contexts include the following: floor levels of the Gonur north (*kremel*) excavations; 1989 Gonur north domestic architecture; and Kelleli 3 and Kelleli 4 excavations. Period 2 excavated contexts include the following: Phases 1 through 4 of the building complex at Gonur south; Togolok 1 and Togolok 21 architecture; and Togolok 1, 21, and 24 burial contexts.

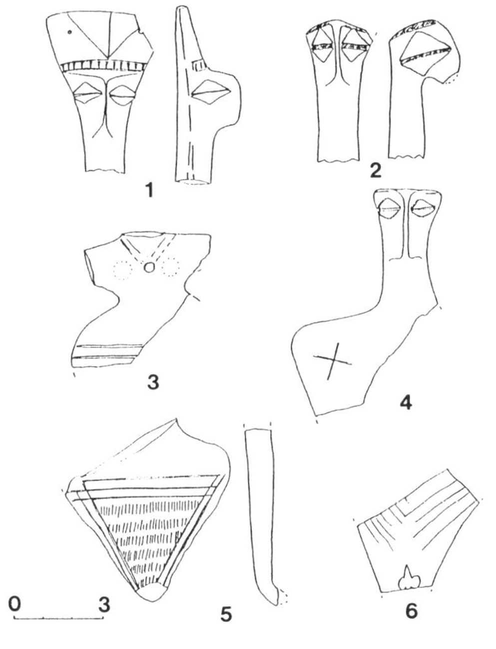

Figure 9.1
Period 1 terracotta figurines. 1) Gonur north, Room 23; 2) Gonur north, surface; 3) Gonur north, surface; 4) Gonur north, domestic architecture, Room 8; 5) Gonur, surface; 6) Gonur north, surface.

LOCALLY AVAILABLE MATERIALS

Terracotta

Violin-Shaped Human Figurines, Period 1

The Margiana figurines are simple, stylized female figures with outstretched arms, violin-shaped bodies, and exaggerated gender attributes. The heads have applied "coffee bean" eyes and beak noses. Two general head shapes are found (fig. 9.1). Figurines in the round are known; small fragments of figurines having legs and male genitalia are also known.

The terracotta human figurines found in the Gonur deep sounding are found only in Period 1 in Margiana and in the foothill sites of late Namazga V.

Margiana figurines often have incised signs on the arms, and some have necklace amulets (fig. 9.1:3). These details relate closely to the well-established sequence of figurines (types I and III) from the foothill zone of southern Turkmenistan (Masson and Sarianidi 1973).

Although the Margiana Period 1 figurines and the Altyn depe upper-level figurines arc very similar, they do not appear to have been exchanged or imported. Crudely formed and finely made figurines are found together in Margiana, based on finds from the Gonur deep sounding. The variation between styles of figurines may reflect different production areas, different individuals, or different ethnic entities (fig. 9.2).

The function of the figurines is not clear. They are found on every Period 1 site in Margiana and in all contexts: refuse, domestic rooms, and monumental architecture. Terracotta figurines of this type have been found in architectural context and in burials in the foothill region at Altyn depe (Burial 60, exc. 5, Masson 1988). This occurrence in the late Namazga V burials indicates that they had symbolic meaning in the belief system of Margiana and the foothill zone. We cannot speak of a central focus for ritual involving these figurines, because they are found on every site, large and small, and in every household.

The similarity of the figurines from Margiana (Period 1) and the Kopet Dag region (late Namazga V period) suggests that these populations had similar self-perceptions and a shared identity. This changes as the figurines drop out of the assemblage abruptly, and not gradually as has previously been suggested (Masimov 1981; Sarianidi 1981a).

Unbaked Clay Figurines, Period 2

At Togolok 21 a pair of male and female figurines was found in a small vessel (fig. 9.3). Made of unbaked clay, the figures may have functioned in ritual since they had pieces of sharp bone flakes stuck into them while still leather hard. Human figures are also found as appliqués on Period 2 ceramics, in the form of a terracotta frieze (Sarianidi 1980). These unbaked figures have a distinctive form unrelated to the violin-shaped figurines of Period 1, but similar to the human figures on the BMAC decorated ceramics (see fig. 9.6).

Figurines from Ceramic Vessels, Period 2

Series of terracotta figurines are found on large open pots of Period 2, such as the complete vessel found at Togolok 1 (chap. 4, figs. 4.22, 4.23).

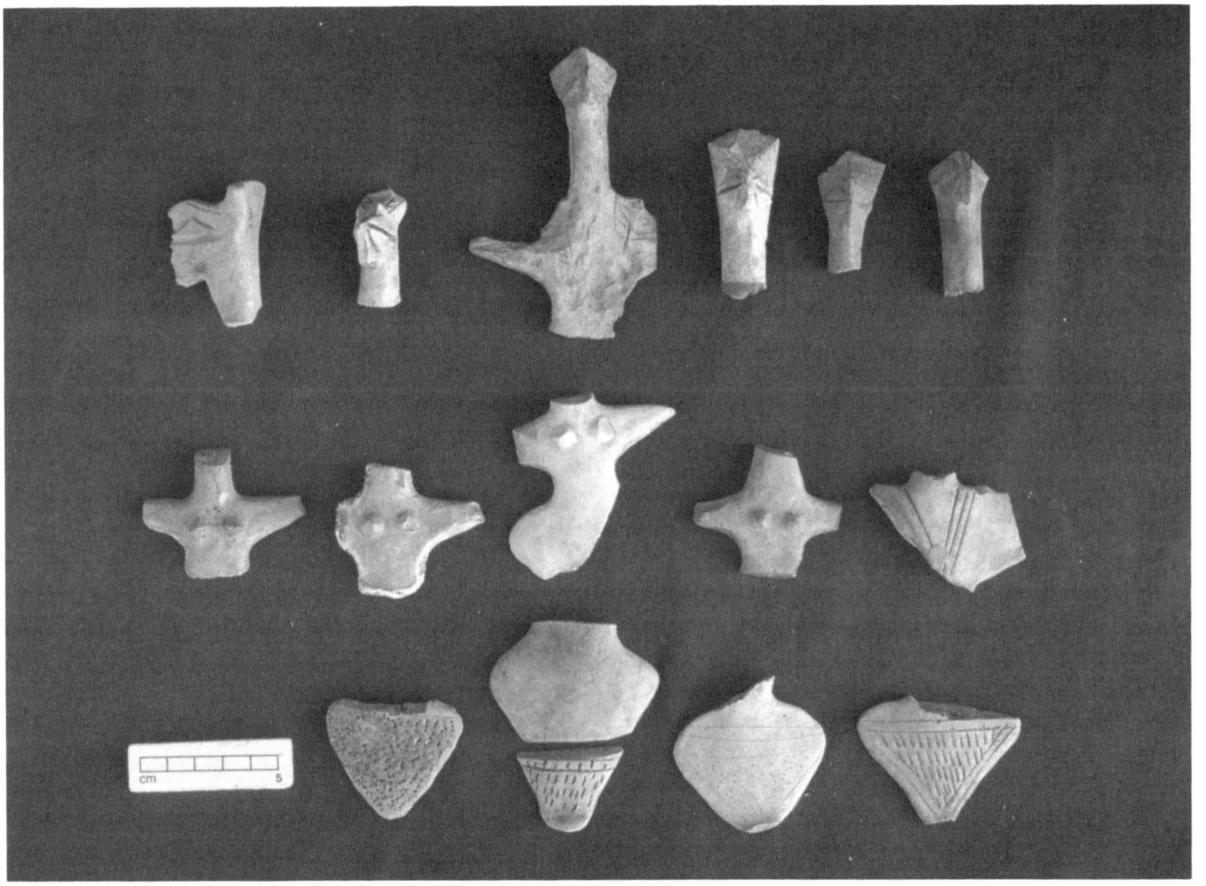

Figure 9.2
Period 1 terracotta figurines from Gonur north.

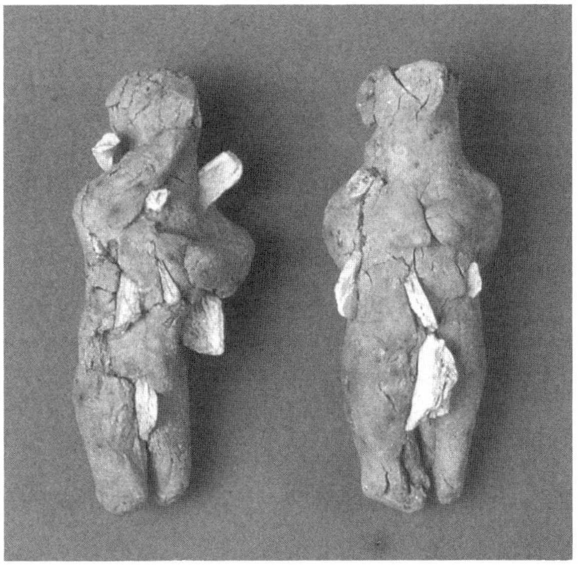

Figure 9.3
Period 2, unbaked clay figurines from Togolok 21 (Sarianidi 1990, pl. XIX:1,2).

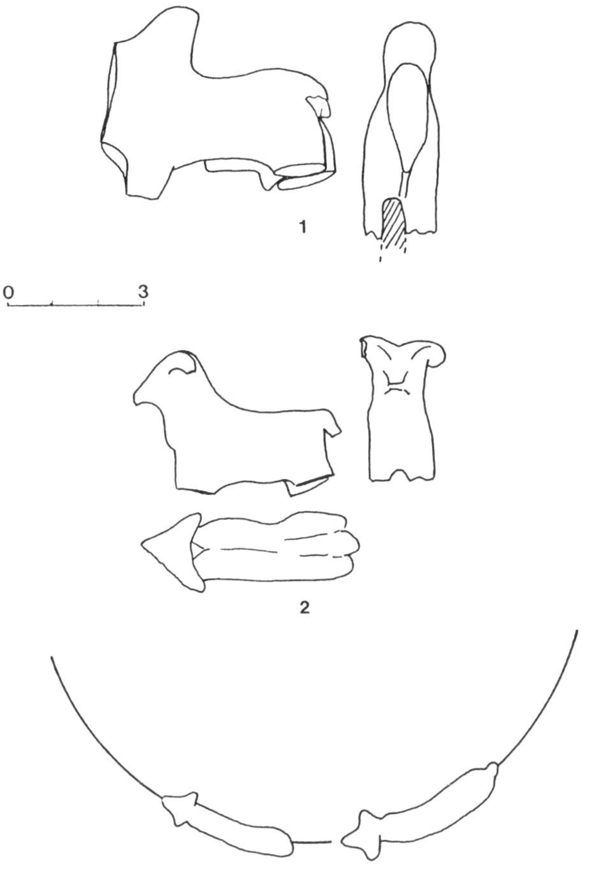

Figure 9.4
Period 2 figurines from ceramic vessels. 1) Gonur south, surface; 2) Gonur south, Room 122; 3) figurines from vessels have a distinctive curve following the diameter of the vessel.

There are two ways to determine if a figurine comes from a Period 2 vessel or was freestanding. First, if the legs are preserved, they will show evidence of being broken off of the rim (animals and humans) or sides (frogs and snakes); some figurines from vessels have fragments of the rim preserved between the feet. Second, figurines attached to the pots are distinctively curved (fig. 9.4). It is clear from excavated contexts that the vessels with terracotta friezes begin only in Period 2. Figurines from ceramic vessels are ubiquitous on Period 2 sites (fig. 9.5), suggesting the general distribution of these vessels in Margiana rather than the limited distribution suggested by the rare occurrence of whole vessels with terracotta friezes.

The figures include humans, birds, and other animals, which together clearly represent a narrative scene (fig. 9.6). Often, applied frogs and snakes are shown crawling upward along the inside walls of the vessels between the widely spaced figures. Like the unbaked clay figures from Period 2, the figures from vessel rims relate to each other, in contrast to the Period 1 figurines which stand alone. They possibly represent a *narrative*, part of the new Margiana ideology.

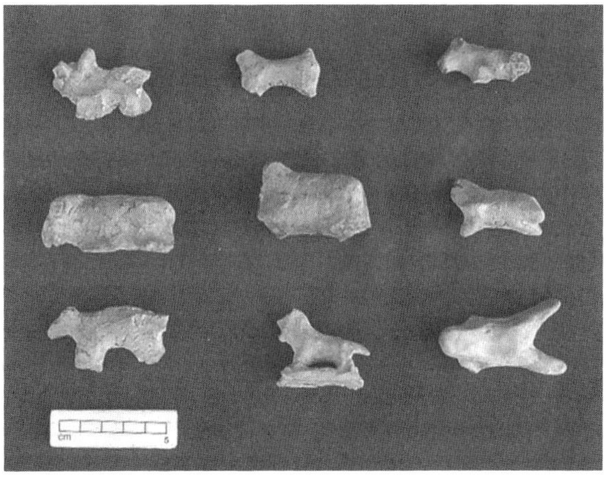

Figure 9.5
Period 2 terracotta figurines from vessel rims and sides.

Freestanding Animal Figurines, Periods 1 and 2

As opposed to the new tradition of human figures applied to vessels, there is a long tradition of freestanding terracotta animal figurines in Central Asia.

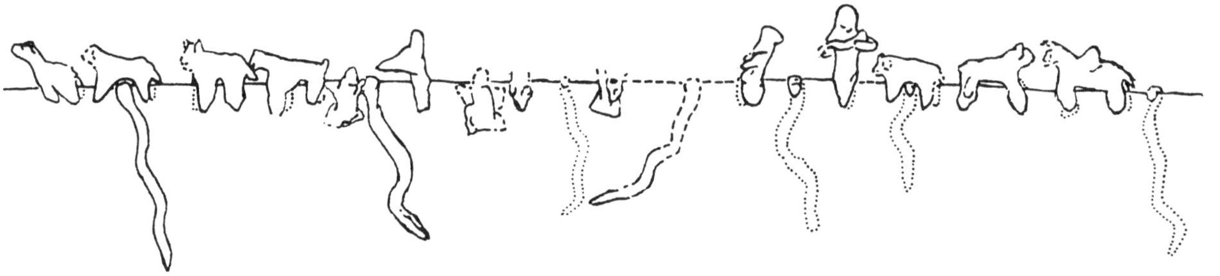

Figure 9.6
Period 2 terracotta frieze from Togolok 1, cenotaph (Sarianidi 1986c:138).

They are found on both Period 1 and 2 sites in Margiana. Naturalistic animal representations that can be identified include large mammals such as humped bovids, two-humped camels, and nonhumped animals (fig. 9.7). There are also generalized depictions of birds, dogs, frogs, snakes, and wild boar (Moore 1993a). Such terracotta animal figurines have been part of the Central Asian cultural tradition since Namazga III times and may be originally related to the painted animal designs on the Namazga III ceramics from Kara depe.

Other Terracotta Objects

Terracotta amulets are common in Period 2 but rare in Period 1. These amulets include miniature versions of stone columns, body parts such as feet and hands, phalli, token disks, balls, and cylindrical and pyramidal tokens (fig. 9.8). In Bactria, similarly shaped amulets are made of metal and of stone, probably because of the proximity of the southern Bactrian oases to the resource areas of Afghanistan, the Chagai Hills, and Badakhshan. Terracotta seals with engraved geometric designs may also be a replacement for or imitation of bronze seals when bronze metal was not available. In some cases it appears that terracotta objects were made in the same form as objects usually found in stone or metal; thus clay was used as replacement material for scarcer resources.

Biconical terracotta whorls are a common object found on the surface and from excavations in Margiana. Terracotta whorls made locally are found in both Periods 1 and 2. Large-diameter whorls were most likely miniature wheels for toy carts; smaller, thicker whorls may have been used in spinning; and smaller, finely finished terracotta whorls appear to be copies of steatite biconical whorls or beads.

One type of terracotta whorl appears to have been imported. Thumbnail-impressed whorls have been found in Period 1 in Margiana (fig. 9.8:5). This type is typical of the western foothill zone at Anau (level 3) and has recently been found in late Namazga V levels at Altyn depe (Udemuradov 1989).

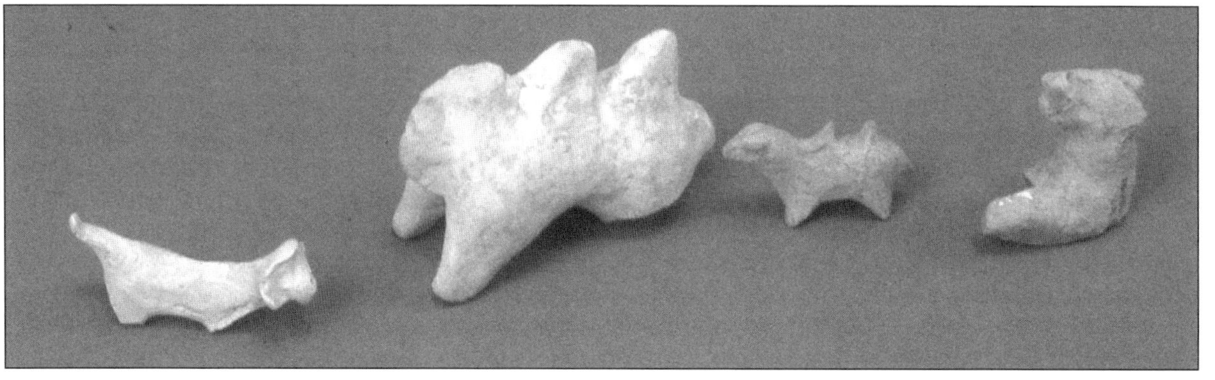

Figure 9.7
Periods 1 and 2 freestanding terracotta animal figurines, Gonur depe.

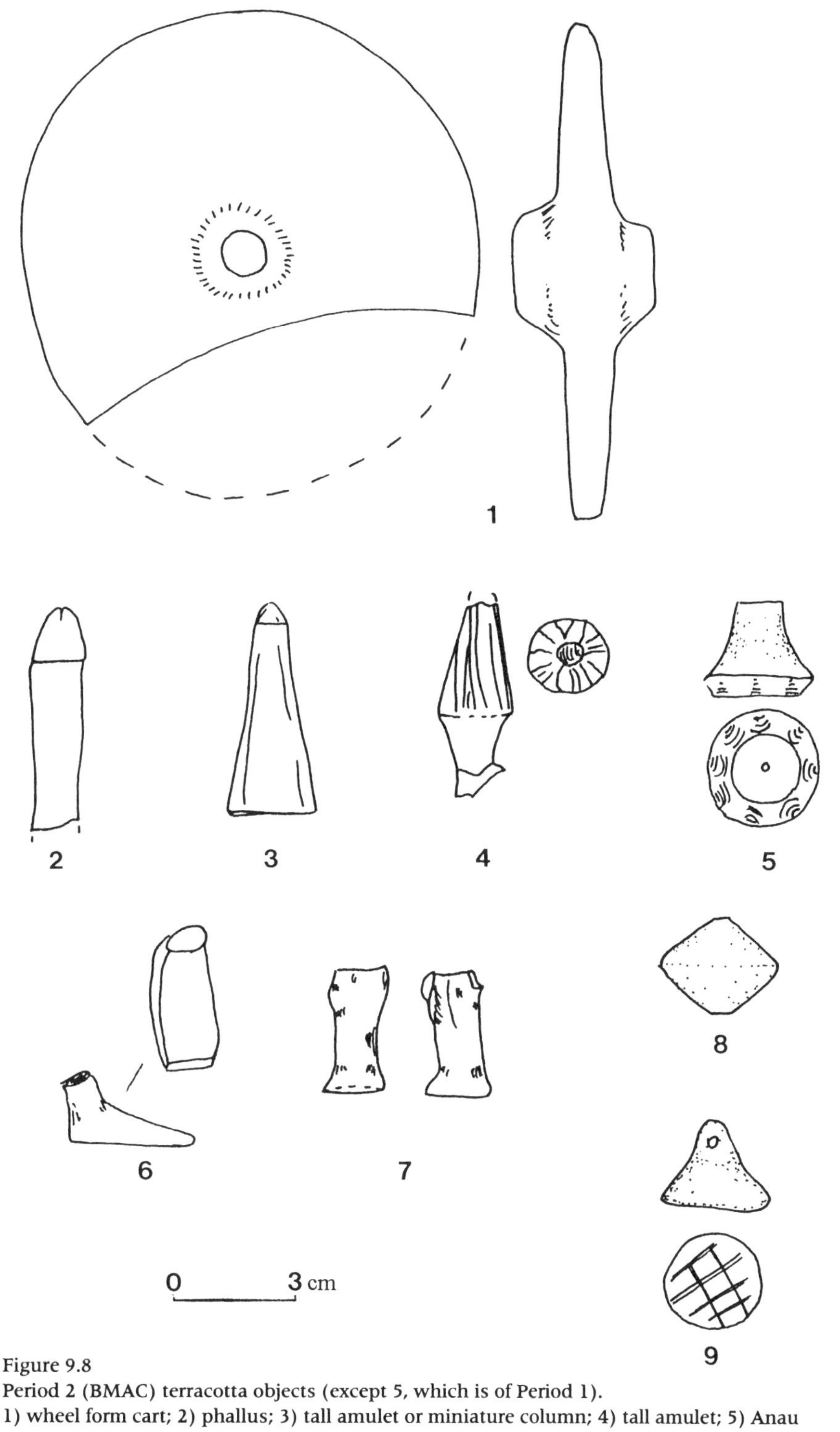

Figure 9.8
Period 2 (BMAC) terracotta objects (except 5, which is of Period 1).
1) wheel form cart; 2) phallus; 3) tall amulet or miniature column; 4) tall amulet; 5) Anau type whorl from Period 1; 6) amulet in the shape of a foot; 7) amulet in the shape of a finger bone; 8) terracotta whorl; 9) terracotta stamp seal.

Bone Objects

Animal bone is an abundantly available local raw material and appears to have been used to make objects otherwise made of stone or metal. Bone objects from the 1989 excavations at Gonur included needles and awls, fleshers, burnishers, worked astragali, incised bone tubes, and bone axes (Moore 1993b).

Bone Tools, Periods 1 and 2

Utilitarian bone tools, such as needles, fleshers, and burnishers, and the worked astragali are typical of the Central Asian tradition as well as part of the greater Near Eastern tradition (fig. 9.9:1–5). Bone object types that appear restricted to the Period 2 assemblage are the incised bone tubes and the bone axes.

Ground and polished astragali were common finds from the excavations of the architecture at the south mound of Gonur. The Period 2 astragali are from sheep/goat (fig. 9.9:5) and wild pig. Astragali have been interpreted as gaming pieces from many sites of the Greater Near East as early as the Neolithic (Watson 1979:199). They may also have been used as tools for grinding.

Worked astragali were found on all of the Margiana sites whose collections I studied, and there is a white crystalline stone (marble) copy of an astragali from Togolok 21, room 50 (Sarianidi 1990). This piece is a faithful copy of a complete sheep/goat astragalus, showing the transformation of a form from one medium to another. The stone astragalus suggests an added symbolic dimension to the astragali in Margiana, which may indicate that the worked astragali are more than simple tools or gaming pieces.

Bone Tubes, Periods 2 and 3

Engraved bone tubes occur in the BMAC in Bactria and Margiana (Period 2 at Gonur) and at Takhirbai (Period 3 at Gonur). The tubes are made from midsections of sheep/goat femora (9 to 11 cm) and have been cut, polished, reamed out, and incised (fig. 9.9:7). The designs consist of large eyes with a stylized headdress above and a collar below. Some of the tubes have dark pigment rubbed into the incisions.

The bone tubes are part of the regional BMAC assemblage, and this specific style is not exported outside of Bactria or Margiana. Partially manufactured bone tubes have been recovered both from Gonur 1 and from Togolok 21, indicating that they were being made there. After being shaped and decorated, the tubes were highly polished either as part of the manufacturing process or during use.

These pieces have been found so far only in architectural context, not in burials. Opium poppy pollen has been recorded from soil inside of the tubes (Meier-Melikyan 1990) leading Sarianidi to interpret them as drinking tubes for sipping an opium-ephedra drink similar to *haoma* (Sarianidi 1990). It must be noted, however, that poppy flowers are a common spring annual in the Kara Kum desert, and that pollen studies have not been conducted from other soils in the Bronze Age sites of Margiana. It is likely that poppy was part of the natural background in the pollen profile of the ancient oases and that the function of the tubes was unrelated to the pollen.

The femur bone shafts of medium-sized mammals (such as sheep) appear to be a natural medium for carving, and examples of similarly carved bones are found throughout the Old World. For example, in Neolithic Anatolia there are similar worked bone tubes associated with clay figurines (with the bone tube as the head on a clay body (Duru 1993). Cut and polished animal femur bones are found in China. Bone tubes from An Yang, for example, are also engraved with faces, although in a totally distinct style (Li Chi 1976, fig. 42). Today, people in northern Afghanistan make bone beads from immature sheep/goat femur bones that appear similar to the Bronze Age bone tubes (Kenoyer, pers. comm.).

In the context of the wide variety of amulets of terracotta, bronze, and stone found in Period 2, it is likely that the bone tubes were another type of amulet, functioning in a symbolic system without necessarily fulfilling a ceremonial function.

Bone Axes, Period 2

Several enigmatic ground and polished bone objects made from the ends of long bones of large mammals (the size of cattle) have been found in Period 2 architecture from Gonur south (fig. 9.9:6). They are carved in the same form of bronze axes, which have been found in both Margiana (Togolok 21) and Bactria (Dashli 3). The bones have been ground and polished on the exterior to form a blade. They have a hole vertically ground out for a handle and a small hole for a pin to hold the axe in the handle. These features provide good evidence that the axes, usually made of bronze, were ceremonial and not for everyday use.

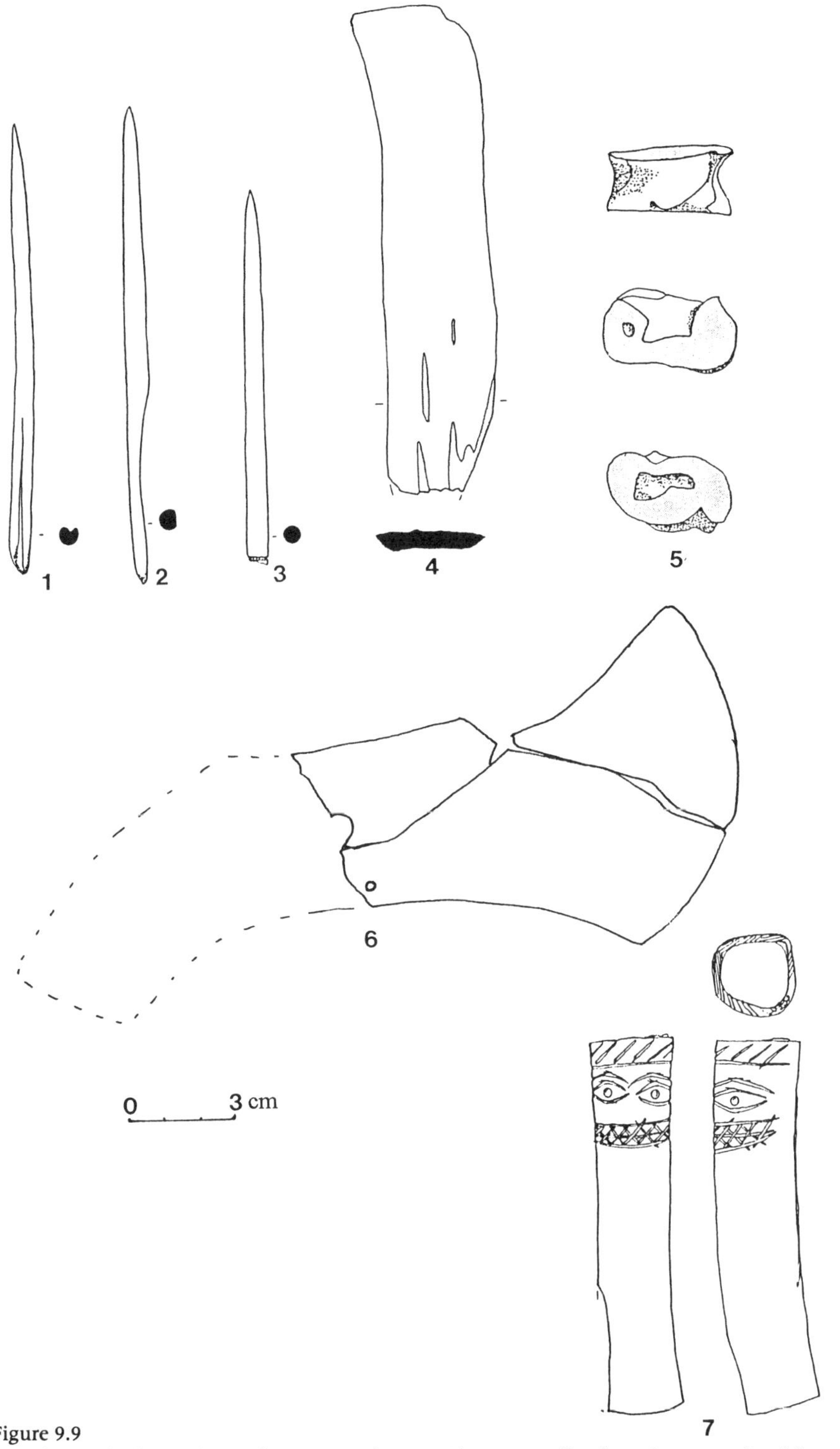

Figure 9.9
Periods 1 and 2 bone objects from Gonur depe. 1–3) Bone needles from Gonur north; 4) bone fleshing tool, Gonur north, deep sounding G-24; 5) worked astragalus, Gonur south, Room 1; 6) bone axe, Gonur south, Room 262; 7) engraved bone tube, Gonur south, Room 88.

IMPORTED MATERIALS

Finished objects in distinctive styles imported from outside Central Asia are very rare in the oases of Margiana and Bactria. Although the desert oasis areas have no metal or stone resources, small artifacts appear to have been locally produced from imported raw materials. Two lines of evidence indicate this: (1) the local distribution of a separate style of the BMAC for the seals, amulets, and small bronze objects found primarily in Margiana (Amiet 1990a); and (2) evidence of local production in Margiana in the form of the unfinished worked small objects and raw materials of steatite, metal, and stone.

Stone

Artifacts made of stone include grinding stones, mortars, pestles, weights, miniature columns, small vessels (primarily of alabaster and steatite), and a wide variety of seals, beads, amulets, and inlay made from steatite, alabaster, and semiprecious stone. The working of alabaster and steatite (softstone), and semiprecious stones, was part of the Central Asian tradition in the foothill zone of southern Turkmenistan since Namazga III times at least. This tradition continued in the desert oases even in the absence of easily accessible raw materials. The wide variety of stone objects, both implements and elite or ceremonial items, indicates an importance for stone objects that is surprising in view of transportation costs.

Steatite is the most common imported stone for small objects of domestic use as well as for ornaments and ceremonial objects. Steatite sources are found in outcrops on the Iranian plateau, and steatite is particularly common from southern Iran (Kohl 1974). Steatite is also likely to be found along the foothills of the Kopet Dag and the Paropamisus mountains, although specific outcrops have not yet been identified (*Encyclopedia of Turkmenistan* 1984:21).

The opaque, yellowish, finely banded alabaster of vessels found in Margiana is similar to that found in the foothill zone. Limestone and sandstone, common in the foothills of the Kopet Dag, were used for the many grinding stones found in Margiana. The use of these resources appears to be a continuation of a long tradition of stone use by foothill populations that continued to exploit the same resources even when they moved to Margiana.

The nearest sources for semiprecious stones such as carnelian, agate, and lapis are in the area around Badakhshan, and not the Kopet Dag or Paropamisus mountains. Such stones are also found in Iran and in the Chagai Hills of Afghanistan (Kohl 1979).

While the desert adaptation did not alter the reliance on stone artifacts, what was previously locally available around foothill settlements had to be imported into the oasis environment.

Stone Vessels: Periods 1 and 2

In Margiana, steatite bowls, dishes, and vials are found in both Periods 1 and 2 (fig. 9.10:1–5). The decorative style of the vessels is included in the *série récente* style of Iran (Miroschedji 1973).

Turned and carved *série récente* steatite vessels from southern Iran (Tepe Yahya IVA) and from the Persian Gulf typically have double circle and dot motif (Potts 1990:106–110). These are different from those found in Central Asia (described below). The styles from the two areas have been grouped together as the *série récente* as found in Iran (Miroschedji 1973). Both the Persian Gulf (and southern Iranian) *série récente* style and the BMAC *série récente* style occur on sites throughout Iran, Mesopotamia, and the Gulf from 2200 to 1700 B.C.

In Margiana, kidney-shaped dishes (part of the previously defined *série récente* corpus) are found in both Periods 1 and 2. Such vessels are also known from Mehrgarh and Sibri, where they are associated with BMAC burials (Jarrige 1989).

Small vials with square bases and round necks are produced in Margiana from imported steatite or preformed blanks (fig. 9.11:3). The finished objects are commonly found in Period 2 in Margiana and in northern and southern Bactria. The carved decoration on these vials includes incised lines, hatched triangles, and single-circle and dot decoration as well as figurative depictions of trees, snakes and so on (figs. 9.10:5, 9.11). This type of vial is also found in Margiana made of other materials such as ceramic, alabaster, and bronze. These vials are known from the looted tombs of Bactria with bronze pins in them and thus have been described as cosmetic bottles (Pottier 1984:28–29). These small vials occur only in Margiana Period 2. This permits a chronological subdivision of the *série récente* style into an earlier period and a later period, the later including these distinctive vials.

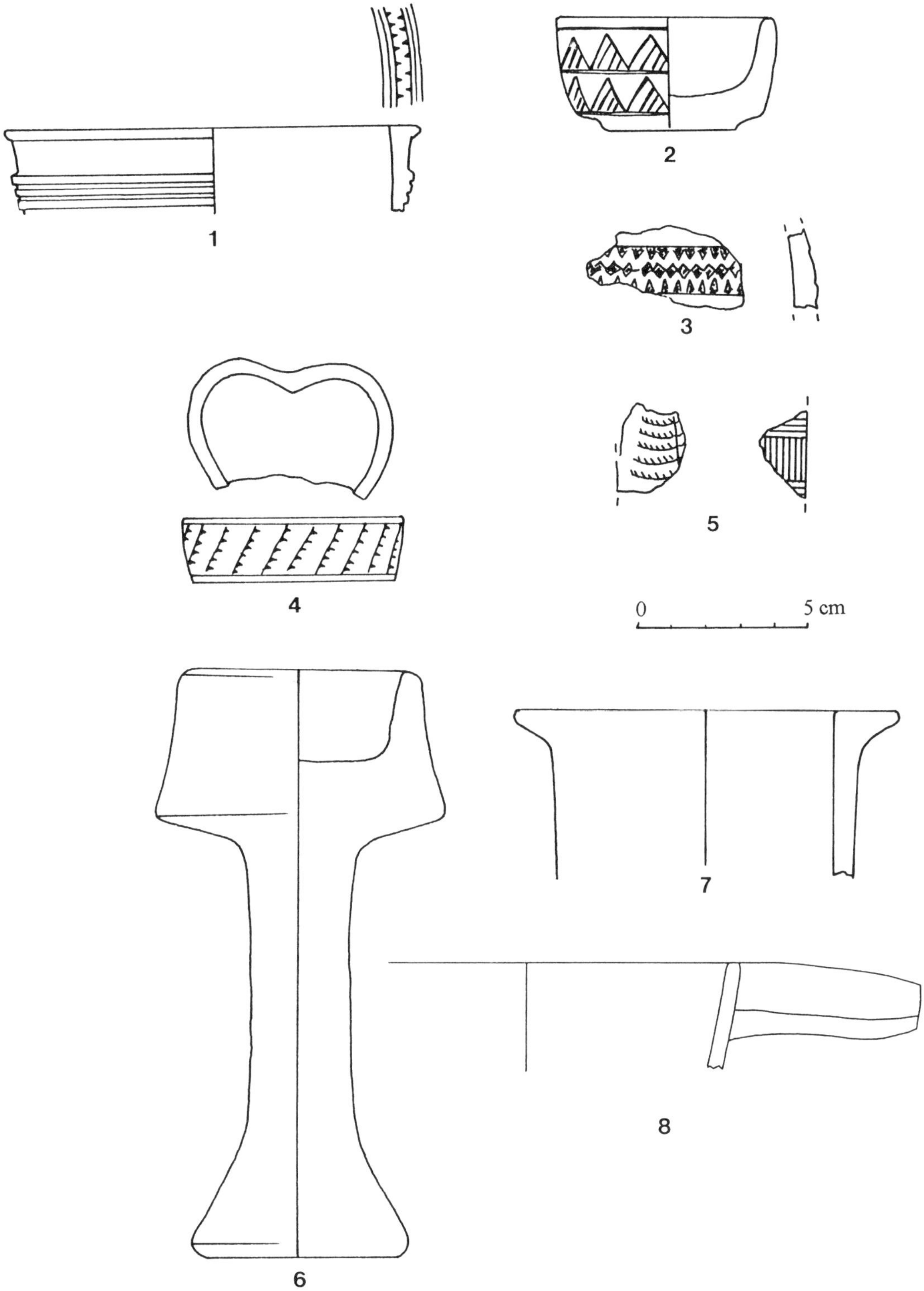

Figure 9.10
Steatite and alabaster vessels from Period 1 (2,3,4,6) and Period 2 (1,5,7,8). 1) Black steatite bowl, Togolok 1, room context; 2) dark grey steatite bowl, Gonur north (*kremel*) Room 35; 3) grey steatite, Gonur north, (*kremel*), room context; 4) grey steatite, Gonur north, Room 1; 5) grey steatite, Gonur south, room context; 6) yellowish alabaster, Gonur north, (*kremel*), Room 4; 7) yellowish alabaster, Gonur south, room context; 8) yellowish alabaster, Togolok 1, room context.

Tall footed alabaster cups are found from Namazga IV to the BMAC (fig. 9.10:6). The stand of the cup becomes thin and elegant, but the basic form is the same over time. The Namazga IV cups had perforated lids and may have served as lamps. Tall alabaster cups become incorporated into the new assemblage of the BMAC and are commonly found in the export contexts of the BMAC.

Turned alabaster bowls are also common in Margiana as part of a continuous tradition (fig. 9.10:7–8). Interestingly, a type of trough spout found in Period 1 and Period 2 ceramics is also made in Period 2 in alabaster, as if in imitation of the ceramics.

Alabaster vials have both square and round bases and incised line decoration. Alabaster vials similar to the steatite forms were also produced or decorated in Margiana in Period 2 (fig. 9.11:2).

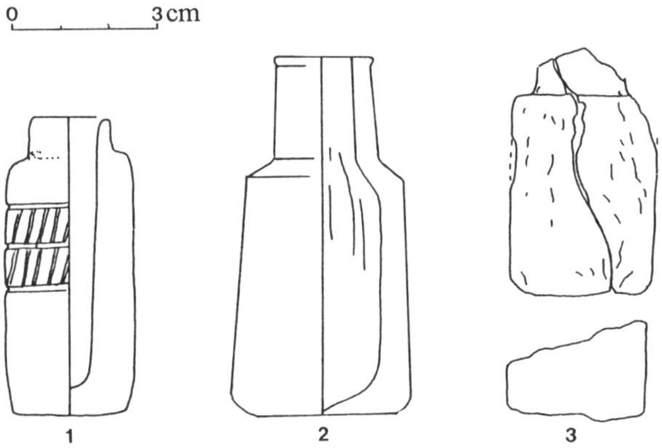

Figure 9.11
Small vials from period 2. 1) Steatite vial, Togolok 21, Room 172; 2) finely banded yellowish alabaster, Togolok 21, Burial 30; 3) unfinished steatite vial, Togolok 21, Room 148.

Stone Figurines, Period 2

Figures, small amulets, and seals made of steatite and alabaster are found in Margiana in Period 2. They are a distinctive feature of the BMAC, although simple geometric steatite and alabaster seals occur in both Periods 1 and 3.

Figure 9.12
Period 2, fragment of body, grey steatite carved in fleece pattern, Togolok 21, Room 148.

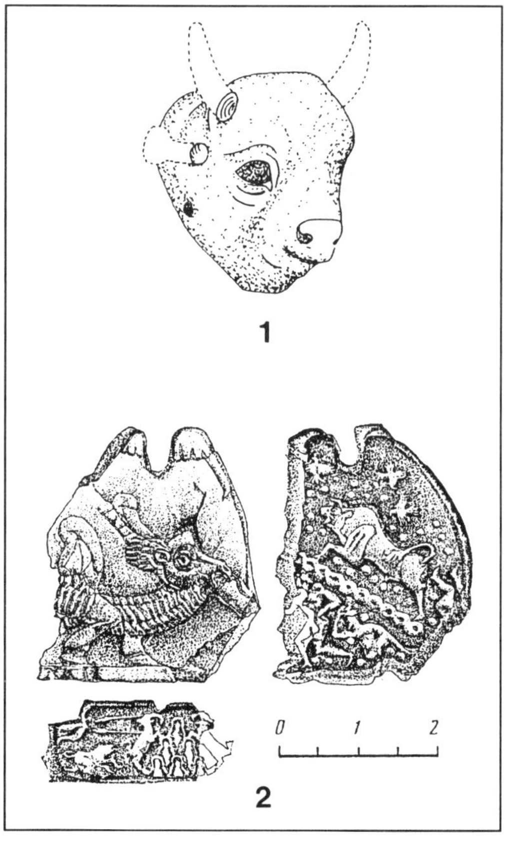

Figure 9.13
Period 2. 1) Alabaster bull's head, Togolok 21, Room 44; 2) reddish steatite amulet in the shape of a Bactrian camel, Togolok 21, southern courtyard.

Stone figures include human and small animal figures carved in the round. Composite multipart human figurines are made with a steatite base and a head and arms of a white stone, usually alabaster. These are best known from the looted tombs of southern Bactria (Ligabue and Salvatori 1990; Pottier 1984), although they have been found only in secure stratigraphic contexts from Margiana (Hiebert 1994, fig. 3). The possibility that they were produced in Margiana is suggested by a fragment of a steatite figurine found at Togolok 21 in a room with other steatite production debris (fig. 9.12).

Period 2 sites in Margiana have a range of small alabaster and steatite figurines, including a bull's head (fig. 9.13:1), an artfully carved steatite amulet in the form of a camel (fig. 9.13:2), and a variety of other animals typical of the oasis environment, such as frogs and boar. Amulets (and some of the bronze seals as well) from Bactria may also have images of mountain goat, monkeys, and bear (Sarianidi 1981b). These animals are native to the foothills and mountains of Afghanistan and reflect the proximity of the Bactrian oasis sites to these areas.

Amulets and Seals

Amulets of the Murgab style (Sarianidi 1981b) are carved in steatite and alabaster on two sides, and were often pierced for a string (fig. 9.14:1). They are not found only from Margiana; many Murgab style amulets and seals are known to have come from Bactria (Sarianidi 1986c). Other amulets common in Margiana Period 2 have a stepped diamond shape (fig. 9.14:5). The stepped design is traditional in Central Asia, where it is found on the painted ceramics from Namazga IV times and on carved stone beads, censors, and disks from Namazga IV levels of Ulug depe. The stepped diamond amulets in Margiana are made of steatite and alabaster and have carved deco-

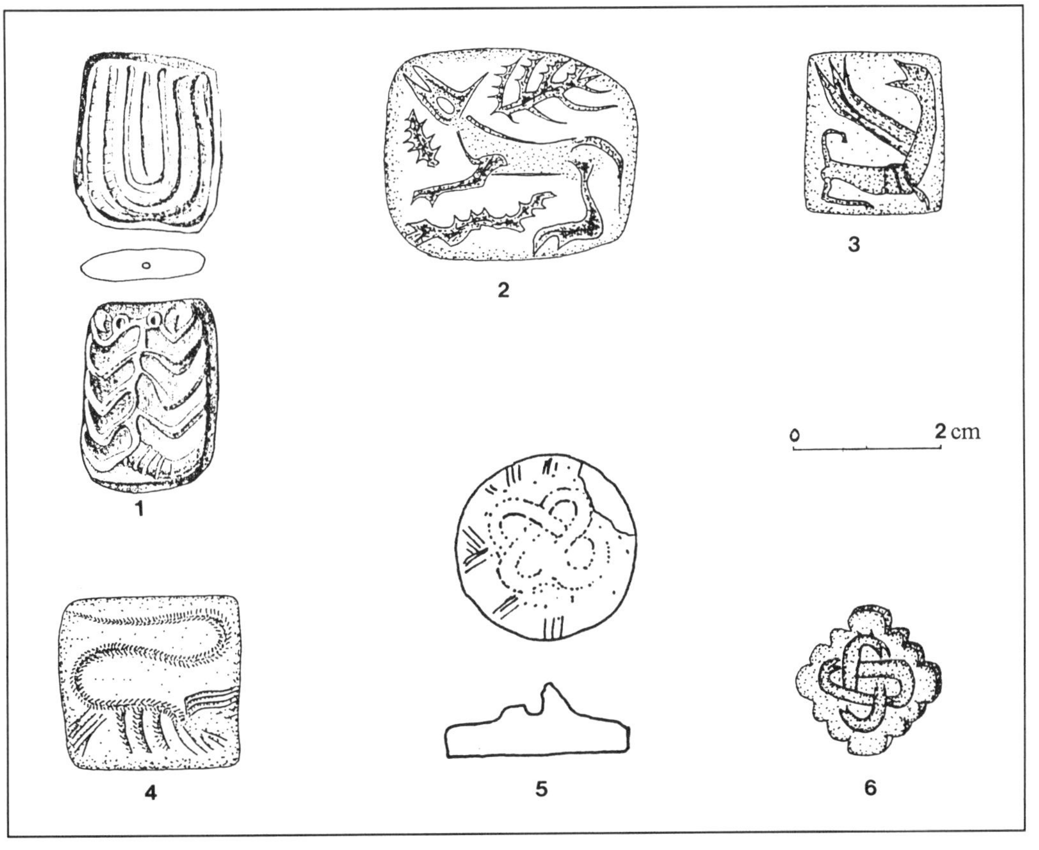

Figure 9.14
Period 2. 1) Reddish steatite, Togolok 21, surface; 2) black steatite, Gonur south; 3) reddish steatite, Gonur south; 4) dark grey steatite, Gonur south; 5) reddish steatite, Gonur south; 6) reddish steatite, Togolok 21, central building, surface.

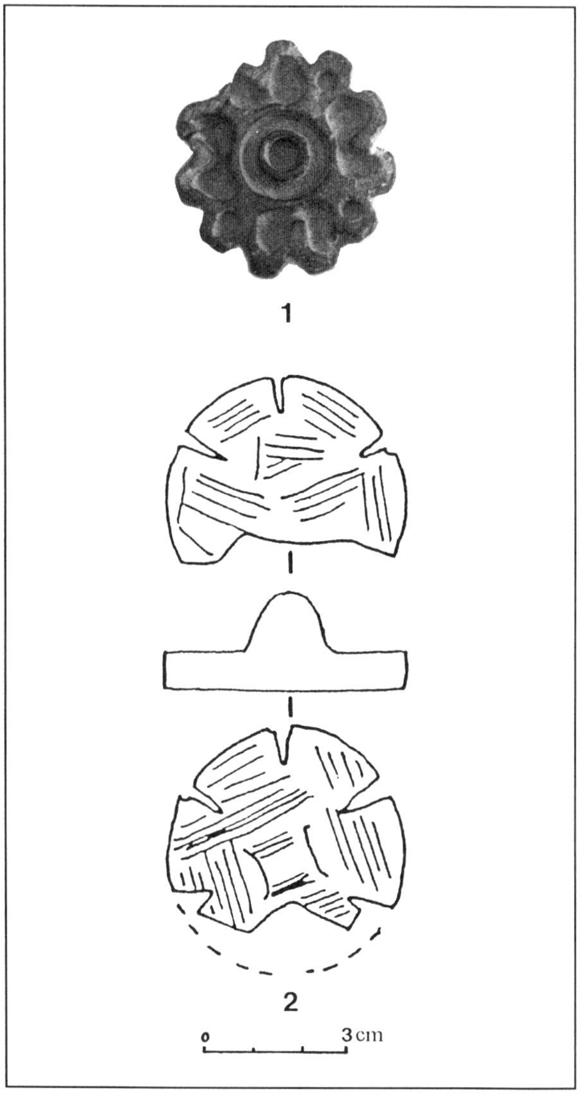

Figure 9.15
Period 2 steatite stamp seals. 1) Gonur north, Room 18; 2) Unfinished steatite seal of the same style, saw marks visible, Togolok 24, burial 40.

ration on either side. One found at Harappa (Vats 1940, pl. XVI, seal no. 255) from the upper level most likely comes from Margiana or Bactria.

Imprints of Murgab style amulets and seals have been found on oval and round bullae. One bulla from Gonur south is oval with a hole for a string, very similar to the much later Parthian and Sasanian bullae (Sarianidi 1993, fig. 12; Hiebert 1994, fig. 8). Bullae from excavations at Gonur 1 and Togolok 21 are evidence for an emerging hierarchy and control system that will characterize the oasis from this time onward.

There are several types of stone seals, including those that appear to be imitations of metal compartmented seals, and others, such as the cylinder seals that are a completely new form in Central Asia (fig. 9.15:1). The stone seals are made primarily of steatite and alabaster and have both drilled and incised designs similar to the amulets. They are classified separately from amulets by having a boss on the back which can be held and is pierced, similar to metal seals. The occurrence of seals and amulets in the BMAC continues a tradition of use from Period 1 in Margiana and from the foothill region, although the images on the BMAC objects are quite different. Unfinished examples of the distinctive BMAC type seals have been found in Period 2 of Margiana, confirming that the "local" form of steatite seal is indeed produced (or finished) in Margiana (fig. 9.15:2). These local designs made on steatite, alabaster, and terracotta continue to be found in Margiana Period 3, following the BMAC.

The cylindrical seals have vivid designs around the cylinder and often have a motif on the base with a loop boss carved on top (fig. 9.16:3). Such seals are reminiscent of later eastern Mediterranean (Mitanni) tradition seals (Salje 1990). The carving on the base is similar both in technique of carving and in motifs to the locally manufactured round amulets. Impressions

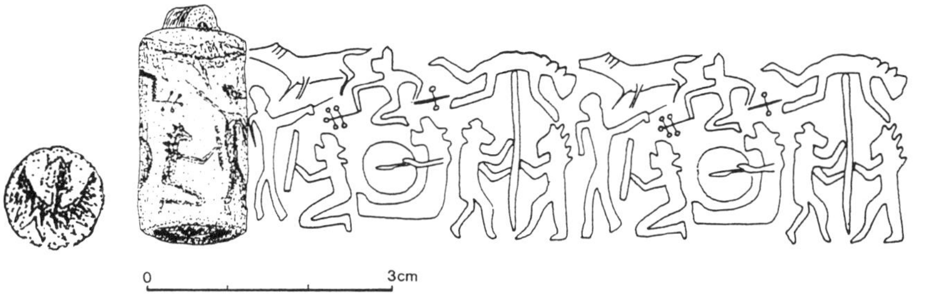

Figure 9.16
Period 2 steatite cylinder seal, Togolok 1, burial 10 (Sarianidi 1989b, fig. 5).

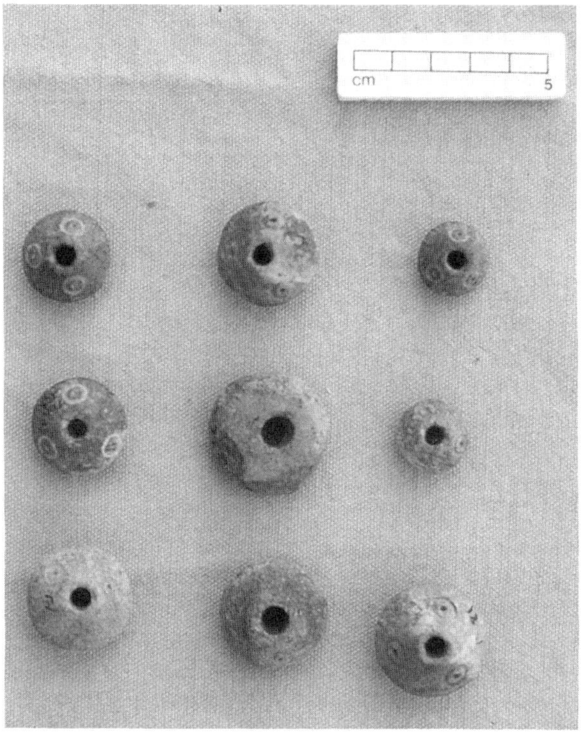

Figure 9.17
Steatite beads from Gonur north, Period 1 (monumental architecture) and Period 2 (south mound).

of the cylinder seals have been found on locally produced ceramics from Taip and from Gonur 1 south (see chap. 4, fig. 4.35:3). Imprints of cylinder seals on the ceramics made prior to firing suggests their use in the control of production.

The BMAC seals appear to have been used as part of a system of administrative control of trade and production in a fashion similar to seals one thousand years older from Mundigak and Shahr-i Sokhta II (Ferioli, Fiandra, and Tusa 1979) and at Shahdad (Hakemi 1977), where seals were stamped on pottery prior to firing. Such seals were not made for a long period following Shahr-i Sokhta II. The *function* of the seals appears to be a reemergence of this older pattern, whereas *the motifs and designs* found in the BMAC are distinctly new.

Beads

Stone beads are frequent finds in Margiana and reflect a high level of craft production and long-distance interaction. Without fine-scale recovery such as screening, however, little information about their relative abundance and context is available. Many beads and bead fragments have been found from the surface. Burials are the main context in which semiprecious stone beads have been found, sometimes in traces of a necklace. The arrangement of the in situ beads demonstrates that various sizes and types were put together in careful patterns.

The most ubiquitous are biconical beads made from steatite, alabaster, or terracotta with the circle-and-dot motif (fig. 9.17). They may have also served as spinning whorls. These are common in the foothill zone and also in Margiana from Periods 1 through 3, and were found in various stages of manufacture at Togolok 21 and at Gonur south. A wide variety of simple spherical, oval, tubular, and flat beads have been found, primarily from Period 2 (BMAC) burials. These finds include paste microbeads, small shell beads of Indo-Pacific origins (*Engina mendicaria*), and of Mediterranean origins (*Nassarius gibbosulus*), and larger beads made of seashell, bone, and semiprecious stones. It is quite possible that shell beads and shell inlay were manufactured at Togolok 21 from cowry (Cypraeidae) and marine shell (*Lambis truncata sebae*) of Indo-Pacific origins (fig. 9.18). Beads made of agate, carnelian, and lapis lazuli indicate source areas from South Asia, the Kopet Dag region, Afghanistan, and southern Iran. Further indications of local production include lapis lazuli debitage on the surface at Togolok 3, which may have been from bead working.

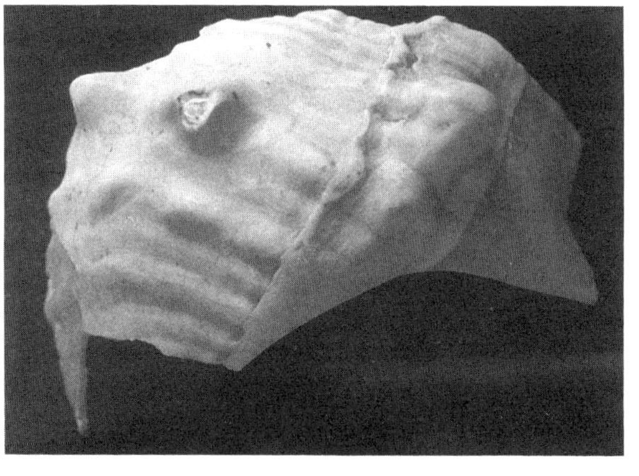

0 3cm

Figure 9.18
Large shell fragment, *Lambis truncata sebae*, Togolok 21, Room 40.

Miniature Columns, Staffs, and Maceheads, Periods 1 and 2

Miniature columns are found at Bronze Age sites on the Iranian plateau, in Central Asia, and in South Asia (fig. 9.19). These distinctive artifacts, made of limestone, alabaster, marble, and steatite, have been carefully carved, grooved, and polished. The earliest example from secure excavated context is from Kara depe in the eastern foothill plain of the Kopet Dag (late Namazga III to early Namazga IV) (Masson 1957). They occur in Period 1 in Margiana as well as in room and tomb contexts of Period 2 (BMAC). They are often part of BMAC assemblages found outside of Central Asia. Due to their high degree of polishing and working, they appear to have been ceremonial in function. However, the possibility that they functioned as weights must also be considered, and they should be weighed.

Twenty-nine whole and broken columns were found in the central building at Togolok 21; this is the largest group of columns from a single site. The distribution of the columns in the building does not show clustering in any room or area (fig. 9.20). Some columns were found on floor surfaces, but others—such as one broken column, the pieces of which were found in two separate rooms—may have come from secondary deposits.

Several of the Togolok 21 columns were found sawed in two pieces, with the ends polished and the two parts kept together. Why the columns were cut is not clear. The sawed portions may indicate that the columns were being modified at Togolok 21. Despite the fact that no stone debitage was recorded from these excavations, other unfinished steatite objects from Togolok 21 indicate that some stone working was being done at the site.

The columns from excavated context at Togolok 21 range in height from 16 to 29 cm. The unbroken columns seem to have been manufactured in pairs of similar size (table 9.2), although none have been found in pairs from burials. Several of the similar sized pairs have contrasting colors. A similar pair of black and white columns was found in a burial

Figure 9.19
Miniature columns in situ on floors of Rooms 19 and 21 (Togolok 1). Photo: Courtesy of V. Sarianidi.

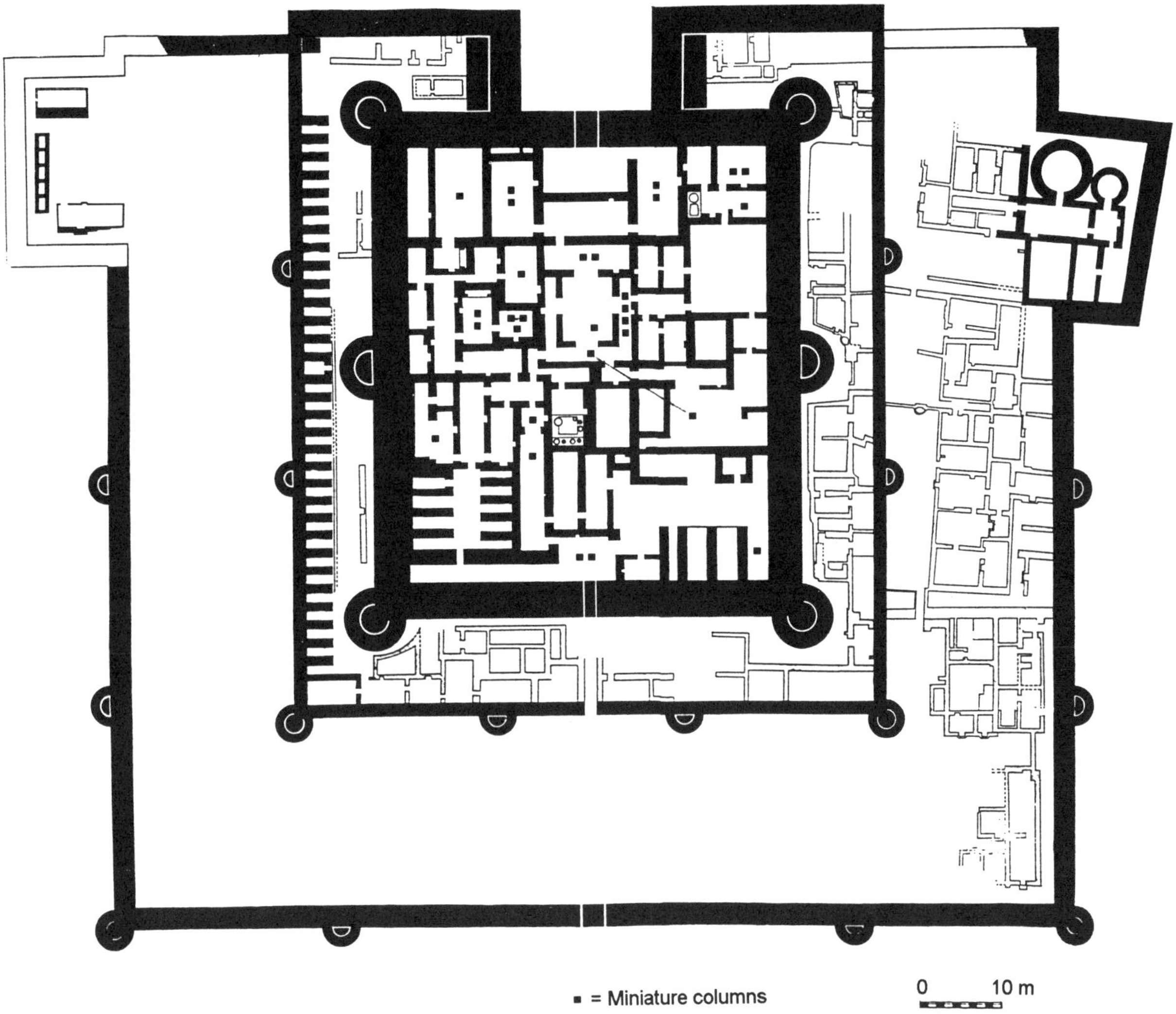

Figure 9.20
Distribution of miniature columns at Togolok 21.

deposit at Quetta (Jarrige and Hassan 1989) (fig. 9.21).

If the columns were paired, perhaps the grooves supported a bar or staff in a fashion similar to later Iranian ritual objects such as the *barsom* mentioned in the *Avesta* (Boyce 1984).

Miniature columns in the BMAC often occur with stone staffs. Staffs (or "scepters"—Jarrige and Hassan 1989) made of marble, alabaster, and schist have been found in many Central Asian burials from Bactria and from the foothill zone. Fragments of schist staffs have been found in architectural context in Margiana from both Period 1 (at Gonur) and Period 2 (at Togolok 21). These are the first architectural contexts documented for the stone staffs. Although the staffs are part of the BMAC found in Bactria, Margiana, and BMAC assemblages outside of Central Asia at Hissar, Shahdad, Mehrgarh, and Quetta, it is clear that they were incorporated into the new assemblage from the earlier Namazga V assemblages of the foothill (such as at Altyn depe Burial 362) and Margiana Period 1.

Round stone maceheads, like the stone staffs, are part of the complex of Bactria and Margiana Period 2, which stems from an earlier tradition. Plain stone maceheads are found in Period 1, whereas in the

```
                                                    X
X                   X X     X     X X     X X X X X
-----------------------------------------------------
I I I I I I I I I I I I I I I I I I I I I I I I I I I
16  17  18  19  20  21  22  23  24  25  26  27  28  29
```

Table 9.2
Height in centimeters of complete columns from Togolok 21.

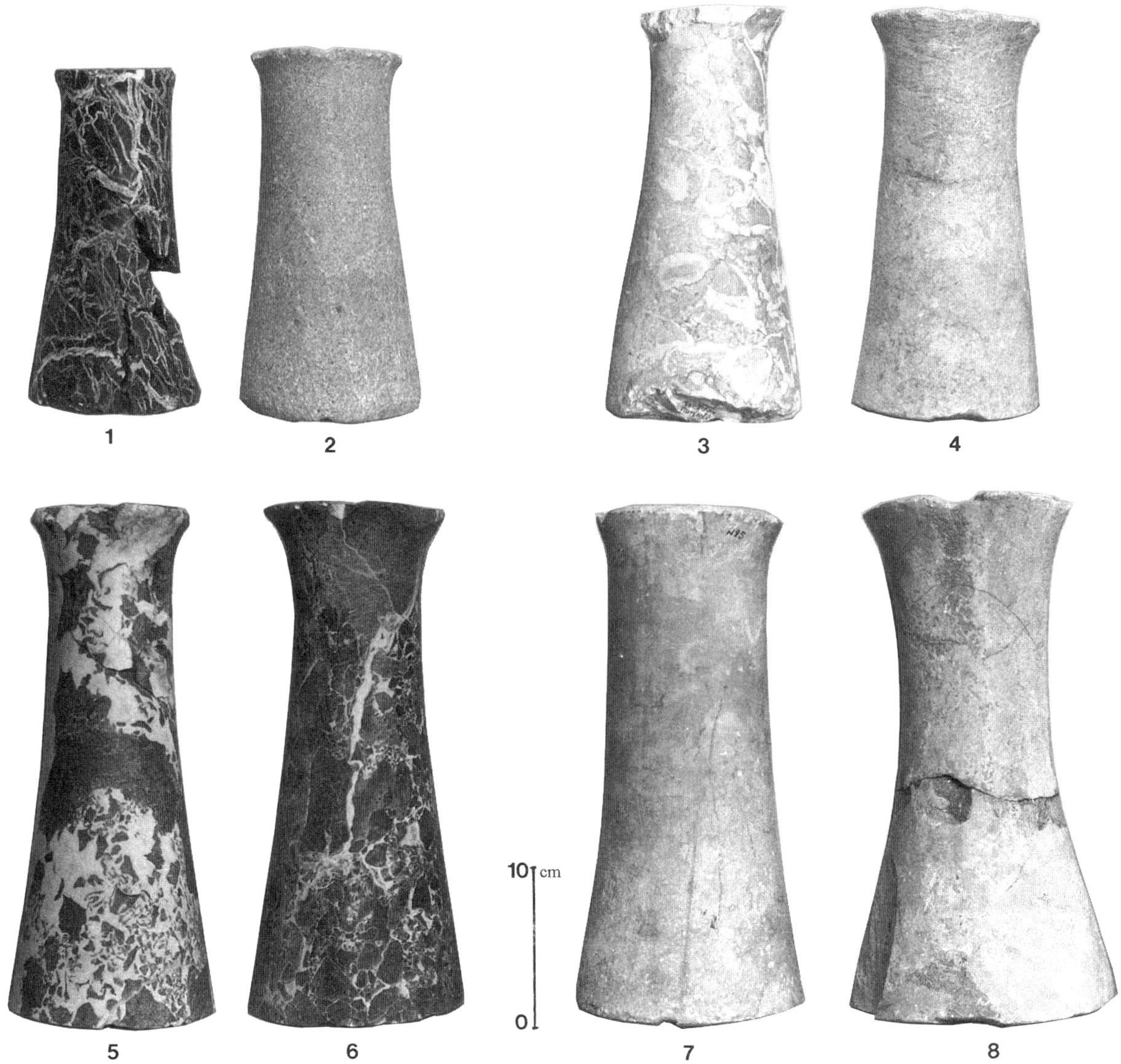

Figure 9.21 Columns paired by size from Togolok 21. 1) 21 cm, black and white marble, Room 39 (bottom half), Room 56 (top); 2) 21.5 cm, grey salt and pepper granite, Room 7; 3) 21 cm, pink limestone with large white round inclusions, Room 20; 4) 24.5 cm pink grainy siliceous stone, Room 15; 5) 29 cm, dark red metamorphic(?) conglomerate in a white matrix, Room 2; 6) 29 cm, dark red metamorphic(?) conglomerate in a white matrix, Room 9; 7) Yellowish pink siliceous rock, Room 25; 8) Yellowish pink siliceous rock, Room 14.

BMAC they are typically ornately carved (fig. 9.22). In Bactria, maceheads are also made of bronze and even lead, and are associated with the staffs and miniature columns.

In the BMAC, miniature columns, staffs, and maceheads appear to have been important symbols, beyond whatever utilitarian function they also might have had. Although each of these objects has been found in earlier contexts, they are grouped together for the first time in the BMAC in both burial and architectural contexts, and probably were incorporated as a set into the BMAC cultural system. Given the difficulties in acquiring and transporting these objects, they would represent considerable value in the oasis context. In this regard, the evidence of stone finishing and the large assemblage of stone objects attest to the central place of Togolok 21 in Period 2 of Margiana.

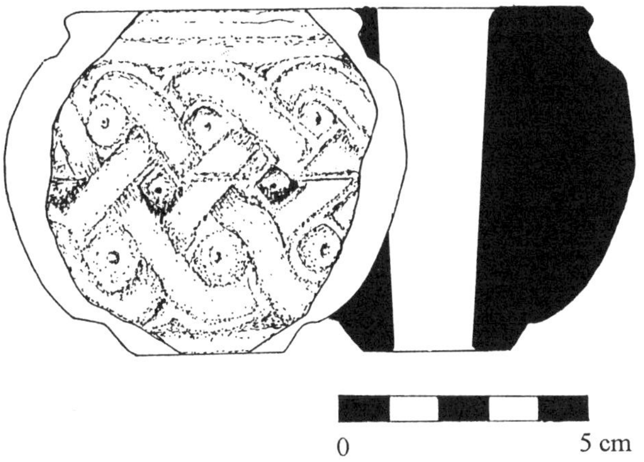

Figure 9.22
Period 2, steatite macehead, Togolok 21, Room 11.

Grinding Stones and Stone Pocketbooks, Periods 1 and 2

Stone pocketbooks are oval or round stones with a hole through the top that serves as a loop or handle. These are close in size and shape to weights from warp-weighted looms for weaving. Similarly shaped stones are illustrated in weaving scenes from Egyptian tomb paintings (Davies 1929); and traditional warp-weighted looms from Iran have weights (*kiseh*) of the *same shape* as the pocketbooks but made of sand-filled bags (Wulff 1966:203). Warp-weighted looms are primarily for the manufacture of cloth (not carpets).

Undecorated stone pocketbooks have been found in Iran and in Central Asia from the third millennium (Namazga III and IV) (Sarianidi 1961). Briefly, during the mid-third millennium ceremonial steatite pocketbooks were ornately carved in the *intercultural* style (Pittman 1984). This presumably ceremonial use appears not to have survived to the transformation of the late Bronze Age. Most of the Central Asian examples, including all from Margiana and Bactria, are undecorated and are found in domestic contexts.

Large grinding stones are found on all of the sites of Margiana as well as the polished hand stones and pestles. In Margiana, many caches of these have been found, as if they were hidden together before being abandoned. They are made of basalt, limestone, and sandstone, the closest sources of which are more than 200 km away in the foothills of the Kopet Dag mountains (fig. 9.23). The numerous grinding stones and pocketbooks found on every site in Margiana, in total, represent an enormous quantity of stone imported to the desert oases.

Chipped Stone, Periods 1, 2, and 3

Chipped-stone arrow points are part of the Central Asian Bronze Age tradition, despite the occurrence of bronze points in the same deposits. The stone points have been found in all agriculturally based sites of the Bronze Age and are not necessarily indicative of a separate hunting or nomadic group. Several points have been found from architectural contexts, and a slight stylistic difference appears between the points of Periods 1, 2, and 3.

Distinctive ripple flaked points have been found in Period 1 of the Gonur *kremel*. Many of these points also have been found from the surface in the area of Gonur (fig. 9.24). The points are similar to those found at Kelleli 4 (Masimov 1981) and at Altyn depe from the upper levels (Masson 1988). The total lack of debitage at Gonur (even with fine screening) indicates that finished points were imported. A wide variety of chipped stone points are also found in situ from Togolok 21, from the BMAC architecture at Gonur south (phases 1 through 3), and together with bronze points at Takhirbai 3.

Figure 9.23
Grinding stones from the floor of Room 84, Gonur south.

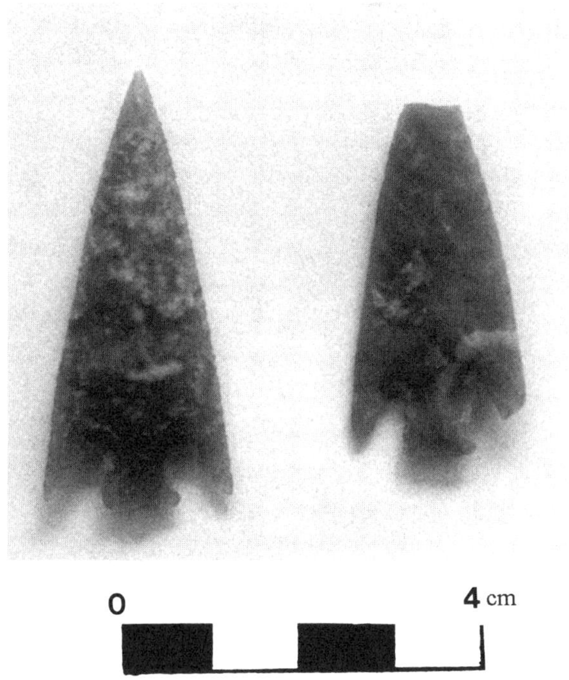

Figure 9.24
Period 2 flint arrowheads. 1) Medium brown chert, translucent, Gonur south, Room 78; 2) Opaque grey chert, Gonur south, Room 80.

Metal

Bronze, copper alloy, and other metal objects and fragments are common in Margiana. More than one hundred metal fragments have been found in situ from building levels at Gonur in a wide variety of forms and styles, indicating a rich metallurgical tradition in the desert oases.

Decorated bronze and copper alloy objects are an important part of the BMAC assemblage, both in the oases areas and in BMAC burials outside of Central Asia. Although hundreds of metal artifacts and fragments have been found on the surface from Margiana, and hundreds more are known from the looted tombs of southern Bactria, an understanding of the development of the BMAC corpus of metals is possible based only on examples from excavated contexts. The metal objects from Margiana can be divided into (1) tools and weapons and (2) ornaments and ceremonial objects.

Period 1

About half of all excavated objects from the Period 1 metal assemblage at Gonur are tools or household objects. Blades include knives and spears. From the excavations at Kelleli 3 and 4 (Masimov, unpublished notes) and from the Gonur *kremel* (Sarianidi 1990) have come undecorated bronze and copper alloy pins, a lead spinning whorl, several adz-type blades, and a long-handled bronze vessel (Kohl 1984, pl. 14 b, c, d).

Compartmented seals, bracelets, and earrings from Period 1 are similar to those from the BMAC (fig. 9.25). For example, the bronze pieces at Gonur north (*kremel*) can be assigned to period not on the basis of style but only on the basis of excavated context. How-

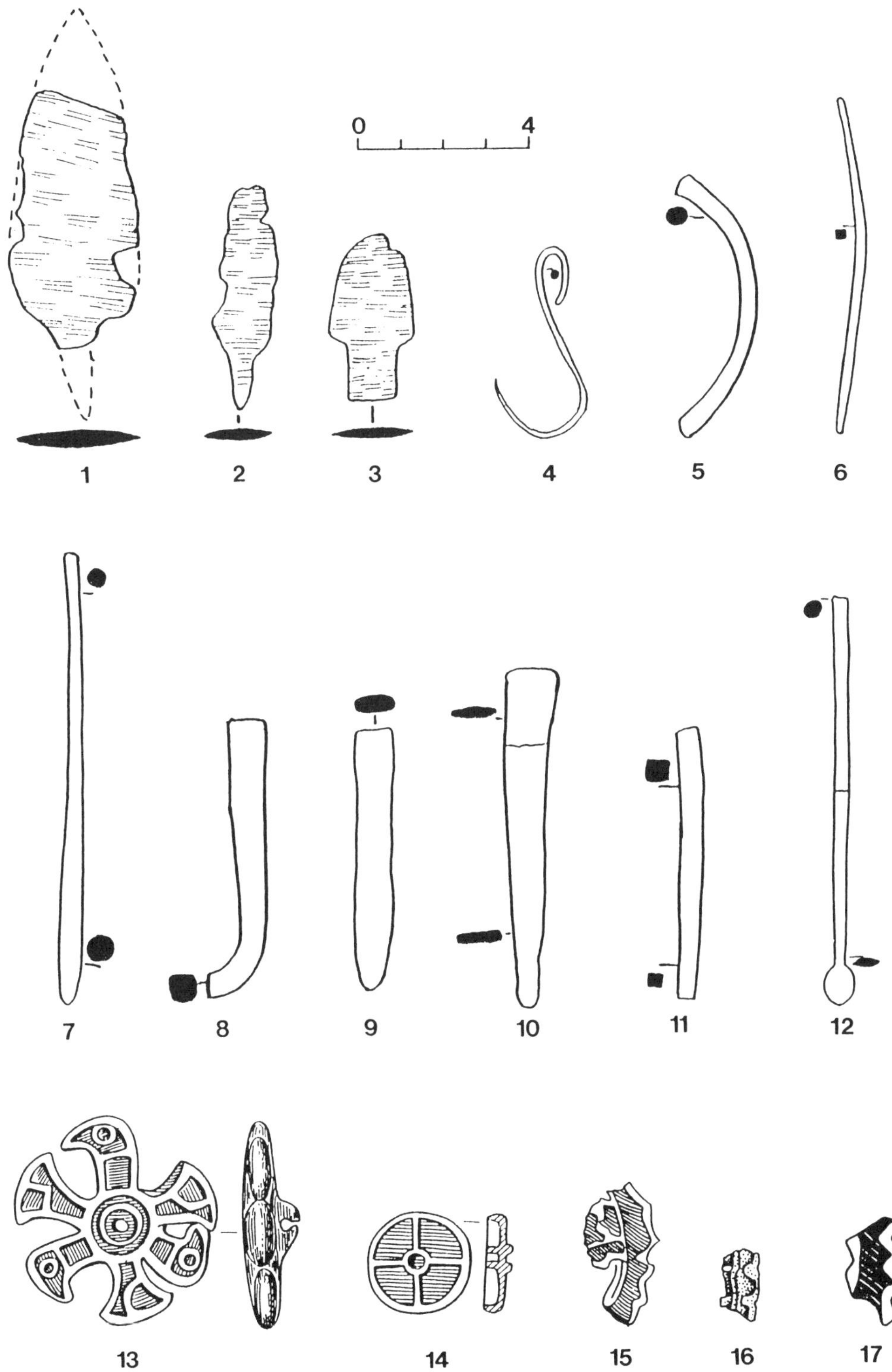

Figure 9.25
Period 1 metal objects from survey and excavation at Adzhi Kui and Kelleli oases. 1–3) Knives; 4) "fish hook"; 5) bracelet fragment; 6) drill; 7–12) large pin fragments; 13–17) compartmental seal from Kellili 1; 14–17) adapted from Masimov 1981, figs. 11–12.

ever, according to Terekhnova's analysis of metal composition, Margiana Period 1 artifacts include some that are alloyed with tin (Terekhnova 1990). Tin bronze has not been found among a sample of twenty-five bronze and copper alloy objects from excavated contexts from Margiana Period 2 (Hiebert and Killick 1993). Most likely this compositional difference indicates a shift in area of origin of the metal ore from Period 1 to Period 2. This is consistent with Margiana's shifting ties from the Kopet Dag foothill plain in Period 1 to the oases of Bactria in Period 2.

Period 2: The BMAC

Half of the metals from Period 2 are also tools or household objects. Blades include knives, spears, arrow points, and razors. There are more tool types in Period 2 than in Period 1, and the types include tools involved in production of other objects. Tools from Period 2 architecture included drills, chisels, and punches which were part of the local production complex (fig. 9.26). Some tools that show signs of use are from burials; an example is the drill found in a BMAC burial at Togolok 24 (fig. 9.26:10).

The ornaments include: cosmetic vials and pins; mirrors and decorative pins, bracelets, and rings; and fragments of compartmented and geometric seals. In general, the jewelry and ceremonial objects were found primarily in burials; some examples, however, also were found on floors in buildings and in midden.

Small bronze and copper alloy vials are found in northern and southern Bactria, in association with decorative pins or sticks. The vials from Margiana differ in form from those found in Bactria, reflecting regional differences in the shape of vessels between Bactria and Margiana. This suggests local centers of metallurgical production, as opposed to itinerant metallurgists. It also emphasizes the lack of exchange of finished objects between oases despite the fact that the raw metal (apparently as ingots) probably came from the Hissar mountains near the northern Bactrian oases.

Large pins (8–14 cm in length) with decorated ends are often found associated with small bronze and copper alloy jars (Amiet 1990b; Salvatori 1990). Round finials are most common in Margiana at Gonur and Togolok. Pins with animal forms or body parts are more common from the Bactrian sites of Sapalli and Dzharkutan (Askarov 1977). Previously it was suggested that the Margiana variant contrasted with the Bactrian variant of the BMAC by its lack of precious metals (Hiebert and Killick 1993). However, large pins made of gold were recently found by B. Udemuradov at Egri Bogaz in Margiana (Udemuradov 1993).

Bracelets and earrings are a very common feature of the BMAC assemblage of metals. Copper, bronze, silver, and lead earrings are common in BMAC burials in Margiana. Bactrian variants of the bracelets have twisted decoration, and the ends are sometimes in the form of snakes' heads (Askarov 1977). These features are evocative of later Iranian bracelets of Luristani and Achaemenid types.

Bronze and copper alloy stamp seals are a distinctive feature of the BMAC. There are two broad categories of seal forms: (1) compartmented—open backed with the design soldered on; and (2) champleve—closed, most likely wax cast, with the design cast and gouged out (fig. 9.26.7).

From Period 2 in Margiana are found geometric and figurative seals, made in both the compartmented and the champleve techniques.

The geometric seals are stylistically undifferentiated from those of Period 1. Bronze stamp seal impressions are found on Period 2 pottery, stamped prior to firing. This practice is similar to that with the stone seals and indicates a similar function.

Bronze and copper alloy axes from Period 2 contexts in Margiana and Bactria are of the cast shaft-hole variety. They have a zoomorphic form, most typically with a prominent eye motif on each side and a tail or a beak (see the axe from the cenotaph illustrated from the excavations at Gonur south in chap. 7). In Margiana these axes have been cast but not hardened for use and thus are considered to have been ceremonial in nature.

Such axes are found both in burial contexts and in monumental architecture in Bactria and Margiana. They are also found in BMAC assemblages outside of Margiana and Bactria, such as at Shahdad and Khinaman.

Axes from Bactria are similar to the Margiana type but more elaborate, with designs of animals and dragons similar to BMAC amulets. These axes are best known from plundered tombs of southern Bactria, which include gold and silver chased examples (Ligabue and Salvatori 1990).

Although undecorated bronze and copper alloy shaft-hole axes have been found in the greater Near East and Central Asia from the beginning of bronze weapon use (Deshayes 1960), the distinctively decorated bronze and copper alloy axes found in Margiana

Period 2 are restricted to the BMAC period in Central Asia and are part of BMAC assemblages found in surrounding areas.

The distinctive styles of metal objects from Margiana Period 2 suggest local manufacture. There are also several direct indicators of local metallurgical production, most notably a copper ingot found in BMAC levels at Gonur south in 1990 (fig. 9.27:1). This, together with a metal casting mold found on the surface at Gonur (fig. 9.27:2), indicates that casting occurred at Gonur. The mold has the form of an eagle engraved on it. Very similar cast eagles adorn the rim of a well-known metal vessel of the BMAC style (Pittman 1984, pl. 30).

Takhirbai 3 (Period 3): Post-BMAC

A small number of bronze objects were found during the excavations at Takhirbai 3 (Masson 1959, pl. 14). Among the bronzes that were typologically similar to BMAC, two were found in situ (a spear point [Masson 1959, pl. 14] and an arrow point [from the 1972 excavations]). Metal fragments from surface collections at Takhirbai 3 indicate that forms of jewelry such as pins and simple earrings continue beyond the BMAC. The metal assemblage from all known Takhirbai period sites in Margiana, although limited, does not include any distinctive nomadic metals that would indicate an intensification of nomadic contacts following the BMAC. This is in contrast to the contemporary (post-BMAC) Molali and Vashkh settlements of Bactria, which are characterized by rich bronze assemblages of the nomadic tradition (P'yankova 1994).

THE BACTRIAN-MARGIANA ARCHAEOLOGICAL COMPLEX

Neither the pre-BMAC period nor the post-BMAC period indicates a strong external influence on the development of the small-finds assemblage. It is thus in the context of local development that we see the BMAC emerge. Sarianidi has documented Bactrian (1977) and Margiana (1990) variants of the style in terms of animal depictions, geometric motif frequencies, types of imported materials, and richness of material culture. There is a specific Margiana local style as well as a regional style found on all of the Bactria and Margiana sites. Of great interest are the small differences in the BMAC style of artifacts from the oases of Margiana, southern Bactria, and northern Bactria. These indicate that although information flowed between oases, little actual exchange of artifacts occurred. Four processes can be identified in the local Margiana development of the BMAC: (1) the replacement or termination of earlier motifs and symbols; (2) the incorporation of old elements into a new interpretation; (3) the transformation of the earlier iconographic system; and (4) the innovation or development of new motifs.

1. Replacement. In Period 1, violin-shaped figurines are the predominant ceremonial artifact. In the development of the BMAC, this tradition comes to an end, despite the clear overall cultural continuity between Periods 1 and 2. Other motifs also change abruptly or disappear; an example is the occurrence of the goat and tree motif found on Period 1 ceramics. This change in ceremonial images is a reflection of culture change within the continuous development in Margiana.

2. Incorporation. Stone staffs, disks, and miniature columns are also found in Period 1, usually individually or in graves. These objects are incorporated into the BMAC, as indicated by the different grouping of them together in both architectural and burial contexts. The incorporation of these objects possibly indicates redefinition and the adding of new cultural meanings to them.

3. Transformation. The large and rich iconography, including zoomorphic, anthropomorphic, and geometric designs, appears to have developed from the earlier Margiana tradition. Period 1 has bronze axes, maceheads, and stone and bronze seals. Such items are transformed in Period 2, where several maceheads from both Margiana and Bactria are ornately carved, and decorated bronze or copper alloy axes are found. The ceremonial aspect of axes in Period 2 is clearly seen in the nonfunctional bone axes found in burials and cenotaphs of the BMAC.

4. Innovation. Motifs on stone, bronze, and copper alloy seals (which come from a foothill tradition) become diversified in Period 2. Motifs include animals, humans, dragons, and some narrative scenes. Amulets made of terracotta, bone, stone, or copper alloy (or bronze) may be indicators of individuals identifying themselves as part of the BMAC. The new artistic and iconographic symbols on the artifacts include snakes, scorpions, and plants typical of the desert around Margiana and images of mountain goats typical of northern Bactria. Images of domestic plants, camel, sheep, and other herd animals are also common on BMAC artifacts.

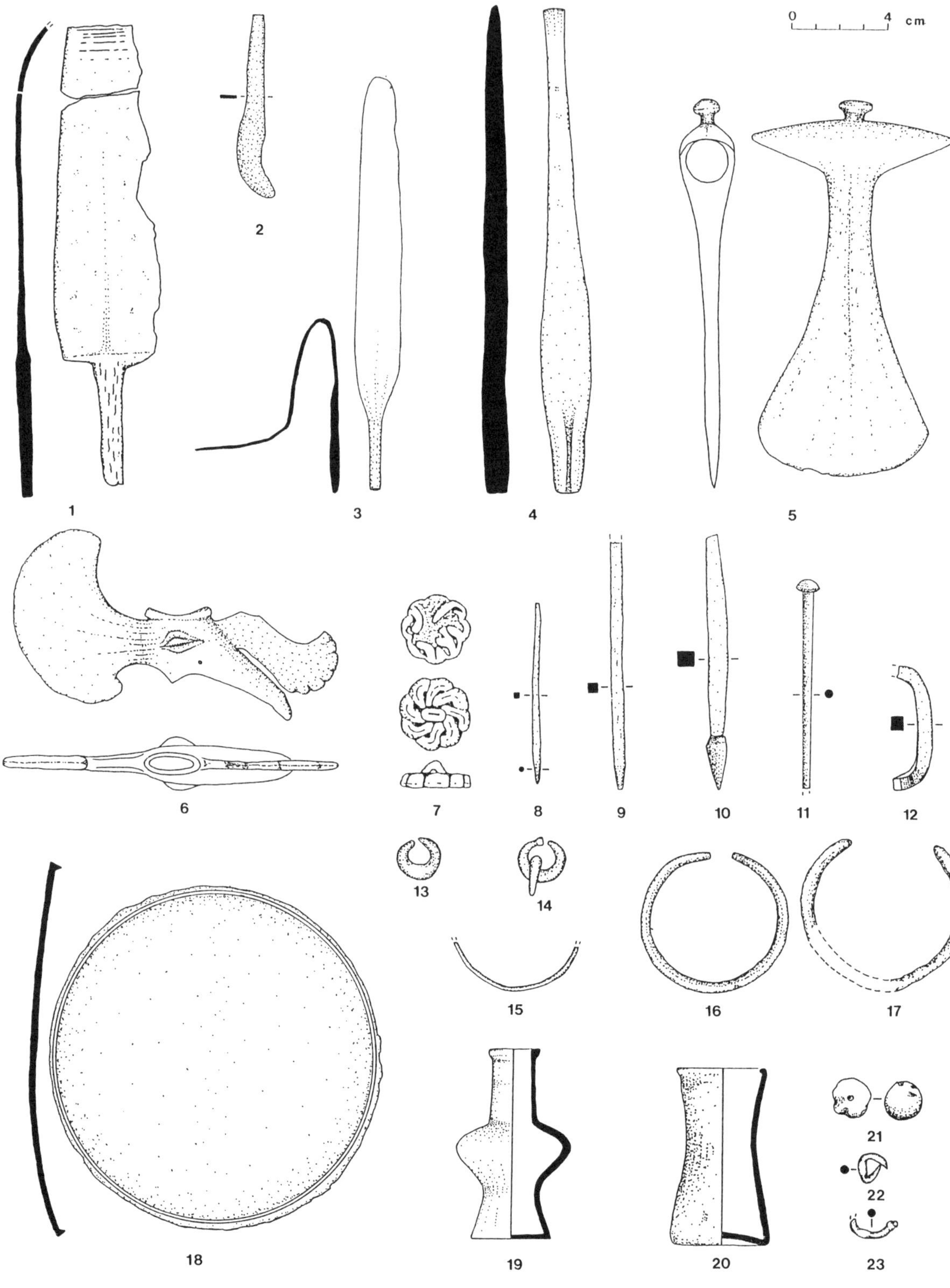

Figure 9.26
Caption on p. 163.

Figure 9.27
1) Copper ingot, Gonur south, Room 141; 2) Stone mold for casting metal in the form of a bird, Gonur north, surface.

Figure 9.26 continued
Period 2 metal objects.
1) Spear or knife blade, Togolok 21, Burial 52; 2) Knife blade, Gonur south, Room 10; 3) Knife blade, Togolok 1, Burial 10; 4) Pick, Togolok 21, Room 75; 5) Tin bronze axe, Togolok 21, Room 180; 6) Copper axe, Gonur south, Cenotaph 41; 7) Champleve seal, Gonur south, Room 10; 8) Drill, Togolok 24, Burial 31; 9) Drill, Togolok 21, room context; 10) Drill, Togolok 21, room context; 11) Large pin, Gonur south, Room 109; 12) Twisted copper fragment, Togolok 21, Room 188; 13) Earring, Gonur south, Room 90; 14) Earrings, Togolok 1, Burial 8; 15) Bracelet, Togolok 21, Room 25; 16) Bracelet, Togolok 21, Burial 10; 17) Bracelet, Togolok 24, Burial 31; 18) Mirror, Gonur, Burial 40; 19) Flacon, Togolok 24, Burial 7; 20) Lead flacon, Togolok 21, Room 161; 21) Lead ball, Gonur south, surface; 22) Silver earring, Gonur south, room context; 23) Lead or silver earring, Gonur south, Room 112.

Production

BMAC style artifacts *are* produced in Margiana as evidenced by the occurrence of unfinished artifacts of these types on the Margiana sites. Many BMAC small finds are made of materials not found in the desert, and production or finishing areas are found in most BMAC building complexes. It would be interesting to focus collaborative excavations on the production areas in the future. Along with Gonur depe—which has evidence for metal and steatite working—there is evidence of steatite and alabaster working at Togolok 21. Copper alloy casting occurs at Togolok 1 (Sarianidi 1990) as well as on many sites in northern and southern Bactria (Askarov et al. 1988). In addition, bronze and copper alloy tools for working other materials are found at every BMAC site.

No production areas have been found within Period 1 buildings in Margiana. It is possible that distinct workshops outside of the habitation areas will be found in Margiana similar to the Namazga V workshop areas in excavation 9 at Altyn depe (Masson 1981b).

The analysis of the Period 2 architecture at Gonur (chap. 7) suggests that in Period 2, production becomes based inside the building complexes themselves. The type of production that develops can be best compared to the *oikos* model. The fundamental unit of *oikos* production consists of members of an extended family or clan (here, all living within the *qala*). The appearance of bullae, and stamp and cylinder seals marking them, indicates the emergence of a new level in the hierarchy of the *qala* economy seen in the local control of production.

Culture Contact

The BMAC assemblage of artifacts (with typical Period 2 type ceramics) is also found well outside of Margiana and Bactria in Iran and South Asia at contemporary sites such as Khinaman, Khurab, Sibri, Mehrgarh, Quetta, Shahdad, Hissar, and Fullol. This export version of the BMAC is typically found grouped together in burials as a complex within the context of a completely different material culture. This is true whether in Iran (Hiebert and Lamberg-Karlovsky 1992), the Levant (Mazar 1990), or South Asia (Jarrige 1989). On the basis of the refined ceramic typology and the definition of BMAC objects, this assemblage outside of Central Asia can be interpreted as a clear indication of the movement of Central Asian people, probably for resource acquisition through conquest or trade. Ironically, because of the late chronology used by the excavators of the Central Asian sites, the finds of Central Asian artifacts far outside of Central Asia have been perceived as antecedents of the BMAC and thus evidence of long-distance migrations into the desert oases.

Indigenous Development

The local development of the BMAC in Margiana is indicated by the continuity in ceramics, architecture, and settlement from Period 1 to Period 2.

Two potential sources of outside influence must be considered in the development of the BMAC: (1) The occurrence of steppe nomadic artifacts inside building complexes in Margiana attests to interaction with Andronovo nomads from the eastern steppe. These nomads could have introduced new stylistic traditions to the area; however, steppe material in Margiana is rare, and the new motifs that appear in Period 2 (e.g., snakes, scorpions, and boar) relate to the oasis environment itself rather than to the steppe nomadic traditions. (2) The distribution of the BMAC outside of Central Asia indicates a wide expansion. People from Bactria and Margiana were in contact with the greater Indo-Iranian region from the Indus valley to western Iran and perhaps beyond. Burials found well outside of Central Asia that have exclusively BMAC goods, including ceramics, are evidence for the contacts of Central Asian people, perhaps involved in acquiring raw materials, with contemporary cultures to the south. However, in Margiana itself there is no evidence of foreign styles or imported objects from the south in either Period 1 or Period 2.

Despite the contacts with nomads to the north and with contemporary Bronze Age cultures to the south, the emergence of the new style in Period 2 appears to be an indigenous process of development rather than the adoption or importing of an ideology or art style. The lack of finished imported objects and the occurrence of imported raw materials are characteristic of an extractive and expansionistic economic system.

Social and economic changes such as we have evidence for in the desert oases culture of the BMAC also affect other aspects of culture, such as ideology, religion, and possibly language. Such ideological changes are reflected in the artistic depictions, ritual objects, and figurines found in Margiana and Bactria. The architectural revolution took place in Margiana in Period 1; the ideological revolution (evident in the iconography of axes, figurines, seals, and amulets) occurred in Period 2.

CHAPTER TEN

Trends and Traditions in Central Asian Culture History

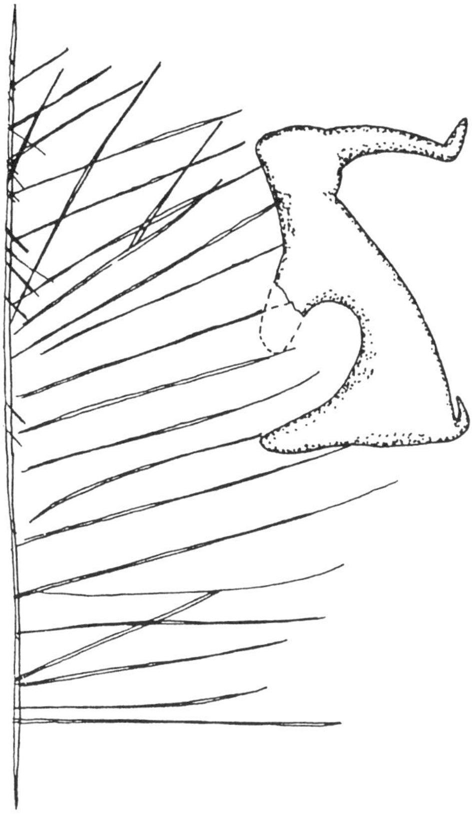

MANY EXPLANATIONS HAVE BEEN PROPOSED FOR THE WIDE-spread distribution of Bronze Age oasis settlements in Margiana and Bactria. These include migrations from the Iranian plateau originally emanating from Mesopotamia (Sarianidi 1987b), evolution from the Baluchistan tradition (Jarrige 1989), nomadic incursions (Alyekshin 1980), migration from the southern Turkmenistan foothill zone (Biscione 1977), and continuous growth of a local population in the oasis areas (Udemuradov 1988). Reevaluation of the sequence using the new data from Margiana does not support any of these suggestions. I suggest a colonization from the urban states of the Kopet Dag foothill plain followed by the local development of the BMAC culture in Margiana and Bactria.

THE CHRONOLOGY PRESENTED IN THIS STUDY

Figure 10.1 presents the chronology for Margiana, the foothills of southern Turkmenistan, and northern and southern Bactria. The ceramic chronology as originally presented by Masson (1956) is based on designs on painted ceramics (P'yankova 1994). Often the main changes in ceramic designs do not correspond with important cultural changes documented from other aspects of the material culture.

In fact, four pivotal transition points in the chronology of Central Asia occur *in the middle* of periods defined by ceramic styles. The Central Asian pattern, as described below, first appears during the late Namazga III period (fig. 10.2). This is a point of wide-scale shifts in society, although the painted traditions of Namazga III ceramics are little affected. A second shift comes in late Namazga IV, with a change toward craft specialization, social hierarchy, regional integration, and monumental architecture. The third transition is late Namazga V, with the development of urbanism and colonization of Margiana. The final transition considered here is the development of the Bactrian-Margiana Archaeological Complex, at the beginning of Namazga VI, again, which has a ceramic assemblage very similar to the preceding (late Namazga V) period.

	Bactrian Desert Oasis Tradition	Margiana Desert Oasis Tradition	Eastern Kopet Dag Tradition	Central Kopet Dag Tradition	Western Kopet Dag Tradition
1500 BC – 1700 BC	Molali Period	Takhirbai Period	?	Late Namazga VI	Anau IV A
1700 BC – 1900 BC	BMAC	BMAC	BMAC burials	Namazga VI	Anau III
1900 BC – 2200 BC	---	Late Namazga V	Altyn depe (Exc 1), 0-2	Late Namazga V	
2200 BC – 2700 BC	---	---	Altyn depe (Exc 1), 3-8	Namazga IV-V	
2700 BC – 3500 BC	---	Geoksyur campsites	Geoksyur	Namazga III-IV	
3500 BC – 5500 BC	---	---	Ilgynly I, II	Namazga II, Namazga I	Anau II Anau Ia, Ib

Figure 10.1
Chronology for Margiana, the foothills of southern Turkmenistan, and northern and southern Bactria.

ESTABLISHMENT OF THE CENTRAL ASIAN PATTERN

By the second half of the fourth millennium in Central Asia (late Namazga III and early Namazga IV), the earliest distinctively Central Asian symbols appear. These specific attributes are found on administrative and elite objects, perhaps related to an increase in interregional interaction with cultures on the Iranian plateau and in South Asia, and it is possible to differentiate regional styles of the central east and western zones at this time. Settlements based on dry farming were located in the central and western foothill zone, whereas settlements based on irrigation agriculture were located in the eastern zone and the Geoksyur oasis (fig. 10.3). In all of these areas, the habitation sites are relatively similar in size and simple burials are typical of village-level agriculturalists.

Traditions of Central Asian Motifs

Sites in the western Kopet Dag zone (Ak depe and Anau) incorporate elements of Iranian ceramic traditions at this time, including both imported and local-

	PRE-NMG III	late NMG III	late NMG IV	early NMG V	late NMG V	MARGIANA OASIS CULTURE Period 1	Period 2
Sheep/goat, wheat/barley village agriculture	—	—	—	—	—	—	—
Irrigation	foothill	oasis	foothill	foothill	foothill	oasis	
Trade items brought in	small objects	raw mat	small objects	trade items	small objects	small objects	raw mat
Contacts		wide Indo-Iranian	few	Indus	local oasis	local oasis	wide Indo-Iranian
Site size (from Kohl 1984)		.6-5ha	5-20ha	5-20ha	5-50ha	.5-15ha	.5-15ha
Stone handled disks, lamps		—	—	—	—	—	—
Terracotta animals and carts		—	—	—	—	—	—
Stepped motifs		---ceramics-->	--stone objects---	—	—	------>	seals>
Stamp seals		------			—	—	→
Terracotta human figurines		sitting	flat---	—	—	—	→
Fortifications			—	—	—	—	→
Status differentiation in burials			—	—	—	—	→
Specialized production areas			—	—	—	—	→
Fast wheel ceramics			—	—	—	—	→
Undecorated ceramics				—	—	—	→

Figure 10.2
Trends in Central Asian culture history.

ly produced grey wares (Sarianidi 1976). At Geoksyur sites and Ilgynly depe (in the eastern foothill zone), typical Central Asian styles such as geometric step and cross patterns and animal images are first found on the painted ceramics similar to South Asian painted motifs, such as from Quetta. These images are similar to those on other media, such as bronze seals during the later Bronze Age of the foothills and the oasis. The beginning of the local exploitation of alabaster and steatite stone to make lamps, handled disks (loom weights), and seal amulets with geometric designs is found in these settlements. Terracotta human figurines, terracotta model carts, and animal figurines are also found for the first time in late Namazga III and early Namazga IV (Masson 1961; Khlopin 1964; Kuz'mina 1980).

Early Oasis Adaptations

Farming in deltaic fans was practiced in the Geoksyur sites of the Tedzhen River delta. The Geoksyur sites were located outside of the dry farming belt and required a simple irrigation system for agriculture (Khlopin 1964; Lisitsyna 1978). The seasonally stable discharge of the Tedzhen River did not require long canals or complex irrigation systems. Simple irrigation systems of the late Namazga III to early Namazga IV period around the Geoksyur sites consisted of parallel canals from a major branch of the delta drainage. Only one or two settlements occurred on each canal system. Thus the ability to transform areas outside of the dry farming belt through irrigation was known one thousand years before the development of irrigation in Margiana.

The occupation of Geoksyur sites has other parallels with the Margiana occupation. Like the oasis areas of Margiana and Bactria, the Geoksyur oasis lacked important natural resources. The Geoksyur sites provide evidence for the first extensive relations with distant areas, bringing imported materials to Geoksyur. For example, metal objects were made from imported ingots, and even Indian ocean shells were imported for the production of bangles (Khlopin 1964). This

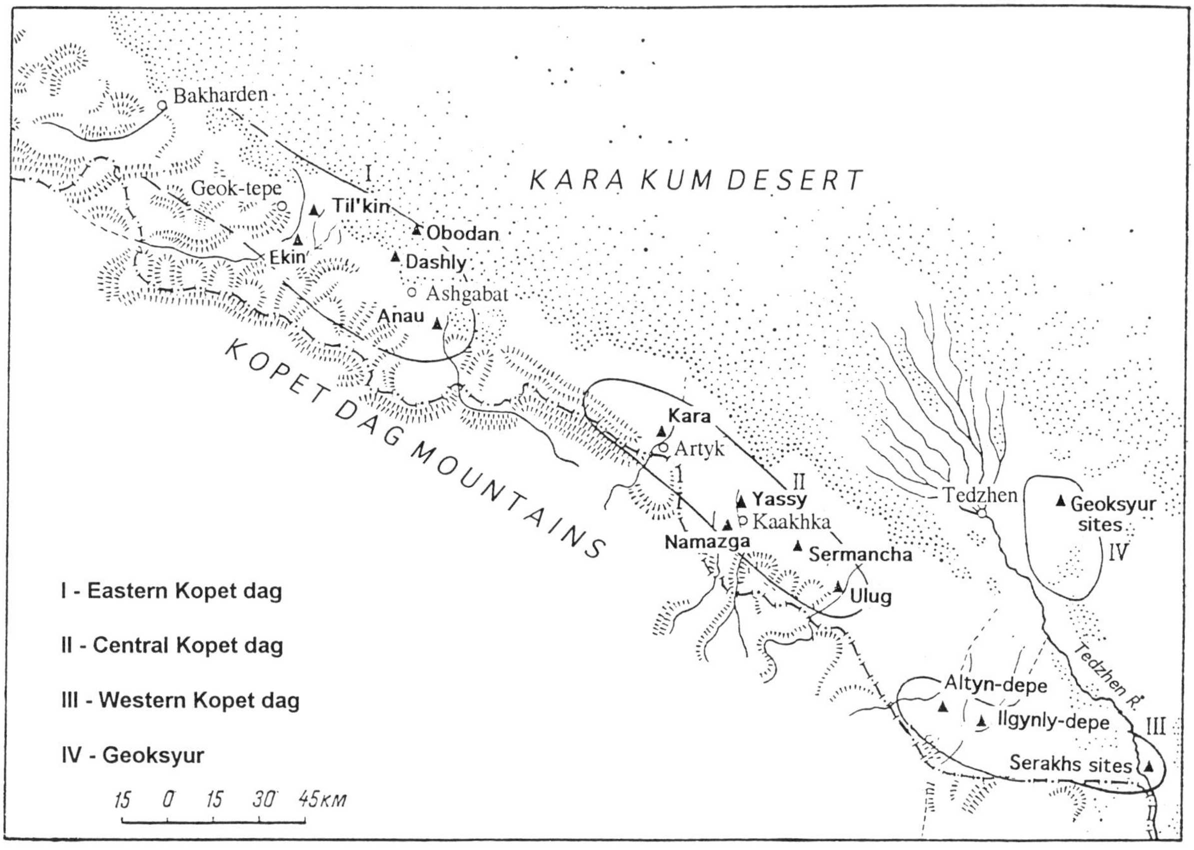

Figure 10.3
Late Namazga III/early Namazga IV regionalization of dry farming culture areas.

pattern is similar to the way craftsmen in the later Margiana sites imported raw materials such as metal ingots and shell.

The network for acquiring raw materials is reflected in the ceramic parallels among the Geoksyur oasis, Baluchistan (Quetta [Piggott 1950], Mehrgarh Period 3 [Jarrige 1989], and Damb-Sadaat 2 and 3 [Fairservis 1975]), Sistan (Shahr-i Sokhta I [Tosi 1983]), South Afghanistan (Mundigak Period III [Casal 1961]), and the Zerafshan valley (Sarazm, levels 1 and 2 [Isakov and Lyonnet 1988]) (fig. 10.4). The connections between Geoksyur and distant areas to the south are primarily reflected in the sharing of motifs on locally produced ceramics. This strongly suggests reciprocal exchange, which is fundamentally different from the later interaction pattern in which actual BMAC items were exported from Central Asia and few finished objects were imported.

Ceramics and small-finds assemblages from Sarazm, however, have very close parallels to material from the Geoksyur sites (Isakov and Lyonnet 1988). Actual importation of the ceramics from Geoksyur is suggested. Small camps or deflated sites in Margiana (Masimov 1979) suggest direct contact between the Zerafshan valley (Sarazm) and the Geoksyur oasis (Masson 1989).

Thus the late Namazga III to early Namazga IV period is of considerable significance, for it indicates the first extensive interaction with distant regions, particularly the Indo-Iranian borderlands. It is important to recognize that the production of finds from exotic materials and long-distance interaction were already characteristic of southern Turkmenistan at the end of the fourth and beginning of the third millennium. However, the simple late Namazga III settlement pattern and lack of site hierarchy indicate a different scale of social complexity from that which characterized the BMAC. It is quite likely that the Geoksyur occupation was short because groups were unable to maintain the canals. The absence of a complex enough social structure to maintain the canals may have contributed to the abandonment of the area.

Figure 10.4
Namazga III–IV (Geoksyur) period.

ORIGINS OF THE CENTRAL ASIAN BRONZE AGE TRADITION

The pattern of resource exploitation, regions of interaction, and iconographic motifs characteristic of Central Asia begin in the late Namazga III period, with the types and forms of ceramics, seals, figurines, tokens, and so on coming only with the late Namazga IV period.

By this time the Geoksyur sites were abandoned, except for the isolated site of Khapuz depe (Masson and Sarianidi 1972). The number of sites in the foothill zone apparently increased, probably reflecting the incorporation of the former Geoksyur population (Kohl 1984). Long-distance interaction between the

Upper Zerafshan and the foothill zone ceased after the early Namazga IV, but sites in both areas continued to be occupied (Besenval and Isakov 1989). The lack of ceramic parallels with other regions and imported objects suggest a much reduced interaction network (fig. 10.5).

By the late Namazga IV period, the following features of foothill sites are documented: the earliest occurrence of specialized production areas (Masimov 1970, 1976), the earliest fortifications on the outer perimeter of the settlements (Masson 1968), and marked increase in status differentiation of individuals in burials (Alyekshin 1979; Masson 1981b). Overall, the Kopet Dag foothill plain sites, from Anau to Altyn depe, have a similarity of ceramic forms and styles forming a stylistic horizon. This horizon suggests greater interaction among these sites and, together with the other indices of increased social

Figure 10.5
Late Namazga IV/early Namazga V period.

complexity, suggests their integration within a state-level society (Kohl 1984).

Specialized production includes the local manufacture of copper alloy objects with shapes typical of the middle and later Bronze Age: metal vessels, pins, earrings, chisels, and punches. Stone objects, including steatite and alabaster biconical beads, alabaster pots, and geometric stamp seals similar to those from the Margiana assemblage, were manufactured locally. It is difficult to differentiate these late Namazga IV artifacts from the Namazga V and BMAC small finds when they are found out of excavated context.

Flat violin-shaped terracotta female figurines, typical of Namazga V, are first found in late Namazga IV levels. Similar figurines are seen outside of the foothill zone in Margiana Period 1. It is possible that the wide distribution of these distinctive figurines represents shared political identity in addition to cultural identity between the two regions.

The Central Asian Bronze Age Ceramic Tradition

The most distinctive development in the late Namazga IV period is the beginning of pottery made on a fast wheel. The carinated forms characteristic of all of the Central Asian Bronze Age ceramics (with fine geometric painted designs) become common during Namazga IV.

The transition to the fast wheel-finished pottery is clearly documented at Altyn depe in the successive excavation horizons 4 through 8 (Masson 1988:23, table 1). The late Namazga IV ceramics (Altyn depe levels 4 and 5) were almost entirely made on the fast wheel, and the forms of the ceramics have the distinctive carinated side and vertical-lipped rims that characterize the forms of the Central Asian ceramic tradition. The development of the fast wheel as a technology and the manufacture of pottery in specialized quarters imply the emergence of a mass-produced ceramics most likely made by specialists.

The wheel-made ceramics of the late Namazga IV, early and late Namazga V, Namazga VI, and the Bactrian and Margiana Bronze Age oases areas share some overall characteristics of form:

1. The open forms (Margiana types 2.A) include vases on pedestal bases and trumpet-shaped cups of all sizes. Both types 2.A.2 and 2.A.3 (vertical-lipped and incised rim forms) are found as early as late Namazga IV.

2. Large closed pots with a concave moldmade base are also first found in late Namazga IV. These forms by definition are made on a wheel and reflect a manufacturing technique that continues until the end of the Bronze Age ceramic tradition in Central Asia.

3. Jars generally have a medial carination and are called "biconical" jars. These range from sharply carinated to rounded in a general trend through time.

4. Cups and bowls have a tall pedestaled base and are first found in early Namazga V levels at Shor depe (Shchetenko 1970, table 1). The form of these bases is made possible by fast-wheel production.

5. Ceramic potstands (*podstavki*) are found in both the Central Asian and Indus valley traditions. These ceramics appear to be used both for the manufacture of the concave base of large closed pots and also as the stands for these vessels.

These attributes of the ceramics of the Central Asian tradition have broad similarities to the Indus valley ceramics, which appear to be parallel developments. The similarities in the two regions' wheel-made ceramics (pedestaled bases, moldmade bases, and *podstavki*) indicate long-term interaction with South Asia during the entire period of cultural development in Central Asia but no indication of a specific period of influence.

THE MATURE BRONZE AGE OF CENTRAL ASIA

The first occurrence of unpainted fast-wheel ceramics so typical of the desert oases of Margiana and Bactria is in the early Namazga V period in the central and eastern foothill zone at sites such as Shor depe (Shchetenko 1970; Masimov 1978), Namazga depe (Masson 1956), Altyn depe (Masson 1981a), and Ulug depe (personal observations).

The ceramics, which often have a sharp carination on the shoulders and rim, are often considered elegant in shape with their distinctive forms. The forms are very standardized, most likely indicating a high degree of craft specialization, especially in comparison with the earlier handmade ceramics.

Two chronological phases of Namazga V ceramics are particularly well documented at Altyn depe, where extensive Namazga V deposits have been excavated (Masson 1967, 1970, 1977; Masimov 1970).

The early Namazga V sites of the foothill zone are dense settlements with differentiated quarters. At both large and small sites the architecture is similarly compact, with multiroomed houses, long alleys or corridors, and courtyards (Shchetenko 1970). These sites are better characterized as large agglomerated villages, since there is no difference in the structure of the settlements between the large sites and the small sites.

The regional interaction of the early Namazga V appears to be a continuation of the late Namazga IV pattern with a limited regional network. The occurrence of isolated exotic small objects in the absence of other evidence of contact is more indicative of a pattern of "trickle trade" than of culture contact (Beale 1973).

The early Namazga V period deposits at Altyn depe include imported (or imitated) mature Harappan artifacts (Masson 1977, 1984). The small seals, beads, and ivory sticks appear to be trade items, and, if not made in the Indus valley, they are of a type at least foreign to the Central Asian small-finds tradition. While the early levels of the Harappan outpost of Shortughai are contemporary with the early Namazga V (Possehl 1989), it must be noted that ceramic parallels between Altyn and Shortughai for this period are negligible.

Late Namazga V

Late Namazga V is a critical period in the development of Central Asian oases cultures because of two important events in the foothill region. First, during the late Namazga V, several extremely large and dense settlements emerge with all of the indicators of state-level urbanism. Second, the oasis area of Margiana is widely occupied.

During the late Namazga V period, Namazga (50 ha) is the largest site in the central foothill zone, and Altyn depe (25 to 26 ha) is the central site in the eastern zone. The architecture at both sites is distinctive, with multiroomed houses, courtyards, and narrow streets (Masimov 1976; Masson 1981b).

Based on the excavations up to 1980, it has been commonly reported that the late Namazga V occupation at Altyn depe (levels 0 through 2) was restricted to a small area of the site (Masson 1981b, 1988). Since the early 1980s, excavation at Altyn depe has been focused on the final phase of occupation, and the area of occupation is now clearly extensive, perhaps the most extensive of the Namazga V period. Areas of late Namazga V include potters' quarters (excavation 10), monumental architecture (the upper levels of excavation 7), and large areas of domestic architecture (excavations 9, 13, and 16). The wide-scale excavation of levels of this period permits characterization of these large sites as "cities," as the word is defined in the Near East (Childe 1953; Adams 1981; Masson 1989).

Evidence of a Food Production Crisis?

It appears now that the late Namazga V period represents the largest extent of urban settlement in the foothill zone and that the sites grew to larger sizes than they ever had before. Future research should focus on the possibility that the sites exceeded the carrying capacity of the agricultural land around them. The rivers of the foothill zone do not allow irrigation, because their discharge is too small. Agriculture is restricted to dry farming with limited *liman* irrigation. Contrary to the evolutionary perspective on agricultural systems proposed by Lisitsyna (1978), no other complex irrigation system developed in the foothill zone until the later introduction of the *qanat* system of underground canals—a development that followed the mid-first millennium B.C.

The refined chronology from the foothill sites such as Altyn depe (Udemuradov 1987) and Anau may make it possible to examine this suggestion of limited prehistoric carrying capacity (fig. 10.6). We can suggest that, given a crisis in food production in the foothill sites, the long-known richness of the desert oases would seem very attractive. People from the foothill sites would then invest the energy necessary to clear the land and settle there.

There may be a correlation between the depopulation of the urban foothill sites of the Kopet Dag at the end of Namazga V and the origins of widespread occupation in Bactria.

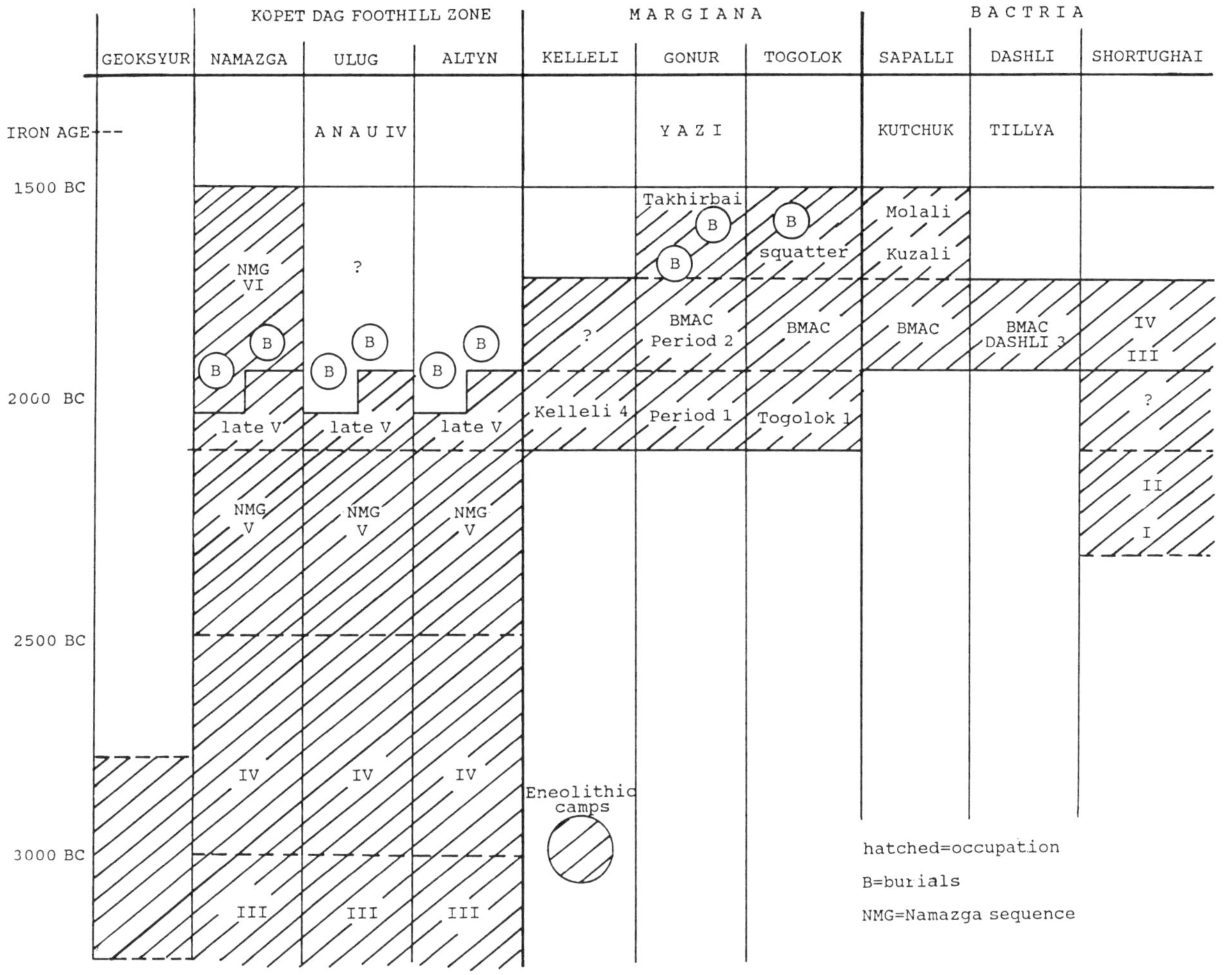

Figure 10.6
Proposed chronology for Central Asia adapted from Hiebert 1992b, fig. 10.1. Based on the following: Geoksyur (Khlopin 1964); Namazga (Masson 1956; Dolukanov, Shchetenko, and Tosi 1985); Ulug (author's observations); Altyn (Masson 1981b; Udemuradov 1987); Kelleli, Gonur, Togolok (this study); Sapalli (Askarov 1977; author's observations); Dashli (Sarianidi 1977, 1990) Shortughai (Francfort 1989).

NAMAZGA VI

The Namazga VI period in the foothill zone is found at very few sites, and where it is found the occupation is very small. Typically this situation has been referred to as a deurbanization. A shift from large-site to small-site occupation has been suggested (Biscione 1977). Migration out of the foothill zone has also been suggested (Masson 1989). Most likely what is called "Namazga VI" is a regionally restricted ceramic assemblage found only at Namazga depe and Anau (Hiebert and Kurbansakhatov 1993). There is no evidence of any interaction between Namazga VI of Namazga and Anau and what has been called "Namazga VI" in Margiana.

Other sites that are considered to have Namazga VI levels (Yangi-kala, Ulug depe, and Altyn depe) yielded "Namazga VI" materials from burials that have more parallels with the Bactrian-Margiana ceramics and small finds than with styles from Namazga depe. Excavations at Anau are resolving questions of the nature of the foothill Namazga VI. Few of the other large sites of the foothill region have any Namazga VI occupation, and the large site of Altyn depe appears to have been abandoned.

THE ORIGINS OF OCCUPATION IN MARGIANA: PERIOD 1 (2200–2000 B.C.)

Late Namazga V materials are found widely in Margiana, covering an area of approximately 3,000 sq km (fig. 10.7). It is important to emphasize that the initial occupation of Margiana occurred at the same time that the foothill site of Altyn depe was in its largest urban phase.

Colonization

Margiana was colonized simultaneously over a large area. Similarities in the ceramics, small finds, and architecture between the sites of Period 1 suggest that

Figure 10.7
Distribution of late Namazga V materials.

these building complexes were built in a single period. The cultural tradition of the colonists appears to have remained very close to the foothill culture during Period 1 in Margiana. The ceremonial objects such as the figurines and the range of types and forms of ceramics, tools, and weapons are indistinguishable from those from the contemporary urban settlements of the foothill zone. However, based on analysis of the ware of the ceramics and the paste of the small figurines, these were not being exchanged.

We have no reason to think that Margiana was "discovered" at this time. The evidence from Sarazm of contacts with the foothill sites from Namazga III times and the scatters of pre-Period 1 sherds in Margiana indicate that the Murgab River delta of Margiana was known, even if it was not considered a worthwhile area for settlement. A point must have been reached in the foothill occupation when the potential involved in investing in the opening of a new area became greater than the risks.

New Agricultural Systems

The first hurdle in occupying Margiana concerned the clearing of the thickets and the cutting of irrigation canals. The second hurdle was the shift from dry farming to irrigation. The settlement pattern suggests a pattern of large canals, dams, and levees characteristic of agriculture in the oasis from this time onward. This man-made oasis environment strongly altered the ecology of the delta. The ethnobotanical record of weed seeds and grains typical of irrigated fields provides evidence for this disturbance from the earliest levels of the deep sounding at Gonur.

Pioneer Architecture

The compact multiroom houses, corridors, and alleyways of the foothill sites appear structurally distinct from Margiana's pattern of domestic structures with shared courtyards packed into a fortified building complex. The new Margiana settlement plan does not reflect the organization of the foothill zone but is something completely new for the region and for Central Asia. These settlements appear to be spaced to maximize the agricultural potential of the canals. Settlements remain isolated in comparison with the contemporary urban settlements of the foothill zone.

THE BMAC OASIS CULTURE: PERIOD 2 (2000–1750 B.C.)

By 2000 B.C., both Margiana and southern Bactria were occupied by cultures using irrigation agriculture and constructing large fortified building complexes. In Margiana, occupation continued within the oases at Kelleli, Gonur, and Togolok, although the location of the building complexes shifted enough between Periods 1 and 2 so that few Period 2 structures directly overlay Period 1 structures. The duration of this second period in Margiana is not clear, but according to Takhirbai period radiocarbon dates, the BMAC sites may have been occupied for about 150 to 200 years.

The Period 2 ceramics are clearly continuous from Period 1, with small changes in existing forms and a few new, distinctive, but rare shapes. The difference between the two assemblages is clear enough to enable differentiation of the grave assemblages associated with the BMAC in Margiana. Period 2 is distinguished by new motifs on steatite amulets, distinctive compartmented copper alloy or bronze seals, handled cylinder seals, and the rich metal and stone assemblage referred to as the BMAC. This includes ceremonial axes and small vials, but *not* the violin-shaped figurines, which no longer are made.

Cultural Continuity and Transformation

The shift from Period 1 to Period 2 in Margiana is seen most clearly in the emergence of a new set of symbols found on seals, metal, stone, and terracotta objects. Apart from these signals of social change, most aspects of the assemblage show continuous occupation by a single population and do not support migration or replacement.

First, the settlement and architectural pattern remains fairly constant, although it is possible that the building complexes become better fortified. Stratigraphically, the deep sounding at Gonur shows deposition without any clearly defined break. The ceramics of Periods 1 and 2 are so similar in ware and shapes that these periods can be distinguished only when assemblages of forms are studied. The *categories* of imported objects and small finds are similar from Period 1 to Period 2. All of these indicators appear to point to the local growth of Period 2 from Period 1.

Second, social identity appears to be transformed in Period 2, with the development of the shared BMAC culture. The oasis adaptation spreads to similar deltaic oases in northern Bactria and southern Bactria. The new aspects of Period 2 iconography often relate to the desert environment: snakes, scorpions, boar. Objects such as axes and maceheads, which were used earlier, are transformed into ceremonial objects. Miniature columns, staffs, and maceheads are found in new contexts, indicating perhaps that they are being reinterpreted in the oasis culture. There appears to be an emphasis on the materials of the imported stones, which leads to the deliberate juxtaposition of exotic materials, such as alabaster and steatite.

The new oasis system includes a reorganization of production to craft activities occurring within the *qala* and the finishing of distinctive objects on exotic materials, such as imported stone and metal. Bullae and cylinder seals are used in Period 2, indicating a sophisticated control of exchange. Sealings on ceramics may indicate control of production as well.

The *Qala* and the *Khan*

The long-term growth of social complexity in the foothill zone of southern Turkmenistan led to state-level society in the mid- to late third millennium (late Namazga IV to Namazga V). Evidence for this rests on the compact, walled urban sites with monumental architecture and burials showing social and economic hierarchy. The social organization of the Margiana colony is more difficult to classify and cannot be placed in the tribe-state-empire political framework (Fried 1967).

The initial occupation of Margiana was very complex and well organized. It is interesting that although the settlements of Margiana Period 1 are fortified, there must have been a high degree of communication and information flow between them. This is reflected in the successful agricultural and irrigation systems as well as in the uniformity of material cultural over the area of Margiana.

If this study had focused primarily on the production of ceramics and locally manufactured items, the high degree of standardization and quality of manufacture would strongly suggest a state-level society. The foothill state-level society has almost the same set of ceramic forms and technology. If production is used as a measure of sociopolitical complexity, one would have to assume that the foothill sites and the Margiana sites had similar levels of complexity.

The exchange of exotic materials presents a different picture of economic and political complexity: the pattern of exchange is entirely one sided, since few finished objects are brought in, although raw materials are imported and consumed. If Period 2 is considered, the pattern of exchange of one area dominating surrounding areas is most characteristic of empires.

If any one of these characteristics (settlement pattern, architecture, production, exchange) of the Margiana oasis is taken as the focus of analysis, an argument can be made for a certain general category of sociopolitical organization. Taking all of these factors into consideration, a new organization can be proposed on the basis of local historical analogy.

From the initial occupation of Margiana, large fortified building complexes contained several household units. These isolated complexes are easily compared to the traditional *qala*. *Qala* of Afghanistan and of medieval Merv were a type of feudal agricultural manor. Tabari described the organization of medieval Merv as containing dispersed villages grouped around *qala*, and bound by feudal bonds to the head of the *qala*, or *dikhan* (*Encyclopedia of Islam* 1988:619). The *dikhan* controlled his lineage and fields around a single branch of the canal. These *dikhans* paid tribute to a regional *khan*, who maintained canals, controlled production, and obtained a considerable amount of basic materials (stone, metal, and so on). The Bronze Age buildings can be best compared to the *qala* architecture and may reflect the origins of a system of landlord *khans*.

One suggestion for the emergence of this system in Margiana is that, in Period 1, the *dikhan* were still subservient to the leaders of the foothill zone. In Period 2 the emergence of an independent oasis culture could reflect the emergence of a *khan* in Margiana. Well-fortified citadels are found both in Margiana Period 2 (Togolok 21) and in southern Bactria (Dashli 3, round building), which can be compared to the later *khanate* architecture of the ark.

This system of *khans* and *qala* is a political and economic pattern that works well in the oasis environment. Once established, this pattern remained in place until the development of long-distance trade, which concentrated power in the hands of the merchants at the expense of the landed *dikhans*. With the introduction of Near Eastern city structure to the

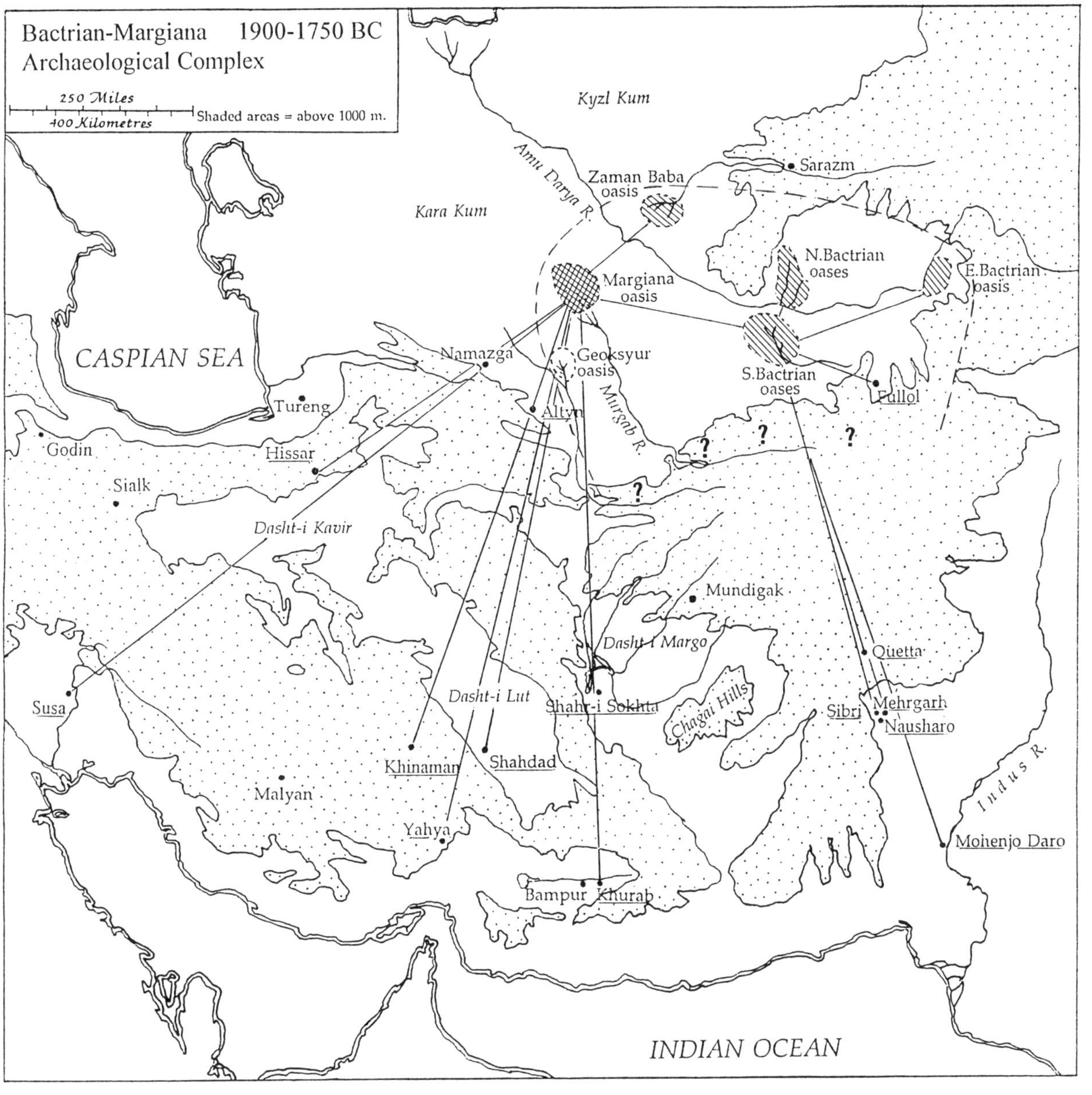

Figure 10.8
Distribution of BMAC objects.

region during the Parthian period (circa the first century A.D.), the social structure changed abruptly (Filanovich 1989). For the first time in Margiana, there was a dichotomy between the urban center and the rural areas. In the development of Parthian and medieval Near Eastern urbanism, the sources of wealth shifted from agriculture to trade and property in the town (Hiebert 1992a). The two systems waxed and waned depending on the personal power of the current local *khan*.

Expansionism

Sarianidi (1990) argues that Margiana was settled from the region of eastern Iran, based on a late chronology for Margiana. With a corrected chronology and a clear antecedent for the BMAC in Period 1 in Margiana, it is possible to flip the center of the BMAC *okione* to its real home in Central Asia. Most of the BMAC artifacts in Iran are found in contexts contemporary with the BMAC in Margiana. The BMAC objects are exotics in the context of the local Iranian or South Asian assemblages (fig. 10.8). I would suggest that the interaction with southern Iran (Khurab), northern Iran (Hissar), and South Asia (Mehrgarh) is an expansion in quest of resources. Raiders or traders from Margiana clearly interacted with the distant cultures. Toward the end of the BMAC time period, urban settlements to the south were dramatically reduced in settlement size. This has often been attributed to environmental change or migrations, but it is possible that the BMAC people raiding and trading on the Iranian plateau and on the borders of the Indus valley also had a destablizing effect on those urban cultures.

CONCLUSIONS

It is possible to outline a series of artifacts and images found in Margiana that are very similar to later Iranian objects and symbols. One great problem in the study of the archaeology of Central Asia has been that these stylistic parallels have been used to cross-date settlement in Margiana. The tradition interpretation holds that these sites were contemporary or that Margiana was slightly later. This attempt at independent dating using radiocarbon determination and detailed comparison of ceramic assemblages has made clear that Margiana predates these distant stylistic parallels by several hundred years.

The origins of the oasis identity in the BMAC provide an example of how culture change occurs within the context of ecological and technological constraints. I have tried to show that the development of the BMAC was not due to a shift in the settlement, technology, or adaptation and that it is not possible to suggest a role for outside influence. Rather, I see a two-stage development: first is a revolution in settlement and architecture and the establishment of a successful farming and herding adaptation in the Namazga V colony from the foothills; second is the development of an independent culture and its spread to other deltaic fans in the desert region, notably in northern and southern Bactria.

Finally, a notable aspect of the Margiana oasis culture is its expansive nature, as seen in the BMAC, possibly due to the quest for raw materials. Long-distance resource procurement also occurred during the occupation of the Geoksyur oasis, suggesting a correlation of oasis occupation and expansionism.

Following the abandonment of the Bronze Age oasis sites of Margiana, the next important occupation of the Margiana oasis is farther to the south during the first millennium B.C. The oasis becomes prominent again only with the founding of Gyaur kala during the early Parthian period. During this period there is a reestablishment of oasis agriculture with wide-scale occupation in Margiana (Nikitin and Sogomonov 1982). This period also coincides with the first major period of caravan trade from China to the Parthian and Roman worlds. The need for imported materials in the oases played an important (possibly fundamental) role in the later development of long-distance overland trade.

Bibliography

Abaev, V. I.
1990 *Izobrannye Trudy: Selected Writings*, vols. 1–4. Vladikavkaz, Irkutsk.

Adams, R. McC.
1981 *Heartland of Cities*. University of Chicago Press, Chicago.

Algaze, G.
1989 "The Uruk Expansion: Cross-cultural Exchange in Early Mesopotamian Civilization." *Current Anthropology* 30(5):571–608.

Al'khamova, Z. A.
1953 "Polevoi otchet VIII otryada IuTAKE po izucheniiu rabada gorodischa starogo Merva v 1947 g." *Trudi Iu.T.A.K.E* 2:404–412.

Alyekshin, V. A.
1979 "Mogila znatnogo goroshanina na Altyn-depe." *Uspekhi Sredneaziatskoi Arkheologii* 4:81–82.
1980 "K probleme geneticheskoi svyazi Iuzhno-turkmenskikh kompleksov epokhi bronzi." *Kratkie Soobshcheniya* 161:24–31.

Amiet, P.
1979 "Archaeological Discontinuity and Ethnic Duality in Elam." *Antiquity* 53:95–204.
1986 *L'Âge des Échanges Inter-iraneans*. Notes et Documents des Musée de France, Paris.
1990a "Elam and Bactria," in *Bactria: An Ancient Oasis Civilization from the Sands of Afghanistan*, G. Ligabue and S. Salvatori, eds., 125–140. Erizzo, Venice.
1990b "Antiquities of Bactria and Outer Iran in the Louvre Collection," in *Bactria: An Ancient Oasis Civilization from the Sands of Afghanistan*, G. Ligabue and S. Salvatori, eds., 157–180. Erizzo, Venice.

Amiran, R.
1969 *Ancient Pottery of the Holy Land*. Mosad Bialik, Ramat-Gan, Israel.

Arne, T. J.
1945 *Excavations at Shah Tepe, Iran*. Publication 27. The Sino-Swedish Expedition, Stockholm.

Arnold, P. J., III
1991 "Dimensional Standardization and Production in Mesoamerican Ceramics." *Latin American Antiquity* 2(4):363–370.

Askarov, A. A.
1977 *Drevnezemledel'cheskaya Kul'tura Epokhi Bronzi Iuga Uzbekistana*. FAN, Tashkent.

Askarov, A., and B. Abdullaev
1983 *Dzharkutan*. FAN, Tashkent.

Askarov, A., I. Buryakov, O. Kvirkveliya, and V. Radililovskii
1988 *Teoreticheskie i Metodologicheskie Problemy Issledovaniya v Arkheologii*. FAN, Tashkent.

Beale, T. W.
1973 "Early Trade in Highland Iran: A View from a Source Area." *World Archaeology* 5(2):133–148.

Besenval, R., and A. Isakov
1989 "Sarazm et les débuts du peuplement agricole dans la région de Samarkand." *Arts Asiatiques* 44:5–20.

Biscione, R.
1973 "Dynamics of an Early South Asian Urbanization: The First Period at Shahr-i Sokhta and its Connections with Southern Turkmenia," in *South Asian Archaeology*, N. Hammond, ed., 105–118. Duckworth, London.
1977 "The Crisis of Central Asian Urbanization in II Millennium B.C. and Villages as an Alternative System," in *Le Plateau Iranien et l'Asie Centrale des Origines à la Conquête Islamique*. Colloques Internationaux 567. J. Deshayes, ed., 113–127. CNRS, Paris.

Bogucki, P.
1993 "Between East and West: Archaeology in the New Eastern Europe." *Journal of Archaeological Research* 1(2):145–166.

Bourgeois, J.-L.
1989 *Spectacular Vernacular: The Adobe Tradition*. Aperature Foundation, New York.

Boyce, M.
1975 *A History of Zoroastrianism*. Handbuch der Orientalistik. Erste Abteilung, Der Nahe und der Mittlere Osten 8. E. J. Brill, Leiden.
1984 *Zoroastrians: Their Religious Beliefs and Practices*. Routledge & Kegan Paul, London.

Casal, J.-M.
1961 *Fouilles de Mundigak*. Mémoires de la Délégation Archéologique Française en Afghanistan 17. Librairie C. Klincksieck, Paris.

Chernykh, E. N.
1989 "Khimichiskii sostav zolotikh izdelii is pogrebenii Tillyatepe," in *Khram i Nekropol Tillya tepe*, V. I. Sarianidi, ed., 237–238. Nauka, Moscow.

Childe, V. G.
1953 *New Light on the Most Ancient East*. Norton, New York.

Chosky, J.
1989 *Purity and Pollution in Zoroastrianism: Triumph Over Evil*. University of Texas Press, Austin.

Cleuziou, S.
1986 "Tureng Tepe and Burnished Grey Ware: A Question of 'Frontier'." *Oriens Antiquus* 25:221–256.

Costantini, L.
1977a "Le Piante," in *La Citta Bruciata del Deserto Salato*, P. Basaglia, ed., 159–228. Erizzo, Venice.
1977b "Introductory Note on the Burnt Wood Residues from Shahr-i Sokhta, Iran." *East and West* n.s. 27:105–110.

Curtis, J.
1988 "A Reconsideration of the Cemetery at Khinaman, South-east Iran." *Iranica Antiqua* 23:97–127.
1990 *Ancient Persia*. Harvard University Press, Cambridge.

Dales, G. F.
1977 "Hissar IIIC Stone Objects in Afghan Sitan," in *Mountains and Lowlands: Essays in the*

Archaeology of Greater Mesopotamia, L. D. Levine and T. C. Young, Jr., eds., 17–28. Biblioteca Mesopotamica 7. Undena Press, Malibu, California.

Dales, G., and M. Kenoyer
1986 *Excavations at Mohenjo Daro: The Pottery.* The University Museum, University of Pennsylvania, Philadelphia.

Dalton, O. M.
1964 *The Treasure of the Oxus with Other Examples of Early Oriental Metalwork*. British Museum, London.

Dani, A. H.
1970 *Excavations in the Gomal Valley*. Ancient Pakistan 5. Department of Archaeology, Peshawar.

Davies, N. de G.
1929 "The Townhouse in Ancient Egypt." *Metropolitan Museum Studies* I.

Davis, W. M.
1905 "A Journey Across Turkestan," in *Explorations in Turkestan*, R. Pumpelly, ed., 23–119. Publication 26. Carnegie Institution, Washington, D.C.

Deshayes, J.
1960 *Les Outils de Bronze d'Indus au Danube.* Paul Geuthner, Paris.
1975 "Les fouilles récent de Tureng tepe: la terrasse haut de la fin du III millénnaire." *Compte Rendus des Séances de l'Académie des Inscriptions et Belles-Lettres*, 522–530.
1977a *Le Plateau Iranien et l'Asie Centrale des Origines à la Conquête Islamique*, J. Deshayes, ed., Colloques Internationaux 567. CNRS, Paris.
1977b "À propos des terrasses haut de la fin du III millénnaire en Iran et en Asie Centrale," in *Le Plateau Iranien et l'Asie Centrale des Origines à la Conquête Islamique*, 95–112, Colloques Internationaux 567. CNRS, Paris.

Desse, J.
1989 "Étude archéozoologique," in *Fouilles de Shortughai: Recherche sur l'Asie Centrale Protohistorique*, H.-P. Francfort, ed., 187–206. Diffusion de Boccard, Paris.

Dietrich, R. V., and B. J. Skinner
1979 *Rocks and Rock Minerals*. Wiley and Sons, New York.

Dolukhanov, P. M.
1988 "Paléoécologie de l'Asie centrale aux âges de la pierre et du bronze," in *L'Asie Centrale et ses Rapports avec les Civilisations Orientales des Origines a l'Âge du Fer*, 215–221. Mémoires de la Mission Archéologique Française en Asie Centrale. Diffusion de Boccard, Paris.
1993 "The ex-USSR:Post-perestroyka Problems." *Antiquity* 67:150–156.

Dolukhanov, P. M., A. J. Shchetenko, and M. Tosi
1985 "Seriya radio-carbon-uglorodnykh datirovok nasilenii epochi bronzy na Namazgadepe." *Sovetskaya Arkheologiya* 1985(4):119–123.

During-Caspers, E. C. L.
1985 "A Possible Harappan Contact with the Aegean World," in *South Asian Archaeology 1983*, J. Schotsman and M. Taddei, eds., 435–452. ISMEO, Naples.

Durrani, F. A.
1988 *Excavations in the Gomal Valley: Rehman Dheri Excavations Report No. 1*. Ancient Pakistan 6. Department of Archaeology, Peshawar.

Duru, R.
1993 "A New Variety of Idol From the Burdur Region: The Bone-Head Idol," in *Aspects of Art and Iconography: Anatolia and Its Neighbors*, M. Mellink, E. Porada, and T. Özgüç, eds., 158–160. Turk Tarih Kurumu Basimevi, Ankara.

Dyson, R. H.
1973 "The Archaeological Evidence of the Second Millennium B.C. on the Iranian Plateau," in *Cambridge Ancient History*, 3d ed., vol. II (1), 686–715. Cambridge University Press, Cambridge.
1989 "The Iron Age Architecture at Hasanlu: An Essay." *Expedition* 31:107–128.

Dyson, R. H., Jr., and W. C. Remsen
1989 "Observations on Architecture and Stratigraphy at Tappeh Hesar," in *Tappeh Hesar: Reports*

of the Restudy Project, 1976, R. H. Dyson, Jr. and S. M. Howard, eds., 69–110. Monographie di Mesopotamia 2. Casa Editrice Le Lettre, Firenze.

Encyclopedia of Islam
1988 E. J. Brill, Leiden.

Encyclopedia of Turkmenistan
1984 *Turkmenskaya Sovetskaya Sotsialisticheskaya Respublik*, N. V. Atamamedov, ed. Glavnaya Redaktsiaya Turkmenskoi Sovetskoi Entsiklopedoi, Ashgabat.

Fairservis, W. A., Jr.
1975 *The Roots of Ancient India*, 2d ed. University of Chicago Press, Chicago.

Ferioli, P., E. Fiandra., and S. Tusa
1979 "Stamp Seals and the Functional Analysis of Their Sealings at Shahr-i Sokhta," in *South Asian Archaeology 1975*, J. E. van Lohvizen-deLeeww, ed., 7–26. E. J. Brill, Leiden.

Filanovich, M. I .
1989 "Istoriko-kul'turnie arkheologeskie tablitsy po gorodishchu Gyaur-kala v Starogo Merva." *Trudi Iu.T.A.K.E.* 19:62–121.

Fitch, J. M., and D. P. Branch
1960 "Primitive Architecture and Climate." *Scientific American* 203(6):134–144.

Francfort, H.-P.
1981 "The Late Periods of Shortughai and the Problem of the Bishkent Culture/Middle and Late Bronze Age in Bactria," in *South Asian Archaeology 1979*, H. Hartel, ed., 191–202. Dietrich Reimer Verlag, Berlin.
1984 "The Early Periods of Shortughai (Harappan) and the Western Bactrian Culture of Dashly," in *South Asian Archaeology 1981*, B. Allchin, ed., 170–175. Cambridge University Press, Cambridge.
1989 *Fouilles de Shortughai, Recherches sur l'Asie Centrale Protohistorique*. Diffusion de Boccard, Paris.
1993 "Dungeons and Dragons: Reflections on the System of Iconography in Protohistoric Bactria and Margiana," in *South Asian Archaeology Studies*, G. Possehl, ed., 179–208. International Science Publisher, New York.
1994 "The Central Asian Dimension of the Symbolic System in Bactria and Margiana." *Antiquity* 68:406–418.

Fried, M. H.
1967 *The Evolution of Political Society*. Random House, New York.

Fry, R. E.
1980 "Models of Exchange for Major Shape Classes of Lowland Maya Pottery," in *Models and Methods in Regional Exchange*, R. E. Fry, ed., 3–18. SAA Papers 1. Society for American Archaeology, Washington, D.C.

Ganyalin, A. F.
1956 "Pogrebeniya epokhi bronzi i seleniya Yangi-kala." *Trudi Iu.T.A.K.E* 7:374–384.
1967 "Raskopki v 1959–1961 gg. na Altyn-depe." *Sovetskaya Arkheologiya* 1967(4):207–218.

Gasche, H.
1986 "Architecture d'intérior Susienne: les cheminees," in *Fragmenta Historiae Elamicae*, L. de Meyer, H. Gasche, and F. Vallat eds., 83–110. Édition Recherche sur les Civilizations, Paris.

Gerasimov, I. P.
1978 "Ancient Rivers in the Deserts of Soviet Central Asia," in *The Environmental History of the Near and Middle East Since the Last Ice Age*, W. C. Brice, ed., 319–334. Academic Press, New York.

Gorodtsov, V. A.
1927 *Tipolocheskii Metod v Arkheologii*. Obshchestvo Issledovatele Ryazanskogo Kraya, Ryazan.

Grenet, F., ed.
1987 *Cultes et Monuments Religieux dans l'Asie Centrale Preislamique*. CNRS, Paris.

Grishin, Iu.
1980 *Drevnyaya Dobycha Medi i Olova*. Nauka, Moscow.

Gupta, S. P.
1979 *Archaeology of Soviet Central Asia and the Iranian Borderlands*, 2 vols. B. R. Publishing Corporation, Delhi.

Hakemi, A.
1977 "Découverte d'une civilisation préhistorique à Shahdad au bord du Lut «Kerman»," in *Sixth International Congress of Iranian Art and Archaeology, Oxford, Sept. 11–16, 1972*, 131–149. Iranian Centre for Archaeological Research, Teheran.

Hiebert, F. T.
1992a "The Oasis and City of Merv (Turkmenistan)." *Archéologie Islamique* 3:111–127.
1992b *Bronze Age Oasis Settlements of Central Asia*. Ph.D. thesis, Harvard University.
1994 "Production Evidence for the Origins of the Oxus Civilization." *Antiquity* 68:372–387.
n.d. "Central Asia, Iran, and the Gulf in the second millennium B.C."

Hiebert, F. T., and D. Killick
1993 "Metallurgy of Bronze Age Gonur Depe." *Information Bulletin* 19:186–204.

Hiebert, F. T., and K. Kurbansakhatov
1993 *Polovoi otchet iz pervie mezhdunarodnie ekspeditsii na Anay*. Akadamii Nauk, Ashgabat.

Hiebert, F. T., and C. C. Lamberg-Karlovsky
1992 "Central Asia and the Indo-Iranian Borderlands." *Iran* 30:1–15.

Hiebert, F. T., and K. M. Moore
1993 "New Stratigraphic Excavations at Gonur Depe (North)." *Information Bulletin* 19:96–108.

Hillman, G.
1984 "Interpretation of Archaeological Plant Remains: The Application of Ethnographic Models from Turkey," in *Plants and Ancient Man: Studies in Palaeoethnobotany. Proceedings of the Sixth Symposium of the International Work Group for Palaeoethnobotany*, W. van Zeist and W. A. Casparie, eds., 1–41. A. A. Balkema, Boston.

Huntington, E.
1945 *Mansprings of Civilization*. Mentor Books, New York.

Isakov, A., and B. Lyonnet
1988 "Céramiques de Sarazm (Tadjikistan URSS): problèmes d'échange et de peuplement à la fin du chalcolitique et au début de l'âge du bronze." *Paléorient* 14(1):31–47.

Isakov, A., P. L. Kohl, C. C. Lamberg-Karlovsky, and R. Maddin
1987 "Metallurgical Analysis from Sarazm, Tadjikistan SSR." *Archaeometry* 29(1):90–102.

Isbell, W., and G. McEwan, eds.
1991 *Huari Administrative Structure: Prehistoric Monumental Architecture and State Government*. Dumbarton Oaks Research Library and Collection, Washington DC.

Itina, M. A.
1977 *Istoriya Stepnyka Plemen Iuzhnogo Prearal'ya*. Trudy Khorezmskoi Arkheologo-Etnograficheskoi, vol. 10. Nauka, Moscow.

Ivanova, I. K., N. V. Kind, and V. V. Cherdyntsev
1963 *Absolutnaya Geokhronologiya Chetvertikhnogo Perioda*. Nauka, Moscow.

Jarrige, J.-F.
1988 "Le complexe culturel de Mehrgarh (Période VIII) et de Sibri: le trésor de Quetta," in *Les Cités Oubliées de l'Indus*, 111–128. Musée National des Arts Asiatiques Guimet, Paris.
1989 "Excavation at Nausharo 1987–88." *Pakistan Archaeology* 24:21–67.

Jarrige, J.-F., and M. U. Hassan
1989 "Funerary Complexes in Baluchistan at the End of the Third Millennium in the Light of Recent Discoveries at Mehrgarh and Quetta," in *South Asian Archaeology 1985: Papers from the 8th International Conference of the Association of South Asian Archaeologists in Western Europe*, K. Frifelt and P. Sorensen, eds., 150–166. Scandinavian Institute of Asian Studies, Occasional Papers 4. Riverdale Company, Riverdale, Maryland.

Kachalova, N. K.
1985 "Periodizatsiya Srubnykh pamyatnikov nizhego Povolzh'ya," in *Srubnaya Kul'turno-istoriceskaya Obshchenots'*. Kuibyshevskii Instituta, Kuibyshev.

Kepinski, Ch.
1982 *L'arbre stylisé en asie occidentale au deuxième millénaire avant J.-C.*, vols. 1–2. Éditions Recherche sur les Civilisations, Paris.

Khlopin, I. N.
1964 *Geoksyurskaya Gruppa Poselenii Epokhi Eneoli.* Nauka, Moscow.

Khlopina, L. I.
1972 "Southern Turkmenia in the Later Bronze Age." *East and West* 22:199–214.
1981 "Namazga-depe and the Late Bronze Age of Southern Turkmenia," in *The Bronze Age Civilization of Central Asia: Recent Soviet Discoveries*, P. Kohl, ed., 35–62. M. E. Sharpe, Armonk, New York.

Kingerly, W. D., P. Vandiver, and M. Prickett
1988 "The Beginnings of Pyrotechnology, Part II: Production and Use of Lime and Gypsum Plaster in the Pre-Pottery Neolithic Near East." *Journal of Field Archaeology* 15:219–244.

Kircho, L. B.
1972 "Stratigrafiya Altyn-depe i kolich estvennii metod opredeleniya otnositelnoi khronologii." *Karakumskie Drevnosti* 4:172–176.

Kirsta, B. T.
1980 *Reki Pustyn.* Ylym, Ashkhabad.

Kohl, P. L.
1974 *Seeds of Upheaval: The Production of Chlorite at Tepe Yahya and an Analysis of Commodity Production and Trade in Southwest Asia in the Mid-Third Millennium*, Ph.D. thesis, Harvard University.
1979 "Physical and Chemical Analysis of Soft Stone Vessels from Southwest Asia." *Archaeometry* 21:131–159.
1981 "The Namazga Civilization: an Overview," in *The Bronze Age Civilization of Central Asia: Recent Soviet Discoveries*, P. Kohl, ed., vii–xxxviii. M. E. Sharpe, Armonk, New York.
1984 *Central Asia: Paleolithic Beginnings to the Iron Age*. Synthèse 14. Éditions Recherche sur les Civilisations, Paris.
1992 "Central Asia (Western Turkestan): Neolithic to the Early Iron Age," in *Chronologies in Old World Archaeology*, vol. 1, R. W. Erich, ed., 179–196. University of Chicago Press, Chicago.

Kuftin, B. A.
1956 "Polevoi otchet: o rabote XIV otryada IuTAKE po izucheniiu kulturi pervobytno-obshchinnykh osedlo-zemledelcheskikh poselenii epokhu medu i bronzi v 1952 g." *Trudi Iu.T.A.K.E.* 7:260–290.

Kuzits, Iu., ed.
1981 *Izotopnie Geokhimicheskie Metodi v Biologii, Geologii i Arkheologie*. Tarty Universiteta, Tarty.

Kuz'mina, E. E.
1966 *Metallicheskie Izdeliya Eneolita I Bronzogo Veka Srednei Azii.* Svod Arkheologiskikh Istochnikov, Moscow.
1980 "Etapi razvitiya kolesnovo transporta Srednei Azii v epokhu eneolita i bronzi." *Vestink Drevnei Istorii* 1980(4):11–35.
1986 *Drevneishie skotovodi ot Urala do Tyan-Shanya*, Ilim, Frunze.

Kuz'mina, E. E., and A. A. Lyapin
1984 "Novye Nakhodki Stepnoi Keramiki na Murgabe," in *Problemy Arkheologii Turkmenistana*, V. M. Masson, ed., 6–21. Ylym, Ashgabat.

Lamberg-Karlovsky, C. C.
1971 "Tepe Yahya—Mesopotamia and the Indo-Iranian Borderlands." *Iran* 10:89–100.
1973 "Prehistoric Central Asia: a Review." *Antiquity* 67:43–46.
1975 "Third Millennium Modes of Exchange and Modes of Production," in *Ancient Civilization and Trade*, J. A. Sabloff and C. C. Lamberg-Karlovsky, eds., 341–368. University of New Mexico Press, Albuquerque.
1981 "Afterword," in *The Bronze Age Civilization of Central Asia: Recent Soviet Discoveries*, P. Kohl, ed., 386–397. M. E. Sharpe, Armonk, New York.

1990 "The Bronze Age of Bactria," in *Bactria: An Ancient Oasis Civilization from the Sands of Afghanistan,* G. Ligabue and S. Salvatori, eds., 13–24. Erizzo, Venice.
1991 "The Search for the Scythians in the USSR." *Symbols* 1991:14–18.
1994a "Central Asian Bronze Age—Special Section." *Antiquity* 68:353–354.
1994b "The Bronze Age Khanates of Central Asia." *Antiquity* 68:398–405.

Lamberg-Karlovsky, C. C., and M. Tosi
1973 "Shahr-i Sokhta and Tepe Yahya: Tracks on the Earliest History of the Iranian Plateau." *East and West* 23(1–2):21–53.

Lapp, P.
1966 *The Dahr Mirzbaneh Tombs: Three Intermediate Bronze Age Cemeteries in Jordan.* Publications of the Jerusalem School, Archaeology 4. American Schools of Oriental Research, New Haven.

Li Chi
1976 *Anyang.* University of Washington Press, Seattle, Washington.

Ligabue, G., and S. Salvatori, eds.
1990 *Bactria: An Ancient Oasis Civilization from the Sands of Afghanistan.* Erizzo, Venice.

Lisitsyna, G. N.
1968 "Rastitel'nost Iuzhnoi Turkmenii v VI-I t.l. do n.e. po dannim opredeleniy uglei." *Karakumskie Drevnosti* 2:51–57.
1978 *Stanovlenie i Razvitie Oroshaemovo Zemledeliya v Iuzhnoi Turkmenii.* Nauka, Moscow.

Litvinskii, B. A.
1952 "Namazga-depe po dannim raskopok 1949–1950 gg." *Sovetskaya Etnografiya* 4:30–52.

Lyapin, A. A.
1975 "Novie pamyatniki epokhi bronzi Iuzhnovo Turkmenistana." *Uspekhi Sredneaziatskoi Arkheologii* 3:73–76.

Mackay, E. J. H.
1943 *Chanhu-Daro Excavations 1935–36.* American Oriental Series 20. American Oriental Society, New Haven, Connecticut.

Marshall, J.
1931 *Mohenjo-Daro and the Indus Civilization.* Arthur Probestan, London.

Maruschenko, A. A.
1959 "Elken-depe (otchet o raskopkakh 1953, 1955 i 1956 gg.)." *Trudi Instituta Istorii, Arkhe ologii, i Etnografii Akademii Nauk Turkmenskoi SSR* 5: 54–109.

Masimov, I.
1970 "Raskopki remeslennogo kvartala epokha bronzi na poselenii Altyn-depe." *Karakumskie Drevnosti* 3:51–63.
1973 "Raskopki svyatilishcha epokhi bronzi na Altyn-depe." *Sovetskaya Arkheologiya* 1973(2):139–145.
1976 *Keramicheskoe Proizvodstvo Epokhi Bronzi v Iuzhnom Turkmenistane.* Ylym, Ashgabat.
1978 "Raskopki zhilikh kompleksov na Altyn-depe." *Karakumskie Drevnosti* 7:12–36.
1979 "Izuchenie pamatnikov epokhi bronzi nizovii Murgaba." *Sovetskaya Arkheologiya* 1979(1):111–131.
1981 "Bronze Age Sites in the Lower Murgab," in *The Bronze Age Civilization of Central Asia: Recent Soviet Discoveries,* P. Kohl, ed., 194–220. M. E. Sharpe, Armonk, New York.
1984 "Zhiloi dom na Kelleli." *Pamiyatniki Turkmenistana* 2/38:16–18.
1986 "Novie issledovaniya pamyatnikov epokhi bronzy na Murgabe," in *Drevnie Tsivilizatsii Vostoka,* V. Masson, ed., 171–181. FAN, Tashkent.

Masimov, I., and A. Lyapin
1977 "Arkheologo-topograficheskie raboti v nizov'yakh drevnego Murgaba." in *Arkheologicheskie Otkritiya, 1976 Goda,* 552. Nauka, Moscow.

Masson, V. M.
1956 "Raspisnaya keramika Iuzhnoi Turkmenii po raskopkam B. A. Kuftin." *Trudi Iu.T.A.K.E.* 7:291–373.

1959 *Drevnezemledelcheskaya kultura Margiani.* Materiali I Issledovaniya po Arkheologii SSSR 73. Nauka, Moscow.
1961 "Kara-depe u Artika." *Trudi Iu.T.A.K.E.* 10:319–463.
1967 "Protogorodskaya tsivilizatsiya iuga srednei azii." *Sovetskaya Arkheologiya* 1967(3):165–190.
1968 "Urban Revolution in Southern Turkmenia." *Antiquity* 42:178–187.
1970 "Raskopki na Altyn-depe v 1969 g." *Materiali Iu.T.A.K.E.* 3:5–24.
1976 "Altyn Depe and the Bull Cult." *Antiquity* 50:14–19.
1977 "Pechati protoindiiskogo tipa iz Altyn-depe." *Vestnik Drevnii Istorii* 1977(4):147–156.
1981a "Altyn-Depe During the Eneolithic Period," in *The Bronze Age Civilization of Central Asia: Recent Soviet Discoveries*, P. Kohl, ed., 63–95. M. E. Sharpe, Armonk, New York.
1981b *Altyn-depe*. Trudi Iu.T.A.K.E. 18. Nauka, Moscow.
1984 "Formirovanie drevnikh tsivilizatsii v srednei azii i indostane," in *Drevnie Kulturi Srednei Azii i Indii*, V. M. Masson, ed., 56–70. Nauka, Leningrad.
1988 *Altyn depe*. Trans. H. Michels. University Museum, University of Pennsylvania, Philadelphia.
1989 *Pervie Tsivilizatsii*. Nauka, Leningrad.

Masson, V. M., and V. I. Sarianidi
1972 *Central Asia: Turkmenia Before the Achaemenids*. Thames and Hudson, London.
1973 *Sredneaziatskaya terrakota epokhi bronzi*. Glavnaya Redaksiya Vostochnoi Literaturi, Moscow.

Mazar, A.
1990 *Archaeology of the Land of the Bible: 10,000–586 B.C.E.* Doubleday, New York.

Meadow, R. H.
1993 "Continuity and Change in the Agriculture of the Greater Indus Valley." *Information Bulletin* 19:63–77.

Meadow, R. H., ed.
1991 *Harappan Excavations 1986–1990: A Multidisciplinary Approach to Third Millennium Urbanism*. Monographs in World Archaeology 3. Prehistory Press, Madison, Wisconsin.

Meier-Melikyan, N. R.
1990 "Opredelenie rastitel'nikh ostatkov iz Togolok 21," in *Drevnosti Strany Margush*, V. Sarianidi, ed., 203–205. Ylym, Ashgabat.

Miller, M.
1956 *Archaeology in the U.S.S.R.* Frederick A. Praeger, New York.

Miller, N. F.
1993 "Preliminary Archaeobotnical Results from Gonur." *Information Bulletin* 19:149–163.

Miroschedji, P. de
1973 "Vases et objets en stéatite susiens du musée du Louvre." *Cahiers de la Délégation Archéologique Française en Iran* 3:9–80.

Molodin, V. I.
1992 "Studies in the Bertek River Valley on the Ukok Plateau." *Altaica* 1:23–34.

Mongait, A.
1951 "Krizis burzhuaznoi arkheologii." *Kratkie Soobshcheniya* 40:3–15.

Moore, K. M.
1993a "Animal Use at Bronze Age Gonur Depe." *Information Bulletin* 19:164–186.
1993b "Bone Tool Technology at Gonur Depe." *Information Bulletin* 19:218–227.

Moore, K., N. Miller, F. Hiebert, and R. Meadow
1994 "Agriculture and Herding in the Early Oasis Settlements of the Oxus Civilization." *Antiquity* 68:418–427.

Mukhamedzhanov, A. P.
1978 *Istoriya Orosheniya Bukharskogo Oazisa*. FAN, Tashkent.

Nachasova, I., and K. Burakov
1993 "Archaeomagnetic Research on the Territory of Ancient Margiana." *Information Bulletin* 19:205–218.

Nikitin, A., and A. Sogomonov
1982 "Archaeological Investigations of the Merv Oasis: Reconnaissance Investigations." *Information Bulletin* 2:30–33.

Niyazklychev, K.
1973 "Zemledel'cheskii kalandar i skotovostvo u Turkmen-chovdurov v kontse 19–nachale 20 v," in *Ocherki po Istorii Khozyaistva i Kul'turi Turkmen*, 87–98. Ylym, Ashkhabad.

Nyerges, A. E.
1982 "Pastoralists, Flocks and Vegetation: Processes of Co-adaptation," in *Desertification and Development: Dryland Ecology in Social Perspective*, B. Spooner and H. Mann, eds., 217–248. Academic Press, London.

O'Donovan, E.
1882 *The Merv Oasis. Travels and Adventures East of the Caspian During the Years 1879–80–81*. Rep. 1970, Arno Press, New York.

Özgüç, N.
1980 "Seal Impressions from the Palace at Acemhöyük," in *Ancient Art in Seals*, E. Porada, ed., 61–101. Princeton University Press, New Jersey.

Parpola, A.
1988 "The Coming of the Aryans to Iran and India and the Cultural and Ethnic Identity of the Dasas." *Studia Orientalia* 64:195–302.

Peake, H., and H. Fleure
1927 *Peasants and Potters*. Oxford University Press, London.

Piggott, S.
1950 *Prehistoric India*. Pelican Books, Harmondsworth, England.

Pilipko, V. N.
1984 "Poselenie rannezheleznogo veke Garrikyariz I, " in *Turkmenistan v Epokhu Rannezheleznogo Veka*, V. M. Masson, ed., 28–57. Ylym, Ashgabat.

Pittman, H.
1984 *The Art of the Bronze Age: Southeastern Iran, Western Central Asia, and the Indus Valley*. The Metropolitan Museum of Art, New York.

Possehl, G. L.
1989 *Radiocarbon Dates for South Asian Archaeology*. An Occasional Publication of the Asian Section. The University Museum, University of Pennsylvania, Philadelphia.

Pottier, M. -H.
1984 *Matériel Funéraire de la Bactriane Méridionale de l'Âge de Bronze*. Memoire 36. CNRS, Paris.

Potts, D.
1990 *The Arabian Gulf in Antiquity*, vol. 1. Clarendon Press, Oxford.

Prickett, M.
1986 "Settlement in the Early Periods," in *Excavations at Tepe Yahya, 1967–75: The Early Period*, T. W. Beale, ed., 215–246. American School of Prehistoric Research, Bulletin 38. Peabody Museum, Harvard University, Cambridge.

Pugachenkova, G. A.
1958 *Puti Razvitiya Arkhitekturi Iuzhnogo Turk menistana Pori Rabovladeniya i Feodalizma*. Trudi Iu.T.A.K.E. 6. Nauka, Moscow.

Pumpelly, R., ed.
1908 *Explorations in Turkestan, Expedition of 1904*. Publication 73. Carnegie Institution of Washington, Washington, D.C.

P'yankova, L.
1989 "Pottery Complexes of Bronze Age Margiana (Gonur and Togolok-21)." *Information Bulletin* 16:27–54.
1993 "Pottery of Margiana and Bactria in the Bronze Age." *Information Bulletin* 19:109–127.
1994 "Central Asia in the Bronze Age:Sedentary and Nomadic Cultures." *Antiquity* 68:355–372.

Redman, C.
1980 "Archeology in a Medieval City of Islam." *Middle East Studies Association Bulletin* 14(2):1–22.

Renfrew, C.
1987 *Archaeology and Language: The Puzzle of Indo-European Origins*. Cambridge University Press, New York.

Rougeulle, A.
1982 "Des «étuves» à dattes a Bahrain et en Oman: le probleme de l'appaition des techniques de transformation de la datte." *Paléorient* 8(2):67–77.

Saiko, E. V.
1984 *Tekhnika i Tekhnologiya Keramicheskogo Proizvodstva Srednie Azii i Istoricheskom Razvitii*. Nauka, Moscow.

Salje, B.
1990 *Der 'Common Style' der Mitanni-Glyptik und die Glyptik der Levant und Zyperns in der Spaten Bronzezeit. Bagdader.* Forschungen 11. Philipp von Zabern, Mainz am Rheim.

Salvatori, S.
1990 "Early Bactrian Objects in Private Collections, " in *Bactria: An Ancient Oasis Civilization from the Sands of Afghanistan*, G. Ligabue and S. Salvatori, eds., 181–188. Erizzo, Venice.
1993 "The Discovery of the Graveyard of Gonur-Depe 1 (Murgab Delta, Turkmenistan): 1992 Campaign, Preliminary Report." *Rivista di Archeologia* 17 (in press).

Santoni, M.
1984 "Sibri and the South Cemetery of Mehrgarh: Third Millennium Connections Between the Northern Katchi Plain (Pakistan) and Central Asia," in *South Asian Archaeology 1981*, B. Allchin, ed., 52–60. Cambridge University Press, Cambridge.
1988 "Aspects matériels des cultures de Sibri et de Mehrgarh VIII (plaine de Kachi, Baluchistan, Pakistan) à la fin du 3è et au début du 2è millénaires," in *L'Asie Centrale et ses Rapports avec les Civilisations Orientales: des Origines a l'Âge du Fer*, 135–141. Diffusion de Boccard, Paris.

Sarianidi, V. I.
1957 "Keramichicheskie pechi drevnei Margiani." *Kratkie Soobshcheniya* 69:72–78.
1961 "Eneoliticheskoe poselenie Geoksyur." *Trudi Iu.T.A.K.E.* 10:225–318.
1965 *Pamyatniki poznego eneolita iugo-vostochnoi Turkmenii*. Svod Arkheologicheskikh Istochnikov, Moscow.
1975a "Novie otkritiya v nizovyakh Murgaba." *Arkheologicheskie Otkritiya 1974 Goda*, 528–530. Nauka, Moscow.
1975b "Stepnie plemena epokhi Bronzi v Mar giane." *Sovetskaya Arkheologiya* 1975(2):20–29.
1976 "Pechati-amuleti Murgabskogo stilya." *Sovetskaya Arkheologiya* 1976(1):42–68.
1977 *Drevnie Zemledel'tsi Afganistana*. Nauka, Moscow.
1979a "K voprosu o kul'ture Zamanbaba," in *Ethnografiya i Arkheologiya Srednei Azii*, A. V. Vinogradov et al., eds., 23–28. Nauka, Moscow.
1979b "Ob odnoi gruppe kul'tovikh izdelii Baktrii." *Sovetskaya Arkheologiya* 1979(3):262–265.
1980 "Kul'tovii sosud is Margiani." *Sovetskaya Arkheologiya* 1980(2):167–179.
1981a "Margiana in the Bronze Age," in *The Bronze Age Civilization of Central Asia: Recent Soviet Discoveries*, P. Kohl, ed., 165–193. M. E. Sharpe, Armonk, New York.
1981b "Seal-Amulets of the Murghab Style," in *The Bronze Age Civilization of Central Asia: Recent Soviet Discoveries*, P. Kohl, ed., 221–255. M. E. Sharpe, Armonk, New York.
1984 "Raskopki monumentalnikh zdanii na Dashli-3." *Drevnyaya Bactriya* 3:5–32.
1986a "Bronzovii vek Margiani." *Kratkie Soobshcheniya* 188:83–91.
1986b "The Bactrian Pantheon." *Information Bulletin* 10:5–20.
1986c *Die Kunst des Alten Afghanistan: Keramik, Siegel, Architectur, Kunstwerke aus Stein und Metall.* E. A. Seeman Verlag, Leipzig.
1987a "Le complexe culturel de Togolok-21 en Margiane." *Arts Asiatique* 41:5–21.
1987b "South-west Asia: Migrations, the Aryans and Zoroastrians." *Information Bulletin* 13:44–56.
1989a "Protozoroastriiskii khram v Margiane i problem vozniknoveniya Zoroastrizma." *Vestnik Drevnei Istorii* 1989 (1):151–170.
1989b "Siro-khettskie bozhestva v Baktriisko-Margianskom panteone." *Sovetskaya Arkheologiya* 1989(4):17–24.

1990 *Drevnosti Strani Margush*. Ylym, Ashgabat.
1991 "Temples of Ancient Margiana." *Pakistan Archaeology* 26:175–187.
1992 *I Zdes' Govoril Zaratushtra*. Vniie, Moscow.
1993 "Excavations at Southern Gonur." *Iran* 31:25–38.
1994 "Temples of Bronze Age Margiana: Traditions of Ritual Architecture." *Antiquity* 68:388–397.

Schmidt, E. F.
1937 *Excavations at Tepe Hissar Damghan*. The University Museum, University of Pennsylvania, Philadelphia.

Schoeberlein-Engel, J.
1994 "Identity in Central Asia: Construction and Contention in the Conceptions of 'Özbek,' 'Tâjik,' 'Muslim,' 'Samarqand,' and Other Gropus." Ph.D. thesis, Harvard University.

Shchetenko, Iu.
1970 "Raskopki melkikh poselenii epokhi bronzi." *Karakumskie Drevnosti* 3:33–50.

Stein, M. A.
1931 *An Archaeological Tour in Gedrosia*. Memoires of the Archaeological Survey of India 43. Government of India Central Publishing Branch, Calcutta.

Steinkeller, P.
1989 "Marhashi," in *Realexikon der Assyriologie und Vordasiatischen Archäologie*, 381–382. W. deGruyter, Berlin.

Stuiver, M., and P. Reimer
1993 "Extended ^{14}C Database and Revised CALIB 3.0 ^{14}C Age Calibration Program." *Radiocarbon* 28:1022–1030.

Struve, V. V.
1949 "Vosstanie v Margiane pri Darii I." *Materali Iu.T.A.K.E.* 1:9–34.

Suslov, S. P.
1961 *Physical Geography of Asiatic Russia*. W. H. Freeman and Co., San Francisco.

Szabo, A., and T. Barfield
1991 *Afghanistan: An Atlas of Indigenous Domestic Architecture*. University of Texas Press, Austin.

Tarn, W. W.
1951 *The Greeks in Bactria and India*. 2d ed. Cambridge University Press, New York.

Terekhnova, N. N.
1990 "Obrabotka metallov v drevnei Margiane, " in *Drevnosti Strani Margush*, V. I. Sarianidi, ed., 177–205. Ylym, Ashgabat.

Tosi, M.
1970 "A Tomb from Damin and the Problem of the Bampur Sequence in the Third Millennium B.C." *East and West* 20(1–2):9–50.
1974a "The Problem of Turquoise in Protohistoric Trade on the Iranian Plateau." *Memorie dell'Instituto Italiano de Paleontologie Umana* 2:147–162.
1974b "The Northeastern Frontier of the Ancient NearEast." *Estratta da Mesopotamia* 8–9:21–76.

Tosi, M., ed.
1983 *Prehistoric Sistan 1*. Reports and Memoirs 19. IsMEO, Rome.

Tosi, M., and M. Piperno
1973 "Lithic Technology Behind the Ancient Lapis Lazuli Trade." *Expedition* 16(1):15–23.

Trigger, B. G.
1989 *A History of Archaeological Thought*. Cambridge University Press, Cambridge.

Udemuradov, B. N.
1986 "Keramicheskii kompleks Kelleli (o genezise i svyazyakh)." *Izvestiya Akademiya Nauk Turkmenskoi SSR* 1986(6):26–33.
1987 "Keramicheskii kompleks verkhnikh sloev Altyn-depe." *Izvestiya Akademiya Nauk Turkmenskoi SSR* 1987(6):26–32.
1988 "K voprosu o proiskhdenii kompleksov epokhi bronzi v Margiane." *Izvestiya Akademiya Nauk Turkmenskoi SSR* 1988(4):19–25.
1989 "K voprosu o poyavlenii ocedlikh zemledel'tsev v srednem techenii Murgaba." *Izvestiya Akademiya Nauk Turkmenskoi SSR* 1989(2):26–29.

1993 *Altyn-depe i Margiana: Suyazi, Khronologiya, proiskhozhdenie*. Ylym Press, Ashgabat .

Vats, M. S.
1940 *Excavations at Harappa*. Government of India Press, Calcutta.

Vinogradov, A. V.
1968 *Neolitiicheskie Pamyatniki Khorezm*. Nauka, Moscow.

Vinogradova, A.V., and E. E. Kuz'mina
1986 "Kontakty Stepnykh i Zemledel'cheskikh plemen srednei azii v epokhu bronzy," in *Vostochnyi Turkestan i Srednyaya Aziya*, B. Litvinskii, ed., 126–151. Nauka, Moscow.

Vishnu-Mittre
1977 "Changing Economy in Ancient India," in *Origins of Agriculture*, C. Reed, ed., 569–588. Mouton Publishers, The Hague.

Vishnu-Mittre and R. Savithri
1982 "Food Economy of the Harappans," in *Harappan Civilization: A Contemporary Perspective*, G. Possehl, ed., 205–221. Aris and Phillips, Warminster, England.

Walter, H., and E. Box
1983 "The Karakum Desert, An Example of a Well-studied Eu-biome," in *Temperate Deserts and Semi-Deserts*, N. West, ed., 105–159. Elsevier Scientific Co., New York.

Watson, P. J.
1979 *Archaeological Ethnography in Western Iran*. Viking Fund Publications in Anthropology 57. University of Arizona Press, Tucson.

Wilhelm, G.
1989 *The Hurrians*. Aris and Phillips, Warminster, England.

Wolfart, R., and H. Wittekindt
1980 *Geologie von Afghanistan*. Gebruder Borntraeger, Berlin.

Wright, G. A.
1971 "Origin of Food Production in Southwestern Asia: A Survey of Ideas." *Current Anthropology* 12:447–477.

Wulff, H.
1966 *The Traditional Crafts of Persia: Their Development, Technology and Influence on Eastern and Western Civilizations*. M.I.T. Press, Cambridge.

Yaneshevich, Z. V.
1977 "O nakhodke yamenya na pocelenii Altyn-depe." *Karakumskie Drevnosti* 5:162–169.

Young, T. C., Jr.
1965 " A Comparative Ceramic Chronology for Western Iran, 1500–500 B.C." *Iran* 3:53–85.

Zhukovskii, V. A.
1894 *Razvalini starogo Merva*. Materialy po Arkheologii Rossii, S. Peterburg.

Concordance of Figures

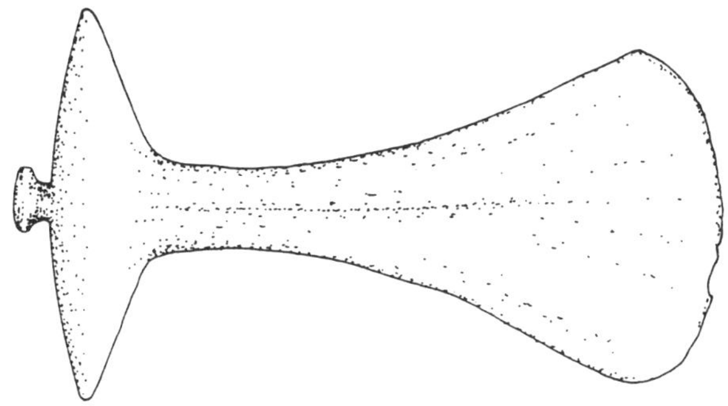

Since many of the figures first appeared in the author's Ph.D. thesis *Bronze Age Oasis Settlements of Central Asia* (University Microfilms #19933 511-825, 1993), this list provides a concordance of the figures in this monograph (ASPR 42) with the page numbers where they originally appeared in the Ph.D. thesis (BAOS).

ASPR 42	**BAOS**
Figure 1.2	p. 23
Figure 1.6	p. 30
Figure 1.8	p. 11
Figure 1.9	p. 19
Figure 2.2	p. 36
Figure 2.3	p. 43
Figure 2.7	p. 50
Figure 2.8	p. 51
Figure 2.10	p. 53
Figure 2.11	p. 54
Figure 2.13	p. 59
Figure 2.16	p. 64
Figure 2.17	p. 67
Figure 3.1	p. 71
Figure 3.5	p. 77
Figure 3.6	p. 80
Figure 3.7	p. 86
Figure 3.8	p. 88
Figure 3.9	p. 92
Figure 3.10	p. 94
Figure 4.2	p. 146
Figure 4.4	p. 149
Figure 4.5	p. 151
Figure 4.7	p. 154
Figure 4.8	p. 156
Figure 4.9	p. 104
Figure 4.11	p. 108
Figure 4.12	p. 160
Figure 4.14	p. 162
Figure 4.15	p. 164
Figure 4.19	p. 167
Figure 4.20	p. 168
Figure 4.21	p. 169
Figure 4.25	p. 172
Figure 4.31	p. 178
Figure 4.35	p. 145
Figure 4.36	p. 191
Figure 4.37	p. 194
Figure 4.39	p. 187
Figure 6.1	p. 230

ASPR 42	BAOS
Figure 6.2	p. 231
Figure 6.3	p. 233
Figure 6.7	p. 247
Figure 6.8	p. 249
Figure 6.10	p. 252
Figure 6.11	p. 254
Figure 6.12	p. 259
Figure 6.13	p. 262
Figure 6.14	p. 264
Figure 6.15	p. 267
Figure 6.16	p. 269
Figure 6.17	p. 270
Figure 6.18	p. 273
Figure 6.22	p. 279
Figure 6.23	p. 284
Figure 7.1	p. 294
Figure 7.3	p. 297
Figure 7.4	p. 304
Figure 7.13	p. 321
Figure 7.15	p. 325
Figure 7.17	p. 329
Figure 7.19	p. 333
Figure 7.23	p. 340
Figure 7.25	p. 344
Figure 8.2	p. 372
Figure 9.1	p. 381
Figure 9.4	p. 385
Figure 9.8	p. 387
Figure 9.9	p. 390
Figure 9.10	p. 397
Figure 9.11	p. 398
Figure 9.20	p. 410
Figure 9.22	p. 413
Figure 10.2	p. 436
Figure 10.6	p. 434

Index

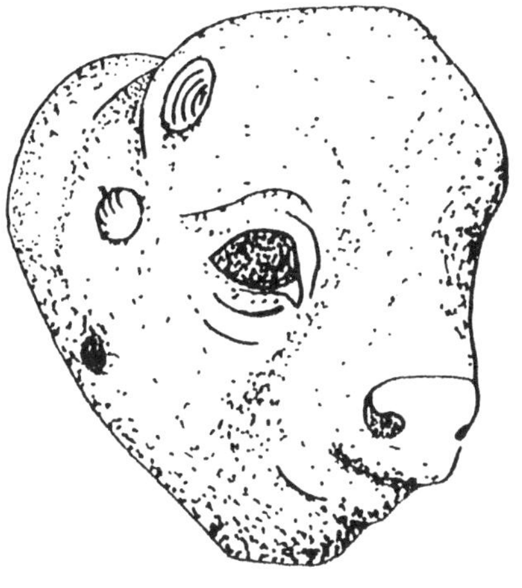